Television in Europe

COMMUNICATION AND SOCIETY
edited by George Gerbner and Marsha Siefert

Television in Europe

Eli Noam

New York   Oxford
OXFORD UNIVERSITY PRESS
1991

Oxford University Press

Oxford New York Toronto
Delhi Bombay Calcutta Madras Karachi
Petaling Jaya Singapore Hong Kong Tokyo
Nairobi Dar es Salaam Cape Town
Melbourne Auckland

and associated companies in
Berlin Ibadan

Published by Oxford University Press, Inc.,
200 Madison Avenue, New York, New York 10016

Oxford is a registered trademark of Oxford University Press.

Library of Congress Cataloging-in-Publication Data
Noam, Eli
Television in Europe
Eli Noam.
p. cm.—(Communication and society)
Includes bibliographical references and index.
ISBN 0-19-506942-0
1. Television broadcasting—Europe.
2. Television broadcasting policy—Europe.
I. Title. II. Series: Communication and society (New York, N.Y.)
HE8700.9.E8N63   1991
384.55′094—dc   90-23042

9 8 7 6 5 4 3

Printed in the United States of America
on acid-free paper

Preface

Like its companion volume *Telecommunications in Europe*, this book deals with the rise and decline of powerful monopoly institutions in the communications field. In television, these are the public broadcasting institutions that have dominated Western European television from its inception. These organizations, though they varied, shared fundamental similarities: most countries had two or three television channels and a handful of radio stations, all operated by a semipublic institution with an exclusive franchise and governed by a body that incorporated many of the significant political groupings in society.

This system was largely stable for about forty years following World War II (and sometimes going back to the 1920s). But in the 1980s, pressures emerged that could no longer be contained. A new media system began to replace the old one, accompanied by extraordinarily bitter political disputes. This was not surprising, because the influence of television over the general population was deemed so significant, and the cultural resources that the traditional broadcasters controlled were so large. On the other hand, European societies were free and open for print media and films, and the monopoly status of the electronic media was therefore an anomaly.

By the end of the 1980s, European television had been fundamentally transformed, and television was opened to private broadcasters in almost every country. If the structure of media affects their content and if media shapes society, then those structural changes must have a significant long-term impact. The democratic transformation of Eastern Europe is frequently attributed, at least in part, to the reach of Western media. It may well be that the cumulative impact of the new media environment on Western Europe will turn out to be as important.

In the past, a scarcity of electromagnetic spectrum allocation (often self-imposed) permitted only a tiny number of program channels. Because of their limited number and cultural and political importance, control over channels was an issue of great significance.

The well educated generally disliked sharing the channel with those of lesser sophistication. In the United States, commercial television's body-count economics were aimed at the peak of the bell-shaped statistical distribution, often but erroneously referred to as the "lowest common denominator." Because it strongly reflects popular tastes, many of the educated elite stopped watching such television. In many European countries, on the other hand, they took control of program content and shaped much of it according to their viewing preferences.

When production equipment became cheap, and when it was recognized that spectrum scarcity could fairly easily be overcome by low-power broadcast and cable transmission, the traditional system was challenged both from the commercial-minded right and the "alternative" left.

As this process evolved, most European countries began contemplating or implementing changes that would have been unthinkable only a few years before. It would be surprising if this process were not to continue for decades and if at its end television were not quite different. These are the issues this book discusses, both in general and in country-specific terms.

One of the problems of social science research on these and other developments in the broadcast field is the fragmentary nature of its analytical apparatus, particularly in its economic approach. The book therefore starts with a series of chapters that provide both the setting and an analytical approach to television issues. The methodology is economics oriented without being technical. There is no claim that other methodologies do not also yield useful insights. The analysis is used for basic concepts of the new media environment: diversity, commercialism, information increase and overload, internationalism, Americanization, media integration, subsidization, and international media flows.

Another line of investigation deals with the impact of an open television system on other and more traditional media, such as theater, film, and books. Here the discussion is essentially empirical; it finds these sectors to be alive and well, at least in the United States, and describes the forces of expansion and integration in the information industry.

Part II of the book is devoted to individual countries. Almost thirty countries are discussed, spanning a wide variety of size, history, and language. (The countries of Eastern Europe are covered in less detail, because their economic and political systems in the past and their rapid transition in the present render them very different from those of the West.) The book serves as something of a handbook on the European broadcasting systems, providing a view of how they developed, how they looked at the end of the 1980s, and how they were changing from a traditional to a new stage. Some chapters include a considerable amount of institutional history because to understand the future one needs to know the past. For example, one cannot analyze Germany's broadcast system without reference to its history. This may seem obvious for the Nazi past, but a closer look reveals that it is actually the years of the Weimar Republic whose dismal lessons in the broadcast field are more relevant for today's environment and explain present-day structures and struggles.

The final part of the book discusses European collaborative efforts in broadcasting on the policy and technical levels, and satellite broadcast transmission. This is followed by the concluding chapter, which identifies the past and future stages of evolution in European television.

The book tries to go beyond theorizing and into the actual institutional detail. This is an enormous undertaking, given the number of countries involved, many of which have little accessible literature provided by parties without a self-

interest. Priorities have had to be set, and several of the larger countries received a more detailed treatment. This book, it should be said at the outset, is
not a comparative study in the sense of contrasting different countries' approaches to a problem or technology and evaluating the best of them. This is
done occasionally, but it is not the central aspect of the book. Although change
in television was partly caused by cross-fertilization across frontiers and
strengthened by the move toward European integration, most change was in-
duced over time within societies.

Although treating an entire continent with some specificity is worthwhile, it
is also perilous. A generalist author can expect rejoinders seeking to discredit
a broader analysis by a critic's superior knowledge of the details in a subplot.
I have tried to deal with the specifics by investing much time in visits, academic and trade literature, and voluminous correspondence. Drafts of the chapters were sent to a dozen or more individuals and institutions in each country,
sometimes in several rounds, and most comments and corrections were incorporated. Often the replies and corrections from the same country were contradictory, mirroring the policy debates in those countries. Despite all the care, I
am sure that national experts will be able to identify some factual disagreements. I invite the reader to keep a perspective. Although an update or additional particulars may be critical to those directly involved, the broader picture
is rarely affected by them.

To be critical of a practice in a European country does not necessarily mean
to approve of its U.S. counterpart. However, this is not a book about American
broadcasting. But it is of course true that the perspective of this book has
benefitted from participation in American policy and research. I should clarify
that most of the book was written before I took leave as a professor at Columbia University and as director of its Center for Telecommunications and Information Studies (which subsequently became the Columbia Institute for Tele-
Information), and before I was appointed to the New York State Public Service
Commission. Nothing in this book reflects the views of that regulatory body
(whose international and broadcast involvements are, in any event, quite negligible). The PSC and its staff of 600 regulate, among other things intrastate
telecommunications and the 10 million lines in the state. It is in frequent disagreement and litigation with the Federal Communications Commission in
Washington. Thus, the views of this book are not necessarily those of official
Washington, nor do they attempt to defend them. The New York State PSC,
for example, instituted low-income telephone service, based on a plan by the
author, that provides basic telephone service for potentially 1.5 million poor
households for $1 per month. I mention this because one of the caricatures of
a liberalized communications policy is that it is by necessity anti-poor and
socially Darwinistic.

A large body of writing sees change in broadcasting as a redistributory challenge by large business interests—many of them American-based multinational
firms—to existing socially motivated and home-grown arrangements. France's
former PTT Minister Louis Mexandeau, for example, discredited a Luxembourg satellite project that would have competed with a high-cost French pres-

tige project as a "Coca-Cola satellite." The reality, however, is much more complex. Domestic structures are less rooted in social benevolence than their defenders claim. A look at their history makes that plain. More important, the imperatives of an information-based economy and a rapidly developing technology do not leave unscathed the institutional structure under which the media system of society functions, and it makes little sense to slay the messenger of that news.

Moreover, this book does not argue for a privatization of public broadcasters or for a reduction of their financial ability to support cultural and social missions. Actual ownership is an issue of secondary concern. Much more significant is the question of the structure of the media sector—exclusivity, entry, flexibility, and choice.

The public broadcasters are organizations of considerable cultural, artistic, and political accomplishment, but this provided no permanent protection before the tides of change. Today these broadcasters are prisoners of their own success. In societies based otherwise on principles of diversity, the notion that virtually all electronic media flows would be squeezed through two or three channels of a single organization seems economically and politically unrealistic if one takes a long-term perspective. The interests of distributors of information cannot predominate for long over those of the producers and users of information.

Such observations, despite their obviousness, are surprisingly controversial in the political and intellectual realms. The political groups in support of the traditional allocation of television are a formidable array of forces. Moreover, they protect a cause of undeniable merit—public-spirited broadcasting—and are opposed by forces of often challenged legitimacy, including publishers with imperial ambitions, Hollywood promoters, and assorted political right-wingers. There are few people without an axe to grind advocating the extension of freedom of speech to electronic media purely on grounds of principle.

Despite its formidable array of support groups, the traditional monopoly system is breaking up. The process of transition is bitter and highly polemical. The integrity of proponents on the various sides is routinely discredited, as if the underlying two principles that must be balanced—information as a public service, and the right of free expression—are not both legitimate societal goals, regardless of the selfishness of their advocates and beneficiaries.

As will be discussed, commercial broadcasting is not bad in the sense of low creativity relative to its self-defined task. It is not necessarily "easier" to create popular entertainment for a huge and fickle audience. Fundamentally, a medium's output is defined by its structure; changing the structure leads to change in the outputs. Private media do not inherently produce low quality. Private book publishers, magazine editors, and film makers have produced both undemanding and excellent creations. When only two or three channels exist, profit- and audience-maximizing broadcasters aim their product at the peak of a distribution of viewers. But when the number of channels increases, economic logic dictates that broadcasters disperse across the task distribution and specialize in programs for particular audience segments. This is what book publishers habitually do.

The emergence of a multichannel option shifts the burden of proof. It is one thing to allocate the only two available TV channels to governmental organizations and to exclude private interests; otherwise the media power and public influence of the few private broadcasters would be unacceptable. But it is another matter to justify the same policy when fifty channels could be available. Now centralized control through a central government seems dangerous, whereas private control over channels can be diffused over a variety of interests. The latter point is a key issue of disagreement. If ownership diversity is economically impossible, the case against private ownership is easier to make. Although many have visions of right-wing media czars, it is important not to miss the forest for the trees. Surely one must also have reservations about a television system in which the creative talents and desire to communicate of a society are restricted into the channels run by the same organization. Johannes Gutenberg's profit-seeking inventive activity was a disturbing element to the late medieval Catholic church. Gutenberg's invention led in time to the empires of Springer and Hersant, but it also led to reformation, enlightenment, science and revolution. In matters of communication, one has to take the long and broad view.

At the conclusion of this project, thanks are owed to a large number of people; only a few can be recognized in these pages, and none should be held responsible.

The project was made possible by the financial assistance of the German Marshall Fund of the United States and later of the Gannett Foundation. Peter Weitz and Gerald Sass deserve the credit for supporting the work and keeping it alive as its scope grew. Without them this book could not have been initiated, written, or concluded.

At Columbia, a lively collection of student research assistants, citation checkers, and typists participated in the project, supervised by Christopher Dorman, Theresa Bolmarcich, and especially Richard Kramer, who contributed much to the completion of this work. Assisting them were Andrew Blau, Barbara Bowley, Laura Bulatao, Andrew Day, Remy le Champion, Sherry Emery, Valere Gagnon, Marilyn Englander, Christine Enemark, Michael McManus, Rhonda Harrison, Erica Simmons, and Mark Young who provided research assistance and editorial help, including fact, quote, and citation checking. Roberta Tasley, Douglas Conn, and Áine Ní Shúilleabháin, as managers of the Columbia Center, provided the necessary organizational structure and often direct help. Les Brown and Barbara Martz provided research materials; Jessica Josephson contributed important editorial help. At the Oxford University Press, thanks are due to Rachel Toor, Steve Bedney, and Herb Addison.

Among academic colleagues and experts from the private and public sectors, both at home and elsewhere, I am grateful to Loretta Anania, Johannes Bauer, Michael Botein, Martin Bullinger, Barry Cole, Richard Collins, John Davey, Wolfgang Edelstein, Martin Elton, Beth Eres, Karl Heinz Fabris, Nicholas

Garnham, Paul W. J. de Graaf, Dina Goren, Shaul Hai, Jaakko Hannuksela, Poul Hansen, Stephen Hearst, Henri Hervé, Wolfgang Hoffmann-Riem (whose excellent annual Hans Bredow Institute yearbook of international broadcasting proved an invaluable source, in particular for some of the smaller countries in the book), Fransisco Pinto Balsemão, Kirsten Beck, Farrell Corcoran, Janos Horvat, Elfriede Hufnagl, Bernt Hugenholtz, Olof Hultén, Knud Jorgensen, Gunnar Karlson, Christian Kobelt, Steven Koltai, Andre Lange, Michael Latzer, Alex Lebanon, Klaus Lintschinger, Claire Manville, John T. Martin, Kjell Nowak, Piero Ottone, Vibeke G. Petersen, Francois Pichault, Richard Pine, Lars Qvotrup, C. J. Rafferty, Karl Erik Rosengren, Herman Santy, Ulrich Saxer, M. Schmolke, Alessandro Silj, Seppo Sisatto, Richard Andersen, Anthony Smith, Matthias Steinmann, Constantinos Stratos, Jeremy Tunstall, Paul Vandebussche, Thierry Vedel, David Webster, Lennart Weibull, and Jürgen Wickert. To those whose names I have inadvertently omitted, my apologies.

Most of all, I owe this book to my wife Nadine Strossen, champion of free speech and human rights in America and abroad; to my mother, who provides the bridge across the Atlantic, and to the memory of my father.

New York   E.N.
April 1991

Contents

Television in Scandinavia and the North Atlantic Countries

Television in the Mediterranean Countries and Eastern Europe

III   THE EVOLUTION OF EUROPEAN BROADCASTING

I

EUROPEAN BROADCASTING: THE SETTING

1

The Emergence of Change

European broadcast policy is rooted in two traditions, both interventionist in nature. One originates in the general treatment of telecommunications, which in turn dates back to the sixteenth century and the establishment of highly profitable state postal monopolies (Noam, 1991). The other stems from the treatment of print publications, with its checkered history of liberalization and restriction.

From the beginning, European governments participated actively in the control of broadcasting. They allocated radio frequencies, declared wireless transmission to be vital to military affairs, and kept a guiding hand on the new communications medium with its considerable political and economic potential. After a brief experimental phase in the 1920s, which included amateur and commercial stations, radio broadcasting was firmly taken under state control in most European countries. World War II provided additional impetus. During the postwar period of reconstruction, dominance over radio served to reestablish social and political controls, and the airwaves became a battleground for the ideological struggles of the Cold War.

When television emerged in the early 1950s (following experimental transmissions in the 1930s), it was resolutely placed into the prevailing scheme of state radio broadcasting. This system was subsequently loosened into independent broadcast institutions, still closely controlled by the dominant social and political institutions.

Although the organizational structures of West European broadcasting varied from country to country, there was much similarity. Typically, broadcasting was centralized in a public institution with a monopoly over television and radio. This organization provided two or three channels of television for the entire country, plus a handful of radio channels. It was (and still is) usually run not under direct government control, but through a semi-independent board appointed directly or indirectly by the government or, more frequently, by the national legislature (i.e., by the major political parties). This assured the major opposition parties of participation, but it was often associated with a heavy internal politicization along party lines. Financing derives from a periodic license fee on television and radio sets, supplemented by advertising revenues. There are, of course, variations on the basic theme. Germany, a decentralized country, allows federal states to control broadcasting. Tiny countries such as Luxembourg and Monaco established themselves early as profitable ''broadcasting havens.'' Britain permitted two commercial television channels. Greece had a military-dominated second channel. France and Sweden made their two or three public channels semi-independent of each other. Finland leased some of the public channel's broadcast time to a private broadcaster. Switzerland and Belgium have separate national broadcast institutions to serve their different language groups. And in the Netherlands, the ideological "pillars" of society collaborate under the umbrella of a single broadcasting authority. But within these variations, for more than a generation the institutions of public broadcasting generally held a domestic monopoly position over television supplemented in border regions by the broadcasts of similar institutions from neighboring countries. Even where more than one public station existed, such as in Germany, they were highly coordinated.

These public broadcasters are generally well financed (especially in comparison with other cultural institutions), highly successful in creating quality programs, and politically and culturally influential. They play important roles in strengthening democratic values and in encouraging the arts. It has been a generally successful system, thus its structure became regarded as the natural order of things, as if exclusivity over a major form of information provision in open societies were not highly unusual. Only in retrospect can one appreciate how anomalous these early decades of television were when entire societies congregated each evening around the limited informational offerings of the one government-influenced giant institution. Such extreme aggregations of mass audiences will likely prove to have been a passing phenomenon, unconnected to the past or the future of media. In time, forces of change began to be felt. For a decade or so they could still be contained; but by the mid-1980s, pressures for opening the electronic media to new participants were everywhere. At the end of the decade, the monopoly position of the public broadcasters had been broken in most countries, either by domestic liberalization or by the entry of foreign program channels delivered over cable television. A chain of events was set into motion. As this process continues to unfold, the traditional system of the broadcasting monopoly is being superseded by a much more complex media structure reflecting the complex societies that underlie them.

Future generations may well consider this opening and diversification of the video media in Western Europe to have been as historic a revolution in the late 1980s as was the democratic revolution of Eastern Europe. And although the drama in Eastern Europe was greater, the long-term impact of the change in West European media may prove to be equally profound for their societies.

Changes in European telecommunications and broadcasting are sometimes viewed as resulting from an offensive by American economic interests. But although American companies played a role in new policies in Europe, most areas of the industrialized world developed home-grown opposition to the monopoly system in quite predictable patterns. Many Europeans struggled with the PTT monopoly since the sixteenth century, and with the broadcast monopoly since the 1920s, and required no transatlantic hand-holding.

For a long time the development of commercial broadcast systems was limited. In Great Britain, a closely regulated private television system went on the air in 1955. In Finland, the private MTV leased several hours of air time each day. And France was surrounded by several "peripheral" commercial ventures in which the French government held substantial control.

Change began with radio, where both the stakes and the entry barriers were lower. An early challenge to traditional broadcasting arose when commercial interests began to focus on young audiences, whose often rebellious tastes had been neglected by broadcast officials, who focused on national rather than on generational culture. The offensive of commercially oriented pirate stations dates back to 1958, when a ship-borne station began broadcasts to Sweden and Denmark. Given the extraordinary paucity of radio channels relative to Swedish and Danish affluence and sophistication (for a long time each country had only *one* radio channel), this was not surprising; other Scandinavian pirate ships soon followed. Despite governmental attempts at suppression, including supranational agreements and official hand-wringing, the practice spread to Holland, Belgium, and Britain. The established broadcasters saw the pirate problem as one of law enforcement rather than of audience dissatisfaction. Changes in program policy were undertaken most reluctantly, as evidenced in the BBC's position referring to the government's view that there was a need for a new service devoted to the provision of a continuous popular music program:

> . . . But it may be pointed out that this need would not have arisen if the Government had dealt firmly with the first pirate stations at an early state in their existence [Robbins, 1967, p.52].

Despite their often devoted audiences, commercial radio pirates had no legitimacy. This began to change when *noncommercial* pirate community stations, heirs in spirit to the early amateur radio operators of the 1920s, and operated by various political and community groups of the late 1960s and 1970s, sprang up all across Europe. The audiences of these stations were small, but they served to undermine the broadcast monopoly and expose its heavy-handedness. Eventually, some of the nonprofit pirates became legalized, since this was politically more palatable than private broadcasting stations operated by business interests. But the limited opening of the monopoly created a breach through which commercial media could eventually enter more easily, especially when the line between community radio and commercial broadcasting began to blur.

Such an opening had been long sought by commercial firms, in particular by publishers and affiliated advertising agencies. Publishing in many European countries is highly concentrated. In Germany, the firms Springer, Burda, Gruner + Jahr, and Bertelsmann have an extraordinary hold over national newspapers, magazines, and books. Springer had in 1989 an 82 percent market share in newsstand sales of national newspapers. The big four publishers' 1988 weighted market share in magazines was 66 percent (*Media Perspektiven,* June 1989). In Austria, one newspaper is read by more than 40 percent of the population. In Switzerland, 75 percent of all advertising is placed by three agencies. In Britain, France, Italy, Sweden, Finland, and Spain, major print media firms emerged. These enterprises had substantial economic and political power;

their further expansion in the domestic print sector had reached the limits of market size and political acceptability. Foreign print markets provided a limited outlet to empire building, but it proved difficult to cross language barriers in newspapers and magazine publishing. An expansion into television seemed a natural horizontal and vertical move. For a while, the more traditionally-minded among publishers viewed commercial television as an unwelcome competition for advertising revenues and public attention. But their more aggressive colleagues began to embrace the notion of participating in private broadcasting and to champion it. Soon they gained the attention of dissatisfied viewers of public television and of politicians, particularly in the economically liberal center and often but not always on the political right.

For the right, the empire building by media firms coincided with its own disenchantment with public broadcast institutions, which they increasingly suspected of having fallen into the hands of the political left. (This attitude mirrors the distrust of American conservatives of the private television networks.) For a while, the rightist criticism was tempered by aversion to the commercial media's emphasis on consumption, entertainment, and sexually explicit content, all of which ran counter to traditional values. A dilemma arose, which eventually forced conservatives to choose between their social values and the protection of their political interest in media control. Increasingly, they supported a commercialization of media, while advocating a number of fig leaves to prevent excesses. This shift also reflected the increasing secularization of societies. In Italy, the Christian Democratic (DC) party had long dominated the broadcast institution RAI. As it lost its control over Italian politics, it had to cede control over the second RAI channel to the Socialists, and accept a Communist role in the third channel. Eventually, illegal private broadcasters emerged, many providing programs that were in obvious conflict with Catholic values. Nevertheless, the DC tolerated and eventually supported private broadcasting.

With conservatives lending greater support to media liberalization, the position of the moderate left was the key. In many European countries, moderate conservatives and moderate socialists possess roughly similar voting strength. For the conservative-supported broadcast reforms to have long-term stability, approval or at least acquiescence from the left is therefore essential. Particular political constellations were necessary to soften the moderate left's initial strong opposition. In Germany, for example, some influential Social Democrats shifted to an acceptance of private television in order to protect the future of the traditional media city of Hamburg. In France, the Socialists embraced media liberalization to assure that the new channels would be controlled by sympathetic rather than hostile interests, and in response to the alienation of the left from the official stations that had long been the tool of conservative governments. President François Mitterrand, like Winston Churchill in the 1930s, had been excluded too often from the airwaves to forget, and put media liberalization on his agenda.

Another factor in the weakening of public broadcast institutions was their increasing financial dependency. In Britain, the BBC in 1987 had a budget of well above $1 billion. The aggregate budgets of the German ARD and ZDF channels were of a similar magnitude. Over time, the broadcasting institutions had become cultural mega-institutions and had gilded the cage of their public service obligations. For a long time, they could absorb their increasing cost of operation through the steady and effortless increase in license-fee revenues that accompanied television's growing penetration. Later, a higher fee was instituted on color television, first as a progressive tax on the presumably richer owners of color sets, but eventually as a *de facto* general increase. Once most households had color television sets, revenues plateaued. Operating costs, however, continued to rise, and the broadcasting institutions became strapped for funds. They responded to the problem by demanding fee hikes, a politically unpopular move, and often by expanding on-air advertising, thus blurring the distinction between the self-commercializing public broadcasting institutions and the private media. Their need for fees led to public debates, which often revealed examples of feather-bedding and mismanagement. While few private firms could withstand similar inquiries, they usually do not make direct demands on the government's taxing power, or at least not as publicly.

In such an economic environment, public broadcasters were especially worried about the entry of rivals. They feared that a reduced audience share would inevitably lead to lower revenues. They also believed that to maintain audiences they would need to lower their program quality. This concern is not altogether persuasive. Although a good number of viewers would probably switch to programs with lower standards, this does not require the broadcast institutions to give up their own excellence. Public broadcasters supported by a license fee could retain quality and socially oriented programs, whether their audience share were 75 percent or 25 percent. The key question is whether their license fees would drop. And here one may note that European countries subsidize a large number of socially beneficial cultural and educational services that are not necessarily used by a majority of the population. Thus, public broadcasters could maintain their programming priorities despite others' rights to receive and transmit alternative programs.

It would be unthinkable if the Oxford or Cambridge university presses, for example, could prevent the establishment of other publishers because they might publish cheap detective novels or gothic romances. Some might argue that television should be distinguished from print publishing as a more powerful medium requiring special restriction. But this argument is circular. A television channel is powerful because of its scarcity. If one press were the only publisher operating in Britain, fierce debates would rage over its control and over proposals to license rivals. Correspondingly, in a television environment of 100 different channel providers, each channel's power would be diffused.

In interpreting the causes of the liberalization of media, many observers point to new technology—the emergence of video cassettes, cable television, satellite transmission. Yet although the new technological options enabled change by providing transmission channels and, importantly, financial mechanisms to charge for their use, they were neither necessary nor sufficient conditions. The opening of terrestrial radio or television broadcasting, for example, did not require new inventions. It was an institutional and political rather than a technological change.

Conversely, the emergence of cable television or DBS did not necessitate their opening to private program providers. Thus, it would be inaccurate to describe media liberalism as technology-driven. Similar changes took place at the same time in the field of telecommunications with monopoly network systems breaking down; here too the underlying dynamics were connected to but were not determined by technology (Noam, 1991).

What can be said about technology is that the introduction of new forms of video distribution destabilized a system whose monopoly status was already under pressure, and that eventually its defenders ran out of fingers to plug the leaky dikes. The technology of cable television reduced spectrum scarcity as an argument for monopoly. Once dozens of channels were available, it was difficult to demand that one state institution should or could program them all. The presumption shifted to private supply, and such supply became available through low-cost satellite distribution. Technology of distribution also made it easier to transform television from a public good, in economic terms, paid for only indirectly, into a private good with buyers and sellers, thus radically altering the economic foundation of the medium.

At the same time, it would be simplistic to view the availability of technology as a *deus ex machina*. Satellites would have become much less of a factor had not several major European countries adopted a political agenda of technology development. Such industrial policy led to state-sponsored creation of rockets and satellites. Once these were technically operational they had to be put to good use to justify the effort. Similarly, in several countries cable television was actively pushed by the PTT telecommunications monopolies as part of their expansion into new functions once they had successfully completed the spread of basic telephone service in their countries. Entry into cable provided some protection from potential rivals in the future, by anticipating them in the market, and it served their affiliated equipment suppliers well. Cable development, too, could be presented as a high-tech policy in pursuit of fiber and broadband switching technologies. Such efforts led to a proliferation of video channels, not as part of media or cultural policy but as a result of economic and development policy in the electronics sector. One part of government promoted activities whose indirect impacts another part of government decried. In the end, economic policy, fanned by the increased globalization of competition, won out over cultural policy, as it usually does, given the relative strengths of their societal proponents.

In the process, however, neither governments nor public broadcasters will become obsolete. The latter continue to have important functions, in particular producing or distributing programs that are not adequately provided otherwise. They are experienced organizations with an important mission and wide support, and they will not vanish. They may even improve as the privileges of their exclusivity vanish. Governments, for their part, will have to seek new approaches. Their task is more complex than before, since an outright ban is easier to enforce than a partial regulation in a complex environment. At the same time, governments' powers are less certain. On the one hand, television program networks are becoming global, reducing control; on the other, local and regional broadcasting is emerging. The notion of the state as the appropriate territorial and regulatory unit comes into question, both from Brussels and the provinces. And from the citizenry, as the notion of freedom of video speech grows familiar, government interference is challenged.

Many people have value preferences against media influence in private hands; they fear the effect of commercial television on consumer attitudes; they shudder at its influence on political values; and they suspect its long-term impact on creativity and perception of reality (McQuail et al., 1986). But in democratic societies, where private interests are responsible for much of publishing and film production, it is difficult to make a principled distinction and explain why the television media should be treated differently from other media, once issues of spectrum scarcity and media concentration have been dealt with.

Clearly, media issues are highly political. Broadcast media are part of our cultural reference and they help to set the political agenda-setting role. Competing groups vie for control over culture because it permits them to influence society. Thus, broadcasting institutions are often embroiled in controversy over values and politics.

The media appeal to each audience segment connotes messages of hostility to other "taste publics" that often correspond to class structure in advanced societies. Pluralism and tolerance are often not well developed here (Gans, 1972). A diverse media environment can serve multiple taste publics. But at the same time, some viewers might not be able to afford certain programs provided in a market environment. Thus, changes in the television system will have negative distributional effects. To keep these effects in perspective, one must remember that such inequality is tolerated in the publication of books and magazines as well as in theater and film. Furthermore, the existing "equality of scarcity" also includes inequities toward viewing audiences that are inadequately served by the small number of existing channels. For other media, a variety of social mechanisms have been established to deal with the equity problem, including public libraries, reduced ticket prices for the young and the aged, subsidized performances and venues, and general income programs for the poor, the elderly, and students. Such mechanisms could also be extended to television programs and their distribution.

Still, it is likely that the distribution of television programming in the future will be less equal than it was in the past. The viewing of arts and culture might become more expensive, and popular programs such as major sporting events will be siphoned off into paychannels. One cannot gloss over the redistributory impact.

By the end of the 1980s, the structure of West European television was very different from what it had been at the opening of the decade. In many instances, the change was embryonic, the public broadcast institutions were still dominant, and barriers were still high. But in most countries private television had been permitted, albeit in a limited fashion and often in a market structure of a public–private duopoly—more open than the previous monopoly, but still a limited television of privileged entry, and of doubtful stability consequently.

These changes form a regular pattern, and one can identify several stages in their evolution, discussed in Chapter 29.

As these changes were taking place, the direction electronic media were taking was unmistakable: television was becoming more diverse, more audience-oriented, more transnational, and more integrated with other media. At the same time, it was less based on national mass audiences, less responsive to political oversight, economically less equitable, and less rooted in national culture. The latter point is the subject of the next chapter.

2

National Culture and the
Iron Law of Hollywood Dominance:
An Economic Critique

Traditionally, an important issue in European media debates is the impact of the liberalization of television on national culture. Critics of change frequently postulate an "iron law" of television, according to which a liberalized television environment would invariably lead to a flood of low-quality imports, typically American. Bad imported programs would drive out good domestic programs. If this were indeed true, one might consider it to be merely a case where the demand for a product is better satisfied by foreign suppliers. But such a conclusion would be mildly subversive to many defenders of the monopoly system, because it suggests that domestic programs are watched only by the grace of some form of cultural protectionism. Hence, a "scientific" argument is usually added to show that it is not the *content* of imported programs that undermines domestic ones, but some underlying *economic logic,* an "iron law" leading to inevitable decline of domestic production absent structural policies.

The argument, in a nutshell, is as follows. A TV broadcast institution, when deciding how to fill its time slots, faces a choice of either costly domestic production or of importing off-the-shelf Hollywood programs that have already been produced and that therefore can be obtained for marginal cost (i.e., for almost nothing). Therefore, given budget constraints or profit maximization (the thesis applies to both public and private institutions), the cheap imports will be economically more attractive than the local production, leaving Hollywood programs predominant. The traditional political pessimism ("The Russians are coming") and economic pessimism ("The Japanese are coming") were joined by cultural pessimism ("Hollywood is coming"). More recently, the political worries have shrunk with the ascendancy of democracy throughout Europe. Yet this has not necessarily led to greater European self-confidence when it comes to film and television. Here the iron law argument is still the staple of discourse, and is shared by many respected media scholars. Hardly anyone bothers to think through its dubious logic. This argument, and a discussion of the reasoning behind it, are the subject of this chapter.

It should also be noted that the treatment of cultural issues by using economic analysis is not likely to be persuasive to those who view an economic approach to cultural issues as a mark of philistinism. Economists are accustomed to various industries or groups denying that economic principles apply to themselves. The author, having only recently served as a politically appointed telecommunications and energy commissioner, is not politically naive as to deny the centrality of noneconomic issues in the media debate. However, if critics to media liberalization make economic arguments, they must accept defending them on the same methodological ground.

It should be noted at the outset that the analysis pursued in this chapter applies largely to the flow of media products between developed countries. When it comes to less-developed or very small developed countries, some of the notions in the following discussion may not be realistic. Moreover, it is not the purpose of this chapter to trace the effects of modernity on traditional societies and the role of information flows in such change. This is important, but has been done by many others. This chapter deals with Western Europe, not the Third World or the new world information order.

Ten Flaws of the Iron Law

A British government White Paper outlines an economic argument that explains the potential for Hollywood programs to drive out British ones:

> [T]he economics of programme production [for cable] will . . . militate for the maximum possible use of the sort of ready-made material of which there are vast archives in the United States available off the shelf at marginal cost . . . an hour of original material can range from £20,000 for a current affairs programme to £200,000 for drama (or even more in the case of prestige projects). Bought-in material from the USA, where the production costs have already been largely if not wholly recovered on the domestic market, can be obtained by the broadcasters for as little as £2,000 [Home Office and Department of Industry, 1983: paragraph 121].

This argument is seriously flawed, for the following reasons:

1. It compares the incremental cost of distributing an existing media product, where investments have already been sunk, to the *total* cost of new production. The statement, "It is cheaper to buy an already produced Hollywood program than to produce a new program domestically" is like saying, "It is cheaper to take a Chrysler-built taxi into the city than to buy a new Austin car." In other words, it compares apples and oranges—the marginal cost of rental with the total cost of production. It assumes that the American program is part of a "distribution sequence," whereas a British program is not. But there is nothing natural about this asymmetry, as will be discussed.

2. The thesis assumes that a Hollywood program would be imported primarily due to its low cost. However, European broadcasters have a choice of programs. Why would a low-quality American program have an advantage? Programs at similarly low marginal cost are available from other English-speaking

countries such as Canada and Australia, as well as from the European continent at the somewhat higher cost of dubbing. Subtitling is quite cheap. Large libraries of motion pictures from around the world are also available at low marginal cost. To a German broadcaster, English-language programs have no cost advantage over French-language ones. Thus, if American programs are indeed of low quality, it would only be necessary to pick from marginal-cost alternatives produced in other countries. (It may be argued that U.S. productions are the "best value," because its domestic market is large; this will be dealt with further.)

The exception would be if, somehow, the entire world could not offer enough programs above the U.S. quality level to fill the program requirements of a country's broadcasters, thus leading to actual dependence on Hollywood. But that is implausible if one simply adds up the film and TV productions in the various countries and then compares them with the program hours needed by a broadcaster, after subtracting time for such domestic mainstays as news, sports, and interviews. The argument further requires a simultaneous abundance of Hollywood productions; otherwise, prices would be bid up above marginal cost by foreign broadcasters in search of product. Finally, it also implies that in the tremendous output, past and present, of Hollywood and U.S. commercial television networks, not enough decent material can be found to satisfy the quality requirements of a foreign channel.

3. Even when imports are cheap, domestic production need not be curtailed. To demonstrate this is elementary. Suppose that there are two types of programs, F (foreign) and D (domestic), and that a programmer has a trade-off schedule for them that is more elastic than Albania's used to be. This, together with the broadcaster's budget constraint, would determine the relative prevalence of domestic and foreign programs.

As foreign imports become cheaper, more resources will be freed up to support domestic production. Depending on the elasticities and prices involved, the *income effect* of the cheaper import could more than offset the *substitution effect* toward the foreign programs. Subsequently, it is possible that *more* rather than less domestic production will take place, unless there is a ceiling on total programs. This shift to increased domestic production is more likely where the preferences for domestic programs are high.[1]

4. The thinking behind the "iron law" is asymmetric. It considers the American product to be exportable to, say, the United Kingdom at low marginal cost, without taking into account the worldwide export value of a similar British production. Indeed, given the global prevalence of public broadcasting, one would expect an even larger international market for public broadcasting-produced programs than for American commercial products. In the United States, too, the advent of cable television systems has created channel packagers with a voracious appetite for programs. Hence, foreign producers would find a large potential market for their productions. This is no mere speculation. In one instance, the BBC switched its program offerings to the United States from the noncommercial Public Broadcasting System to the commercial Arts & Entertainment channel, which promised a higher price. This is not surprising, because all large public broadcasters are under budget pressures and thus want to raise revenues by distributing their production most profitably.

Hence, the potential earnings of international exports must be factored into the economic analysis of whether or not to produce a program domestically. The American market has major barriers to entry. For example, American audiences are accustomed to slick production quality and are uncomfortable with subtitles, British accents, or unfamiliar comedies involving French families. But such barriers may become lower as familiarity increases, audience fragmentation reduces the need to appeal to vast majorities, and foreign producers pitch their programs to U.S. audiences.

This last point leads to the problem accompanying exports. They are a cultural double-edged sword, since they lead both to greater domestic production and to a greater internationalism of the exporting country's media products in order to make them more attractive to foreign markets. British films, for example, often cast well-known American actors, because their presence provides an easier entry to U.S. audiences. The low-budget Italian "spaghetti Westerns" of the 1960s were an extreme case, promoting American imagery.

5. The argument is frequently made that the large U.S. domestic market is able to support many exportable products. It is of course true that the United States is a large and wealthy market. But to conclude from this that producers in that market have a natural advantage requires significantly greater explanations than have been offered. Larger market size may permit production budgets larger than those in small markets and can thus lead to products of greater appeal. Market size does not consist simply of the number of domestic viewers, or else the numerous Indian films would be more successful internationally. Even factoring in wealth, the U.S. market does not give the obvious advantage one might initially assume. The total U.S. audience is far more fragmented among the much larger number of films created in the United States than in West European countries. In 1989, U.S. film production was 472; French, 135; Italian, 124; British, 54; German, 65; and 47 in Spain. Thus, there were 1.92 films per million population in the United States, 2.42 per million in France, 2.16 per million in Italy, 0.95 per million in the United Kingdom, and 1.06 per million in Germany. Thus, the domestic market in the United States may be largest only in a potential sense; in reality, it is quite crowded, and attention is short-lived, especially given the larger number of television productions in the United States, which is not included in the figures above.

Even in absolute terms, European language markets are not small. Counting overseas countries, English, Spanish, Portuguese, French, and German—the main languages of ten European countries—are spoken or understood by over 100 million people. Given these market sizes, it is by no means clear why Hollywood producers should have more production money at their disposal than a European counterpart, considering that Western Europe is a rich region. If European film financing and production budgets are lower than those in the United States, it may reflect caution in European financial markets' willingness to support risky ventures without governmental subsidies, a problem that has also plagued European high technology.

6. It is similarly argued that because Hollywood programs can recover their production costs domestically, they can export them at a low price. But such two-stage thinking—that a film must first make money domestically, with exports considered only as an added windfall—is flawed, for it leads one to consider the size of the *domestic* market as opposed to total potential market as determinative of production decisions.[2] With that kind of thinking, nobody would produce watches in Switzerland or grow Kiwi fruits in New Zealand. And General Motors would dominate the Italian and Swedish automobile markets.

If size of domestic markets alone predetermined export success, the United States would control most world markets. But clearly, there are many types of goods and services where medium- and smaller-sized countries are successful. Presumably, in their investment decision they take the follow-up international markets into account. Moreover, one could expect the opposite—that small countries would be more successful in media exports than large ones because their relative revenues from international sales are greater than those of large countries. Hence, their media products would be expected, at least for profits-maximizing private firms, to be *more* universal and less national in scope. And this would make them, at least as a percentage of revenues, more successful in exports than a large country like the United States.

7. The "iron law" does not take into account the effect of competition for imported video products within a foreign country. It assumes that the price of a product is governed only by its cost characteristics, without regard for the structure of demand. But the nature of demand for television programs is quite strange, except that most participants have become so used to it that they have ceased to notice. If a multichannel environment existed in a European country, an attractive program with some scarcity value from the United States would fetch much more than the low marginal cost broadcasters currently pay. Under any reasonable scenario of competition among program channels, the price for the imported American show would be bid up and would be *above* what conventional wisdom believes is an invariably low standard rate.[3]

At present, a number of cartel arrangements prevent such competition, making rival bidding practically nonexistent. In countries where several public channels are programmed independently, joint organizations exist for the purchase of foreign materials. In the United Kingdom, the ITV companies purchase programs centrally and operate an elaborate allocation mechanism if several companies are interested in the same item. A tacit arrangement of noncompetition exists between the ITV companies and the BBC. This arrangement broke down in one instance when an ITV company acquired the rights to a new season of the American soap opera "Dallas," at the time a highly popular BBC offering. A confrontation and much debate ensued, eventually forcing the ITV company to retreat and leaving "Dallas" with the quality-conscious BBC for another season. In Italy, similarly, government rules against real-time broadcasting by commercial networks kept the bidding for sports events artificially low.

These domestic arrangements are further buttressed by international purchase cartels that prevent competitive bidding between countries' broadcasters and deny program suppliers the option to hold out and seek higher prices from at least some nations in the cartel, especially where cross-border broadcasting could reach many viewers. Foremost among such organizations is the European Broadcasting Union (EBU).

From the beginning, the EBU established a common bargaining position toward copyright holders such as music publishers, denying them a competitive environment for negotiation. The EBU set several standard agreements.

The EBU is also the sole negotiator on behalf of its member organizations for the rights to international events, and it controls program distribution between them. If one sells to an EBU organization in one country, one must deal with EBU members in other countries. For example, the EBU purchases the rights for the Olympic Games for all its members, assessing individual costs according to a certain formula. This allows it to restrict bidding for events and squeeze out potential buyers who seek rights for one country only, thereby limiting payments to the owner of the events. In contrast, the various U.S. networks compete with each other for broadcast rights. This has led to payments that are extraordinarily higher than the ones paid by the EBU for all West European countries.

In 1975, the EBU threatened not to carry the Olympic Games rather than accept the modest $18 million price asked by the Montreal Olympic Organizing Committee (which, along with the Canadian taxpayers, had incurred billions of dollars of expenses to stage the event). After protracted negotiations, the EBU acquired the rights for approximately $10 million. Thus, a three-week event watched intensely by much of EBU's 240 million television viewers was compensated at less than $0.01 per day per household, while Canadian taxpayers contributed huge subsidies. In 1984, the American TV rights to the Los Angeles Summer Olympic Games were acquired by ABC, after competition among the three major networks, for $1.67 per household; the EBU, in contrast, acquired the rights for $0.17 per household without facing competitors (Crane, 1987). The difference between the two reflects monopoly powers.

Some people, shortsightedly, believe that such a squeeze on program production is actually a mark of a superior system. But they fail to make the connection between compensation and production. The EBU system is, in effect, a ''beggar thy neighbor's producers'' system. It is a protectionist cartel in which the interest of the broadcast institutions in receiving programs cheaply dominates over the goal of encouraging cultural production. When each country's broadcast institution tries to minimize its program acquisition cost, they collectively depress the market for program productions. There is only limited independent production, because incentives to invest are low under the traditional system. Furthermore, national broadcast institutions end up subsidizing the cost of domestically produced programs more than they otherwise would have to if adequate international compensation mechanisms existed, or they resort to coproduction rooted in the need to access another market rather than in an inherent logic of production. This increases the dependence of film makers and artistic talent on ''their'' national institutions, because they must operate in an environment characterized by subsidies from one major patron. In 1988, the entire European independent production industry had revenues of only $1.4 billion, in contrast with the in-house production by the broadcast institutions of $7 billion.

8. The fear of an Americanization of media overlooks changes in the supply of American media programs themselves. It assumes a static trend in American production: low quality today, low quality tomorrow. Any potential for variation is overlooked by such spokesmen as the BBC's former Director General, Alasdair Milne, who claims that,

> We at the BBC already know, from years of experience and buying only the best American entertainment programmes, what an immense amount of inferior programming is being offered. To imagine that it is possible to buy additional American programs and maintain a broadcasting standard we are used to, is not to live in the real world [Milne, 1983].

Such a statement seems hard to accept, considering that the BBC, under Milne, had broadcast series such as "The Dukes of Hazzard," which are lowbrow even by the standards of American commercial television. The BBC's selection of some of the least intellectually demanding American shows, while ignoring more notable U.S. programming, is presumably based on the need for broad audience appeal to maintain rating shares comparable to its commercial rival, ITV, and not become one scraped the bottom of the barrel of U.S. productions.

Milne's view is essentially static. Yet the American media are experiencing fundamental changes. In the past, the scarce resource of electromagnetic spectrum permitted only a tiny number of program channels, resulting in program content that attempted to serve the viewing interests of numerous groups. In America, the three major commercial television networks aimed at the peak of the bell-shaped statistical distribution, which is often—but mathematically erroneously—referred to as the "lowest common denominator." This strongly reflects popular tastes.

Commercial broadcasting is not bad in the sense of lacking creativity relative to its self-defined task. High brow productions can have as many relentless cliches and formulas as situation comedies. The outputs of a medium are defined by its structure; change the structure and the outputs will also change. When there are only two or three channels, profit and audience-maximizing broadcasters will aim their product at the peak of a Gaussian distribution of viewers. When the number of channels increases, economic logic dictates that broadcasters disperse across the distribution. Some will specialize in programs for particular audience segments. This will be discussed in greater detail in Chapter 4.

The proliferation of channels in recent years in America changes the medium's structure, leading to increased production and greater differentiation of the overall fare. Fragmented audiences demand both higher-quality shows and lower-quality ones, presenting foreign broadcasters with much more variety to choose from (and to supply to) than in the past. Audience segmentation also led to ethnically oriented channels.[4] Some empirical evidence for diversity is presented in Chapter 3.

9. The argument that American imports constitute a change implies that American exporters do not take international program preferences into account, but view Europe as merely a dumping ground for Hollywood studios and New York networks. Again, this is flawed economic thinking. Before making a substantial investment decision for a series, program producers calculate costs and compare them with expected revenue flows. The latter includes the probability of the series being ordered by a network and becoming an ongoing success, as well as the potential for subsequent syndication revenues in the United States and abroad. In recent years, most series have not broken even financially in their network runs, becoming profitable only through subsequent syndication broadcasts. Thus, the anticipated purchase decisions of foreign broadcasters directly affect the nature of the programs offered by the American producers. A show that clearly has no appeal beyond the United States may not be produced, and therefore not offered to a U.S. network. Therefore, a view of the BBC and other European broadcasters as mere passive recipients of the hand-me-down programming decisions of American producers who inflict them on the international market as an after-thought assumes economic irrationality. Yet a flawed business sense is not usually part of the indictment of Hollywood.

In deciding on the approach, script, casting, and so on, of a film, a rational Hollywood producer will take the foreign market into account. Let us assume that a film has three "content inputs"—D (domestic), F (foreign), and U (universal)—and that the world consists of two countries. Domestic and foreign inputs are those that touch and illuminate familiar experiences specific to their respective societies; universal ones touch upon both cultures. If only the domestic market is served, the producer will utilize inputs D and U up to the point where their marginal cost is equal to the expected marginal revenue they generate. Content input F is assumed to have a negative effect domestically and will not be included. If the second country is now included, where the content input D has a negative audience effect (the "cultural discount" often commented upon), the producer will shift more toward universal inputs. Furthermore, there will now be inputs of F, as long as the value of the audiences gained in the second country is greater than the negative impact in the first country. In other words, the economically rational production decision will be more universal, less domestic, and more foreign-oriented than when the markets are segmented from each other.

Of course, it could be argued that although this model of behavior is theoretically true, reality is very different. In particular, the argument goes, the U.S. domestic market is so competitive that a program must be a superachiever in it; otherwise it would not be produced at all. Thus, even potential success in foreign markets would not help the survival of a program that is not a top hit with American audiences. Hence, foreign audiences play no role in shaping them. This notion of a two-stage maximization is probably empirically true at present, but only because foreign television markets are not yet very profitable.

When reasonable profits can be generated from foreign television distribution, the two-stage model will no longer be rational. Still, would an American network buy only the programs that maximized the domestic audience, without concern for follow-up foreign audiences, thus skewing the producers' choice of the mix of D, F, and U program inputs?

There are two answers to the preceding question. First, if this is the case, it is a by-product of the U.S. rules against network syndication that are defended by the Hollywood producers. Preventing the networks from follow-up gain has the side-effect that they are more likely to choose programs without regard to the after-markets. Second, program producers can offset network preferences by proper substitution of input and budget factors. Suppose that a producer sells an episode to a network for $1 million, the network's expected advertising revenue beyond its own expenses and required profit. This amount provides the cost ceiling for the episode's producer, assuming for the moment there is no follow-up syndication or after-market. For a $1 million total budget, the cast will not include "name" stars, special effects will be limited, and so on. Suppose now that foreign syndication is introduced, and that it could be expected to yield another $1 million. To serve the foreign audience, the program input may have to shift relatively more toward U and F. Although this mix will not be optimal for the network's domestic audience, the producers can use the higher potential revenues to increase the overall production budget, and can hire "name" stars, larger casts, and use more expensive special effects. Consequently, the program will be more attractive for the domestic market, and the network may well acquire it.

Many television network executives deny that production costs affect their selection among programs offered to them; given the cost sunk into programs, this may be true. Still, the fact remains that made-for-TV films have noticeably lower production budgets than theatrically distributed films and that the latter are presented as television program highlights. The mechanism at work is the producer's implicit realization of upper limits on network revenues, which also creates a ceiling on the expected payment from the network for a production and hence on the production budget.

Moreover, current foreign broadcast revenues are relatively small for Hollywood television producers. But when the revenues obtained abroad increase, as they invariably will in a more varied foreign multichannel environment, the impact of global feedback on U.S. decisions will become even more important than before. Hence, the "Americanization" of foreign television environments would be accompanied by a "universalization" of Hollywood television programs, and the end result may be various forms of "mid-Atlantic" programs produced on both sides of the ocean.

10. The "iron law" implicitly assumes that the American head start prevents entertainment-oriented television programs from being produced in other countries. Actually, many non-American media empires emerged, especially once foreign media were liberalized: in Italy, Berlusconi; in Britain, Maxwell; in Germany, France, and Benelux, the Luxembourgeois CLT; in Germany, Kirch; in Sweden, Stenbeck; in Australia, Britain, and the United States, Murdoch; in

Brazil, Teleglobo; in Mexico, Televisa. All have extensive international activities that go far beyond the scope of American networks, and several are also active in production. In 1986, Berlusconi's subsidiaries accounted for 62 percent of all Italian film production, arguably a greater cause for concern than American imports.

Many of the problems of large-scale American program exports result less from American media offensives than from the underdeveloped state of independent film production in the importing countries, which are usually dependent on the monopoly broadcast institutions that are its main clients and financial patrons. The weak state of media financing and the absence of profitable foreign outlets for media products also contribute to the major imperfections of domestic markets. One could argue that some "infant industry" protection would improve this situation. But to confer the status of "infant" upon the cultural sectors of Germany, Italy, France, or Britain is to make a mockery of that term.

The traditional broadcast system reduced the number of outlets that would compete for productions and limited bidding among them. The result favored distribution (i.e., broadcasting) over production. In such a system, distribution was cheap and was thus popular with the fee-paying public and with governments. One could often even afford to take the high road and refuse all advertising. But at the same time, this system contributed to an anemic production sector that existed by virtue of bureaucratic graces. No doubt there are independent producers who will swear that but for the public television system, they would not exist; of course, there will always be beneficiaries from any system. What is more instructive, but much more difficult, is to hear about the unrealized plans and the unproduced programs, the stillborn creativity that is attributable to a restricted system of information production and distribution.

If the traditional monopoly broadcasting system has squeezed program production, how could it have the high program quality it usually exhibited? The answer to that question is the little understood secret of public European television: its attractive existence was based on an unintended subsidy from the despised Hollywood. Countless program hours are acquired for broadcasting at the minimal prices a purchase monopsony can command. The notion that Hollywood employs a system of price discrimination is correct only as a supply analysis. But it entirely ignores demand conditions, which are based on industry structure. In a monopsony system, the price of programs will be lower than where competitive demand exists, assuming a normal upwardly sloping supply curve. This can be seen, for example, in Italy, where program prices are higher per capita than elsewhere. In most countries, programs for which American networks paid a million dollars were acquired only months later for large European audiences at a price of only thousands and sometimes hundreds of dollars. Commercial American producers, advertisers, and audiences thus propped up the European public system. Every time that an American audience endured another commercial message, it made it economically more possible for a European audience to watch the same program without the advertising. Every time a program could be acquired for a trivial compensation based on market power rather than end user demand, American creative talent was in fact being un-compensated. The sincerity with which criticism against low-price "dumping" of Hollywood programs is advanced by the stewards of European broadcast institutions, as if producers seek low-price sales as desirable, shows that they themselves rarely grasp the economic foundations of their own activity, or the extent of its fleeting privilege.

The Paradox of Hollywood Advantage

The export success of Hollywood studios is unusual insofar as they are, by a wide margin, the world's highest-cost producers. Over the years and for a variety of reasons, production costs have grown steadily. Labor unions established high compensation schedules and restrictive work rules. Name actors grew more expensive, since such stars are usually necessary for a film's visibility. The essence of a star is rarity, and scarcity commands economic rents. In the days of the old studio system, actors had long-term contracts with the production companies. As a result, a studio reaped the benefit of early investment in an actor's reputation since it controlled subsequent compensation. But under the current Hollywood system of unrelated deals, actors are the primary beneficiaries of early investments in their reputation, and this is one source of increased production cost.

Another factor is the escalation of the public's expectations: Special effects in a new film set a standard that future films must match or surpass, leading to ever-increasing costs. There are occasional breaks in this escalation when some elements becomes too expensive (e.g., animation or mass battle scenes). But overall, aggregate production costs generally increase with the number of highly specialized skills in production and distribution.

Hollywood's high-cost environment is partly offset by its advantage of econ-omies of aggregation, which are related to, but distinct from, economies of scale. These economies arise not from a single firm's size, but from an entire industry operating in close proximity. As with automobiles in Detroit, financial services in New York, microelectronics in Silicon Valley, silk in Lyon, and cutlery in Sheffield and Solingen, such clustering offers advantages. It makes possible highly specialized firms, shortens communication flow, and provides efficient labor markets. Clusters may be the industrial form of the future, com-bining the control efficiency of small firms with the economies of scale of providers of specialized inputs.

If the Hollywood firms are the high-cost producers and if many non-American programs are offered in the world market, what explains Holly-wood's global success? It is not within the scope of this chapter to answer this question in detail, but some reasons can be suggested.

1. Hollywood programs are squarely aimed at the broad middle peak of dis-tribution of tastes, rather than at more elevated tastes. This also seems to appeal to the broad audiences in other countries. In many European countries there is a gulf between the tastes of producers and the audience, making it more difficult to span the gap between the elitist and the banal. The relative attractiveness of Hollywood programs to European audiences, even after a "cultural distance discount," suggests that the tastes of these audiences, despite decades of higher-quality television, are not markedly different from American ones.

2. America is a country of significant ethnic and cultural diversity; thus, a program that proves popular across its population tends to have many universal themes that appeal elsewhere.

3. By force of America's economic, political, and scientific influence, its themes have reached a global audience, making its own issues universal.[5] This is not simply the might of America that puts its images forward. For example, among the most popular books in Germany have been the 80-plus volumes by Karl May, written around the turn of the century, many of whose adventures take place on the American frontier. These books were written well before the American political ascendancy, and by an author who had never traveled across the ocean.

4. American film production has been at the technical forefront almost from the beginning, creating entertainment on a highly professional level. Its business has moved entertainment production from individualized, small-time operations to mass production with tremendous technical sophistication. Any visitor to Disney World must marvel at the ingenuity with which technology and imagination are harnessed into creating a leisure-time experience (Pryluck, 1986). Entertainment arts are, for better or worse, one of America's best exports, just as wine is one of France's. It is an industrialized process, far removed from the paradigm of the starving artist supported by an official benefactor, which is the model in many other societies.

5. Film and television are part of the broader U.S. service economy. Throughout the developed world, manufacturing-based economies are shifting toward a service base, and this trend is most advanced, among the larger countries, in the United States. Hence, the leadership of the American film production industry is no more surprising than that of the American computer software industry. As its manufacturing loses ground to Pacific Basin countries, the U.S. economy relies on such services for its present comparative advantage. From the American perspective, this makes restrictions against its own media products especially unfair: although it is flooded by foreign manufacturing products, its own export strength in information is stymied on grounds of cultural domination.

6. Of course, there are also organizational reasons for the global penetration of U.S. films, most notably the distribution networks of Hollywood producers that provide them with superior access to theaters worldwide. The practices of Hollywood firms for decades were also the target of U.S. antitrust lawsuits. Unfair distribution practices can be restricted by other countries' laws and regulations on unfair business practices, if evidence of such practices can be demonstrated. There is no reason to assume that European states would be unable to protect themselves. Indeed, power can be exercised against Hollywood producers. An illustration: until 1986, film imports to South Korea of American movies were handled by a Korean national monopoly, which distributed part of its profits to the domestic film industry. When the monopoly was abolished, film makers, their subsidies threatened, began to disrupt theaters showing American films by releasing live snakes and liquid ammonia.

Generally, one should not overestimate the power of a distribution system. Like other forms of vertical integration, discrimination in favor of one's own product is sensible only as long as that product is not inferior. It rarely makes sense for a distribution organization to push its own unpopular films into theaters and reject other producers' blockbusters. Ultimately, the market power of Hollywood distributors depends on their access to Hollywood programs, not vice versa.

The Issue of National Culture

Using the nation as a cultural unit is to some extent arbitrary. If cultural disaggregation is a central value, its logic can be carried on to units smaller than nations, such as regions and cities. There need not be a congruence of political and cultural borders, as national minorities such as Basques or the Welsh demonstrate. Conversely, there are instances in which the cultural unit transcends borders that may well be a historical accident, as was true for a long time of Poland.

Groups and their cultures can be divided into categories that are not based upon geography or language (Morgan, 1985). Class is an important dimension, as in "proletarian culture," and so is age, as in "youth culture." Today, upper culture is substantially transnational when it comes to classical music, ballet, opera, the visual arts, or architecture, and even many literary classics and plays. Culture is often more alien across social classes and age groups than across borders.

For a long time, civilization in Europe was exemplified by clergy and scholars who spoke Latin rather than national languages. Later, it was defined by a highly internationalized nobility (and its bourgeois imitators) whose members had more in common culturally with each other than with their respective subjects. For a time this class spoke primarily French.

The strong emphasis on national culture was largely the creation of the nineteenth-century nation-state, part and parcel of the aggressive nationalism for which Europe eventually paid so dearly. The identification of nationhood and culture became part of a justification for external expansion and internal homogenization. National differences were drawn out to considerable lengths in that era. In Germany, for instance, there was a major conflict between adherents of "sports," viewed as an alien import from England, and "Turnen" (gymnastics) which was seen as genuinely German, largely because its exercises were developed during the Prussian War of liberation against Napoleon. Two separate and hostile athletic associations existed, with the Kaiser's sympathy strongly in favor of the German form of exercise. Is German national culture today being eroded by attendance at a soccer game rather than at a gymnastics event? How many of its citizens know or care?

Linking culture and the nation-state was a concept close to the heart of governments. Cultural creation and distribution were typically centered in the national capital rather than in the provinces or periphery. Some clustering of cultural activities creates economies of scale and of aggregation, but this is not the whole story. From the dawn of civilization, those in power glorified their rule through cultural productions. Artists flocked to the place where subsidies and buyers for their services were most plentiful. Hence, culture tended to flow from the center outward. To a government, influencing cultural activities was crucial, as its producers were among the most generally articulate voices in society. The pen is not only mightier than the sword, but much cheaper. Artists of national culture could be used to articulate the state's agenda, whether it was reducing a division among social classes, increasing harmony among regions, instilling a yearning for lost territories, creating religious conformity, or fostering imperialism. Those artists and intellectuals who opposed the dominant political dogma of the time were usually ostracized as outside the national culture. When their nonconformist politics had ceased to be a threat, possibly after their death, they were often eulogized as exemplars of the same culture

Today the stress on the protection of national culture by various officials in Europe is at odds with the parallel stress on the importance of European integration. Surely no one imagines that the historical removal of intra-European barriers will leave cultures unaffected. The notion of a "European culture" is being officially promoted in furtherance of a laudable political goal (Commission of the European Communities, 1984). Yet it is far from clear why it should make sense in terms of cultural identity for Spain to favor a German television program over an Argentinean one, or for Britain to look to Italy rather than to Australia or America for programs. Furthermore, a European culture should, if anything, be more susceptible to American culture, because the latter has already fused many European countries' cultural influences.

Efforts to create a common European cultural front against Hollywood are not new, and their motives have often been suspiciously economical. Already in the 1920s, for example, Erich Pommer, the head of Ufa, Germany's near-monopoly producer, argued for "European films" and established a European distribution collaboration. His partner, Charles Delac, vice-president of the French film trade association, declared that without a European film cartel the concept of the "European film" would be unattainable (Knops, 1989). Various restrictive contractual arrangements were agreed upon, supplemented by import restrictions enacted by governments. The profit motive behind such policies was recognized at the time. When the German Ministry of Interior drafted a law to "protect the cultural interests in the German film sector," the city of Hamburg argued that this must primarily be used to raise the cultural level of film and not be solely aimed at the one-sided support of the German film industry (Knops, 1989).

Underlying the question of national culture is the difficulty of enforcing group loyalty to societal norms and state control. Loyalty is easier to maintain in small groups such as a family or a platoon. As the group grows, so does the incentive for an individual to free-ride on the group, because the ratio of contribution to direct benefit decreases. The possibility of divergence and coalitions increases, and subsequently, centrifugal forces arise. Stressing the national culture is one way to establish a cohesive force and is an important one for large and heterogenous states with smaller subcultures. Television played a central role as an ideal vehicle for this cohesive culture. For a long time, the nation as a whole, both geographically and socially, was television's measure of reference in terms of reach and control. More recently, the new generation of video transmission technologies has undermined the concept of the national electronic hearth around which the national family gathers. Some of the new media are highly individual, such as videocassettes and records; others are local, such as cable television and low-power TV; still others are transnational, such as satellite transmission. Each rearranges the national audience into more specialized groups, just as magazine publishers have done, reaching different subgroups. Hence, television becomes transformed from the medium of national culture to that of subcultures, often cutting across frontiers, and from a nationally cohesive force to a differentiating, localizing, and internationalizing one.

This is not to deny the obvious, that cultural activities and traditions vary significantly from country to country, and that they are worthy of support. Rather, they aim to instill a healthy skepticism for eager invocations of the concept of "national culture" and "cultural identity" by governments and representatives of powerful institutions, including the broadcasting establishments, arguing for restrictions on media. Cultural politics are real politics, and cultural dominance is real dominance. Notions of protecting national culture are not necessarily benign; they may well mask a form of information protectionism that serves entrenched interests as much as it purports to help the general population.

In the field of television, these protected groups include the state and the political parties (both governmental and opposition) controlling programming policy, personnel, and budget allocation of public broadcast institutions. For a long time the newspaper publishers, particularly medium- and small-sized ones fearing the loss of advertising revenues to commercial television, were among those protected. Other beneficiaries were cultural influentials, as well as journalism unionists, who have achieved links of patronage with the broadcast institutions employing or supporting many thousands of them, often under civil service-like conditions of employment and income security. Although their employment potential would be greater in a larger media landscape, it would be less secure and comfortable, particularly at the upper levels, where political connections are vital. A program of liberalization would mostly help outsiders and newcomers.

Outlook

Protectionism to preserve a new domestically based cultural industry or restrictions on distribution outlets within a country will not work in free societies.

Given the technological changes, information products will cross national boundaries and domestic legal barriers with ever-increasing ease. The era when television consisted of a tiny number of outlets, limited and controlled by the state, will prove to be a brief historical episode.

What are the implications of this growing internationalization and diversification on media production? As discussed in Chapter 1, consumers end up paying more than they have in the recent past, leading to concerns about income distribution.

On the positive side, the change encourages the production and supply of a larger number of TV programs, books, plays, and films. Some works that would not have been created at all are now being produced; but not *all* works benefit equally. The system favors media products that can be distributed through multiple stages, such as popular fiction, and thus aids integrated firms that can shepherd such works through each phase, or that at least can professionally deal with those stages in which they do not participate. This incentive structure extends not only into film and television production, but also into book publishing and theater, as production decisions become dependent on further distribution stages. Similarly, the incentives render productions that are specific to any particular country less attractive than works of global appeal that are distributed internationally.

Where, then, are media headed? The media mix of the future will not be American; it will rest on two foundations: a private sector and a public one. The private sector will consist of a variety of large and integrated international media companies originating in several countries, as well as numerous small producers, often arranged in clusters. This structure will not always result in enough productions of a type that is desired domestically. Therefore a public system based primarily on the traditional public broadcast institutions will continue to exist. Its role, however, will be to *add* programs, not subtract them. A book publisher cannot protect its circulation by preventing the publication or importation of popular books by others. Its survival is based on quality of its output, possibly supported by subsidies, but not on restricting others. Similarly, television productions in Europe are subsidized through the license fee mechanism, channeled through the public broadcasting institutions and through their ability to obtain programs at monopsonistic prices. The license fee mechanism is likely to be maintained even in a liberalized television environment and to be diversified, both through other sources of funds and through additional destinations of subsidies. It is likely, however, that the present public broadcasters' dual role as mass distributors and as producers will become much more separated.

The opening of mature European countries' borders to foreign cultural products will not cause their own cultures to disappear. The presence of Tolstoy, Dickens, and Balzac did not spell the end of German literature. British, American, or Japanese cultures are not undermined by an enjoyment of the music of Bach, Beethoven, or Mozart. Today Latin American literature is among the world's most admired, despite (or perhaps because of) the proximity to the United States.

Ultimately, the popularity of Hollywood glitter does not negate the popularity of domestic productions. Familiar program inputs and the treatment of issues close to home enhance the attractiveness of domestic programming. Audiences are not passive recipients of information and program inputs, but they interpret and process content selectively in light of their own values and priorities.

This chapter has argued that the "iron law" of media Americanization, according to which television liberalization leaves foreign countries to be flooded by Hollywood programs, is seriously flawed in its economic analysis, at least where developed countries are concerned. (The reader should be reminded, again, that the analysis does not claim that economics provide a full explanation of cultural matters.) This is not to say, however, that there will be no impact of liberalization. Important groups in society will lose part of their hold over the process of cultural production, at least that part expressed through television programs. More likely than an Americanization is an increasing cultural homogenization in which programs move in various directions, and their content becomes more universal. These trends will be reinforced by the emergence of integrated media firms controlling many stages of distribution across media and countries. But there is no evidence—theoretical or empirical—that these firms will be predominantly American.

3

Basic Concepts for the New Television Environment

To analyze the changes in the media environment it is necessary to understand some of the basic concepts and forces that affect it. The preceding chapter looked at the forces of internationalization in television media. This chapter continues the analysis of television more generally.

The Shift of Information Products from Public to Private Goods

What is the setting for communications media? The changes in mass media have to be viewed as part of the underlying shifts in the economy and society toward information. Information, broadly defined, is becoming the major input and output of advanced societies. Their economies are in the midst of painful transitions from an industrial to an information base. Mass production is moving to less developed countries, and the manufacturing that does remain in the First World has a high information content. In highly developed nations, the core of economic activity increasingly centers on producing, manipulating, and distributing information. But politicians still tend to think largely in the traditional categories of industrial production and of information as something in need of control. Consequently, public policies tend to favor the producers of hardware rather than the producers and users of information, and to seek the increasingly unattainable goal of gatekeeping its distribution.

Technology and labor productivity directly affect media. Originally, entertainment was only produced live. Theater, song, dance, opera, and vaudeville productions were expensive, because of their relatively small output in terms of audience-hours. As industrial productivity rose, and with it the general wage level, live shows became still more expensive. But technology created substitutes; and the advent of film recordings radically reduced the cost of repeat performances. The economies of information distribution were further boosted with the advent of broadcast technology, which permitted the reaching of a mass audience at extraordinarily low cost, and this reach was later extended further by satellites. But the advances in distribution were not matched by an ability to establish orderly markets for broadcast information, because of the limits to the number of distribution channels and because of the impracticality of charging users for a program they watched. This tended to transform video programs into quasi-public goods (i.e., services not offered through a market mechanism and necessitating cumbersome financing schemes—either the sale of viewers' attention time to advertisers or a governmentally enforced user tax—instead of regular exchange transactions). Much of this has changed through the new forms of distribution media, which permitted an increase in the quantity of programs offered at any time. Even more important, they made it possible to extract payments from viewers directly, thus turning the public good back into a private good, similar to theater, film, magazines, and books. With television back as a private good, the consequences cannot be contained in market-based economies. An expansion of the realm of the market into what Arthur Okun has called the "realm of rights" is always painful, because it offends our basic democratic and egalitarian sensibilities (Okun, 1975). But a similar expansion of the realm of the market was equally resisted when it challenged feudalism and mercantilism. This, of course, provides no dividing line or justification, only a perspective on the ceaselessly shifting and overlapping domains of economics, politics, and culture.

Media Integration

One of the most important economic forces in the present evolution of media is *integration* in the various modes of information production and distribution. Publishing, film, television, and computer applications are merging to form the information industry. Computers, for example, already play a media role in videotex and in generating graphics; they are emerging as a major tool for video editing and special effects; and they may become an element in open-architecture television receivers, which can handle any technical transmission standard, and in the down-loading, storage, selection, and 3-D applications of video media.

Integration means that alternative pathways for the delivery of information are not neatly segregated, as they have been in the past. Video programs can be distributed via terrestrial transmitters (using conventional UHF/VHF frequencies as well as over microwaves), from various types of satellites, over coaxial and fiber cables, over upgraded telephone wires, and by cassettes, records, computer disks, and photographic film. The written word, similarly, can reach users by a variety of paths. This inevitably leads to turf battles among the various interests allied with one form of delivery or another. The disputes, however, are not typically between the public and private sectors. In America, private broadcasters opposed private cable television. In Australia, the public ABC and the private broadcasters were united in their dislike of satellite broadcasting, public or private. It is often more useful to analyze new media issues not along the dimension of private versus public, but along that of newcomers versus incumbents that do not wish to share their favored position.

The various transmission paths are not economically equivalent. Cable tele-

Table 3.1 Theatrical Film Release Sequence: Price, Revenues and Audience Data for Major Media in the United States[1] (1985)

Media	A Effective Retail Price per Viewer	B Net Distributor[2] Revenue per Movie	C Estimated Total Audience	D = B × C Estimated Total Distributed Revenue
Theaters	$3.00–$5.00	$0.75–$1.25	5 million	$3.75–$6.25 mil.
Pay-Per-View Cable	$0.67–$1.33	$0.30–$0.60	10,000–20,000	$3000–$12,000
Pay Cable/Sub-scription TV (prorated)	$0.50–$1.00	$0.11–$0.14	10–15 million	$1.1–$2.1 million
Network Television	free	$0.04	65 million	$2.6 million
Syndicated Television	free	$0.01	45 million	$450,000
Videocassette sales	$4.17–$12.50	$1.04–$3.12	8,000–24,000	$8320–$74,880
Videocassette rentals	$1.25–$2.50	$0.31–$ .62	480,000–960,000	$148,000–$595,200

Source. Waterman (1985).
1. Assuming a $20 million theatrical grossing film.
2. Net of distribution expenses (but excluding advertising).

vision, because of its technological and economic advantages, emerged in the United States as the central medium of distribution, though some of the others hold market niches. In Europe, cable distribution similarly became a main form of multichannel video delivery in several countries.

In addition to the increasing technological overlap of the various forms of delivery, there are strong economic incentives for their integration. The key element is the importance of controlling and coordinating the release of a media production in distribution. Book publishers have traditionally sold hard-cover books first and released lower-priced paper-back editions later; movie distributors initially screened films at major ("first-run") theaters and then at secondary theaters. In America, new television programs went first to the major networks and later to independent station syndication. The underlying principle is the attempt to price-discriminate between classes of viewers of different demand elasticity. Table 3.1 shows the relative revenue per viewer at various distribution modes in the United States.

The ability to price-discriminate is important, because many viewers receive what economists call a "consumer's surplus"; that is, they have to pay less than they would be willing to (e.g., certain sports events, for which audiences would pay substantial sums if they were forced to). The magnitude of this surplus was estimated in 1973, before television became a private good, as $20 billion in the United States (Noll et al., 1973). The significance of most of the new media is that they permit the extraction of this significant consumer surplus by a refinement of price discrimination in which a cascading chain of distribution is set up from low-elasticity audiences down to high-elasticity ones. The former are served first and at higher prices. This requires a coordination and separation of distribution media. A possible release sequence for a work of fiction with popular appeal is as follows:

Hard-cover book or Broadway theatrical production

Soft-cover book or traveling theatrical productions

First-run movie theater exhibitions

Videocassettes

Pay-per-view television

Regular pay television

Network television

"Second-run" pay television

TV syndication to independent stations

Late-night TV

Reducing the previously existing consumer surplus contributes to inequality, because it creates pricey versions of formerly free products. But a historical perspective is necessary. The present consumer surplus has been a temporary rather than a typical arrangement, and it is attributable to the peculiarity of conventional TV as an excellent distribution channel but a highly inefficient collection mechanism for program providers. Television became a public good (i.e., there was no charge for usage). By contrast, few people attend movies, major sporting events, or arts performances for free. Even the Bolshoi Ballet charges for tickets. Between 1948 and 1972, the share of income devoted to movies fell considerably, from 8.7 percent to 2.2 percent, suggesting that viewers, if forced to, would be willing to pay a similar share today for video programs, and probably more, given increased leisure time, greater convenience of home media, and more viewing choices. This dormant demand was targeted by the producers of the new media.

With the incentives for sequential discrimination, there are strong economic reasons for a producer of a program to control, directly or indirectly, the stages of its distribution, because they can establish the most profitable sequence of releases. A series of contractural arrangements could serve a similar role, but their transaction costs in a dynamic environment with constantly varying products are high.

Furthermore, there are externalities from one stage of distribution to the next. Advertising and promotion for the theatrical distribution stage, for example, benefit subsequent cable and broadcasting distribution. There are advantages, therefore, for media firms to be present in every phase of distribution, from books and motion picture to cable and broadcasting (at times offset by the benefits of specialization). This leads to large, diverse, multimedia firms such as Time Warner in America; Bertelsmann in Germany; Murdoch (News Limited) in Australia, Britain, and the United States; Havas in France; Berlusconi in Italy; and CLT in several European countries. Such incentives are not unique to private firms. They affect public broadcasters too. Although they are not profit maximizers, they operate under budget constraints, and they seek to expand their revenue and diversify its sources. Public broadcasters are affected by a greater variety of integrated distribution modes in two distinct and contrary ways. In their capacity as producers of programs, they benefit by being able to sell them more expensively according to the logic of a release sequence. But in their capacity as distributors of others' production, they will be further down the release sequence than before. To maintain their previous position, they would have to pay more than before or else accept a delayed access to programs. In the future, and with more channels under their control, they are likely to establish a release sequence of their own—pay TV, cable channels, over-the-air broadcasting, rebroadcasts, and syndication.

The Distinction Between Distribution and Production

Most discussions of broadcast issues make the analytical mistake of failing to separate the roles of television distribution and production. But these roles are quite distinct. In their purest form, broadcasters are simply outlets for programs produced by others. In that sense, a national market fragmented among "too many" broadcast outlets would not prevent the production of high-cost programs. To claim the opposite, as broadcasters frequently do, is analogous to claiming that books would not be written and published if there were "too many" book stores. The opposite should usually be true: the greater the number of outlets, the more demand would be generated and the more production would be encouraged. Only where significant monopoly rents could be extracted would a more limited number of outlets, under certain demand conditions, provide for greater revenue to support production. In actuality, however, most broadcasters fulfill more than the pure distribution function; they are also producers of programs. Such a function may make sense for productions such as local news or sports, for which they are the only outlet. (Even here, local or regional production companies could take over.) But for more general productions, such as films and national events, the vertical integration of program production and distribution is a much more tenuous affair. In purely economic terms, it does not make sense for a broadcast institution to be a large-scale producer, unless it also tied into a strong international distribution and marketing system, enabling it to defray production costs beyond its immediate range of viewers. Although the primary articulated reason for integration, production, and distribution is the public broadcaster's cultural mandate to produce programs of value and importance, the fulfillment of these obligations does not require in-house production. Programs could be selected from those offered by outside producers, whether public or commercial; when offerings prove to be insufficient, they could be commissioned on the outside. Moreover, it is not necessary that the financing of such productions be the broadcaster's responsibility. This is merely one possible arrangement among several.

Although some cultural and organizational arguments can be made in support of a vertically integrated system, such a system is basically a garden variety vertical extension of a monopoly. In this case, the monopoly over distribution is extended into a substantial role in production. Because viewers (and program producers) have nowhere else to go, broadcast institutions can "buy" more of their own programs, and possibly pay for their own productions' higher prices, than they would otherwise.

It might be argued that a broadcast monopoly would not favor itself, but would let its programs be produced by the cheapest bidder, relative to desired quality. But this implicitly assumes a perfectly elastic (i.e., horizontal) supply curve. As soon as one allows for the more realistic upwardly sloping supply curve, in which a higher market price increases the supplied quantity, a "producer's surplus" exists (i.e., equilibrium is reached at a price where many program producers are able to sell their product at a price higher than the minimum they would accept). This is also known as "economic rent." By purchasing from his own program subsidiaries, a broadcast monopolist can therefore appropriate part or all of this rent or surplus to himself (unless it could discriminate perfectly with regard to price).

Thus, the argument that the existence of vertical integration is necessary to finance the creation of worthwhile programs involves much fuzzy thinking. The basic issue is how to subsidize productions that the market would not undertake. Vertical integration coupled with monopoly in transmission is one way to do so. It shifts monopoly rents of distribution downstream into the program production stage. These rents can be either due to advertising revenue that is higher than that in an open system, because neither advertisers nor audiences have easy alternatives, or due to an undivided hold over the TV set license fee. But as has been argued, other support mechanisms for worthwhile programs other than monopoly rent and vertical integration are possible. For example, the TV license fee could be used to fund a program foundation that would support worthwhile productions by various sources. A monopoly system is not a necessary condition for the creation of quality programs that the market does not provide.

The Supply and Consumption of Information

Although there is much talk about the information society, changes in the media information available to households are rarely quantified. Nor is the shift from print to electronic media measured. Yet it is useful to look at some numbers. One approach to investigate the changes in information that reaches households and its distribution over different media was created for Japan by Tomita and applied comparatively for the United States and Japan by Pool, Inose, Takasaki, and Hurwitz (Pool et al., 1984). They show that the average American "consumed" in early 1980 about 60,000 "words" of mass media every day, about 4000 per waking hour, one word per second. Total TV consumption doubled over two decades from about 20,000 to 40,000 words per day, a growth of 3.3 percent annually. In terms of words consumed, electronic media were gaining, and print media, mostly newspapers, were losing. Television in 1960 accounted for 50 percent of information consumption. By 1980, this had risen to 64 percent. Because only words and not graphic images have been counted, this calculation even tends to understate the informational role of television. These figures relate to *consumption* of information. *Supply* of information is much higher. In 1960, mass media supplied about 3 million words per capita per day—including unwatched TV, unread papers, and so on. By 1980, this figure had increased by 267 percent to 11 million words per capita per day! The ratio of words consumed to those supplied fell in two decades to less than one half of what it had been (from 1.4 percent to 0.6 percent), and this ratio declined for each mass medium. Over the two decades, TV words available daily per person grew from 0.5 million to 2.18 million at an annual rate of 8.8 percent, for a total increase of 436 percent. It further accelerated significantly in the 1980s, because of the penetration of cable.

Radio is the cheapest mass medium in terms of production and consumption, and the most verbose in terms of the total words supplied to the typical household (75 percent of all words in 1960 and 72 percent in 1980). Radio proffered 2.2 million words in 1960 and 7.8 million words in 1980, growing by 252 percent. Consumption grew 150 percent through the period to 14,000, a stable 23 percent of total words consumed.

On a per-word base, books are easily the most expensive of mass media. But they have the highest ratio of words consumed relative to supply. This figure was declining (46 percent in 1960, versus 35 percent in 1980). It is lower (15–20 percent) if one subtracts students and professional browsing and leaves only leisure reading. The number of words supplied is fairly low (4738 in 1960, 6090 in 1980), and growing at 1.3 percent for a total of 29 percent. Home consumption is static, with 2160 words per week per person in 1960 and the same rate twenty years later.

The new viewing options lead to an increase in total viewing time. According to the Nielsen figures for 1985, U.S. households with television but without cable watch television forty-five hours and twenty-two minutes per week, whereas cable households (about half of all TV households), watch a remarkable fifty-eight hours. (Of course, the latter may be self-selected heavy viewers.) Researchers at Michigan State University found that greater viewing options change viewing styles. Viewers tend to move rapidly from channel to channel, watching several programs almost simultaneously. This viewer-active channel hopping is likely to favor programs that are visually arresting and whose plot line is simple to move in and out of. Some TV sets and cable channels permit the simultaneous watching of several channels, and viewers can select the audio signal of the visual image they prefer. Of course, newspaper- and magazine-reading is similarly nonlinear insofar as stories compete for attention and lack a coherent plot.

Just as households allocate time to different media, they also apportion money for them. In 1976, expenses per typical U.S. household were $40 for books (11 percent of total media expenditure); $90 for newspapers and magazines (25 percent); $33 for movie admissions (9 percent); $179 for TV sets, records, etc., plus $16 for TV repair (55 percent) (Sterling and Haight, 1978, p. 117). Thus, more than half of the media budget was spent on electronic media, but this was still less than their percentage in total words consumed (67 percent). Books, on the other hand, were consumed much less (4 percent) than their share in a household budget (11 percent). With movies, the discrepancy was 0.3 percent versus 9 percent, and with newspapers and magazines it was 10 percent versus 25 percent.

Thus, radio and television "words" are a bargain relative to those of movies and print. It is not surprising, in economic terms, that the consumption of TV "words" increased and that attempts were made to raise their price.

Program Diversity: Empirical Observations

Many analyses of the media environment seem to prefer reinterpreting old data to collecting new ones. According to one frequently made assertion, multichannel television (i.e., cable TV) is essentially the same as traditional commercial broadcast television, except that there is more of it. But this view is not empirically based. The diversity of programs available on American cable TV, for example, is much greater than that under the earlier restricted systems, particularly in smaller towns and cities, because additional and specialized program channels provide more variety. In 1990, there were in the United States sixty national satellite-distributed basic channels, five pay-channels, six pay-per-view services (some in the planning stages), thirteen audio services, eight text services, four computer-download services and two cross-channel promotion services over cable (*CableVision Magazine*, 1990, communication). These channels provide programs such as news (CNN), public affairs (C-SPAN), popular movies (HBO, Showtime), special movies (USA, Cinemax, TNT), performing arts (Arts & Entertainment, Bravo), documentaries (A&E and Discovery), children programs (Nickelodeon, Disney), Black-oriented (BET), Hispanic (SIN), sports (ESPN), business (FNN), health (Lifetime), soft-core pornography (Playboy), religion ("pray-TV," such as CBN), music (MTV, VH-1, Nashville), and shopping (CVN, HSN).

It is useful to compare the evolution of viewing options over time, and across the Atlantic. Table 3.2a shows program availability in New York and London in 1969. Table 3.2b, prepared for the British cable industry in 1982, similarly compares viewing options. The table illustrates the program diversity of cable, in terms of quantity, diversity, and quality (Veljanovski and Bishop, 1983).

At that time, London offered three channels, and New York (Manhattan) had twenty-six. In 1990, the number in New York, depending on location in the city, was as high as 70. In London, in the areas where cable television was available, there were 15 channels. The program choice in 1990 is shown in

Table 3.2 TV Viewers' Choice in New York and London

(a) **Wednesday, November 5, 1969 at 9:00 pm***

New York

Channel	Program
2	Sinatra (music)
4	Music Hall
5	David Frost Show (talk)
7	Movie: Man and a Woman
9	Rouge's Regiment
11	Ben Casey
13	News in Perspective
21	University of the Air:
	Eye of Universe (documentary)
31	All About TV (documentary)
41	Mas Alla de la Muerte (Spanish)
47	Secuesto en el Cielo (Spanish)

London

Channel	Program
BBC1	Wednesday Play: All Out for Kangaroo Valley
BBC2	Rowan and Martin (comedy)
ITV	Special Branch: The Children of Delight

(b) **Monday, June 7, 1982 at 9:00 pm**

New York
Manhattan Cable

M*A*S*H (sitcom)
Black Ghetto Life (documentary)
Sister, Sister (film)
Merv Griffin (talk show)
The Kennedy Years (documentary)
Baseball
Spanish Play
Variety Show
Adam and Eve, with Nureyev (dance)
Spanish Drama
Orpheus (opera)
International Education (public access discussion)
Seminar on Nuclear Arms
Baseball
Bye, Bye Birdie (film)
Danger UXB (drama)
Dog Day Afternoon (film)
Gymnastics
Classified Advertisements
Royal Ballet
Folk Art (discussion)
Chinese Cooking
News

London

BBC 1	News
BBC 2	Hitchhiker's Guide to the Galaxy
ITV	Minder

(c) **Wednesday, November 28, 1990 at 9:00 pm**

New York[1] *(Queens—BQ Cable: Time Warner System)*

Channel	Network/Service	Program
1	Preview Guide	Program guide
2	WCBS	Jake and the Fatman (detective)
3	The Weather Channel	Weather Watch
4	WNBC	Dear John (sitcom)
5	WNYW	Movie: Stripes (comedy w/ Bill Murray
6	MTV	"Prime" Music
7	WABC	Doogie Howser, M.D. (Sitcom)
8	ESPN	College Basketball (Kentucky v. Cincinnati)
9	WWOR	B.B. King: King of the Blues (documentary)
10	CNN	Larry King Live (talk)
11	WPIX	Movie: Night of the Fox (George Peppard)
12	USA	Movie: Silhouette (Faye Dunaway)
13	WNET	Power of the Past w/ Bill Moyers: Special about Florence
14	A&E	Our Century: The Vietnam War (documentary)
15	Nickelodeon	Green Acres (sitcom from 1960s)
16	VH-1	Prime Time Music
17	TBS	Professional Basketball (Atlanta Hawks v. Boston Celtics)
18	TNT	Movie: Gone with the Wind
19	Family Channel	Movie: The Man in the Iron Mask (Dumas novel)
20	Lifetime	Six Ladies Laughing (comedy)
21	WLIW	The Unforgettable Nat King Cole (documentary)
22	CNN Headline News	News
23	FNN	Business Tonight
24	HBO	Movie: Descending Angel (George C. Scott)
25	WNYE	Ko-Hyang (Korean)
26	BET	Video Soul (Black Entertainment)
27	TDC	"Wings" (aviation documentary)
28	MSG	Professional Hockey (Wash. v. N.Y. Rangers)
29	Sports Channel Am	College Basketball (Indiana v. Notre Dame)
30	Sports Channel	Professional Hockey (Philadelphia Flyers v. N.J. Devils)
31	WNYC	New York Hotline (talk)
32	TLC	Quarks: Lecture by Leon Lederman (science)
33	CUNY (City Univ. Ch.)	The Constitution (documentary)
34	QPTV Pub Access	Community Bulletin Board (non-profit announcements)
35	QPTV	Is this Your Neighborhood? (documentary on zoning)
36	C-SPAN	Senate Armed Services Committee Hearings
37	C-SPAN II	House Banking Committee Hearings on the Economic Impact of the Persian Gulf
38	TNN	Nashville Now (variety show)
39	E!	Entertainment
40	Comedy Channel	Young Comedians
41	WXTV	Mi Pequena Soledad (Spanish telenovela)
42	Showtime	Movie: Beaches (Bette Midler, Barbara Hershey)
43	TMC	Movie: Karate Kid, part II (Ralph Macchio, Pat Morita)
44	QVC	Diamonique jewelery (shopping)
45	MAX	Movie: L.A. Bad
46	Disney	Movie: Chariots of Fire (Ben Cross, Ian Charleson)
47	WNJU	Movie: La Fichera Mas Rapida del Oeste (Spanish)
48	AMC	Movie: Broken Arrow
49	Bravo	La Gazza Ladra (by Rossini, Cologne Opera Company)

Table 3.2 TV Viewers' Choice in New York and London (*Continued*)

50	WNJM	Movie: All Creatures Great and Small
51	CNBC	America's Vital Signs (medical)
52	JC Penney	"Junior's" (fashion/sales)
53	Prayer Channel	Religion
54	Jukebox Network	Country Music
55	TV55	Movie: Interiors (Woody Allen)
56	QPTV Public Access	Belle of New York (local entertainment/interview)
57	QPTV Public Access	coverage of local events in Greek community
58	HSN	Home Shopping Network
59	PPV	Movie: The Guardian
60	PPV	Movie: The Last of the Finest
61	PPV	Movie: Grave Secrets
62	The Korean Channel	KBS: Korean News via Satellite
63	NATV/Sinovision	Chinese Program
64	ITV/Indian Channel	Movie: Atithee (Indian)
65	The Greek Channel	Sports Programming from Greece
66	Shalom America	Hebrew/Jewish Program
67	Playboy	Fantasies
68	HSN II	Sports Emporium
69	Travel	Video Visits (travelogue)
70	Galavision	El Chavo del Ocho (Spanish)
71	HSN	Electronics (shopping)
72	MSG	Professional Basketball (N.Y. Knicks v. Detroit Pistons)
73	Country Music TV	Country Music Videos

London[2]

Network/Service	Program
BBC 1	Nine O'Clock News
BBC 2	M*A*S*H (U.S. sitcom)
ITV London	Medics
Channel 4	Dispatches: Profile of Margaret Thatcher's Press Secretary, Bernard Ingham
Sky One[3]	Moonlighting (U.S. detective drama)
Sky News	News
Sky Movies	Movie: Cherry 2000 (Sci-fi)
Eurosport	Boxing
Screensport	Boxing
MTV	Music Videos
Lifestyle	JSTV
BSB Movies[3]	Movie: The January Man (Kevin Kline)
BSB Galaxy	Baby Boom
BSB Sport	Motorcycling
BSB Now	Sex, Lies and Love
BSB Power	Music Videos

Sources: New York Times (1969).
        London Times (1969).
1. For Queens. Similar upgrade for Manhattan system required by 1992.
   Sources: Preview Guide, TV Guide, N.Y. Times.
2. Where cable available.
   Source: Time Out Magazine.
3. BSB and Sky merged in late 1990 into a single 5-channel system.

Table 3.2c. It is difficult not to conclude that the diversity of program choice has increased considerably, and that it includes programs of high quality.

On a randomly picked evening at 9 P.M., one could watch in New York's borough of Queens the movies "Chariots of Fire," Woody Allen's "Interiors," "Gone with the Wind," Dumas' "The Man with the Iron Mask," and "The Karate Kid." There were thirteen other films shown at that time, starring Faye Dunaway, George C. Scott, George Peppard, and Bette Midler. There were films in Chinese, Spanish, and Indian. One could watch at that time separate documentaries about the history of Florence, the Vietnam War, the singer Nat King Cole, another famous blues singer, aviation, physics, the U.S. Constitution, and medicine. There was an opera by Rossini, two channels of popular music, three of country music, and one of soul. There were variety and entertainment (2 channels), comedy, soft-porn, and shopping (4). There were channels in Spanish (2), Greek (2), Korean, Chinese, Indian, and Hebrew. There was basketball (3), hockey (3), and a Greek sports program. There was religion, news (4) including in Korean and Greek, talk, business, weather, congressional hearings (one channel for the Senate and one for the House). Local programming was served by community bulletin board, a program on local zoning, a local interview program, and a local Greek program. Of traditional T.V. series, one can count five.

As large as this diversity is, it was scheduled to be doubled, with an announced upgrade for Queens to 150 channels, to start operation in 1993.

Comparisons of program content are difficult to make. For example, one study compared the share of informative and entertaining programs during the late 1970s in Germany, Great Britain, and the United States (using New York as the American sample point). The findings were that the percentage of informative programs was clearly higher for the public broadcasting authorities (Kellner and Schmidt, 1979). The two public German networks ARD and ZDF had, respectively, a very high 62 percent and 58 percent of programs in the informational category. In contrast, the British commercial ITV and the New York commercial station had 47 percent and 36 percent respectively of such programs. At the same time, New York had eleven over-the-air and twenty-six cable channels, whereas German and British television had only three or four channels. Therefore, in *absolute* terms, the study finds a larger quantity of information programs available in New York. This is an important point. As the number of channels goes up, the likelihood of audience satisfaction, including demanding segments thereof, increases, even if the additional channels are largely "more of the same." A good test is to take a program guide for a multichannel cable system and to check off the programs one deems good and interesting. Even discerning viewers will come up with a surprisingly large number of such programs, probably many more than they could actually watch. Furthermore, as will be shown in Chapter 4, it is unlikely that new channels would merely duplicate existing offerings.

The Center for Telecommunications and Information Studies at Columbia University (now Columbia Institute for Tele-Information, C.I.T.I.) conducted several analyses of the program diversity in American cities by comparing a typical week's programs in 1985 with those of 1970. The results show tremendous change. In 1985, a medium-sized heartland city like Tulsa, Oklahoma, had a program diversity and quantity far beyond anything that existed only a few years earlier in a much larger city like New York. During the fifteen-year period, Tulsa added two broadcast stations to its initial four, while building a thirty-five-channel cable system that carried the broadcast stations as well as additional channels. In 1990, forty-one channels were active. To analyze changes in program quantity and distribution, broad categories of programs, such as "Informational" and "Feature Film," were defined. These were then subdivided into forty-two subcategories, such as "Police, Mystery, and Suspense" and "Current Issues Documentary." The numbers show that total program hours increased elevenfold from 1970 to 1985 (See Table 3.3) (Jackson, 1985). Of major program categories, informational programs increased tenfold, from eighty-seven to 1015 hours per week; entertainment quadrupled, to 768 hours; news increased tenfold to 612 hours; and religious programs popular in the Bible belt community, increased fortyfold to 400 hours. These are phenomenal quantities. Among subcategories, there are major quantity increases in every segment. Even where the percentage is small, the absolute number of hours is high: performing arts were offered 54.5 hours during the week, up from 4.5 hours. Public affairs were 181.3 hours per week, up from 2.3; money and finance were 120 hours, up from 1.0; children's informational programs were offered 30.8 hours, up from 13.0; arts documentary had 9.8 hours, up from zero. Every program type had at least 43 percent more time, and ten new program types appeared. On the other hand, programs specifically aimed at American Indians, who comprise a part of Oklahoma's population, fell from one hour to zero. Thus, even by 1985 not all segments of the population were equally served, which raises the question of how such programs can be provided. A similar analysis—see Table 3.4—was conducted for New York City, for the years 1970 (precable) to 1985 (twenty channels). The increase in the staples of popular programming was huge: movies, 1098 percent; music, 3764 percent; religion, 864 percent; science, 188 percent; and sports, 970 percent. But other program categories also had major increases, though of a lesser magnitude: children's programs, 142 percent; cultural programs, 127 percent; documentaries, 95 percent; drama, 194 percent; financial, 867 percent; foreign language, 354 percent; news, 224 percent; and science, 188 percent. In contrast, the popular categories of variety fell by 73 percent and games and quiz shows stayed unchanged.

Barriers to Entry

Even in the absence of legal restrictions there are economic barriers to entry. New entrants must bear a substantial cost to establish themselves alongside incumbent public broadcasters. Barriers can be created, for example, by cost structures that are hard for newcomers to meet. Labor agreements are one such

Table 3.3 Changes in Television Program Availability, 1970–1985, Tulsa, Oklahoma

Program Type	Total Hours			Proportion of Total Hours		
	1970	1985	% Change	1970 (%)	1985 (%)	% 1985 / 1970
CHILDREN'S	43.5	297.2	683	9.60	5.62	56
Animated Ent.	15.0	170.4	1136	3.43	3.22	94
Live Entertain.	15.5	96.0	619	3.55	1.22	51
Live Information	13.0	30.8	237	2.97	0.58	20
ENTERTAINMENT	149.0	768.0	515	34.11	14.52	43
Situation Comedy	38.0	172.0	453	8.70	3.25	37
General Drama	4.5	125.5	2789	1.03	2.37	231
Adventure, SciFi	6.5	76.5	1177	1.49	1.45	97
Quiz, Game	24.9	70.5	283	5.70	1.33	23
Police Myst. Susp.	8.5	70.4	828	1.95	1.33	68
Daytime Drama	37.1	60.0	162	8.49	1.14	13
Performing Arts	4.5	54.5	1211	1.03	1.03	100
Western	8.0	44.5	556	1.83	0.84	46
Variety	12.5	39.5	316	2.86	0.75	26
Humor	4.5	29.8	662	1.03	0.56	55
Adult		24.8	na		0.47	na
INFORMATIONAL	87.2	1015.0	1164	19.95	19.21	96
Classrm. Instruc.	32.8	187.0	570	7.51	3.54	47
Public Affairs	2.3	181.3	7883	0.53	3.43	652
Finance, Money	1.0	120.2	12020	0.23	2.27	994
Instruct., Advice	6.3	113.0	1794	1.44	2.14	148
Health, Fitness		112.1	na		2.12	na
Conversation	33.0	98.6	299	7.55	1.87	25
Wildlife Nat. Doc.	0.5	27.5	5500	0.11	0.52	455
Travel	0.5	25.5	5100	0.11	0.48	422
Entertain. News		23.6	na		0.45	na
Biography Docu.	1.0	23.3	2330	0.23	0.44	193
Auction, Sale		20.0	na		0.38	na
Curr. Issue Doc.		16.0	na		0.30	na
Medical Instruct.	1.0	15.5	1550	0.23	0.29	128
Law Documentary	0.5	10.5	2100	0.11	0.20	174
General Document.	4.5	10.0	222	1.03	0.19	18
Arts Documentary		9.8	na		0.19	na
Foreign Language		7.3	na		0.14	na
History Document.	0.5	4.8	960	0.11	0.09	79
Local Affairs	2.7	3.8	141	0.62	0.07	12
Hearing Impaired		3.0	na		0.06	na
Farm	0.8	2.3	288	0.18	0.04	24
SPORTS	25.7	361.2	1407	5.88	6.83	116
Spts. Event Report	2.0	136.0	6800	0.46	2.57	562
Sports Anthology	4.1	131.2	3200	0.94	2.48	265
Sports Event Live	19.6	94.0	480	4.49	1.78	40
UNPROGRAMMED						
Off Air	235.2	564.3	240			
To Be Announced		31.3	na			
TOTAL PROGRAMMED HOURS	437.0	5284.6	1209			
TOTAL HOURS	672.0	5880.0	875			
CHANNELS	4	35				

Source. Jackson, 1986.

Table 3.4   Changes In Television Program Availability, 1970–1985, New York City (Manhattan)

Program Category	Hours		Absolute Change	% Change	% of total	
	1969	1985			1969	1985
Children's	127	307	180	142	12.5	9.0
Comedy	46	169	124	271	4.5	4.9
Cultural	25	43	18	73	2.4	1.2
Disc./Talk/Int.	138	315	177	127	13.6	9.2
Documentary. Biog.	22	43	21	95	2.2	1.3
Drama	77	227	150	194	7.6	6.6
Financial	17	166	149	876	1.7	4.8
Foreign Language	47	213	166	354	4.6	6.2
Game/Quiz	54	74	20	4	5.3	2.2
General News	69	239	169	244	6.8	7.0
Health/Medicine	11	90	79	718	1.1	2.6
Movies	258	540	282	1098	25.4	15.7
Music	11	425	414	3764	1.1	12.4
Religious	14	135	121	864	1.4	3.9
Science/Nature	13	37	24	188	1.3	1.1
Soaps	30	65	35	117	3.0	1.9
Sports	31	337	305	970	3.1	9.8
Variety	26	7	−18	−73	2.5	0.2
TOTAL	1016	3432	2416	340	100.0	100.0
Herfindahl Index (Program Diversity)					0.1207	0.0874
(1.0 = Total Concentration)						
Concentration (top 4 categories as % of total)					59.1	47.1

Source. Fleischmann (1986).

factor. Another way to deter entry is for the incumbent to possess excess capacity (Spence and Owen, 1977), such as the expansion of its previous broadcast activities into additional channels (terrestrial and satellite) and additional times of the day. Entry barriers are higher in a monopoly market, since a new entrant will qualitatively alter the industry structure much more than where no monopoly exists. Adherents of contestability theory (i.e., of the view that a monopoly does not necessarily translate market share into market power) argue that a potential entrant can affect a monopolist's behavior as much as an actual entrant (Baumol, et al., 1982). However, this theory entails the absence of irreversible (sunk) costs for entry as well as other assumptions about the incumbent's reaction (Brock, 1983; Shepherd, 1983). Applied to television, a public broadcaster could move to a centrist programming policy in order to preempt commercial entry. But as the program model described in this book demonstrates, there will be room on either side for rival program supply. The only way to ward off rivalry would be for the public broadcaster to operate multiple channels covering the entire taste·spectrum. This would expand the broadcaster's scale of operations, its political influence, and its financing requirements.

One entry barrier policy is to permit only a small number of private broadcasters to operate by strictly limiting licenses and frequency allocations. This is the cautious, evolutionary approach that several European governments have taken, with the exception of Italy, where events could not be contained. This limited barrier policy leads to a tiny number of highly profitable and influential private channels, at or near the center of the preference distribution.

Whereas a wide-open system would eventually lead to a broad diversity, a limited license policy creates centrist program approaches. Furthermore, the scarcity of such licenses turns their distribution into a high-stakes game of politics and money, as the French experience demonstrates. The holders of scarce commercial licenses quickly become staunch opponents of further liberalization. In Britain, the ITV companies hold highly profitable regional monopolies over television advertising, and they opposed the entry of newcomers with almost as much fervor as the BBC. In the United States, commercial broadcasters fought the FCC's intention to add stations by spacing them closer to each other. U.S. broadcasters also succeeded, for a decade, in blocking the expansion of cable television's transmission of programs otherwise unavailable over the air.

Although limited licensing is often justified by the scarcity of frequencies, this argument has always been overstated. First, if the huge segment of spectrum that governments assign to themselves were reduced, a great deal of room would be immediately available for additional television channels. This would be much more possible in Europe in the 1990's with the reduction in military forces. Second, a surprisingly large number of low-power television stations can fit within the existing frequency allocations. Third, the microwave range has been opened to low-cost broadcasting, both terrestrially and by satellite. Finally, but perhaps most important, cable television has thoroughly overcome over-the-air spectrum limitations. A coaxial cable can carry, depending on the associated hardware, over 100 video channels; if more channels are needed, several cables can be run in parallel. Fiber-optic lines have an even greater potential capacity and a dramatically smaller size. Twenty-six-gigabit transmission rates over a single fiber were achieved in 1988 in the laboratory, which would be enough for hundreds of channels. Soon both cable and telephone companies will use fiber video transmission. For all of these reasons, any "scientific" argument for a limitation of television licenses lives on borrowed time.

A government can try to diversify centrist program offerings of limited private broadcasters by imposing entry conditions that aim at opening up diversity. Grantees of licenses can, for example, be required to provide programming that appeals to minority tastes. Yet if experience is a guide, such obligations are subsequently opposed by commercial broadcasters, because they lead to lost profits. Another strategy to assure program diversity is to award licenses to a diverse set of operators. The Netherlands provides the best example; there, several ideological "pillar" organizations are licensed to share broadcasting.

This chapter provided an analysis of several basic concepts of the new television environment—the shift of TV from a public to a private good, release sequencing and the vertical integration of media, the distinction between distribution and production, the quantitative supply and consumption of information, the empirical extent of program diversity, and barriers to entry. With an understanding of these elements, we can now proceed to the next chapter.

4

A Model for the Analysis
of Broadcast Structures

Given the heated rhetoric surrounding broadcasting and new electronic media, it is surprising how few analytic tools exist for an evaluation of media structure and its change. A television set is enshrined in almost every home, and households allocate extraordinary portions of their disposable time to its viewing. Few disagree that television is a major factor in modern society, with a pervasive influence on politics, culture, economics, and social affairs. Economists, however, have taken little interest in the study of the medium, particularly in the more theoretical aspects of program choice.

In a sparse literature, one can discern two approaches. The first, by Steiner (1952), dates back to an analysis of radio programming; it was continued by Rothenberg (1962), Wiles (1963), and Beebe (1977). The basic concept is the assignment of viewer preferences to fixed program categories.[1] That approach does not analyze different arrangements of control, except for the difference between a competitive and monopolistic broadcaster, and excludes political considerations. The second approach, taken by Spence and Owen (1977) and developed further by Wildman and Owen (1985), provides a comparative welfare analysis, incorporating viewer demand functions. That approach too does not deal with the political dimension of broadcasting control and its impact on program diversity.

This chapter attempts to carry this discussion further and to integrate program choice with public choice theory in a third type of approach. In the past, public choice theorists have analyzed the optimal political platforms that parties would adopt to maximize their political support. This can be extended to analyze television programming, particularly, the relationship between program diversity, channel capacity, and institutional structure. Establishing such an analytical model is important, given the increasing complexity of media and the current discussions concerning its structure worldwide.

As discussed earlier, broadcast policy is distributional policy. Setting up a system that satisfies the taste patterns of one group is in a way like giving that group free movie passes or producing the films it favors. Different allocations result from different structural regimes of the broadcast system. The conclusions of this chapter are that the allocations of an advertiser-supported market system are not different from the political outcome in a populist direct democ-

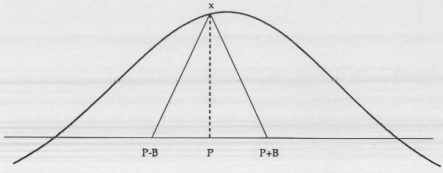

Figure 4.1.

racy; both are squarely at the center of the taste distribution. To provide higher-quality programs, one must institute different structural policies—for example, independent public broadcast authorities, program regulations, and entry restrictions. However, the need for such policies to assure quality programs declines as the distribution of television programs increasingly relies on regular economic exchange transactions. Constituencies supportive of quality programs can be served outside the political system. Hence, the importance of politics in broadcast issues declines, because the redistributive role of the medium is less important than before. This helps explain the growing acceptance of television's commercialization that can be observed in Europe.

The Model

Television programs come in a great variety. We assume for purposes of the model that they can be ordered along an axis ranging from "low culture" to "high culture," using the terminology of Herbert Gans (1974). An ordinal rather than a cardinal ranking is sufficient. For most programs, such classification is possible; some programs may have several content levels, so that an ordinal assignment is more difficult. But it is in the nature of any modeling to simplify.

Any given average quality level, which will be denominated the "pitch" of the program, appeals to a segment of the television viewing audience such that it would designate that particular "pitch" as its first viewing preference. Viewers can thus be ranked by pitch preferences in an ordinal fashion. These preferences are distributed unevenly across the population. Few households prefer a program on modern poetry over all other alternatives. At the other extreme—despite H. L. Mencken's observation that nobody ever went broke underestimating the taste of the American public—one arrives at a pitch of such simple-mindedness that it is the first preference of only a few. Most preferences are somewhere in between. We assume that preferences are distributed normally across the spectrum of program pitches, as depicted in Figure 4.1, with the dimensions defined for a standardized normal distribution. Of course, other dimensions to a program affect preferences, such as technical sophistication, "name" actors, and so on. These elements could be modeled into a multidimensional distribution, but that would complicate the model without adding much to the conceptual analysis.[2]

Although viewers prefer a particular program pitch, they are willing to watch programs in a general range of their first preference, though at a declining rate. This probabilistic assumption permits a relaxation of unrealistic, binary yes–no decision rules of the previous models, which applied a choice to viewing by a given group. We assume that a program of pitch P will be watched within a band of $\pm B$ around P; the audience is represented, on Figure 4.1, by the triangle bounded by $(P - B)$, $(P + B)$, and X. B is not infinite; that is, individuals will not view programs that are too distant from their preferred pitch. There are, of course, anecdotes about people who watch anything, including the test pattern, but these stories go back to the days when television was a novelty. We make no assumptions on the width of B, we assume only that it is constant across the taste spectrum.

Programs are delivered to households by broadcasting organizations under a variety of institutional and regulatory settings. A broadcaster's fundamental programming policy decision is to select its pitch of the programming. Although the selection of programs spans a range, there is an average pitch for a given broadcaster. An illustration is provided by the noticeably differing pitches of an American public broadcasting station versus those of commercial stations (or in Italy, those of the public RAI versus those of the commercial stations). In radio broadcasting, these pitches are often referred to as "formats," such as all-news, classical music, and "easy listening" (Howard and Kievman, 1983). Broadcasters may vary their program pitch over the hours of the day, responding to change in the underlying distribution of program preferences. For example, the pool for daytime audiences has a different composition than that for evening audiences. This leads to different pitches over the day (e.g., soap operas in the daytime) but does not alter the analysis for each given time period.[3] We assume, furthermore, that the cost of acquiring programs for broadcasting is independent of the program's pitch. This assumption will later be relaxed. Also, we assume that once the station's power is set, the marginal cost of broadcasting to an additional household is zero within the station's reach, but that such reach is fixed.[4] We also assume that taste preferences are independent of program pitch.

Single Channel Broadcasting

Limited Commercial Broadcasting

The first case discussed is an unconstrained, commercial, advertising-supported broadcaster X, operating on the only television channel available. Program choice is based on a maximization of advertising revenue, which in turn means—to simplify for the moment—a maximization of audience.

X must thus find the pitch P_1 that maximizes triangle A in Figure 4.1. This triangle represents the total audience. Its height at P_1 is given by the normal distribution.

$$H_{P_1} = (2\pi)^{-1/2} e^{-1/2 P_1^2} \tag{1}$$

Readers unfamiliar with statistical distributions need not understand more of this formula than that the vertical height H_p at any given horizontal point P in Figure 4.1 is determined according to an equation featuring the constants π and e.

With audiences ranging between $\pm B$, total audience A is then

$$\begin{aligned} A &= 1/2 \cdot H_P \cdot 2B = 1/2(2\pi)^{-1/2} e^{-1/2 P_1^2} \cdot 2B \\ &= (2\pi)^{-1/2} e^{-1/2 P_1^2} \cdot B \end{aligned} \tag{2}$$

It is obvious from Figure 4.1 that the maximum area A is reached when $P_1 = 0$.

Strictly speaking, advertising revenues will not be related simply to the size of the audience; rather, the audience will be weighed by its "consumption power," since this is what advertisers seek (Poltrack, 1983). We assume that consumption power equals income, and that income and preference for upper culture are, on average, positively and linearly correlated because of the higher educational levels commonly associated with higher incomes. The pitch P_2 that maximizes C is then determined by maximizing the audience triangle weighted by its median "consumption power" c.[5] The greater the income weight, the more the maximizing pitch will be shifted to the right. In other words, when audience income is factored into the broadcaster's profit-maximizing quality pitch, the program pitch is actually raised in terms of quality.

State Broadcasting

Suppose, alternatively, that the single channel is operated by a government-controlled broadcasting organization. Depending on the policy goals of the government, different programming choices will occur.

Public Benefit

A first strategy is a policy in which the government, in a pursuit to please as many citizens as possible, aims to provide a maximum audience with programs they like; this will be at $P_3 = 0$, identical to the unweighted commercial solution P_1, and in fact at a lower-quality pitch than the income-weighted commercial P_2.

Vote Maximization

A second alternative is that governmental television program policy is not selfless, but designed to serve the interest of the party in control. Let us, for simplicity, assume that electoral contests are carried on by political parties

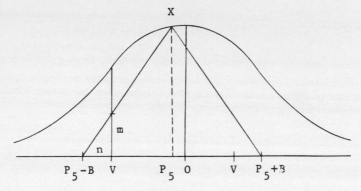

Figure 4.2.

competing for supporters who have various degrees of program quality preferences. Voters with elitist tastes vote for elitist parties, and voters with popular
tastes vote for popular parties. If television programming policy is the only
electoral issue differentiating the parties, they will promise policies designed to
maximize voters (i.e., viewer). Voters will vote for the party promising the
program pitch closest to their preference. In a two-party system, if each party
tries to maximize its votes, this will result in both parties promising a centrist
pitch, aiming for the peak of the distribution, $P_4 = 0$. (Children would be
served only to the extent that enough adults do value television programs for
their own or their neighbors' offspring.)

Any one party's moving off-center would permit the other party to shift in
the same direction and become the first choice of a majority. One may think
that a party's electoral strategy should be not to maximize votes, but to achieve
a simple majority of 51 percent (i.e., a minimal winning coalition) and to
benefit its members as much as possible, rather than dilute benefits across a
large majority. This would be achieved by moving the promised program pitch
off center (e.g., by a distance of up to B). However, the other party, also
seeking a majority, would not move symmetrically into the other direction. To
the contrary, merely by staying at the center or moving toward it, it would gain
a majority. (In fact, it could even move beyond the center toward the other
party's voters.) This would therefore induce the first party to adjust and move
right back toward the center, if it wants to win. Hence, in a two-party system,
program pitches that are off center are not stable platforms.[6]

Spoils System

A third variant is a governmental program policy in which the government
rewards its supporters by providing a program pitch of *their* preference (in
contrast to a centrist one, which also benefits voters of the other party). This
"spoils" system assumes that an election has been conducted on issues other
than television. A winning party controls government and broadcasting, setting
programming policy to please its followers. Let us assume that the victorious
grouping comprises voters with taste preferences to the right of V. (See Figure

4.2.) If the government has a spoils policy, it will set P_5 to satisfy the maximum number of its supporters. It will set programming pitch at

$$P_5 = 0, \text{ if } |V| \geqq \frac{1}{2} B \tag{3}$$

but where the majority is slimmer ($|V| < B$), the general solution is to maximize the triangle defined by P_5 minus the smaller triangle on the left of V. It can be shown (Noam, 1985) that this simplifies to the solution[7]

$$P_5 = -(1 - B/2 + V_0/2) \pm [(1 - B/2 + V_0/2)^2 - 1]^{1/2} \tag{4}$$

Propaganda

A fourth policy would be to take into account that programming is also a propaganda tool that can be consciously wielded in order to influence the hearts, minds, and votes of viewers. It is largely for that potential that control of television has been so fiercely fought over in many countries. Television is thus not merely a governmental public service but also a means of widening and securing its voter base. By choosing a certain program pitch, it can influence viewers' values and eventually their voting preferences. In pursuit of an optimal propaganda strategy, a trade-off must be made between the "purity" of the pitch (i.e., its being squarely within majority preferences) and its reach of opposition viewers. The more "pure" and distant a pitch is from the opposition voters' preferences, the less likely they are to watch the programs. On the other hand, the closer the pitch is to these voters, the less propaganda impact will be made on the actual audience. The optimization problem of propaganda can be stated as selecting a pitch P_6 that maximizes the product of opposition viewers reached, weighted by the distance of P_6 to them. It can be shown that moderate pitch is an optimal broadcast propaganda policy, because of its high reach of opposition audience. Analogies can be found in the international broadcasts of various countries that are aimed at influencing public opinion abroad. For example, the BBC's approach, in its international news, has been to be close to the equivalent of V, projecting a position that is relatively moderate in relation to that prevalent in other countries. In contrast, the Voice of America, for a variety of reasons, aims its programs more at audiences already on its own side of V and thus is reputed to be less effective.

These results have their symmetrical equivalents if the majorities as majority coalitions are on the other side of the spectrum. Then a change in the electoral result in a spoils or propaganda system would lead to a considerable shift in the program pitch. To avoid such instability, the institutional structure of a public broadcast institution must be changed. What that means is that instead of having broadcasting whipsaw back and forth, parties may agree to a form of broadcasting that they will never fully control, even if they have an electoral majority; however, the other party will not control it either. This attitude is more likely where the strength of voting blocs is relatively similar, majorities change periodically, and the ideological differences between the parties are bridgeable. The latter is represented by the single peaked normal distribution, which moves parties toward the center.

The establishment of independent broadcast organization has also another effect beyond stability. We have shown that a two-party electoral system results in a centrist program pitch identical to (or even lower than) the commercial solution. Hence, for viewers in a single-channel broadcast system with a preference for high quality programs, neither the market nor the democratic process leads to satisfactory supply. For their tastes, there exists either a market failure or a "political failure." They do not get their favored programs under either system. To assure their supply with high-quality programs therefore requires a different institutional set-up, in which neither the market nor the populist democratic process is dominant. This would mean the creation of a broadcast system that sets a program policy that is different from the pure democratic one and contains enough insulation to pursue other optimization goals. Hence, independence is not simply the prerequisite for political outspokenness, or balance, which is the typical justification for such a system. Balance will be achieved under a centrist system and recognition of more extreme views could be achieved by regulatory rules by the broadcaster access. More significantly, the independence permits a program pitch that is higher than that of the centrist-populist.

This higher-than-centrist pitch would be reached if the program preferences of an independent broadcast authority were set in a way that corresponded to those of its board, management, and staff. Most of these tend to have fairly high educational levels and above average program preferences. They will view their preferences as those that others should share. But there are limits to their tastes becoming dominant for the program pitch selection. Viewers cannot be forced to watch programs outside their preference; thus, high program pitch is accompanied by an audience loss. Beyond a certain point, further cultural refinement will lose the intended audience. Even though the independent broadcasters could ignore audience figures altogether, this is unlikely. Therefore, an attempt to combine quality with audience numbers through a maximization of "quality-weighted" viewing is likely.[8]

One function of the independent form of governance is to set such a quality weight. The greater it is, the more the programming pitch will be to the right. This optimal pitch is not the extreme of program quality. The model shows that even high weights for culture shift it only up to one standard deviation to the right.

Multichannel Television

The model is now extended to systems that provide more than one channel. Let us again begin with a commercial system including multiple stations. A new commercial broadcaster Y will position itself, relative to an incumbent broadcaster X, so as to maximize audiences. (We ignore the weighting by consumption capacity in the following.) For a given program pitch P_y, audience range is again $2B$. Depending on the choice of P_y, there could be an overlap with X's audience (see Figure 4.3). We assume that within the area of overlap, audiences are evenly split between X and Y. This does not mean that they are

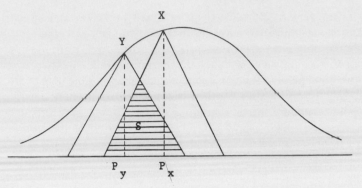

Figure 4.3.

equally shared at a given pitch of overlap, since, depending on audience location, there are unshared audiences above triangle S at any point except for the point of intersection.

The decision rule for a choice of P_y, given P_x, then is to maximize the triangle defined by P_y, minus half of the triangle of overlap S.[9]

The optimization problem for y is then to find P that maximizes area A. This relation is a function $P_y = f(P_x)$, since P_x has been assumed as given. But once chosen, the previous P_x would be modified, since y cuts into its audience. Thus, there is also $P_x = g(P_y)$, creating a simultaneous relation. X and Y settle in an equilibrium at opposite sides of the peak of the distribution. In other words, they do not have the same pitch. Much of the conventional interpretation of television sees commercial broadcasting as inherently striving for identical "lowest common denominators" (Mander, 1978). However, one can see from the model that differentiation is the rational policy.

The addition of further broadcast stations repeats the process, placing stations $x, y, z_1, \ldots, z_n$ across the audience preference distribution. As the number of stations increases, their spread across the distribution widens (i.e., more "outlying" program tastes are reached). At the same time, the spacing between chosen program pitches decreases, and viewers find closer substitutes for their favored program pitches. In the process, the "band" of primary audience tuñed to a station is narrowed, without a shift in preferences. The implication is that program channels become more specialized and that they "narrowcast" to their actual audience. This can be observed in U.S. cable television, where segmented program channels have emerged. Furthermore, the proximity of spacing is closest near the peak of the distribution; these audiences will have the greatest choice of programs appealing to their taste.

Two important measures for programming diversity can be defined. The first is the "spread" of programs from the right-most to the left-most pitch. ($S = P_R - P_L$). "Spread" deals with the reach to outlying preferences but does not measure the extent of satisfying more centrist ones. In Figure 4.4, the areas T_1 and T_2 are regions of substantial nonviewing in a hypothetical three-channel spread-maximizing system (i.e., various segments of the audience are not es-

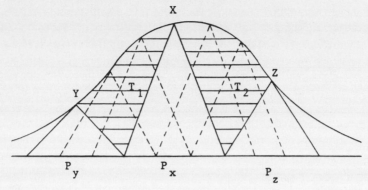

Figure 4.4.

pecially satisfied with the programs that are delivered). T_1 and T_2 are reduced as more intermediate channels emerge.

Therefore, a second useful measure is that of viewer "preference satisfaction," measured by the extent of viewing participation within the entire population. The definition for viewer preference satisfaction is to find the total area under the program triangles as a share of total population. Spread and preference satisfaction grow with additional channels. If entry is limited to a small number of commercial broadcasters, their program offerings will be largely centrist in pitch. Only if entry barriers are lowered and the number of entrants is increased will the spread widen and diversity grow.

It is possible to calculate the change in spread of S and the number of stations that would be required to reach a desired pitch P_E. One question is at what point certain programs that are deemed socially meritorious in terms of quality would be provided by market mechanisms. The model permits an analysis of when such an outlying point will be reached.

A certain symmetry exists in a market provision of program pitches. As the spread moves (rightward) toward higher quality with larger channel capacity, it also moves leftward on the graph toward the lower-pitch offerings, and it also adds centrist programming. (The inclusion of income as a factor is likely to lead to a somewhat greater expansion toward greater quality.) Therefore, it may take a large number of additional channels in a market system to reach an outlying point of high pitch. This may create the impetus to create or maintain regulatory or public ownership solutions as a shortcut to assure the continuance of quality programs. For example, a government may set up a channel with the requirement to have an outlying pitch P_2 (see Figure 4.4). A good example in the United States is the Public Broadcasting System (PBS). Similarly, government regulations may require each commercial station to devote part of its broadcast time to programs of pitch P_2, thus in effect creating the equivalent of a channel of type P_2. The latter policy is imbedded in the U.S. licensing requirement to "ascertain the public interest" by providing programs that deal with issues of concern to the community.

One observation is that one side-effect of a high-pitched public channel is to push commercial stations toward lower-pitched programs. Profit-maximizing commercial television would be somewhat higher in program pitch if the high-quality audience were not served by a public station. Hence, a casual comparison between commercial and public stations can overstate the "inherent" difference in their program pitches. Similarly, an increase in commercial stations reduces, after a point, a public-type station's audience by providing programs that are near substitutes. If that public station has flexibility in selecting its program pitch, and if it did not have to care about increasing its audience, it could move to a higher P. Hence, increased commercial offerings can raise the program quality of a public station too.

This illustrates that the introduction of a commercial television channel that competes with a previously monopolistic public channel does not inherently push the public station lower. If the public station had been initially closer to the center of the distribution, a commercial station near it would push it toward higher-quality programs. If the public station was already fairly far outward in pursuit of a quality goal other than audience maximization, new commercial channels need not take much of its audience. And if they did, by their offering high-quality programs, it is not clear what the social harm would be.

A monopolist (including a cable operator with control over all channels), would be more effective than a coalition of broadcasters in containing channel expansion, because it could limit channel supply beyond the point of net overall marginal audiences, in contrast to the free-entry system continually carving up the same audience into ever-finer slices. A monopoly system can also cover a broader variety of program pitches with a lower number of stations, because it can choose to avoid duplication. For example, Figure 4.4 shows schematically that it takes three monopoly channels to reach a program diversity that would require more channels in a competitive commercial system. This would seem to make a monopoly system more efficient in terms of diversity, in that one range of viewer preferences can be served with fewer resources and less duplication. (We assume for simplicity that the cost of operating n independent channels is the same as that of an n-channel monopoly system.) This is the strongest justification for a governmental system if a maximization of program spread is sought. A maximization of spread may make sense for a government if it corresponds to the spoils systems of several parties in a government coalition. For example, in Italy the public channel RAI-1 is controlled in an almost official fashion by the conservative Christian Democratic party, whereas the RAI-2 channel is similarly allocated to the Socialist party, and RAI-3 is allocated to the Communists. But the Italian system has not proven stable, because the incentives for private providers to serve the centrist audience niches are too strong.

A full monopoly is not necessary to achieve program diversity. Thus, the channel X in Figure 4.4 could be commercial, with different public channels Y and Z serving the outlying areas.

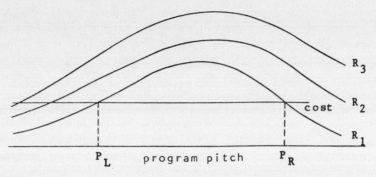

Figure 4.5.

New Media

The so-called new media of cable television, direct satellite broadcasting (DBS), microwave multipoint distribution systems (MDS), and videocassette recordings (VCRs) change the availability of distribution channels. VCRs, in particular, permit the satisfaction of outlying tastes.

To say that more channels of program provision than previously provided are technically possible does not mean that they are economically feasible. To analyze this it is necessary to introduce a measure of cost and relate it to audience size. We assume initially, as before, that the programming cost for each program channel is the same, regardless of pitch. In Figure 4.5, this is represented by the horizontal line C. The bell-shaped curve is that of revenues. If each audience represents equal worth in terms of advertising revenues, with a constant "per thousand" advertising charge, revenues are also distributed normally. This defines the range of economically feasible quality pitches. For a one-channel system, this range is between the intersection points of cost and revenue curves. Further out, cost exceeds revenues, P_L and P_R.

If the upper-quality audiences are more valued than the lower-quality ones, the revenue curve tilts upward around its peak, resulting in the feasibility range shifting to the right. Conversely, if high-quality programs are more expensive to produce than low-quality ones, the cost line tilts upward and shifts the feasibility range toward lower quality.

The emergence of new distribution technologies has several effects. First, it shifts the cost line down by reducing distribution costs. For example, with a satellite transponder that can be rented for a few million dollars, all of North America or Europe can be covered for reception by cable TV systems, master antennas, or direct reception. Second, the new technologies expand the number of available channels, which have been severely restricted by national governmental allocations as well as international frequency agreements that ignore the economic value of the scarce resource of electromagnetic spectrum. These administrative steps have thus created an artificial scarcity for civilian uses (Levin, 1971) and raised entry costs. The new distribution media partly avoid such costly bottlenecks by using either nonbroadcast forms of transmission (cable, fiber-optic distribution, cassettes) or other parts of the frequency spectrum.

By providing added channels, total audiences increase up to a point, because the unserved audiences are being reached. In Figure 4.5, this is shown by R_2, the revenue curve for two channels and varying average pitch. On the other hand, this increased total revenue has to be split among more channels. Because average audiences are decreasing with number of channels, revenues decline with expansion. Furthermore, competition for programs drives up costs of operating a channel. Hence, the economically feasible range of program pitches may shrink in a multichannel environment, if the channels' source of revenues is conventional. It therefore becomes necessary in a multichannel system to create new sources of revenue in order to "stretch" the smaller per-channel audiences. Media liberalization in terms of greater program options is therefore tied to a liberalization of the channels' financing options. Thus, the new types of channels, after a point, may require direct market relations. Audiences can acquire television programs in a regular market setting through basic cable subscription, pay cable, subscription TV, satellite signal unscrambling charges, and cassette rentals and sales (Owen, 1975).

As a consequence, program providers can take into account viewer demand elasticities for different program pitches. For example, outlying program preferences held by only small audiences (outside the feasible set of Figure 4.5) can be satisfied if the demand is sufficiently price inelastic. (In terms of the graph, the revenue curve would be much flatter and less bell shaped.) This also reduces the need for public broadcasting to serve the outlying taste areas and transforms the question of adequate supply to these taste minorities to the one existing in publishing.

Because of the introduction of a market mechanism, income differentials make themselves felt. If income determines willingness to pay and if quality preferences rise with income, the revenues for the right segment of the revenue curve rise higher than those on the left. Thus, although the economically feasible set of program options increases in both directions, it does so most on the higher-quality part of the program distribution. In such a media environment, the higher taste preferences are better served than before, by permitting the superior economic position of their holders to make itself felt.

Conclusion

This chapter established a framework for the analysis of program diversity and audience shares under different regimes of ownership, regulation, and channel quality. The model lends itself to analytical solutions and may serve as a tool to clarify programming decision making and the impact of various institutional arrangements. The audience maximization of commercial broadcasting leads to program quality similar to that of a direct democratic process. To create a bias toward quality, alternative mechanisms have to be introduced. That, together with the potential for the propaganda use of broadcasting and the potentially large rents of controlling a scarce channel, makes questions of broadcast policy extraordinarily contentious for European countries. However, the emergence of alternative distribution channels and payment mechanisms has moved television programs more into the mainstream of economic transactions. In consequence, the need to use the political arena to assure the supply of certain programs has declined, the marginal loss to incumbent channels has successively decreased, and the propaganda reach has been reduced by the growing spread of programs in distribution. Therefore, liberalization of new entry is less resisted, because the stakes have become lower.

Because even in a multichannel environment some program categories are still inadequately served, government action may be needed to assure the production and distribution of programs with a high social value. There is a place for public broadcasting or subsidies for the production of valued programs. Program diversification can be achieved by additive policies of production and distribution support rather than by subtractive entry barriers.

5

Electronic Media and Their Impact

Joseph Schumpeter's metaphor of the creative destruction of capitalism is a useful backdrop in looking at the perceived dangers to culture caused by "new" media. There has always been a tendency by any group of creative people and institutions to identify their own role, and the technology on which it is based as central to culture. When sound was introduced into motion pictures, the German musicians' associations agitated publicly, holding that "sound movies are tasteless" and "sound movies are economic and spiritual murder." When radio was introduced, American researchers noted that the "popularity of this new pastime (radio) among children has increased rapidly . . . (and) has brought many a disturbing influence into its wake. Parents have become aware of a puzzling change in the behavior of their children . . ." (Eisenberg, 1936). In Britain the headmasters of Rugby complained that "Instead of solitary thought . . . people would listen in to what was said to millions of people, which could not be the best things" (*Daily Telegraph*, Oct. 22, 1926; in Briggs, 1961, p. 14). In earlier days, fiction and theater, too, had often been considered as harmful to moral and intellectual values. In Cromwell's England there was no room for the frivolities of a Shakespeare. Even story-telling was suspect at times. Thus, Plato warned that "Children cannot distinguish between what is allegory and what is not . . . it is therefore of the utmost importance that the first stories they hear shall aim at producing the right moral effect."

Today the entry of new forms of television delivery are accompanied by fears that they will harm traditional values of culture and their carriers—traditional broadcasting, books, theater, and film. Are these fears well-founded? Will traditional media decline in their significance and financial viability? This chapter looks into this question. It arrives at an outlook for the future of traditional media that is optimistic, at least based on the experience of the United States.

Film

Because film is the closest substitute for television, the film industry has been concerned with the introduction of new delivery media. The industry—composed primarily of producers, distributors, and exhibitors—still remembers the traumatic years after the introduction of television. In the United Kingdom, attendance fell from 1.2 billion in 1955 to 500 million in only five years, and to a miniscule 55 million in 1984. (By 1988, attendance had risen again to 84 million.) In Germany, movie attendance fell from 600 million in 1960 to 124 million in 1977, while half of the theaters closed (Plog, 1987). Attendance increased slightly thereafter, but the introduction of videocassette recorders dealt the industry a second blow. By 1988, attendance was around 109 million. In France, a country with great enthusiasm for films, attendance dropped from 450 million in 1956 to less than 200 million twenty years later. It rose slightly thereafter, but was similarly hit by the videocassette recorder boom and was 122 million in 1988. In Italy, attendance dropped steadily until 1970, when it stabilized at about 520 million; it then increased, but the advent of private television caused dramatic declines after 1977. By 1984, movie attendance in Italy was 162 million, falling to 100 million in 1988. In per capita terms, attendance in France fell from 3.78 in 1975 to 2.19 in 1988; in Italy it plummeted from 9.63 in 1970 to 1.74 in 1988; in the United Kingdom it dropped from 9.62 in 1960 to 0.98 in 1984, but rose to 1.48 in 1988; and in Germany it declined from 2.67 in 1976 to 2.30 in 1984 and to 1.78 in 1988.

In the United States, too, attendance dropped sharply in television's first years, from 3.4 billion in 1948 to less than 1 billion in 1968. On a per capita basis, theater admissions fell from 32.3 to 9.9 in 1968, and 7.8 in 1972. Box office revenue declined, in real terms, from $2.1 billion to $1.0 billion. The number of movie theaters decreased from 18,000 to 12,000. During those fifteen years, the percentage of homes with television sets increased from 0 to 93 percent. Declines in cinema outlets ended by 1968, with numbers of theater screens increasing since then, from 12,652 in 1963 to 23,132 in 1989. Cinema attendance rose from its 1972 nadir to 1.2 billion in 1984 and 1.13 billion in 1989. Theater receipts showed a similar increase, with box office receipts rising to $5.03 billion in 1989 (MPAA, 1989).

In the United States, as in Europe, the film industry's attitudes toward television progressed in three stages. First, movie studios underestimated television by analogizing it to the radio with its comparatively slow penetration and initially dubious technical quality. Television, however, established itself almost overnight on the foundation of the already existing broadcast industry infrastructure. The film industry was immediately and severely affected by television, with profits at the ten major Hollywood studios falling from $122 million in 1946 to $30 million three years later. The total number of theatrical features produced declined from an annual average of 488 in the years from 1927 to 1947 to 253 in 1954. Labor costs, however, did not fall, partly because of union protection, which raised Hollywood actors' minimum daily wages from $35 in 1945 to $80 in 1956; journeyman prop-makers' hourly wages rose from $1.80 per hour in 1945 to $3.14 per hour in 1956, and writers' weekly minimum from $125 in 1945 to $350 in 1956 (Sterling and Haight, 1978, p. 261).

When the movie studios finally realized the severity of their problem, they went to the other extreme, preparing for battle with wholesale reorganizations of their structure. They abolished the stock company system, with its galaxy of

contract stars and immense fixed costs. (One actor who lost his film studio job
and moved down the prestige ladder to television work was Ronald Reagan.)
Producers also sought a more attractive product through CinemaScope and special effects, such as 3-D and Cinerama. Big budget movies were produced, and
taboo themes television did not dare to touch were taken up by films. In Germany, the film industry fought the new medium under the slogan "Not one
meter for television" and blacklisted actors who participated in TV productions
(Plog, 1987).

During this period of hostility toward television, Hollywood perceived its
audience as the movie-going part of the population. Although the 1948 *Paramount* decree had divested the studios of thousands of their theaters (24 percent
of the U.S. total), the founders of the movie business were still economically
and emotionally attached to theatrical distribution.

The hostility toward television began to crumble in the mid-1950s as producers realized their economic interests were not committed to any particular form
of distribution. They began to produce television shows such as "MGM Pa-
rade" and "Warner Bros. Presents," ostensibly to promote their latest theatrical releases. Eventually, the pretense was dropped and the studios began openly
producing for television, though still through differentiated subsidiaries (e.g.,
Screen Gems for Columbia and Sunset for Warner). This part of their business
rapidly became indispensable, and their market share in network series reached
one-third by 1978. The studios also discovered the enormous value of their
film libraries to the new media and the public's voracious appetite for programs. Despite massive opposition by theater owners, films began to be less of
an exception on television. The resistance of theater owners to TV screening
was breached in 1955 when RKO left theatrical productions altogether, concentrating solely on TV films and offering all of its old films to television. By
1958, almost 10,000 pre-1948 Hollywood films were available to television;
audiences spent 25 percent of their TV time viewing movies, more than four
times the time spent at the theaters. Shortly thereafter, the restriction against
newer movies was dropped, as the studios reached agreements with the unions.
Within a few short years the mighty film studios had become television's clients,
fiercely competing among themselves and with upstart independent producers
to supply the networks. In Germany the vertical relations became so strong that
the television institutions bought up the two largest production studios. The
first channel (ARD) financed 100 films between 1974 and 1985, including the
internationally noted "The Lost Honor of Katherina Blum," "The Tin Drum,"
"Das Boot," and "Paris, Texas."

Like the Bourbons, who had learned nothing and forgotten nothing, U.S.
movie producers repeated virtually the same mistakes with cable television.
First, they ignored cable television and let others take the lead in program
distribution. When they finally realized the importance of the new medium,
they went on an ineffective counter-offensive. The next stage was accommo-
dation: In "pre-buy" arrangements, feature movies were increasingly co-fi-
nanced by cable program channels. The studios began to produce special "for-

cable'' movies, just as they did for the networks, and their film libraries were rented or sold to cable program services.

Despite their myopia, the film producers were helped by the emergence of the new media; the real losers were the traditional broadcasters and networks. Instead of squeezing through only a few main television distribution channels, program producers could reach audiences in many new ways, either by finding alternatives to network distribution or by preceding network distribution with a release sequence moving from low- to high-demand-elasticity audiences. Thus, producers improved both their bargaining position and the potential profitability of their operations. Motion pictures became easier to finance, with a line-up of presold television rights, cable networks co-financing production, advance contracts with theater exhibitors, and cassette deals.[1] Consequently, motion picture production rose in the U.S.; counting movies released by all distributors, film production almost doubled from 258 in 1975 to 472 in 1989. Jobs likewise increased, with 19,700 more people employed in the motion picture industry in 1987 than five years earlier, a 9 percent increase. Production and services personnel increased, from 64,000 in 1975, to 80,800 in 1980, and 132,600 in 1989 (Motion Picture Association of America, 1989 communication).

Because of the increased number of media outlets and for related reasons, the value of film libraries also rose considerably, and this was reflected in the high prices at which several studios were subsequently sold. The steady video rental, cable, and television revenues from these libraries shelter studios from the effects of a few unsuccessful movies in a season.

Demand for foreign films increased, and American cable channels responded by showing movies that would be theatrically exhibited only in a few major cities. Sparse local audiences were aggregated nationally through cable. Cassette recordings can be targeted to still more specialized audiences.

Hence, the new media environment has been a positive development for movie production, employment, and diversity; (on diversity, see also Chapters 3 and 4). These benefits extend not only to major producers but also to the many independent producers, and thus also reduce the client dependence of artists and producers upon a few networks. A certain parallel was the creation of Britain's commercial Channel 4, which strengthened small independent film producers who created artistically respectable programs at a fraction of the cost of the ITV companies, the BBC, or American network programs.

The question arises of whether all types of film production benefit equally. As previously discussed, an integrated media system encourages the creation and production of works with appeal across various delivery media and national boundaries. There is also an increased production incentive for programming suited to middle- and upper-income audiences, whose income carries greater weight for producers' decisions. This situation is no different from the traditional state of book publishing or the performing arts. Furthermore, the production of films appealing to relatively older age groups rather than to the fairly young movie-going audiences is likely to increase.

Weighed against the increases in private production must be potential reductions in the support of independent producers by public broadcasters because of the emergence of new distribution outlets that might lead to a financial squeeze on the public institutions. In 1981, German film makers received only DM 51.6 million in revenues from movie theater ticket sales, whereas they obtained seven times as much (DM 361 million) from German broadcasters (Renz and Taubert, 1983). Negative developments are therefore possible if the public funding mechanism is unwilling to maintain its previous level of support.

Concern about the fate of movie theaters in a multichannel environment is frequently expressed. But it appears that theatrical exhibition will continue despite the pressures it faces. In the United States cinema attendance rose in the 1980s, primarily due to teenagers: more than half of the movie audience was under twenty-four years of age. Similar trends exist in Europe. In Germany, for example, 80 percent of all moviegoers are under thirty years of age. For this age group, the social aspect of movie theater entertainment cannot be replaced by pay cable. Since much of the cable audience is middle-aged or older, they are not significantly diverted from the movie theaters. A second major role for theaters is their promotional role in creating familiarity with and anticipation for a film, which benefits later distribution stages. Theaters also permit distributors to differentiate between customer types, with net distributor revenues per movie viewer ranging from $0.75 to $1.25 (Waterman, 1985). If distributors were to skip this stage they would lose this high-revenue audience to pay cable, which brings in only $0.11 to $0.14 per viewer. (Revenues for videocassette *sales* are higher, but not for rentals.) Because the "first-sale doctrine" in the United States makes it impossible to separate the cassette sales from the cassette rental markets, theater distribution remains at the top of the chain. Cassette recordings and pay cable follow hard on its heels, in some cases only 90 days later, benefiting from the publicity generated for and by the theatrical release. However, much of the second-run theatrical distribution is squeezed out in the sequence, and is the main loser to cable television and cassettes. In the United States, as mentioned, the number of movie screens has almost doubled, from about 12,652 in 1963 to 23,132 in 1989.

Theater

Although they are rivals for audience attention, electronic media and theater are symbiotically intertwined. The theater functions as one of the major training and revitalization grounds for actors, playwrights, directors, technicians, and other creative personnel and their productions. Similarly, work on television productions—even on televised advertisements—provides some economic sustenance to theater artists. Thus, television and theater support each other economically.

The major blow to theater was dealt not by television but by sound films; introduced in 1927, they displaced silent films in about two years and caused a rapid drop in theater attendance, and this was not all. In Europe as in the United States, the booming theater of the early 1920s was hit almost simultaneously by the emergence of radio broadcasting, sound movies, stage labor unionization, and the Great Depression.

It is difficult to get a statistical grasp on the decline in theatrical productions due to television. In the United States of the 1920s, 250 new Broadway commercial theater productions a year were common. Throughout the years of the Depression, the figure was slightly above 100. After 1945, the downward trend was slow but steady, productions dropping in the 1960s to less than forty and to thirty-one in the 1989–90 season (Moore, 1968, p. 14; Poggi, 1968, p. 61; League of New York Theaters and Producers, communication, 1989). This can be partly explained by a trend toward longer-running, "safe" shows, because the total number of playing weeks is similar to 1947 levels. On the other hand, revenues for Broadway shows have quadrupled, to $283 million in 1990, and those for road shows almost quintupled to $367 million in 1990. Off-Broadway theater also picked up considerably, from forty-one productions in 1954–55 to 131 in 1964, and from 1883 performances to 9296 (Baumol and Bowen, 1966, p. 438). The more recent development and spread of new multichannel television media coincides with greater expenditures on theater, particularly among the affluent, educated, so-called yuppie generation, whose movie attendance as teenagers raised film theater ticket sales in the 1970s.

The main problems faced by theaters are financial, and there are only the indirect result of electronic media. During the last twenty-five years, general economic and technological trends have raised the productivity of the industrial sector. As William Baumol noted, the productivity increase raised wage rates first in the industrial sector and then unavoidably in the service and nonprofit sectors, which were forced to match them, although their productivity had not increased. Consequently, operation costs of artistic institutions increased, requiring admission charges and government subsidies to keep pace.

In Germany, governmental subsidies contributed over $40 to each ticket sold during 1980 in the eighty-three public theaters (which offer three-quarters of all theater tickets). The contribution of ticket sales to total revenue was only 16.6 percent. Most of the rest was a governmental subsidy (*Media Perspektiven,* 6/81, p. 494). In the period 1976–82, audiences for plays declined by 8.6 percent (*Media Perspektiven,* 9/83, p. 653). But during 1970–82, administrative personnel increased by more than 20 percent, whereas the number of actors increased by less than 1 percent, and that of singers declined by more than 4 percent (*Media Perspektiven,* 1983, p. 654). In a tight budget situation, theaters became vulnerable to the budget process, and their artistic independence was subject to interference.

Commercial theater has had traditionally close relations with the film industry, but as with publishing, this relationship tends to skew the selection of new plays in favor of those with a certain film and television appeal.

The advent of television has generally benefited the theater community more as individuals than as institutions. In America, commercial broadcasters regarded theatrical drama as lacking in mass appeal. Cable television seemed to offer a solution, and several cultural cable channels were established with ambitious plans for the performing arts. Hopes ran high, but there were early financial failures. Some problems were due to managerial miscalculations and extravagance, others lay in their timing: it requires multichannel cable systems with much capacity in order for cultural channels to be included in a commercial setting, and these were initially not available across the country. It was also hoped that the performing arts could be helped by pay-per-view cable television: opera and theater enthusiasts might pay to watch special events. But it is unlikely that they would be interested in anything less than spectacular productions, big events, and name stars. The same logic applies to videocassette recordings of theater productions.

Although new media can help theater, it can also harm it by undermining public television, whose sheltered position permitted the subsidization of arts and drama. In Germany the ARD broadcasting authorities employed in 1979 eighteen orchestras and four choirs, at an expense of DM 127 million ($70 million), not counting the cost of administrative overhead, technicians, instruments, conductors, copyright payments, and guest soloists. The fear is that the opening of media to new commercial entrants would create financial pressures on public broadcasting, forcing it to become more oriented toward mass audiences, and reduce the support that television provides for the arts. But this fear is based on an asymmetrical perspective. It assumes that new commercial multichannel systems would have no interest in drama productions. Yet the British experience with ITV program companies and with Channel 4 does not support such pessimism. There is also an implicit assumption that the public would not subsidize cultural productions on television by methods other than through a monopoly distribution system. Societies that care about preserving and supporting the performing arts can and will undoubtedly continue to do so. Nevertheless, the artistic community has tended to rally around the existing restrictive structure of broadcasting, believing it to provide stable subsidies for their work. However, to embrace the arrangements that restrict demand is to take a very short-term view. The arts benefit most from many stages and many outlets for talent, rather than from artificial limitation.

Books and Publishing

There has always been great concern about electronic media displacing books. Empirical studies that television watching negatively affects reading have been provided (Noelle-Neumann, 1973). American children's watching more TV and spending less time reading was viewed as having alarming implications for the future of book publishing.

Reading and television watching are not, however, a zero-sum game. A television program can stimulate interest that leads to the reading of a book, and vice versa. According to one study at Michigan State University, fifth-grade children in households with cable access read 2.6 books per month out of school, whereas children with no cable access read only 2.1 books. Similarly, the children in cable households read 1.6 magazines per week versus the 1.3 magazines of children without cable. They were also found to be more active viewers and more exploratory in program seeking. They did not spend more time watching television than noncable children. Moreover, they were less likely to regard TV as mysterious and remote and more likely to feel that acquaintances and children like themselves could appear on television. Of course, factors of family income and residential location are likely to have skewed these findings that are so favorable to cable television. But they suggest that despite numerous studies, the relationship between reading and television is full of contradictory observations. Therefore, it may be more instructive to examine the health of publishing as an indication of how books are faring in a television-rich environment.

During the period since the introduction of television in the United States, the book publishing industry has increased in terms of the total number of titles and books sold. From 1946 to 1980 the number of new titles increased at an annual rate of 5.2 percent from 9746 to 35,651, whereas in the "TV-less" period from 1911 to 1945 it actually declined by an average of 0.8 percent per year, from 11,200 down to 8496 (Paine Webber Mitchell Hutchins, 1982). In 1980, more than 538,000 books were listed in print; by 1989 this figure had increased to 800,000 (R.R. Bowker Company, 1990, communication).

American publishing companies increased from 655 in 1947 to 1652 in 1977 (Noble, 1982, p. 105), and then to 2180 in 1989 (R.R. Bowker Company, communication). In dollar terms, book sales are 0.25 percent of the American GNP, and this percentage has remained remarkably stable since 1960. In the 1930s and 1940s it was only about half as large. Of course, the growth rate of books might have been steeper without television.

A study of information flows into the home (discussed in Chapter 3), found a stable consumption of about 2100 book-words per person per week over the two decades from 1960 to 1980 (Pool et al., 1984). Supply (i.e., books entering the home) rose slowly to about 6000 such words per person per week. The high ratio between consumption and supply of book-words shows that, in contrast to other media, people on average do not buy many more books than they actually read, perhaps because of their relatively high cost.

The nonconsumer segments of book publishing increased rapidly. In the 1970s, textbook consumption grew by an annual rate of 11 to 27 percent of all revenues. Technical, scientific and professional books grew 13 percent annually to capture market share. Religious books had an even steeper growth rate of 15 percent to a 5.0 percent share. The share for general reference texts and university presses totaled 8 percent (Noble, 1982). None of these segments, together almost 54 percent of book publishing, are particularly touched by competition from television. The publishers of trade books, however, are vulnerable to competition. Operating margins, which in 1980 were over 20 percent for college textbooks, were only 1.4 percent (and falling) for mass market paperbacks, 3.8 percent for adult paperbound trade books, and 5.6 percent for adult hardcover trade books.

Specialization allowed small publishers to avoid being pushed aside by large houses. According to U.S. Census of Manufacturing Data, in the period of economic recession from 1972 to 1977, these publishers actually grew from

604 to 1001 (Doebler, 1981, pp. 1–51). As of 1987, according to the U.S. Census of Manufacturing Data, 2180 book publishers were in business in the United States.

Book publishing has become increasingly embedded in a general media system. Because of the low fixed cost book production relative to films or television programs, and because of the low payment of authors unprotected by minimum rates, books are an efficient vehicle for new ideas and plots. More than 40 percent of screenplays for American feature films are derived from novels and short stories (Sterling and Haight, 1978, p. 295). In accordance with the general trend toward interrelated media, several television firms established a presence in book publishing. The relationship benefits publishing because the potential for a subsequent film encourages book production.

Books also receive television promotion through the symbiotic relationship that has developed between authors and television talk shows, with their insatiable hunger for subjects and experts. At the same time, however, the television connection favors the publishing of works lending themselves to capsule discussion on a popular program. It favors the author with a winning personality and ready solutions, shifting the success of a book away from the mediating function of the book critic's expertise and standards.

Beyond trade books, scientific and technical literature has expanded enormously around the world. The economics of this market segment are peculiar. For many scientific and academic authors, book writing is a means to professional recognition, creating a supply of manuscripts that is relatively independent of demand. Such a system has led to a vast increase of publications whose sheer output threatens to undermine traditional publishing, since libraries cannot afford the ever-rising quantities and costs of books written for increasingly specialized audiences. The average library acquisition price index more than doubled from 1974 to 1982 for American hardcover books and somewhat less than doubled for foreign books (Ehresman, 1984, p. 392). The index increased another 38 percent between 1982 and 1987 (*The Bowker Annual,* 1990). Library acquisition budgets in 1982 were only 1.7 percent higher than those in 1975, but acquisition costs rose by 2.15 percent per unit during the same time. Library acquisitions of books fell in the face of the hyperproduction of new titles. Compared with the year 1978–79, book acquisitions by U.S. libraries were lower in 1987 by 9.1 percent in terms of volumes, and 11.6 percent in terms of titles. Book acquisition costs increased 60 percent between 1982 and 1989 (*The Bowker Annual,* 1990).

Although information technology has the potential to reduce administrative costs, especially of cataloguing, the introduction of these systems entails huge investments. Computers were first employed as reference tools and were then interconnected by telephone lines to distant bibliographical on-line data bases, giving birth to an electronic publishing industry. Though at present electronic publishing does not significantly affect traditional book publishing, the electronic handwriting is on the wall. The legal data bases offered electronically are already used by a large number of law firms as a partial substitute for costly law libraries. Similarly, libraries can provide terminals for access to the data banks of central library systems or of publishers themselves, instead of buying reference books and storing them on shelves. Users who at present typically use expensive books at zero marginal cost will be charged on the basis of usage and may end up paying substantially more to conduct their research. This is a mixed blessing for researchers and publishers. Production costs for a "book" will fall, and the lengthy production schedule will be shortened, but the fairly constant number of books sold to libraries will decline, particularly for reference materials, in favor of usage fees that are highly sensitive to the competitive nature of the offerings and to the actual demand of present (as opposed to future) researchers.

The United States and Europe have different approaches to electronic publishing. In Europe the development of public interactive videotex systems such as Prestel, Antiope, and Bildschirmtext (Btx) was emphasized. In the United States more stress was put on the ability to integrate data bases into existing computer and word processing software, terminals, and printers. In consequence, a system of decentralized and technically disparate data bases developed, accessible through the microcomputers and modems that proliferated in offices and homes. In effect, the American approach (to call it "policy" would be a considerable exaggeration) is to allow electronic information publishers to develop as they please, using any available hardware, with the operational role of telephone companies limited to their common carrier function and to optional "gateway" facilities. In Europe, in contrast, the national telecommunications monopolies established large-scale efforts at standard systems. In France the widespread distribution of free Minitel terminals created a critical mass of users. Most other countries' videotex systems were far behind in usership.

Gutenberg's Medium

It is fitting for this more general section of the book to close with a look at what was once, a revolutionary new medium—book printing—and at its inventor, Johannes Gutenberg. Even a brief glimpse reveals a medium borne out of a profit motive, subject to capitalist machinations from the beginning, and almost immediately supplying more fantasies than bibles.

The earliest media of transmission were ceramic tablets and papyrus scrolls. Paper making in China goes back to the second century. In Europe during the Middle Ages, sheets of very fine leather were bound together, forming the first books. Both the material and the writing were extraordinarily expensive and permitted only high-value usage. Although most of the copying work was done by monks for religious purposes, there were also secular scribe shops. In time, some of these enterprises used woodcuts of entire pages to print "block books." The technique became popular with manufacturers of playing cards, and, in 1380 and 1397 led to the authorities' prohibitions of the printing of cards.

The next step in the development of mass media—and Johannes Gutenberg's contribution—was to develop a practicable system of movable type. Strictly speaking, Gutenberg was not the inventor of such printing. Block printing of Chinese books is documented as far back as the year 868 and is attributed to Wang Chieh (*Encyclopedia Britannica,* 1937). Movable printing is credited to Pi Sheng in the years following 1041. From China, the technique spread to Korea, where metal type was documented in 1241 and where development was supported by the state. With their thousands of ideograms, the Chinese language was less favorable for the development of printing than languages using a more limited alphabet. Hence, the impact of movable type was much greater in Europe than in Asia. There is no indication that Gutenberg knew of the Chinese and Korean techniques. Full-page block printing in Europe, however, is documented by 1470.

Gutenberg was far from a revolutionary in terms of his political views. While young he was exiled from his native city of Mainz for siding with the patricians against the middle class guilds. His subsequent political and commercial alliances were with conservatism, wealth, and commerce. Gutenberg's interest in printing arose from his fascination with mass production. Producing hundreds of identical pages was a process similar to his previous major business venture, the manufacture of hundreds of identical mirrors for sale to pilgrims at a shrine. He became keenly aware of the commercial potential of printing, as evidenced by his selling some of his knowhow, shrouded in deep secrecy, for significant sums of money. But his deal soured, and he was soon enmeshed in lawsuits with several of his partners. The records of the lawsuit clearly show that Gutenberg was not pursuing printing for reasons of religion or detached scientific interest; rather, he viewed it as a better means to wealth than mass-producing mirrors. (Gutenberg's entire life also dispels the popular notion that commercial litigation is a curse of the twentieth century. But for the records of his numerous lawsuits we would know little about him.)

The basic idea of movable type was fairly simple, but its practical implementation—finding effective inks, fashioning the right types, and selecting the best paper—turned out to be long and expensive. After his return to Mainz, Gutenberg approached the wealthy merchant Johannes Fust for support in an ambitious project, offering a share of future profits in return for the capital to print the current bestseller, the Bible.

From today's perspective, Gutenberg's first book was extraordinarily ambitious. His Bible had 1280 large pages, with a total of more than 3 million letters. Considering that it was the first real book ever printed, the quality is amazingly high. But this emphasis on excellence proved to be Gutenberg's undoing. During the first three years, he needed an estimated fifteen to twenty assistants to print his Bible, and Fust's financial infusions grew. In 1455, the Bible was completed, but with the aid of the courts Fust took control almost immediately. Gutenberg was left impoverished and embittered, and he died largely forgotten in 1468.

Gutenberg was less successful as an entrepreneur than as an inventor. His printing technology spread rapidly across Europe as some of the printers from Mainz, often Gutenberg's assistants, moved elsewhere or taught their secrets to others. By 1500, 270 different European cities had printing shops that collectively issued 40,000 different titles and 10 million volumes. In some cities there were thiry to forty print shops. Many of the early printers functioned as publishers by securing manuscripts, but they were often unqualified for this responsibility. Soon the scarcity of manuscripts created a bottleneck and competition in book publishing began to depress prices.

Some of the early books were large compendia of information, such as medical tracts, handbooks on various herbs and popular cures or magical animals and their special powers. But in terms of volume, fictionlike books soon predominated, such as the "peoples' books," featuring the adventures of various saints. Fantastic travel stories with horrors of dubious accuracy were also very popular, as were tales of noblewomen's faithfulness or lack thereof. Books of serious literature and poetry were in the minority.

Soon church and state intervened in printing. Alexander VI issued a papal bull in 1501 against unlicensed publishing, and in 1559 the "Index" of proscribed books was established. France controlled printers strictly, and in 1547 one of them was burned at the stake. In 1556, the English government put printing under the charter of the Stationer's Company; in 1583, the Star Chamber limited printing to Oxford, Cambridge, and twenty-one London shops, with rights given to the Stationer's Company to control the printers and to prevent offending publications (Eisenstein, 1968, p. 52). In 1637, England also established restrictions on type founding.

Book printing started with a visionary entrepreneur who published a major book but also led the way to increasingly cheap fantasies. But does it matter? About 500 hundred years later, in one country alone, the United States, 800,000 different book titles were in print.

Johannes Gutenberg was a disturbing element to the late medieval institutions. He put many scribes out of a job and led to the supply of works that may not have been useful. True, Gutenberg's invention led in time to conservative media moguls, but it also led to reformation, enlightenment, science, and revolution. In matters of communication, one has to take the long and broad view.

II

TELEVISION SYSTEMS OF EUROPEAN COUNTRIES

6
Germany

Considering Germany's legacy of an apolitical and PTT-dominated broadcasting system during the Weimar years and a totalitarian system during the Hitler period, the modern German public broadcast system has evolved well in many respects. The public broadcasting system is structurally superior to those of most European countries, because its decentralization provides a greater diversity of approaches to broadcasting and a certain rivalry in performance and quality. The legal status of German broadcasting is more independent than that of the BBC, over which the British government has retained a variety of important residual powers. In practice, however, the German institutions are heavily politicized along party lines. This problem is the cancer that has weakened the system's independence and legitimacy. The absence of institutional self-reform, together with the ascendancy of the highly concentrated publishing industry and the cable construction strategy of the telephone monopoly, led to a limited opening of broadcasting to private interests.

History

German broadcasting has been dominated by the state from its early days. This did not happen by itself; control had to be established. It is therefore instructive to look in some detail at how total state domination was accomplished, even under a democratic constitution.

The 1872 Telegraph Law and its 1908 amendment provided that "electrical telegraph facilities, which distribute information without metallic wires, may be erected and operated only with the permission of the state." When the technology of radio transmission became available, the powerful postal and telecommunication administration, the Reichspost, immediately laid claim to its monopolization. World War I demonstrated the importance of wireless technology. During the war, many soldiers were trained as military radio operators, and some of them participated in the democratic revolution of November 1918. Rebellious military units established their own radio transmission network. The Social Democratic government that came to power sought stability and acceptance and quickly reestablished the wireless monopoly. But many former military signalmen became enthusiastic radio amateurs. In a chronicle of his family's firm, Georg Siemens writes about the consternation of the Reichspost at

the prospect of electronic communications outside of its control: "The Deutsche
Reichspost . . . was aghast: what about the telegraph privilege of the Reich?
Its mood was of a mother hen which had hatched chicks and which was now
excitedly clucking, scurrying back and forth . . ." (1957, p. 92).

The Reichspost was aided by the absence, throughout the Weimar Republic,
of a constitutional provision for broadcasting; therefore, policy could be determined by a complex system of regulations, decrees, and concessions. The scene
was dominated by Hans Bredow, originally a director of Telefunken, the radio
cartel company of the two electric industry giants AEG and Siemens & Halske.
In 1919 Bredow moved from the private sector into government service and
assumed responsibility at the Reichspost for broadcast matters.

Under his tutelage, the Reichspost exercised a highly restrictive regime. It
required the licensing of every single broadcast receiver, as well as approval
for every receiver type sold to the public. For years, it granted licenses to only
three companies, Telefunken, Lorenz, and Hutch, arguing that foreign equipment would make it impossible to prevent individuals from listening to "unauthorized" parts of the spectrum, thus violating the secrecy of communications. Only trustworthy and approved German manufacturers were allowed to
produce receivers. Firms had to meet financial and personal conditions, ostensibly to assure production of adequate quality. Every set had to receive an
official stamp of approval. When the Ministry of Finance argued that the exclusivity of the three closely linked firms could lead to monopolization and higher
prices, the technical office of the Reichspost claimed that only particularly sophisticated firms could meet its strict technical criteria. Soon afterward, the
three firms, free of competition, merged their radio set interests.

Similarly strict rules applied for the mere reception of radio broadcasting,
but they were widely ignored by the amateurs. The Reichspost became adamant
about establishing control over "unregulated reception," claiming that a
receiver could be rebuilt into a transmitter. In 1924, it obtained a government
decree to deal with unauthorized radio listening, based on the public emergency
provision of the Weimar Constitution. It was accompanied by an explanation
by the minister of posts:

> The number of secret wireless facilities is steadily increasing. The existence of such
> facilities seriously endangers the security of the state and of the public order, be-
> cause they provide revolutionary circles with the opportunity to create a compre-
> hensive secret communication network, which in cases of peril can seriously en-
> danger the execution of appropriate action of the constitutional government. The
> government departments involved are unanimously of the conviction that the pre-
> sent legal regulations are not sufficient for the necessary protection of broadcast
> facilities. The Reichsminister of Posts is of the opinion that the existing conditions
> in the wireless sector already represents a disturbance and an endangerment of the
> public safety and order [Lerg, 1980, pp. 99–100].

The decree made the unauthorized reception of radio signals a criminal offense, punishable with prison and large fines. Law enforcement and the Reichspost officials could enter and search for unauthorized radio receivers in any

suspected dwelling without a search warrant. The draconian measures were sought and applauded by the three-firm set manufacturing cartel.

During the same period, the principle of payment for radio reception was established. The purpose of payment was not primarily to establish funding for broadcasting, but to help the state treasury and to demonstrate that radio reception was a privilege and not a right.

Initially, Germany was divided into nine broadcast regions. Private business interests received licenses for a concessionary regional monopoly. They also had the right to sell or rent receivers. They initially received 60 percent of the license fees collected in their territory, though this was reduced in the following years unilaterally to 39.5 percent by 1931.

The umbrella State Broadcasting Corporation RRG (Reichs-Rundfunk-Gesellschaft) was positioned above the regional companies and was financed by mandatory contributions from the regional companies. The RRG received all profits above 10 percent (later 8 percent) from most regional broadcasters.

For all practical purposes the Reichspost became the regulatory commission for broadcasting. For example, in 1924 it permitted advertising in broadcasting, provided that it was in "moderate amount and in the most cautious form" and that the Reichspost's own advertising agency was used. Total advertising revenue, however, was small.

The Reichspost was not the only part of the state with claims to control over broadcasting. From the beginning the Ministry of the Interior, in charge of internal security, was adamant about its desire to prevent independent news and political programs from being broadcast. To make this less blatant, it arranged for the establishment of the "Corporation for Book and Press," which later became DRADAG, the news service provider, which was independent from government only in the most nominal terms. The Ministry of the Interior held a 51 percent share and the German press association held the rest. Thus, news broadcasting was provided by an organization dominated by the highly political Ministry of the Interior. The regional companies were left with entertainment, culture, and education, but no politics.

The government also held direct ownership shares in the regional broadcast companies themselves. The Reichspost had a 17 percent share in each, and DRADAG and a quasi-official umbrella program supplier, the Deutschstunde, each held another 17 percent. The remaining 49 percent was held by private investors. Furthermore, the Reichspost had a 50 percent share in the Deutschstunde. Thus, the Reichspost, together with the Ministry of the Interior, had voting control over all regional companies.

The federal states became strongly opposed to this concentration in the hands of the central government and demanded participation. After bitter negotiations, they received the minor rights to establish "supervisory committees," which were shared jointly by the state governments and the Reichs Ministry of the Interior.

Bredow was unrelenting in his efforts to further increase the Reichspost's influence through administrative means. (Only in 1926, three years after the commencement of regular broadcasting, did the German parliament have a chance to consider broadcast issues.) For example, studio equipment of the original companies and other technical facilities had to be operated by postal employees, but they were purchased and paid for by the companies themselves.

Next, Bredow began to exercise control directly. He became chairman of the administrative board of the RRG. He left his civil service position and was appointed to serve as the broadcast commissioner of the Minister of the Reichspost. Although technically a private person serving a private company, in reality he was a state employee in a state company. For the Reichspost, and for Bredow personally, it had been a remarkable tour de force. After three years of ceaseless manipulation, the Reichspost was in control of broadcasting, with the private companies acting as a fig leaf. Six years later, they formally became state administrations.

In fairness to Bredow, he sincerely believed that an important function of the Reichspost and of the RRG was to keep politics out of the broadcasting system as much as possible. Since the Weimar Republic was highly fragmented politically, the establishment of state control would allow the broadcasting system to remain as nonpartisan as possible. He hoped that preventing the regional broadcasting companies from controlling news programs would contribute to this goal. This "apolitical" position reflected the statist attitudes of Prussian traditionalism, and in that sense was actually quite political.

In 1932, Germany was governed by a series of conservative governments without a parliamentary majority, based on emergency decrees. In this politically confused situation, an official of the Ministry of the Interior, Erich Scholz, began a complex set of bureaucratic intrigues to achieve a political decision in favor of full nationalization and centralization of broadcasting. Scholz, together with the German majority, had been migrating toward the political right. By 1932 he had quietly become a member of the National Socialist party. Under Chancellor Franz von Papen the government decided that the private shareholders in the regional companies had to transfer nominal control. RRG now became 51 percent owned by the Reichspost and 49 percent owned by the states. The regional companies themselves became 51 percent owned by the RRG and 49 percent owned by the states and were supervised by state commissioners. Bredow and Scholz served as commissioners over the RRG. In the following months, broadcasting institutions began dismissing leftist and Jewish employees, even before Hitler's assumption of power. A few weeks later, Hitler became chancellor. Bredow, a representative of the old order, resigned. But the broadcast institutions, shaped under his leadership for centralized state control, required little reorganization.

After 1934, several of the leaders of the previous broadcasting system were brought to trial. The trials focused on financial improprieties and operational competence. The hearings were supposed to be "educational," but they did not proceed well because of the flimsy evidence. Bredow and his two codefendants received light prison sentences and fines, but the case was so weak that an appellate court, hearing the case in 1937, set aside parts of the judgments, a highly unusual occurrence in a political trial at the time.

Until 1932, no Nazi leader had ever spoken on German radio (Diller, 1980).

Although Hitler was a major candidate for Reichs-President in early 1932, he was denied access. After 1933, broadcasting became a major instrument of Nazi propaganda, with Hitler's speeches being constantly broadcast while all other spokesmen were silenced.[1] To increase the reach of radio, an inexpensive "Volksempfänger" (people's receiver) was designed and produced. It was designed to receive mostly German stations. (During the war, listening to enemy broadcasts became a major crime.)

Bureaucratic disputes about control of broadcasting occurred throughout the twelve years of the Nazi regime (Roß, 1986). At the end of 1933, state control remained, but Reichspost control, patiently accumulated by Bredow, was terminated in one fell swoop and transferred to the newly established Propaganda Ministry of Goebbels. Goebbels thereby got his hands on over 55 percent of the Reichspost's license fees for receiving sets. These funds were disposed of for other propaganda activities as well and were the major financial source for his operations. Commercial radio advertising was prohibited in 1936, but the political propaganda aimed internally and externally was unrelenting for twelve years, and provided a major tool for Nazi control (Diller, 1980).

After the Allied victory, German broadcasting was completely revamped by the occupying powers, each influenced by its own broadcast tradition and by a desire to provide a system for a reeducation of Germany. British views were shaped by the BBC model, which was centralized and de facto independent from the state. Particularly influential in conceiving a new model for Germany was the BBC veteran Hugh Greene (Tracey, 1982). Myths to the contrary, the United States did not strive to export its own domestic model of commercial broadcasting; media based on commercial advertising in a totally destroyed country with rationed consumer goods would have made little sense. The United States instead favored a BBC-like model, but more decentralized in the American tradition. The French were willing to follow the British and the Americans because they judged their own system of close relations between state and broadcasting to be an inappropriate model for Germany. The Soviet Union, on the other hand, created broadcasting as an instrument of the new socialist regime it was establishing its occupation zone. All the Allies agreed that the pre-1933 broadcast system was undesirable.

In seeking new forms of organization the Western Allies disagreed with German politicians of virtually all democratic parties, who basically wanted a return to the Weimar system of state radio control, though with control wielded this time by democratic forces. The British and American occupation administrations, in contrast, wished broadcasting to be not merely a voice of the democratic state, but also an independent factor within a democracy. For the new democratic German politicians these concepts were alien, and their acceptance required massive allied pressure on some German state parliaments, sometimes under protest. General Lucius Clay, the U.S. military governor, who became greatly admired by Germans, wrote in 1950 about his efforts on behalf of press and broadcasting freedom: "The German inability to truly comprehend democratic freedoms has not shown itself as much in any other area, except perhaps that of the school reforms. It seemed to be impossible to reach legislation in

which the press was not left to the good or bad graces of the ruling power''
(Bausch, 1980, p. 22). In some cases the Allies simply decreed the new system. During this time, Hans Bredow reemerged and played, to his credit, a
constructive role in popularizing the new concept.

The Allies were also determined to eliminate the Deutsche Post's role in
technical transmission services and to give these services instead directly to the
broadcasters. The occupation forces also wanted to have only minimal governmental representation on the administrative boards and to include participation
of societal interest groups. They were only partly successful in achieving these
goals. In the British zone, in particular, state politicians retained considerable
influence in the establishment of a huge, centralized broadcast institution, the
North-West German Radio NWDR, which the British were setting up. In the
American zone, broadcasting was overseen by a more decentralized system of
several institutions. Most significantly, the West German federal government
which was soon established received no role in broadcasting; the power of the
states over broadcasting continues to be jealously guarded to this day (Bausch,
1980) and is unique within Europe. A discussion of East German (GDR) broadcasting is provided later in the chapter.

Among the most active advocates for the *status quo ante* were the officials
of the Deutsche Post, who actually claimed some form of redress as victims of
the Third Reich, since the Nazis had taken their authority over broadcasting.
Referring to the still intact Telecommunications Facilities Law of 1928, they
laid claim to their old right of broadcasting, and particularly its lucrative broadcast license fee.

As soon as the post offices were reopened after the war, the Post began
collecting radio license fees again. In Bavaria, it returned only 25 percent of
the license fees to Radio Munich and kept 75 percent in return for operating
the transmission and collecting the fees. In 1946, the Deutsche Post went a
step further and proposed a reorganization of broadcasting, with state-
controlled program companies but with Post ''responsibility'' for the operation
of the studios for reasons of ''uniformity of technology.'' The Deutsche Post
maintained its claim to fees not only for program transmission, but also for the
program trade between studios.

The Post petitioned the military governments to revoke the broadcasting authority of the newly formed states in its own favor. The postal unions were
mobilized, opposing a transfer of broadcasting as a ''manipulation of private
capitalist interests.'' The postal unions also demanded that the entire management of broadcasting be controlled by the postal administration.

The postal officials next brought in Bredow, asking him to provide a supportive expert memorandum to the Allied authorities. Bredow, a man with far
broader horizons than his former colleagues, told them that a connection of
broadcasting with the postal system would be superior in purely operational
terms, but that the question was more one of politics than of technical operation. The postal administration was unavoidably centralized, and if it controlled
broadcasting, then broadcasting would also become centralized. Bredow commented, ''Whoever controls the transmitters also practically controls broadcast-

ing. Without transmitters, the best programs are useless. After the experiences of recent years, it is conceivable that in future central administrations [of the Post] an authoritarian spirit will again predominate which would then affect broadcasting'' (Bausch, 1980, p. 29).

In rear-guard action during late 1947, the head of the Deutsche Post demanded at least compensation for the ''expropriation.'' But General Clay was unpersuaded. He directed the postal authorities in his zone to transfer the transmitters and studios to their respective state governments within three weeks. Compensation was not mentioned. Since its foundation in 1490, the postal system had never been rebuffed in such unequivocal fashion by a governmental authority, and it never has been since (Noam, 1991).

Thus the role of the post in broadcasting came to an end. Or so it seemed, for a short time. But the Bundespost, succeeding the Deutsche Post when the Federal Republic was established in 1949, continued to dispute the financial arrangements concerning the viewer license fees and never gave up in its efforts to regain its authority over broadcasting. In 1961, the German Constitutional Court gave it the right to new broadcast transmission, while leaving the existing transmitters to the states. Since then, all new transmitters have been controlled by the Bundespost.

Television Institutions

The first German experimental television broadcasts of still pictures were undertaken in 1929. In the Third Reich, control over the emerging television medium became subject to bureaucratic dispute. Goebbels, the minister of propaganda, was in charge of radio broadcasting. But in 1934 Hitler was persuaded television should be controlled by Hermann Göring, the minister of aviation and a rival of Goebbels, on the flimsy grounds that television broadcasting implicated issues of aviation communications. Only later did Goebbels receive a role in television.

Television began operating in Germany in March 1935. Two months later, TV broadcasts from the station ''Paul Nipkow'' commenced for five hours daily, receiving wide attention during the 1936 Olympic Games held in Berlin. It used a 180-line system. In 1937 a 441-line standard was established. During World War II, television development came to a standstill.[2]

Experimental television broadcasting resumed after the war. On Christmas Day of 1952, NWDR commenced regular TV broadcasting. In 1954, a loose arrangement of the regional broadcast institutions under the name ARD (Arbeitsgemeinschaft der Rundfunkanstalten Deutschlands, or Working Group of German Broadcast Institutions) began operating the joint ''first'' channel.

Radio advertising existed since 1948. Given the financial difficulties at the time that advertising was first proposed, there were no strong objections. Television advertising, however, was more controversial when it began in 1956. It was limited to a few blocks in the early evening, none of which interrupt a program.

In 1959, Chancellor Adenauer and the majority Christian Democratic party proposed the creation of a second German television channel that would operate under central government authority rather than under states control, via a licensed private law institution, Deutschland Fernsehen, with private program providers and advertising support. The states, including the Christian Democratic ones, rallied in opposition. Two explosive issues, the nature of federalism and the role of commercial television, were raised in one action and created a national constitutional crisis. The Federal Constitutional Court ruled in favor of the states, which soon thereafter set up their own second channel, ZDF.

This "First Broadcast Decision" of the Constitutional Court was followed by several more cases. Together they established a remarkable assertion of judicial power into the quasi-legislative area, and their significance extends far beyond the subject matter of broadcasting.

Whereas each state maintains jurisdiction over the structure of broadcasting in its territory, broadcast regulation must be consistent with Article 5 of the Germany Basic Law (Grundgesetz), the fundamental free speech clause, which states:

> Everyone has the right to freely express and disseminate his opinion by speech, writing, and pictures, and to freely inform himself from generally accessible sources. *Freedom of the press and freedom of reporting by broadcast and film are guaranteed.* There shall be no censorship [emphasis supplied].

However, the German Constitutional Court interpreted in 1971 this "broadcast freedom" narrowly:

> As a result of development in television technology, broadcasting has become one of the most powerful means of mass communications which, because of its wide-reaching effect and possibilities as well as the danger of misuse for one-sided propagandizing, cannot be left to the free play of market forces [BVerfGE, 1971].

Broadcast freedom must therefore serve society as a whole (Witteman, 1983).

The nine West German public broadcasting institutions are roughly but not completely analogous to the federalist structure of the country. The absorption of the German Democratic Republic modified this structure somewhat. Several of these institutions cover more than one state, and one state is served by two institutions, one of which also serves another state. These irregularities resulted from the Allied occupation zones after World War II that led to the establishment of broadcast service areas whose territories have remained the same ever since, even if political boundaries have not. The exception is the northwest German system that had covered the entire British occupation zone, which was split into several components (Kleinsteuber et al., 1986).

Additional participants in the German broadcasting system are the federal government's Deutschlandfunk and the Deutsche Welle. The Deutsche Welle provides long-distance international broadcasting. The Deutschlandfunk was aimed, in theory, at East Germany and nearby European countries, but also has a presence with West German audiences, operating an FM frequency whose low signal range suggests that it is a de facto domestic broadcaster. Also part of the broadcast system has been the American-controlled station RIAS (Radio in the American Sector) in Berlin, with semi-independent status and broadcasts in German (including, since 1989, television), unlike the U.S., British, French, and Canadian military stations AFN, BFN, FFB, and CFN, which are apart from the civilian broadcasters.

German broadcasters collaborate in a variety of ways. In particular, they jointly provide the first German television channel. Programs are provided according to a complex formula, with the individual stations transmitting regional programs in certain time windows. ARD, the umbrella organization of the collaboration, is relatively weak. Feature films are centrally acquired, which serves to reduce the competition for rights. The regional stations also operate, separately or in a small group, another set of channels, known as the "Third Program," intended for regional broadcasts but increasingly becoming supraregional (Bullinger, 1987).

The vertical integration of the broadcasting institutions into film production is strong. Most German films are prefinanced by the television institutions, establishing public broadcast institutions as the patron of the film industry. In addition, the broadcasters own the major film production studios directly. Bavaria, the largest studio, is 75 percent owned indirectly by the two public broadcasting authorities, WDR and SDR. Studio Hamburg, the second largest, is owned by the northern German broadcast authority, NDR, through a subsidiary. The second channel, ZDF, in contrast, obtains most of its programs from independent producers, though it has a smaller production studio in Munich (Riva).

In the broadcast institutions the central person is the director general (intendant), who is supervised by a general broadcasting advisory council and a smaller but more important administrative board. The broadcasting advisory boards are composed of parliamentary (i.e., party) representatives, in addition to representatives of socially relevant groups, mostly aligned with one of the political parties. Attempts at interference in political programs are frequent. The intendants, though often professional journalists or media experts, have increasingly included political types (Kleinsteuber et al., 1986, p. 60). But the process can also become a two-way street, when the representatives of the parties in broadcasting councils become the representatives of broadcasting in the parties (Martin Bullinger, communication).

The second German television program channel, ZDF, was created in 1961 through a compact of the German Länder that followed the previously mentioned constitutional crisis.[3] Born in controversy and poverty, in 1985 it was able to afford Europe's largest, most modern, and most expensive broadcast center, located in Mainz, the birthplace of Western printing.

The party "proporz" system has been part of ZDF's reality, too. When the institution was established, the various party representatives agreed that the intendant would be appointed by the Christian Democrats, with the further proviso that he would be a Catholic. In return, the centrist Free Democrat party was allotted the administrative director's position. The program director was also a Christian Democrat party member, and the editor-in-chief was a Social

Democrat "sympathizer," though not a party member. Similar party proportionality exists further down the management ranks. Most of these positions are already filled before the appointment of the intendant, who must then work with a management team that is predetermined by party representatives. Appointments to most jobs, including clerical, editorial, and foreign correspondent positions, are similarly affected by party affiliations. A good number of positions are filled by former press officers of the party organizations.

The supervisory board of ZDF consists of a large number of representatives of pluralist interest groups, various federal states, the federal government, and the political parties. Also represented are nongovernmental groups such as churches, trade unions, employers' associations, farmers, craftworkers, newspaper publishers, and journalists. Many of the "nongovernmental" groups are, in fact, party affiliated and together form powerful caucuses. Some of the most influential political figures are members of the supervisory boards of the ZDF, including the German Foreign Minister, Hans-Dietrich Genscher, and several state prime ministers.

One intendant, the respected Klaus von Bismarck of the West German broadcast institution WDR, commented on his experience:

> I've come to realize that where the professional politicians [on the governing boards] are concerned the political party balance of power is in the final analysis decisive. To assume anything else would put idealistic gloss on the situation. What does this mean? . . . A pressure of these parties, in practice above all of the party groups in the Land Diets on the members of the broadcasting bodies has grown in intensity . . . as a result, the freedom of the majority of these members, who depend on party support, to take decisions that are in the best interests of broadcasting is strictly limited . . . [Grosser, 1979, p. 132].

Disillusionment was also expressed by Klaus Simon, an editor of the southwest German broadcasting institution:

> I regard the belief that representatives of the socially relevant forces will treat the common interest as more important than the interest of their own group as a superstition—I know of only few exceptions to this rule. I regard as a nightmare the idea the Farmer's Union should appoint the editor of the Agricultural Programme or the Trade Union should appoint the person responsible for programmes dealing with social problems [Grosser, 1979, p. 133].

In the aggregate, the institutions of German public broadcasting provide some of the world's best television, particularly in the areas of the documentary and the performing arts. Quality is particularly high in areas that the influence of party loyalty has not penetrated. And even on political issues, there has been independence where the intendant was strong. Efforts are made to air programs for minorities, special interests, and the millions of foreign workers in Germany (though far below these groups' numerical share in the population during the major viewing hours). With its decentralized structure of professional and well-financed institutions, the German system works quite well in many respects and has been a strong force for democracy.

The politicization of the broadcast system is partly due to restrictiveness. If more outlets existed, control over each would probably be less important. As in Italy, the emergence of private television in Germany was partly due to the inability of the existing system to reform itself and expand. For a long time the existing institutions were too tightly balanced to permit a meaningful expansion within the established structure. The decision-making process was not geared toward change, partly because of the complexities of the federalist structure and partly because of the split between the left and the right on the issue. The absorption of East Germany adds new dimensions to complexity. This situation may well continue despite the complex legal framework that was established to assimilate new private and public participants. German broadcasting is hence an unstable system in the sense that smooth transitions are not easily achieved.

The Long March to Private Television

Advertising on German public television was limited to twenty minutes per channel each day and was not permitted after 8 P.M. or on Sundays.[4] Even though rates kept rising, there has been substantial excess demand for advertising time. Using the United Kindom as a model, it was clear that private television would be profitable, and various interests sought to establish private channels. But it took twenty-five years of agitation before this finally happened. In 1961 the German Constitutional Court struck down Chancellor Konrad Adenauer's private television, because it was sponsored by the central government. In 1964, when the states' nascent ZDF television was in financial difficulties, the publishers' association offered to take it over. As a result of the publishers' barrage, two government panels were established in 1964 to investigate the media (Mestmäcker, 1978).

Private television obtained its first legal foothold in the small state of Saarland. Saarland had an arrangement that dated back to its special postwar status and permitted the French "peripheral" commercial broadcaster Europe-1 to transmit French language radio and later TV programs. In 1967, in a remarkable legislative coup, a new media law was introduced and voted on in three readings in rapid succession during the Six-Day War in the Middle East, which absorbed public attention. It was later disclosed that the private broadcast company was to be controlled by the three major political parties, which held 58 percent of the shares, with the remainder held by several important banks and publishers. In effect, the three major political parties were about to establish a private television company in whose profits they would directly participate. The use of parliamentary powers by party organizations created such an uproar that the state government became too embarrassed to act. One applicant, the free broadcasting corporation (FRAG), demanded an affirmative decision by the state government and went to court to obtain it. Thirteen years later (!), in 1981, the federal constitutional court decided the case against the plaintiff in its landmark FRAG (or third broadcasting) decision.

In 1972, another major battle took place in the state of Bavaria when the conservative Christian Socialist Union party introduced a bill that sought to increase the legislature's representation on the broadcasting council, thus increasing the degree of authority that the state would have over future private broadcasting. After the law was passed by the state government, the liberal Free Democratic party organized a citizen's movement and public opposition. The group collected signatures of more than 10 percent of the state's citizens, enough to put a plebiscite on the ballot, an unusual event in Bavaria. The plebiscite proposed that broadcasting be entirely operated by public institutions under safeguards from government or parliamentary domination. In light of the public outpouring of support, the Christian Socialists relented and accepted most of the plebiscite terms. The compromised proposal was overwhelmingly approved.

After the 1967 Saar debacle, it took ten years for serious advocacy for private broadcasting to rise again. Christian Schwarz-Schilling, the Christian Democratic party's media spokesman in the federal parliament, began to speak strongly in favor of private broadcasting as a supplement to the public service system. The Christian Democrats also argued for the participation of private firms in several cable pilot projects that were being planned. These proposals were fiercely opposed by the Social Democrats. The Free Democrats took a centrist position by opposing commercial over-the-air broadcasting but advocating the establishment of a new set of regional public broadband cable institutions that would supervise private program providers.

In 1981, the German Constitutional Court finally struck down the heart of the 1967 Saarland media law that had permitted private broadcasting under certain conditions. The court established that private broadcasting as such was constitutional, provided that the proper legal framework was set up. Specifically, private program suppliers could receive a broadcast license if the channel was "internally pluralistic" by providing a diversity of opinions in its programs, and if it was supervised by an institution similar to public broadcast councils, which include various socially relevant interest groups. Also acceptable was an "externally pluralistic" model, where overall balance was achieved through the multiplicity of channels containing unbalanced programming (Bachof et al., 1983). This decision was highly significant, and it established the constitutional parameters for any reform and media liberalization by the states. All the subsequently drafted state media laws were based on these principles. The first of these laws was that of the state of Lower Saxony, passed in 1984. The state of Rheinland-Palatinate followed with legislation on cable television that permitted private programs, supervised by an independent public state broadcasting commission.

As the tide began to shift, the Social Democrats started to modify their opposition. The signals were given by Peter Glotz, who had significant influence as the party's media expert as well as, later on, its secretary general. Glotz pragmatically argued that any change in the communications field requires cooperation across the political spectrum rather than the pushing through of a plan by a majority:

The left must understand that the Federal Republic of Germany cannot be considered an isolated island. Capital moves across borders, and whoever wishes to simply block the capital utilization will sooner or later be outmaneuvered. Therefore, in the second half of the 1980s neither the ramming through nor the blockading strategy are sensible. . . . . A stubborn anti-capitalism, whose major goal is that media entrepreneurs should not make any money, would be in the coming phase ahead of us as damaging as a blind overreliance on the new technology [Glotz, 1983, p. 24].

Glotz did not continue in this vein, but his opening was picked up in 1984, when his party colleague Klaus von Dohnanyi, the Lord Mayor of Hamburg, proposed allowing private media under public supervision. Hamburg's role in the change was not coincidental. The city-state had been West Germany's media capital; with its harbor in decline, it wanted to link its economic future with the health of its media industry. Munich had been promoting itself as a rival media center, and Hamburg could not afford to fall behind.

In 1985, the national congress of the Social Democrats party narrowly approved the basic outlines of Dohnanyi's position. The Social Democrats' concern thereupon shifted to internal pluralism and to the prevention of a "dual monopoly" of both print and television media on national and local levels by newspaper publishers.

Represented by Wolfgang Hoffmann-Riem, a noted legal media scholar, the Social Democratic deputies in the Bundespost challenged the law passed by Lower Saxony in 1984, and in November 1986 the German Constitutional Court ruled on the case in its *Fourth Broadcast* decision. Although the earlier FRAG decision required public broadcasting institutions to assure diversity, commercial broadcasting was not required to be quite as balanced as the public broadcasters. The 1986 decision gave private interests greater flexibility, but also emphasized that public broadcast institutions were the key elements in the system and that they were responsible for assuring external pluralism in programs. Consequently, it established an obligation of the states to assure their technical, organizational, and especially financial integrity (Hoffmann-Riem and Starck, 1987).

After five years of wrangling among the states, an important agreement was reached in 1987 on the basic framework of private television, cable television, and DBS. The states undertook to tolerate each other's private broadcasting, to establish universal programming principles for such broadcasts, and to monitor the quality of TV advertising. The compact also permits the prime ministers to raise advertising time, which gives them a considerable level of power (Martin Bullinger, communication).

In time, all states passed comprehensive media laws. One approach, adopted by Baden-Württemberg and Bavaria, was to permit local and regional private broadcasting. Lower Saxony and Hessen permit statewide but not local or regional stations.

Nordrhein-Westfalen separates advertising and distribution from program provision, which is undertaken by an organization encompassing all socially relevant forces. In Bavaria, private broadcasters have been placed under the legal umbrella of the existing public institution. Several of the state laws require external pluralism and others, internal pluralism. All require overall balance (Wolfgang Hoffmann-Riem, communication). Each state established a Media Agency (*Medienanstalt*) to regulate private broadcasting and award licenses. These *Anstalten* are financed by a slight increase in the TV license fee of viewers. Lower Saxony awarded Germany's first private radio license in 1985 to FFN, a consortium of eighty-three publishers. Other states followed. A checkered private broadcast system emerged, creating some legal, technical, and commercial problems given the medium's characteristics of propagation beyond state borders and the national aspects of consumer markets. It is therefore not surprising that large media firms have advocated national media laws as application of federal commercial laws. But absent such changes, Germany has a unique system of decentralized broadcast regulation.

Cable Television and the Breakdown of the Traditional System

Traditional telecommunications law in Germany was based upon several dichotomies: between the states and the central government, between broadcasting and telecommunications, and between content and transmission. This system was unable to deal with cable television and the changes in its wake.

Cable television in Germany is less rooted in private initiatives than in the efforts of the monopoly telecommunications administration Deutsche Bundespost to promote, design, finance, and construct it. Its pro-cabling policy led to sharp criticism that it created technical and economic realities—"Sachzwänge"—that tended to predetermine media policy.

Master antenna cable systems have long existed in Germany, usually with a capacity of about five channels. Efforts to establish private cablecasting started in 1970, when the tiny cooperative Senne TV began operating over the master antenna systems, using a small studio in an apartment house in Bielefeld. The studio was almost immediately shut down by the authorities, who labeled it an impermissible private broadcast facility and a "danger to public safety." Soon thereafter the Bundespost became increasingly interested in expanding its activities into broadband cable television. In 1971, the Bundespost prepared a cable television study that aimed at defining a uniform technology. The first Bundespost cable networks were set up on a trial basis in Nuremberg and Hamburg, and without an existing regulatory or political framework. For example, the Bundespost did not consult the states on matters of standard setting, although standards of channel capacity directly affect media policy (Scherer, 1985).

In 1974, the Bundespost decided on regulations concerning the technical standards for community antennas. These included its right to force private community antenna systems to use the Bundespost's broadband links if their facilities crossed public rights of way.

In the same year the government established a blue-ribbon commission (known as the KtK) headed by Professor Eberhard Witte, who a decade later also played the leading role in opening up the monopoly in German telecommunications. The Christian Democratic opposition strongly criticized this as an attempt to establish government control over new forms of media and as a denial of role for the private sector. Ironically, the KtK report contained the proposal and structure that made the introduction of private media possible. Issued in December 1975, the report recommended that several cable pilot projects be established and that cable network operations be separated from control over programming. The report also recommended the establishment of electronic mail, videotex, and telefax service. (KtK, 1976) These proposals led to the introduction, after years of political debates, of prototype cable projects in Munich, Ludwigshafen, Berlin, and Dortmund, all of which required model legislation as well as the creation of a system of program supply that would allow the projects to be readily expanded into a nationwide system.

The federal cabinet approved much of the KtK report in a forty-page position paper and also strongly supported the Bundespost's assertion of monopoly, by claiming that cable distribution and videotex were under the jurisdiction of the federal government.

In 1977, five years after the Bundespost began its cable television activities, it finally asked its own administrative council for regular authorization. The states protested vehemently, but the Bundespost went ahead anyway and embarked on the extensive cabling of eleven cities. However, the federal cabinet, under the leadership of Chancellor Helmut Schmidt (at the time an opponent of almost any form of television), decided two years later to stop the Bundespost in its tracks. But the cabinet decision permitted the Bundespost to supply cable service where there was an "acute public demand," such as in areas with poor over-the-air reception or in historical areas where TV antennas were prohibited. The Bundespost, left with such a loophole, came up with a very generous criteria for "acute public demand."

Critics of the Bundespost's pro-cabling policy correctly anticipated its impact on private television. With over-the-air broadcasting, only public television was shown and initiatives for private broadcasting could be rejected. But spectrum scarcity would not be persuasive with multichannel cable systems. It was therefore likely that the various states, in particular the conservative ones, would license some cable channels for private program provision. This development was opposed by the political left, which feared the social impact of commercial television on German society and on the electoral process. Many rightists, too, were apprehensive about the implications. Still others feared that the cabling of Germany would prove an uneconomical investment; a study by Eberhard Witte reduced that particular concern (Witte, 1984).

Many of the critics were placed in an intellectual quandary, because they normally supported the desirability of a telecommunications monopoly, but now experienced the exercise of its power. The opposite was also true: some proponents of telecommunication liberalization became supporters of a Bundespost activism in cable television in order to promote private media.

With the pilot projects slowly on the way to realization, the Social Democrats' strategy shifted from opposition on policy grounds to a go-slow position that stressed the superiority of future optical fiber over the existing coaxial copper lines. Partly as a result, the federal government approved in 1981 a futuristic concept of the postal ministry to wire eventually all of Germany with fiber-optic broadband cable.[5] This led to the introduction of the Bundespost's BIGFON development project only one month later.

In the same year the cabinet also decided to appoint the special Inquiry Commission, chaired by Christian Schwarz-Schilling, to investigate new information and communications technologies. From the beginning this commission was highly politicized along ideological, jurisdictional, and party lines. The federal states refused to cooperate. While the commission was working, the federal government changed to Christian Democrat, and Schwarz-Schilling became federal minister of posts and telecommunications. The commission disbanded in disarray with an interim report and numerous dissenting views.

Schwarz-Schilling, an advocate of private television, gave high priority to cable development in order to advance the new multichannel medium, to increase the influence of his ministry by giving it new areas to develop, and to create an opportunity for the Bundespost to play a significant role in technological development and employment creation.

Satellite reception can serve as an alternative to cable television. Until mid-1985, it was not permissible to receive satellite broadcast signals without a license by the Bundespost, and such permission was not given for use in satellite master television antenna (SMATV) systems. In 1985 this policy was liberalized under certain circumstances.

The cable pilot projects established models for organized German cable television. In 1984, the prime ministers of the states agreed on a framework for feeding programs into cable, based on the Ludwigshafen model, and the two major broadcasting channels began to cooperate with the cable pilots.

The Ludwigshafen project began operations on January 1, 1984, almost eight years after the basic decision of the federal cabinet. It had taken all this time of intense political debate and technological preparation to provide the legal basis for a service that had been offered by amateurs in Bielefeld in 1970. In 1986, it moved from trial project to regular operation.

The pilot project in the city of Dortmund was a trial for a more public and less commercially oriented concept of cable. It emphasized its "open" access channel and included a large number of imported public broadcasting channels as well as community-generated programs.

Progress in cabling was being made steadily. In 1988, 11.7 million homes were passed by cable, with some 40 percent of them (4.6 million households, about 17 percent of the population) actually connected. Almost all of those received satellite-fed programs. Growth in subscriptions accelerated when more of the actual cabling and marketing was left to private firms. In 1987, the Bundespost established fifty-five regional mixed public and private cable service companies (RKS) (Logica, 1987). By 1991, 16.1 million households were passed (60%), of which half were subscribers. Total investment by what became the semi-independent Deutsche Bundespost Telekom was $16 billion since 1983, most of it not yet covered by revenues.

The first Bundespost high-power direct broadcast satellite SAT-1 was launched in 1987 and failed almost immediately. SAT-2 was successfully launched in 1989. Allocation of its five transponders was highly controversial. After prolonged wrangling among the states, the two public broadcasters (ARD and ZDF) received channels for their satellite programs 1-Plus and 3-SAT, and the private SAT-1 and RTL-Plus received two others. A fifth channel is allocated to a third private broadcaster. The next generation DBS system is planned to have twenty broadcast transponders.

TV-SAT2 utilizes the D2–MAC transmission standard for its five transponders. However, competition from the PAL compatible Kopernikus satellite, and the lack of readily available receivers dampened the prospects for success of the D2-MAC standard and TV-SAT2 itself.

Another form of video delivery that changed the scene is videocassette recordings. In the mid-1970s the blue-ribbon KtK commission overlooked the explosive effect that VCRs would have. Ten years later there were more than 10 million recorders in German households. In 1984, rental of cassettes overtook theater viewing in terms of revenue. Soon there were more than four thousand videotheks plus about 2000 bookstores and gas stations that offered cassettes (Wolfgang Hoffmann-Riem, communication).

Private Program Ventures

As Germany was wired up by the Bundespost and as the legal and institutional status of programming control was resolved in the various states, actual program provision became at last a concrete issue. To understand the various subsequent activities, one must recognize the extraordinary concentration of the German publishing industry. The big four firms in German media and publishing are the Axel Springer group, Burda, the southern German firm of a divided family; the Bauer group, another family firm; and Bertelsmann, which in turn controls the media giant Gruner + Jahr and is owned by the Mohn family.

In Germany many large publishers are not (yet) the relatively centrist and anonymous corporate managers that they tend to be in America. They are shaped by their founders or their heirs. Springer was a vocal conservative, keeping the idea of German reunification alive, and a bête noire of the left. Burda and Bauer are also distinctly conservative family-run businesses. German Social Democrats have no difficulty recognizing that these publishers are not on their side.

Bertelsmann, the largest publishing firm, is more centrist and corporate. Starting out as a provincial publisher of hymn books, the firm now owns numerous book and magazine publishers, book clubs, the filmmaker Ufa (historically a big name in German movie production), record companies, software houses, and cable program channels. It had $7.2 billion in 1989 revenues. Reinhard

Mohn and his family own 89 percent of the firm during their lifetimes, and it will later pass to the nonprofit Bertelsmann Foundation (Protzman, 1989). Bertelsmann has expanded sharply in U.S. media markets by acquiring Bantam, Doubleday, RCA Records, printing plants, and various magazines. U.S. operations accounted for 29 percent of Bertelsmann's 1989 revenues of $7.2 billion.

Axel Caesar Springer was a powerful, controversial, and conservative figure in German public life. Shortly before his death in 1985, 49 percent of his holding company was offered to the public for subscription. This was the first time that a major German media firm was traded on the stock exchange. The stocks were triply oversubscribed and rose within the first day of issuance by almost 100 percent. (The price had been set far too low by the cautious Deutsche Bank.) Of the shares, 10 percent were acquired by the influential film dealer Leo Kirch, who subsequently increased his holding to 26 percent. The remaining 51 percent of stock was shared in almost equal parts by Springer family interests, as well as by Burda. Thus, the Springer firm came to be partly controlled by three of the most powerful media entities in Germany. In 1988, Axel Springer Verlag A.G. became one of the first German corporations to face the prospect of a hostile takeover, when Kirch and Burda bid—unsuccessfully—for full control.

Kirch, who had the foresight to invest in film rights since the 1960s, has a virtual lock on German film distribution. Most foreign producers and distributors deal exclusively through his Beta and Taurus companies. His movie rights have been estimated as worth almost $2 billion. From distribution, Kirch expanded into production, both directly and through coproduction consortia with Seydoux and TF1 in France, Berlusconi in Italy, and American interests. One of his more interesting production activities is Unitel, which records major artistic performances for future broadcasting. Kirch also moved into distribution through video and book clubs, and most important, through satellite channels. After several reorganizations, Kirch holds a major share, about 55 percent, in SAT-1, one of two major private German channels. (PKS, which holds 40 percent of SAT-1, is controlled by Kirch and his allied DG Bank.) He is a major supplier of programming for SAT-1, for a long time at nominal prices in order to nurse the channel to profitability, which it reached in 1990. He also established a pay-TV channel (Teleclub) in Switzerland and Germany, eventually merging it with Canal-Plus and Bertelsman interests into Premiere. Kirch's son also controls another satellite channel, Pro 7. Kirch also tried to enter print publishing through direct and indirect acquisition of 26 percent of Springer, but was rebuffed from taking control by the Springer family. Kirch outpaced the slower Springer, Burda, and Bauer media giants and established himself with Bertelsmann—both rival and partner—as Germany's most dynamic media presence (Ahrens, 1990).

These publishing interests and others formed in 1983 the commercial television venture SAT-1, on the air since 1985. SAT-1's structure was of a mindboggling complexity reminiscent of the Holy Roman Empire. It can best be described as a publishers' consortium of partners, some of whom, in turn, were joint ventures of others. Some of the owners were also programmers, sharing the same frequency and programs within allocated time slots. Initially, the major owners were the movie distributer, PKS (with the strong involvement of Kirch), which held 40 percent of the stock, several large publishers with a combined share of 40 percent, and the publishers' news channels APF (Aktuell Presse Fernsehen), with 20 percent. Almost immediately, Bertelsmann, one of the founding participants, switched to an alliance with the rival Luxembourg CLT for the RTL-Plus channel and was consequently forced out of SAT-1. Medium-sized shares in APF were held by the large publishing houses Springer, Burda, Bauer, and Holtzbrinck, among others. There was also a small amount of participation (less than 2 percent of shares) by dozens of other publishers. After a period of internal stalemate at SAT-1 Kirch acquired control with 58 percent, with Springer left with 20 percent.

The programming independence of the partners quickly led to problems. In effect, the organizations providing programs created positive and negative externalities for each other by reducing or increasing viewership for the channel. Because of lack of coordination, the same actor sometimes appeared on the same evening on several different programs. Occasionally, the partners also competed against each other in program acquisition, thus increasing cost. Because the complex time formulas had to be negotiated among a large number of parties, it was difficult for SAT-1 programming to respond flexibly to an event requiring program modifications. SAT-1 operates out of Mainz, also ZDF's headquarters city. Eventually the structure and ownership were simplified. By that time, it was no longer necessary for publishing industry to present a united front.

SAT-1's major competitor is RTL-Plus, delivered since 1985 by satellite and increasingly also terrestrially. The channel operated by a partnership of the Luxembourg private broadcast monopolist CLT (and its broadcast arm RTL) with Bertelsmann, which was subsequently joined by fellow publishers WAZ, Burda, and FAZ, as well as the huge Deutsche Bank. It operates primarily out of Cologne and Munich. CLT's ownership, in turn, is highly complex, and includes numerous French and Belgian economic and governmental interests. RTL is an experienced broadcasting organization with wide audience recognition and access to the European Broadcast Union's international feeds, which helped the new channel.

3-SAT, another satellite programming channel, is a joint venture of the second German television channel, ZDF, the Austrian Broadcasting Corporation, ORF, and the Swiss Broadcasting Corporation, SRG.

ARD, too, established a satellite-distributed television channel, 1-Plus, also in collaboration with the public broadcast institutions of Switzerland and Austria. It has operated since 1986.

As more channels became available, the typical cable viewer could receive (just among public channels) the two major networks ARD and ZDF, several third programs from the regional institutions, the public 3-SAT and 1-Plus, plus public stations from neighboring countries such as Switzerland or Austria. This can come to eight or more public channels. In terms of presence, therefore, public television is alive, well, and more diverse than ever from the viewers' perspective. The commercial channels typically carried are RTL-Plus and SAT-1. Other television channels often carried on cable include Schleswig Holstein's Eureka, Lower Saxony's Impulse TV, Tele-5 (a youth-oriented channel owned by Tele München, CLT, Berlusconi, and ABC/Capital Cities), Pro-7, and the United Kingdom's BSkyB. Public access, or "open channel," programs are rarely used. Because of their low advertising revenues, local channels have often failed (Tonnemacher, 1987).

Both SAT-1 and RTL-Plus were initially delivered by cable operators via satellite transmission (RTL was also beaming from Luxembourg into a corner of Germany). However, both were also increasingly awarded terrestrial frequencies by the various state media agencies (*Anstalten*) in charge of private broadcasting; license awards were usually based on preventing discrepancy in the viewing options of cabled and noncabled areas. But this policy also led to increased concentration of program supply and made de facto SAT-1 and RTL-Plus into regular national channels.

Faced with program competition, the mighty ZDF fell for a time to fourth place in ratings (17 percent) among cabled homes, behind ARD (22 percent), RTL plus (20 percent) and SAT-1 (17.1 percent) (Ahrens, 1989, p. 12). Informational programming suffered audience declines because of the added entertainment-viewing options available (Woldt, 1989, p. 7). Subsequently, ZDF recovered to 21 percent. (For the entire population, ARD and ZDF's audiences were 33 percent and 32 percent, respectively; RTL had 10 percent, SAT-1 had 8 percent, and the ARD's third channels 11 percent.) Pay TV was started in 1986 on a trial basis, operated by Teleclub, a joint venture of Kirch (Betafilm), Bertelsmann/Ufa, and Springer, and eventually Kirch controlled the channel. Undaunted, Bertelsmann combined in 1990 with Canal Plus to form the Premiere pay-TV channel. The two pay channels merged, and Bertelsmann ended up with Kirch and Springer as partners. Commercial TV revenues began to soar in 1990, with RTL-Plus growing 137% and SAT-1 by 68%.

Broadcasting in East Germany

Until the 1990 unification of the two Germanies, the broadcast system in the German Democratic Republic was radically different from that of the Federal Republic. After World War II, East German radio service was swiftly established by the occupying Soviet forces. The Democratic Radio was established already in May 1945 (Fuchs, 1986, p. B113), and continued after the creation of the GDR in 1949.

In 1952, radio and television were placed under the State Committee for Radio Broadcasting and the State Committee for Television, both subject to the Council of Ministers. Transmission and technical services, on the other hand, were under the aegis of the PTT, Deutsche Post. What made the structure in the German Democratic Republic unusual in comparison to other East European countries was the degree of control exercised by the PTT over the administrative committees.

In 1952, regular television transmission was established in East Berlin, making the GDR one of the first European countries to begin operating a public channel, mostly in order to keep up with the Federal Republic of Germany. By 1955, about 15 hours of programming were available per week to the 0.1 percent of the population that owned television receivers. But in 1987, most households had a television. In 1969 a second channel, DDR2, was launched. There were three regional studios (Gerber, 1990). The radio system had five national channels and twelve regional windows. GDR broadcasting was a massive apparatus—over 1,000 state radio dramatists and musicians alone were employed (Task Force, 1990, p. 53).

East Germans, along with the Eastern Bloc, chose a variant of the French SECAM color-TV standard, partly in order to differentiate compatibility from West Germany and its PAL system. But there was no way to prevent the population from tuning in to West German and West Berlin broadcasting. Partly for that reason, television ownership was high among East Germans in comparison to the rest of Eastern Europe, well in the 90 percent range (Logica, 1987, p. 65).

In the transformation from Stalinism to democratic statehood during 1989 and 1990, changes in broadcasting were at first primarily cosmetic. In early 1990 the Fernsehen der DDR was renamed Deutscher Fernsehfunk (DFF); its former Communist (SED) head of operations was ousted and jailed in a purge (Ahrens, 1990). The Department of Agitation and Propaganda of the SED Politburo became the Department of Media Policy and Information. However, most of the remaining bureaucratic personnel remained in place.

Commercial advertising was introduced for financial reasons. Like in most Eastern European countries, there already had been advertising for state products and services (Kleinwächter, 1990, p. 221). Now, restrictions on commercial advertising were modeled on EC regulations. For example, the daily commercial time was 30 minutes, and there were restrictions on the promotion of alcohol and tobacco. An advertising booking agency was sought; West Germany's ARD and ZDF offered to negotiate the deal on behalf of the DFF, but instead the firm "Information et Publicité" was chosen, a subsidiary of Luxembourg's CLT.

Programming content began to change, too, and Western-style investigative reporting appeared as the Propaganda Department of the Central Committee of the ruling SED was forced to relinquish its role as censor. But the broadcast institutions' primary activities centered on protecting the members of its discredited huge bureaucracy who clung to their positions (Task Force, 1990, p. 53).

In general, the pre-unification reform period saw little cooperation and long-range planning between the East and West broadcasting, particularly in comparison to the more rapid pace of general economic and political integration and of telecommunications. Efforts to reform the East's broadcasting system were initiated by the East's coalition government, without substantial input from the West. While the East's actions did serve to bring the broadcast media out of its state-owned and party-controlled status, the broadcast institutions themselves were a conservative force in this process.

With only limited success in initiating major institutional reform, a vacuum existed that both public and private interests in the West rushed to fill.

In the print media West German firms vied for control of the new market with the four largest publishers pressing to take over newspaper publishers.

The public media were no less active, despite cautioning against the process of "media colonialism" (Ahrens, 1990). West Germans eagerly looked to the East as a means of expanding market share and acquiring additional terrestrial channels, most easily obtained by co-opting existing East German channels rather than investing in the costly process of upgrading outmoded equipment and facilities and working with inexperienced (and intransigent) Eastern management.

Several competing visions emerged. The West German media institutions, particularly ARD and ZDF, looked to incorporate the DFF as a public broadcasting station into the West German public structure either as coequal with ZDF and ARD and in a mirror image of its federated structure (the proposal supported by DFF), or to have one or both of the DFF channels merge with one of the West German public stations (a solution highly unpopular with DFF). Another possibility was the phasing-out of DFF entirely, to be replaced by a new public broadcasting organization, essentially in competition with ARD and ZDF, but situated in Berlin, and with a mandate to focus on East German issues. A further option, proposed by private interests such as SAT-1, was to incorporate DFF within the existing West German broadcasting structure, thereby freeing terrestrial channels for West German private broadcast use (*Intermedia,* 1990). Yet another proposal recommended the continued operation of DFF in conjunction with the development of one or two East German private channels in a dual private-public system. In the end, three of the newly formed south East German states formed the broadcast institution MDR, as a member of ARD. ARD agreed to major upgrade investments in the East, as did ZDF. Both had also to pay more for their movie rights, since their reach included now the former GDR. As these efforts were slowly progressing, video rental took off exponentially, becoming East Germany's fastest growing business sector.

7

France

Early French broadcasting was a mixed public and private system. After Liberation, it became solidly centralized by the government and a tool for its political control, especially under Presidents Charles de Gaulle and Georges Pompidou. Only after 1974, under the more centrist Valéry Giscard d'Estaing, was the state's grip somewhat loosened. But it took a government of the left to create diversity, openness, and greater independence. When François Mitterrand became president in 1981, French broadcasting consisted of three solidly government-dominated television networks and similarly centralized radio stations. In the next few years three television channels were added, one semi-public (Canal Plus) and two commercial (La Cinq and TV-6). In addition, hundreds of independent radio stations, many of them legalized pirates, were licensed, and a semi-independent regulatory agency was established. When the right returned to power in 1986, it went a step further and privatized the major public channel, TF1, and the media firm, Havas, which controlled both Canal Plus and influenced Luxembourg's popular RTL station. After 1988, the Socialists continued the trend and strengthened the independence of regulatory supervision.

As this evolution progressed, the broadcast system that had at the beginning of the decade been totally state dominated and limited was now primarily private and diverse. What is remarkable about the transformation is that it was initiated and guided by Socialists, as part of shifting priorities to cultural producers and away from bureaucratized distributors. Given France's cultural influence, this was important, for it gave liberalization a broader legitimacy in the rest of Europe.

History

Radio transmission was developed in France under the partnership of the army, the PTT, and the private wireless company Compagnie Sans Fils (CSF). There are some claims that a French physicist preceded Marconi in building a receiver for electromagnetic waves. Private radiotelegraphy was attempted in 1902 for shore-to-ship service but was quickly stopped by the authorities, which invoked national interest concerns. In 1919, the government passed a law giving the

PTT power over public wireless telegraphy (Bertho et al., 1984). In 1920, Radio France, an affiliate of CSF, was licensed to provide international service. On June 21, 1921, CSF undertook the first radio broadcast transmission in France. To promote the sale of its receivers, CSF created in 1922 the broadcast company Radiola, later known as Radio-Paris. By 1923, private stations proliferated, and the PTT was charged with policing the air waves. The various interwar governments did not attempt to change this situation because the private stations permitted the survival of the radio manufacturing industry and were appreciated by listeners. Private stations coexisted with the government stations that were subsequently established by the PTT. In 1931, the state acquired the CSF Radio-Paris transmitter and replaced it with a powerful station located in central France. In 1933, under publishers' pressure, the government prohibited advertising on the state-owned stations and instituted state funding for radio. Two years later the Conseil Superieur de la Radio Diffusion was established to coordinate and control program choices. In 1937, the Popular Front government passed the first Statute on French Radio, strengthening the state network while still allowing private stations.

Domestic turmoil increasingly caused the Popular Front government to extend state dominance over broadcasting. In 1938, it established its political control over governance and news; in July 1939, shortly before the outbreak of World War II, radio was taken from the PTT and placed in an autonomous administration directly under the presidency of the council (Vedel, 1987).

The PTT also developed a television service. In November 1935 it installed the first state TV transmitter, using a 441-line standard. By the start of World War II, fifteen hours of weekly television were broadcast in the Paris region, some of which continued during parts of the German occupation (Bertho et al., 1984).

The private radio licenses, by then eleven in number, were held in abeyance during the Vichy period and were canceled in 1945 after the Liberation, in conformity with the statist conception of the new government. The state then operated French broadcasting exclusively for almost forty years, until 1982. However, several private stations on the French periphery—in Luxembourg, Monte Carlo, Andorra, and the Saar—survived or were set up later, though they, too, had strong state involvement.

One of General Charles de Gaulle's first decisions after the liberation of France was to establish a Direction Générale de la Radio under the Ministry of Information. Its purpose was to rebuild stations destroyed during the war and construct powerful new transmitters under the control of the government. Television transmission quality was improved in 1948, when a new standard of 819 lines was implemented. That decision, made under the young State Secretary of Information, François Mitterrand, was a victory for engineers but later impeded the export of French technology and raised the cost of TV receivers to French households (Missika and Wolton, 1983).

De Gaulle's views of broadcasting were deeply affected by his own wartime experience when he broadcast to France from England in a battle of words with Vichy (Kuhn, 1980, p. 54). Control over broadcasting became even more important to him when he returned to power in 1958 and ruled France partly by the force of his ability to communicate with the French people. During the turmoil of the Algerian War in 1960 and 1961, de Gaulle went on the air to appeal directly to the population and soldiers. De Gaulle's use of broadcasting played a central role in the 1961 referendum on Algerian independence: he was a master at using his carefully orchestrated televised press conferences to speak to the public and to send signals to his own government. He viewed television as serious business and went to great trouble in rehearsing his TV speeches (Werth, 1967, p. 361). In defense of de Gaulle's control over television, his supporters argued that such domination was necessary to counterbalance the opposition's hold over the print media (Kuhn, 1985). The same argument, however, was also made by the Socialists when they came to power in 1981.

In suppressing the coverage of opposition views, de Gaulle followed precedent. During the Fourth Republic, the Socialist government of Guy Mollet was inhospitable to opposition views in the news. Once de Gaulle was in power, Minister of Information Jacques Soustelle appointed Gaullists to all important positions in the reorganized broadcast institution, Radio-diffusion Télévision Française (RTF). For example, the former general secretary of the Gaullist party became the Director of News. Yet ministerial responsibility for broadcasting in the Fifth Republic was subject to great flux. Between 1958 and 1979, there were no less than twenty ministers responsible for broadcasting.

In 1964, the RTF was reorganized into the Office de Radio-diffusion Télévision Française (ORTF). Under this new organization, French television became slightly more open. In the next presidential elections, opposition candidates could actually appear on television. But this modest liberalization ended abruptly after the leftist uprisings of May 1968, when the ORTF general staff and journalists went on strike to protest governmental interference in news reporting and to demand a more democratic ORTF board. Once general order had been restored, the government dismissed more than sixty broadcast journalists and transferred thirty others. Other estimates put total dismissals between 200 and 300 employees. Still, the government did increase the employees' representation on the board of governors.

When Georges Pompidou became president in 1969, a more balanced television policy was pursued at first. The Ministry of Information was abolished and broadcasting regulation was moved to the prime minister's office in a more technically oriented Service Juridique et Technique de l'Information. By reorganizing ORTF, the government planned to make the news more independent. Prime Minister Chaban-Delmas, a moderate reformer, allowed each of the two television networks to have a separate and autonomous news team, thus creating some diversity and potential rivalry between television channels. But Chaban-Delmas' ORTF reforms and appointments soon encountered opposition from Gaullist traditionalists and proved to have little presidential support. Pompidou dismissed Chaban-Delmas in 1972 and appointed one of the Gaullist critics of his reforms to the ORTF leadership. He reestablished the Ministry of Information and curbed the independence of news departments. A second ORTF statute, passed in 1972, reestablished the predominance of the government. Even such a national symbol as Jacques-Yves Cousteau was for several years unable to air his films on industrial pollution (Williams, 1985, pp. 60–61).

In 1974, Valéry Giscard d'Estaing, a non-Gaullist centrist, was elected president. Giscard sought to implement broad reforms. Broadcast reorganization was a high priority and was addressed almost immediately. In so doing, Giscard followed de Gaulle and Pompidou, both of whom had reorganized broadcasting soon after their elections and, not coincidentally, had used these reorganizations to move their supporters into key positions.

However, the new president did not approve a liberalization that would have permitted commercial television (though his own brother had been one of its main parliamentary advocates). There were also proposals to make one of the television channels semiprivate by having it run by the governmental Sofirad holding company, which already controlled several peripheral radio stations. These notions ran against the strong opposition of Gaullist traditionalists, and Giscard opted instead for the devolution of the ORTF and the establishment of a set of successor private-law companies owned by the state. Seven companies were rapidly established: Telediffusion de France (TDF) as a transmission company; the three television networks, TF1, A2, and FR3; Radio France, or the public radio service; SFP, a production company; and INA, for research, archives, and training. The government's monopoly over broadcasting was reaffirmed.

Functional separatism, it was hoped, would increase organizational and economical efficiency, introduce limited competition between state-controlled networks, benefit program quality, and reduce government influence over broadcasting. Both the left opposition and the hard-line Gaullists attacked the reforms as a step toward private broadcasting. The trade unions were similarly critical, charging that the reform was an "unprecedented aggression against the staff of a national enterprise" in order to strengthen government domination.

Giscard once again abolished the Ministry of Information and shifted responsibility for broadcasting to the office of the prime minister and the Ministry of Culture, which was eventually upgraded to the Ministry of Culture and Communications.

The Haute Conseil de l'Audiovisuel was established in 1973 as an advisory body on broadcasting and new media, composed of members of the two chambers of the legislature as well as outstanding people from the arts professions. Giscard appointed his son-in-law in 1976 as its general secretary. The organization was tiny and merely advisory, but in time it provided the seed for an independent regulatory body overseeing the broadcast sector.

Government control over television news was somewhat offset by the political preferences of the journalists themselves. In 1977, after two decades of conservative governments, a survey of the political opinion of broadcast journalists in France showed that almost 40 percent classified themselves as left or extreme left, whereas only 12 percent classified themselves as right. At Radio

France, 53 percent of journalists classified themselves as on the left; only 8 percent indicated voting for Gaullist candidates, and only 2 percent in favor of Giscard's were centrist (Cayrol, 1977).

For all of his reformist intentions, Giscard soon resorted to attempts at influencing television coverage, especially where it appeared that the left would win the 1978 parliamentary election. His government also cracked down forcefully on pirate radio stations. But programming became less elitist and didactic and more oriented toward entertainment This change occurred in spite of the fact that competition for ratings between the three television channels was not primarily motivated by economics, since budgets and revenues were only trivially affected by them.

The most complicated part of the system was its financing arrangement. Advertising was introduced in 1968, but there were time limitations and ceilings on the percentage advertising could contribute to a channel's budget. Excluded from TV advertising for a variety of reasons were publishing houses, retailers, tourist trade businesses, and temporary employment agencies. The bulk of financing still had to come from license fees. Until 1982, advertising revenues were limited to 25 percent of overall revenues of the French broadcasting system. The distribution of these fees was subject to a complicated formula, linked partly to audience size and partly to program quality. Program quality was determined by a confusing system of audience surveys and gradings by a twenty-seven-member quality control commission. The operation of this mechanism cost almost as much as the redistribution it administered.

Although Giscard d'Estaing was increasingly opposed to liberalization of broadcasting, especially to demands to legalize local and citizen radio, he also presided over the "telematics" initiative of 1978 whose elements were videotex, and soon thereafter, the direct broadcast satellite project TDF-1. There was, however, no contradiction: on both issues Giscard was pro-state. The TDF satellite was viewed not as media liberalization, but rather as state-guided support for the electronics industry.

The 1982 Liberalization Law

All this changed after the Socialists took power in 1981. An expert commission was appointed, chaired by Pierre Moinot, a high-level judge. Within a few months, the commission reported and recommended changes that were quickly, with some restrictions, passed into the landmark 1982 Law on Audiovisual Communications. The basic framework permitting the reorganization of the entire French broadcasting system was created in only one year, from the appointment of the commission to legislative enactment. Articles 1 and 2 state "Audiovisual communication is free" and "Citizens have the right to free and pluralist communication." The law provided a flexible instrument for the state, which could use it to liberalize and control. It was the fifth major broadcast reform of the Fifth Republic, to be followed by two more before the decade was out.

The 1982 law reordered not only broadcasting, but also the entire audiovisual sector. It established a semi-independent commission, the High Authority (Haute Autorité), to control the broadcast organizations while assuring their independence from the government. Its mission was also to establish program recommendations for the broadcast institutions and program production companies. It was to assure pluralism and balance of programs; absence of racist, sexist, and discriminatory programs; rights to reply; fairness in the electoral process; and general guidelines for advertising. The High Authority was also in charge of frequency allocation and licensing of private local radio roadcasters and cable program providers. Perhaps most important, it was to appoint the heads of the broadcast organizations. Of the High Authority's nine members, three were appointed by the president of the National Assembly, three, (including the Authority's President) by the president of the Senate, and three by the president of France. The Haute Autorité de la Communication Audiovisuelle appeared to discharge its independent function relatively fairly. However, it found itself enmeshed in public pressures in the appointment process and had no budgetary or sanctioning power over the channels.

The 1982 law also organized the broadcasting system into ten independent national organizations, plus twelve regional stations: TDF, as before, was the transmission and technical authority; Radio France operated radio broadcasting; TF1 and A2 were the national and FR3 the regional TV channels, the latter with twelve regional companies serving program windows; and Radio France Outre-mer (RFO) was a new organization for broadcast in overseas department, Société Française de Production (SFP) for production of television material programs, and Institut National de l'Audiovisuel (INA) for archives, training, and research. In addition, Radio France Internationale (RFI) was established for international radio and France Média-International (FMI) for international marketing of French television productions. It was also planned to transform the twelve regional stations of FR3 over time into an independent regional program and production organization, but this did not happen.

The 1982 law on broadcast communications restructured the regulatory regime in an important way: although a governmental role in broadcasting was maintained, no monopoly was claimed anymore. A private organization could enter broadcasting, provided it had licenses for (1) frequencies, (2) transmission facilities, and (3) conducting program activities. Cable licenses were granted by the High Authority. Concessions or licenses could therefore be granted to independent radio, television, and cable program networks.

The Emergence of Private Radio

For a long time the French government had been hostile to radio communications outside of its control. For example, it severely restricted citizens' band

(CB) radios, declaring them to be worthless. Even the noted French scholar Jacques Ellul found CB communication lacking in merit because of the shallowness of its dialogue (Rogers and Balle, 1985, p. 105)—a standard that would condemn much of humanity to silence.

An integral part of French radio is the surrounding foreign radio and television stations broadcasting French-language programming into France. These peripheral stations include Europe-1, Radio Tele Luxembourg (RTL), Radio Monte Carlo, and Sud Radio. They are accepted by the French government and in many instances are even under its control. They are, for all practical purposes, French stations with French ownership. Much of their production takes place in facilities in Paris, and their signals are relayed by wire or microwave across the border (or close to it) for broadcasting back to France.

The government controls these stations through its Société Française de Radio Diffusion (SOFIRAD), established in 1942, which owned 97 percent of Sud Radio, 83 percent of Radio Monte Carlo, and 35 percent of Europe-1. When Prime Minister Chirac protested an interview on Europe-1, the station's director general was quickly dismissed. Furthermore, through Havas (subsequently privatized), as well as several banks and other institutions, the government held a major share in the Luxembourg broadcast company CLT, which operates Radio Télé Luxembourg.

Television broadcasting from Monaco, an independent principality straddling France and Italy, is conducted by two stations. The private Globo Monte Carlo has been owned since 1985 by Tele-Globo, Brazil's major media firm; the station, formerly named Tele Monte Carlo, is aimed primarily at Italy. The public station, also named Tele Monte Carlo, broadcasts in French into France. Pirate television broadcasters, including Canal 5, TIME, Canal 35, and Antenne 1 comprised another segment of French broadcasting. These and many other stations aggressively took to the air after 1977. After being closed down by the police, they reasserted their right to broadcast. A lower court agreed with them that the government had no authority to stop them.

When the Socialists came to power, they had no detailed plans for new media or electronics development, but they inherited a public opinion that had been sensitized on issues of the electronic environment through the Nora and Minc report (Nora and Minc, 1978) on telematics. They also found a number of plans developed during the previous administration (Vedel, 1987). Thus, their position was flexible and permitted them to pursue a pragmatic liberalization of media of the kind moderate socialists in northern Europe were unwilling to pursue.

In legislation passed in 1981 and 1982, the new government liberalized radio broadcasting by legalizing the pirate stations. After all, the Socialists themselves had operated a pirate station of their own, Radio Riposte. By 1983, almost 900 local radio stations were licensed by the High Authority and were operating, providing access to the airways to groups that had not previously been heard. Power was limited to 500 watts, and reach was restricted to a maximum of 30 kilometers. No networking was permitted, pursuant to the goals of decentralization. At first, advertising was also prohibited, and subscriptions, donations, and government subsidies were required for the stations to survive. However, indirect advertising proliferated and the restrictions proved unworkable. Although hundreds of stations were run by nonprofit community groups, many operated commercially in violation of advertising and networking rules. In other cases, local radio, because of its weak economic base, ended up dominated by local government politicians or newspapers. All this led, predictably, to further liberalization. In 1984, local commercial radio was officially permitted, with up to 80 percent of its budget based on advertising revenues. Nonprofit community radio meanwhile received governmental start-up money and operating subsidies.[1]

When the conservatives regained power temporarily, they lifted restrictions on signal reach and networking and reoriented licensing criteria, making them more economic and less cultural. Stations were permitted to own and operate their own transmitters, or to buy the service from other firms. The government also established anticoncentration rules.

In 1986, 400 to 500 stations had opted for the community radio status, whereas about 1400 chose the commercial route (Vedel, 1987). In 1988, there were some 1600 FM outlets, eleven private national radio networks, and seven public radio networks (*Variety*, 1988), a huge increase over the previous handful. The most active networks were Europe 1 and 2, RTL, Radio Monte Carlo, Skyrock, and especially NRJ. Many of the networks used a program satellite feed, reducing the local role of affiliated stations. Other networks (régies) are more in the nature of advertising cooperatives. Communities and cities control about one third of stations.

Canal Plus

With radio being liberalized, television was not far behind. The first new national television channel was inaugurated by the government in 1984, when the pay television channel, Canal Plus was started on a commercial basis. Canal Plus was not an upstart organization, but rather the result of an initiative by the governmental transmission authority, TDF, which wanted to use the frequency of the 819-line transmission standard that was no longer in use. The French electronic industry eagerly eyed a potential market for millions of decoders and adapters in the future. It was also seen as a way to stem the Japanese VCR invasion, because it would provide its viewers with a fare of movies similar to that sought by VCR owners (Kuhn, 1985a). Initially, the influential Minister of Culture, Jack Lang, had opposed subscription television as discriminatory to the poor; but he subsequently changed his priorities, arguing that payments would help develop the culture industry.

To mollify movie theaters, the three regular French broadcasting networks agreed not to show recent motion pictures. Of the 470 films shown in 1982 over the three channels, 434 were older than three years and none were less than two years old (Rozenblum, 1984a, 1984b). For Canal Plus, less stringent rules were agreed upon; it refrained from showing films within their first eleven months or in several prime movie attendance periods. It was also agreed, after acrimonious negotiations with the powerful French film industry, that at least one-half of the films would be of French origin and that Canal Plus would invest in French film productions.

The film industry received other government concessions as well. A new system of tax shelters for film production was established that created investment companies, so-called *soficas* (sociétés de financement de la communication audiovisuelle). Engineered by Jack Lang over the opposition of the Ministry of Finance, this tax shelter was similar to one in the United States that was so badly abused by wealthy individuals that it was abolished. There was also a long-standing system to subsidize film production by a tax on every movie ticket. Support to French films was provided by the Centre National du Cinéma through a "support account" from a tax on television revenues that provided $68 million in funds in 1987. Such measures supported independent producers and reduced the power of the Société Française de Production (SFP) (Epstein, 1988).

Canal Plus's owners included at the time a majority of companies, some controlled by the government. The advertising group Agence Havas (initially state owned and subsequently privatized) at first held more than a 40 percent stake, later reduced to 25 percent. Havas' president was André Rousselet, a Mitterrand confidant and formerly one of the highest officials of the presidential office. Havas was and remained one of France's major communications firms, with holdings also in Luxembourg's CLT, in advertising (Information et Publicité; Eurocom; Avenir), directories, publishing, and tourism. Rousselet was a major force behind the establishment of the channel and became its president. Other utility shareholders were the Compagnie Générale des Eaux, with 21 percent in 1990 (TBI, 1990, p. 38). Smaller stakes were held by private firms, the largest of which were Société Générale (5 percent) the cosmetics company L'Oréal (6 percent), headed by another friend of Mitterrand, and the Caisse des Depots (6.8 percent).[2]

The monthly subscription charge was a relatively high $32, yet Canal Plus became Europe's largest pay-TV operator with a terrestrial network reaching 85 percent of the population and the opportunity to reach the other 3 million homes by transmission from the TDF-1 satellite. It had about 3 million subscribers in 1990.

In 1989 Canal Plus expanded across Europe with joint ventures in Germany (forming Premiere with the large media firms Kirch and Bertelsmann), Spain (with El Pais), Belgium (with RTBF), Sweden, and Africa. Canal Plus revenues rose to over $900 million in 1989. But expansion works in both directions. In 1991, Luxembourg's CLT planned satellite-direct broadcasting, which would compete with Canal Plus in price and content and without the restrictive French rules on the showing of recent movies.

The Establishment of Private Television

Pay TV on a subscription basis was not the only form in which the Socialist government opened commercial television. A report on the subject was commissioned by the government from a commission headed by Jean-Denis Bredin and delivered to Prime Minister Laurent Fabius in 1985. The report noted that significant portions of the country could be served by three supplementary frequencies. Bredin suggested dividing the country into sixty-two broadcast zones, which would permit two new national networks to reach immediately 17 million viewers each, and 22 million if the frequency plans were adapted (Bredin, 1985).

Concessions for the two national networks would be granted by the state for five years, extendable at the end of each year. For local stations the High Authority would be in charge of licensing. To prevent networking, local stations would not be permitted to obtain more than 40 percent of their programming from the same supplier. The report also recommended that the transmission monopoly of TDF be retained.

The Conseil National de la Communication Audiovisuelle agreed with much of the Bredin report but felt that there would be room for only one national private network, which would have about 50 percent of the potential audience. The council also stated that no local station was viable in the face of a national network and that local stations would rapidly disappear. The High Authority opposed the Bredin recommendations, preferring a more regional approach based on local publishers.

Prime Minister Fabius recommended a modified plan to Mitterrand, including three networks, run by large radio stations and influenced by the government-controlled Sofirad organization, and one private, non-pay channel. Of the three state-owned channels, one would function as a basis for a satellite-delivered European cultural program. In the end the government did not formally adapt any particular plan, but instead moved rapidly and pragmatically to license two commercial national networks.

One reason was the waning electoral fortunes of the Socialist government, which led it to pursue a quick and controlled liberalization and to license friendly private interests, thereby preempting the licensing of hostile interests by the conservative government that was expected to follow.

The government also committed itself in 1984 to lease two channels of the TDF broadcasting satellite (which was to be launched in 1986) to the Luxembourg broadcasting firm CLT-RTL. CLT linked these in a terrestrial broadcasting consortium with two other private peripheral broadcasters, Europe-1 and Radio Monte Carlo. In 1985 Luxembourg's prime minister, Jacques Santer, visited Paris for talks with Mitterrand and Fabius. Santer declared that the "signature which a French minister puts under a declaration of intent is always valid." But only one week later the French government gave a broadcast license to a consortium of French and Italian interests including Silvio Berlusconi, the Italian TV czar. This consortium was authorized to commence broadcasting nationally by February 20, 1986—in other words, before the parliamentary elections. Its program would be carried on TDF-1 when the satellite became available. No mention of CLT was made. The government had come to the conclusion, following the prediction of Jean Riboud—the late president of the Schlumberger Group, a close friend of Mitterrand, and an insider in CLT affairs—that the French influence in CLT would decrease in the future. Riboud died in 1985, but he had begun to put together a French-Italian consortium with Berlusconi. In that consortium French interests were primarily held by Jérôme Seydoux (40 percent), known among other things for his sympathies for Mitterrand, and another 20 percent was owned by Riboud's own son, Christopher. Seydoux, a grandson of Marcel Schlumberger and heir to a substantial part of the Schlumberger fortune, was chairman of one of the largest private French companies, Chargeurs Réunis S.A. He also owned a part of the left-leaning *Nouvel Observateur* and in former days the (now defunct) *Matin de Paris*. Berlusconi, for his part, had been recommended to Mitterrand by Prime Minister Bettino Craxi of Italy, a fellow socialist who was on good terms with the media mogul. Berlusconi controlled 40 percent of the consortium and much of the actual operation. Legislation was rushed through the National Assembly,[3] and four days later the license had already been assigned. Negotiations and license decisions were held in strictest secrecy. There was never any public call for license applications; selection criteria were never specified; and no public debate on the merits of the candidates took place before the decision. The consortium also received a channel on the TDF-1 DBS satellite. Berlusconi and Seydoux were also part of a consortium, with the British and German media giants Robert Maxwell and Leo Kirch, that received two other TDF-1 transponders. Maxwell too was the kind of left-leaning capitalist with whom the Socialist government liked to deal.[4]

Awarding the license for La Cinq was politically clever because it put the opposition in an awkward position. It had to argue against the establishment of new broadcast channels at no charge to the viewers and under private control with major French and Italian business interests represented. It had to charge, in effect, that its own business friends should receive the license for La Cinq rather than Mitterrand's.

Within the Socialist party, Minister of Culture Jack Lang worried about the impact on French culture and its protection from American influences. On the other hand, conservatives and centrists found the plan too restrictive. The Council for the Future of France, headed by the former President Giscard d'Estaing, produced a lengthy report on communications, arguing against too much interference and recommending disengagement of the state from the entire audiovisual sector. It also recommended inserting into the Constitution the following sentence: "The state does not manage, does not finance, does not regulate information."

A second broadcast channel was awarded two days later to TV-6, a group controlled by the advertising firm Publicis, the film production company Gaumont, the advertiser Gross, and the commercial radio station NRJ. Gaumont's head was Nicolas Seydoux, brother of Jérôme Seydoux, the president of La

Cinq. TV-6 operated a music channel aimed at a young audience and went on the air in March 1986, two weeks before the election. CLT was again left out (Opitz, 1990).

The TDF-1 satellite channels, too, were assigned. One would go to a European-oriented cultural channel, which the government decided to set up with public funds. A second channel was given to interests including Robert Maxwell, the publisher of the Mirror Group newspapers in Britain, who had aggressively entered cable television in the United Kingdom.

The conservatives came to power in 1986. The new government introduced media reform legislation within three months of taking office and passed the sixth such law since 1958, after extensive discussions in the Senate. (The opposition brought 1700 amendments.)

In a significant shift from traditional Gaullist policies, the 1986 law no longer defined audiovisual communications as a public service. In the words of then Communications Minister François Léotard, "What principle gives the state any rights to take charge of broadcasting, television, and radio programs?" (Vedel, 1987, p. 25). The law also extends to telecommunications.

The government privatized Havas and, thus, indirectly, Canal Plus and RTL. It also sold off the public channel TF1 and announced its intention to privatize FR3 in the future. Thus, in a very short time French television evolved from an all-government lineup of three public broadcasters and no private broadcasters into a system in which four private channels (plus the popular peripheral broadcasters) faced two public networks. In addition, private broadcasting proliferated on the radio, and private satellite-delivered channels on DBS and on cable were about to become a reality after years of discord over implementation.

The conservative government challenged the terrestrial and DBS television concessions granted by the Socialists. But in the end the fifth channel was reconfirmed to Berlusconi (with a 25 percent interest, from an earlier 40 percent), Seydoux (10 percent, down from 30 percent), but they included the dominant conservative publisher and radio chain owner Robert Hersant, a political ally of Chirac and parliamentary deputy for his party, who received an interest of 25 percent and was named president of the company. Ribaud was dropped, and several financial institutions and publishers substituted. Channel 6 was also partly reallocated, with a 25 percent interest going to Luxembourg's CLT (after the French government earnestly impressed on the CNCL the foreign policy importance of such an assignment), 25 percent to the water and cable operator Lyonnaise des Eaux, 39 percent allocated among five major investors (Omnium Gesgion, 9 percent; Union Assurance de Paris, 8 percent; UEI, 8 percent; Bank Paribas, 8 percent; Financière Suez Compagnie, 5 percent), and the remaining 11 percent divided among ten small shareholders. The group transformed TV-6 into the music-oriented M6, a general entertainment channel.

Two DBS channels were awarded to a new consortium involving Berlusconi, Seydoux, the English publisher Robert Maxwell, and the dominant German film dealer Leo Kirch. The law also transformed the government transmission organization TDF (Télédiffusion de France) into a private company whose stock can be traded. TDF's traditional rival, France Télécom, acquired 49 percent and later 100 percent. TDF can offer competitive transmission services to private broadcasters.

Another liberalizing action of the 1986 law was partly to abolish the SFP production monopoly. French broadcasting had traditionally been burdened by regulation forcing the networks to buy programs from the public production company SFP at high prices that reflected SFP's very generous staffing levels. SFP was responsible, only a few years ago, for 75 to 80 percent of all fiction production in France. But the networks, short of funds, were increasingly trying to bypass SFP's high-cost productions. The major share of SFP is owned by the state; the remainder is held by the public broadcasters and TF1. After it lost $160 million from 1986 to 1989, the government granted SFP an additional $100 million in 1990.

Léotard—a member of the younger generation of French politicians, a leader of the right-of-center party, and a man with presidential aspirations—adopted as his main initiative the privatization of the first and prime French television channel, TF1, marking the first time that any major country had privatized a public television channel. The government met opposition from broadcast journalists and trade unions, who went on strike soon after the announcement, stopping all television in France except for limited news and films. The private channels La Cinq and TV-6 remained on the air, gaining more visibility than they might have had otherwise.

One-half of the shares of TF1 was offered to major investors, 40 percent was sold to the public at large, and 10 went to the employees. Individual groups were limited to 25, and foreigners could purchase only 20 percent of the total shares.

Obligations imposed upon TF1 included broadcast quotas (60 percent of programs to be of EC origin and 50 percent to be from Francophone producers) to investment in new French media products (at a minimum, 15 percent of revenues generated). These regulations have changed repeatedly since 1987, partly because TF1 did not meet them.

The dominant concession was awarded by the CNCL to the French construction magnate Francis Bouygues (25 percent), Maxwell Interests (12 percent, sold later to interests close to Bouygues) and various publishers, banks, and conglomerates. Bouygues beat out Jean-Luc Lagardère, despite the latter's inside track in media (the giant Hachette-Matra publishing/electronics, Europe-1 radio station, MMPP news agency, Elle Publishing, Grolier, Diamandis, Salvat, etc.). Thirty percent of the stock was sold to the public. Little of the 10 percent option assigned at preferential rates to employees was exercised, and Bouygues was able to add more than 7 percent to his holdings (Opitz, 1990). Berlusconi, too, acquired about 5 percent in the rival network. Maxwell, however, later sold his share. Hachette, in turn, acquired 25 percent (the maximum permissible) in "La Cinq," the fifth channel, which required the absorption of major losses in the operations of that channel.

In 1991, TF1's national audience share was a very high 41 percent, Antenne 2 had 24 percent, FR3 had 12.5 percent, La Cinq had 10.5 percent, and M6 had

7 percent. (The latter two did not yet have full national coverage.) TF1 revenues increased by 10 percent over 1988 (to Ff 5.3 billion) and net profits (Ff 220 million) rose by 37 percent (*EBU Review* 1990, p. 31). Because of the competition of several networks for advertising, the remaining national broadcasters had financial problems (TBI, 1990). Publicly owned Antenne 2 lost $43 million in 1989, and the private organization La Cinq lost $78 million (Siritzky and Stuart, 1990, p. 39). The latter station's problems, including total losses of $400 million, were aggravated by repeated fines for its failure to meet domestic program quotas. La Cinq further suffered from a bitter struggle over its control; Robert Hersant fought off a 1989 attempt for control by Berlusconi and Seydoux, but then announced he would step down in 1990, selling out his 25 percent share to Hachette and a bank consortium. Seydoux had already sold out. M6, also privately owned, with a program schedule of rock videos and American programs designed to complement those of the larger networks, showed small profits for the first time in 1990 (*EBU Review*, 1990, p. 38).

The government also replaced the High Authority with the regulatory commission Commission Nationale de la Communication et des Liberté (CNCL) whose thirteen members were mostly government officials serving five- to ten-year terms. The CNCL also had some power in telecommunications and cable television. It was given stronger powers for enforcement and establishment of program quality guidelines. Politics provided one justification for its establishment: the High Authority had been designed to extend the majority of Socialist appointees beyond the election; but for the new CNCL, a conservative majority could be appointed.

The new law empowered the CNCL to establish cable operators' obligations concerning retransmission of terrestrial broadcasts, domestic programming content, and rental payments. In the sphere of public broadcasting, the CNCL was responsible for selecting the presidents of A2 and FR3 and important program personnel. In the domain of private broadcasting, it granted licenses for radio (up to five years) and television (up to twelve years). Foreign capital was restricted to 20 percent involvement in these operations; any individual's ownership was limited to 25 percent (Opitz, 1990).

Throughout the Conservative period of government the Socialists attacked the CNCL as partisan. President Mitterrand, who had always taken a very active interest in media issues, publicly characterized it as partisan in its composition and decision making and criticized it for permitting a political witchhunt in the public broadcast institutions (Opitz, 1990). According to Mitterrand, the CNCL had never done anything worthy of respect. When the Socialists returned to power in 1988, the Rocard government declared its intention to establish greater regulatory and institutional independence. It replaced the CNCL, of whose thirteen members eleven were close to the government, by what it termed a less political body. In 1989, it created the Conseil Superieur de l'Audiovisuel (CSA) as a replacement for CNCL—the third regulatory body in seven years. Appointed by the presidents of the Republic, the National Assembly, and the Senate, each of its nine members has specific areas of responsibility, such as radio, satellites, program production, and private TV and serves a nonrenewable six-year term (Munich, 1989). Its powers have been extended beyond those of its two predecessors. It can issue penalties and suspend licenses. It proposes guidelines for the allocation of license fee revenues to the public broadcasting networks. It controls the performance of private commercial broadcasters via licensing privileges. In one of its first actions it chose as the joint president of the ailing public Antenne 2 and FR3 channels a moderate conservative, Phillippe Guilhaume, thereby demonstrating its independence, even though Guilhaume did not last long. On issues of ownership concentration and cross-ownership, the CSA shared some responsibilities with another regulatory body, the Conseil de la Concurrence.

The CSA also set up a new system to promote independent film production and to increase program budgets and quality. However, a French government report in 1990 suggested that the initiative had so far been unsuccessful: Although subsidies had contributed modestly to film funding, private French financing dropped from 46 percent to 38 percent between 1988 and 1989. Public broadcasters also cut their spending (Siritzky, 1990).

Direct Satellite Broadcasting

The evolution of the French direct broadcasting satellite TDF-1 and TDF-2 followed a 1980 agreement in cooperation with Germany's TV-SAT and reflects political fluctuations in France throughout the last decade. Originally scheduled for a 1983 start-up, TDF-1 was launched in 1988, followed by TDF-2. However, the satellites experienced major technical difficulties. Details are provided in Chapter 28 on DBS.

Cable Television and Teletext

Wire-transmitted "broadcasting" actually preceded wireless broadcasting in France. One of the earliest uses of the telephone in Paris was the *theatrophone*, which permitted subscribers to listen to live transmissions of opera and theater in their homes. This service was demonstrated in 1881, only five years after the invention of the telephone (Bertho et al., 1984, p. 80), and this "telephonic drawing room" for opera listening created an enormous demand. In 1889, the Theatrophone Company was founded; one of its early subscribers was Marcel Proust, who wrote about the experience. Theatrophone survived until the 1920s, when one of the newly emerging broadcasters acquired the company, largely for its contracts with theaters (Bertho et al., 1984, p. 81).

Half a century later, in 1973, following the introduction of broadcast television, the government authorized experimental cable television projects, hoping to develop cable television as a local communications medium. No specific legislation accompanied the plans, and of seven planned projects only one in Grenoble became active and permanent. The government also established the Société Française de Télédistribution (SFT) to develop French cable under joint control of the ORTF and the PTT Ministry. In 1975, the government changed course and stopped cable development, largely because of opposition from important regional newspapers, cinema theaters, and the existing broadcast channels (Vedel and Dutton, 1988, p. 26). A national committee was established in 1977 to study cable, but it had a very limited scope. President Giscard d'Estaing, having campaigned as a reformer, now stated that the "risk in fact is that the organs of information will destroy each other, as we can see happening with the present difficulties of the press. The three state television channels have not yet reached the stage of full development. Therefore, we have to wait for the full use of the present media before asking the question about the future role of alternative media." As he did in the case of local radio, Giscard eventually supported France's status quo and centralized tradition in cable, too. A regulation was pronounced in 1977 that strictly prohibited the transmission over cable of programs not receivable over the air.

It took the new Socialist government to open the way for cable television. Although the state transmission organization, TDF, opposed the project, fearing its effect on its pet satellite project, the PTT Ministry and the telephone administration, DGT, recognized the potential of the new medium for their own activities and supported the efforts. In 1982, the government asked the DGT to submit a cable report. The Plan Câble was a creative hodge-podge of political agendas such as modernization, high technology, social concerns, culture industry development, decentralization, and media diversity. The DGT argued that cable television made sense only in the context of French leadership in electronics, particularly in switched-star network technology. Since this technology was costly and unproven, it would require DGT leadership and the economies of scale that a national effort would entail.

An ambitious cable plan was adopted soon thereafter. It included the use of optical fibers and switched-star architecture, the connection of 6 million subscribers by 1992 at a cost of FFr 1.2 billion, the creation of 15,000 to 20,000 jobs, and substantial local and citizen participation. Two domestic technical development efforts were launched. PTT Minister Mexandeau declared that France had no intention of opening its market to foreign cable equipment.

About 150 municipalities applied to receive cable service. High-tech enthusiasm cooled, however, when fiber and star switching were found to be significantly more expensive than coaxial cable and tree-and-branch architecture. Since the DGT was increasingly required by the government to subsidize the electronic and space industries (FFr 2.8 billion in 1982, 2.4 billion in 1983, 8.4 billion in 1984, and 15.5 billion in 1985 [Vedel 1987, p. 34]), it could provide less investment money than expected to the local cable projects.

The municipalities also discovered the limits of the government's decentralization policy. They could not design or own "their" cable systems but were expected to contribute heavily with interest-free loans. This led to acrimony, slow progress, complex local management, and politicization. In 1983, cable penetration had reached only 0.6 percent of the population (including master antenna systems), largely in areas of bad reception (Vedel, 1987).

The DGT was flexible enough to compromise. In 1985, it dropped the requirement of fiber on the subscriber loop and of local financial contributions. Even so, the actual cabling of France fell dramatically behind the government's plan. Instead of 1.4 million homes wired by the end of that year, as PTT Minister Mexandeau had promised, only 100,000 households were actually linked. It was only in 1987 that substantial systems came on line: Paris, with 55,000 initial subscribers; Rennes, with 20,000; and Montpellier, with 25,000. But even this achievement represented only about 20 percent of the previously planned subscribership for 1987.

The Chirac government held up the cable plan, except where agreements had already been signed. Its 1986 Communication Law abolished the DGT's monopoly on installation and operation of cable. It created the CNCL and gave it powers of licensing and franchising. CNCL permitted municipalities, as well as private and even public firms, to operate cable systems, as long as they conformed to technical standards and program regulation. France Télécom (successor to the DGT) was expected not to involve itself further in cable TV networks (Brailliard, 1988). This new law led to two coexisting approaches: one using the existing network, the other developing new private sector networks. In both cases, local and CNCL authorization for twenty-year periods of construction and operations is required.

As mayor of Paris, Chirac advocated the establishment of a mixed cable venture to operate the Parisian system. The municipality held 51 percent, a governmental water utility 39 percent, and a governmental savings bank the remaining 10 percent. The system became operational in 1986. It had fifteen channels, including the six French terrestrial networks, a local Paris channel, teletex services, public channels from Italy and the United Kingdom, commercial terrestrial television from Monte Carlo, the satellite channels Sky, TV5, and at times the Cable News Network. It aimed at a capacity of thirty channels.

Another satellite channel is TV-5, a low-power satellite operation that was started in 1984 as a joint operation of the French-speaking broadcasters in France, Belgium, and Switzerland, later joined by Canada. Other pay-TV services offered are Télé-Lyon Metropole and Ciné-Cínema. Satellite networks are Canal Bis (1989), Canal Infos (1988), Canal J (1986), Canal Humour (1989), Canal Santé, and Planète.

Beyond Paris, the most noteworthy cable development was in Biarritz, where the DGT tested with several hundred subscribers an advanced broadband fiberoptic system, involving an integrated transmission system that included picturephones, regular telephones, television, videotex, FM stereo, and video conferencing. The project, which was inaugurated in 1984, for several years of trial, cost about FFr 660 million (Beck, 1985; Dutton, et al., 1987). The architecture was a remote switch star configuration, allowing on-demand video programming. Subscribers could dial into a "television club" and access more than 2000 videocassettes directly through fiber optic telephone lines.

For cable television distribution, new, locally based institutions, known as Sociétés Locales d'Exploitation du Câble (SLECs), were established. SLECs were usually headed by local politicians for marketing, programming, and regulating local cable television. A commissioner appointed by the central government to each SLEC was to ensure that the operating conditions were respected. France Télécom was to install cable networks by agreement with municipalities, and the SLECs were to pay for use of the facilities on a per-subscriber basis. France Télécom would also control transmission of distant programs to the cable networks.

For locally originated programming, the SLEC needed authorization by the audiovisual supervisory body; permission for nonlocal program channels came from the Communications Ministry. To mollify cultural and movie theater interests, the government required at least two-thirds of cable programs to be French, and a minimum of 15 percent of programs to be of local origin. Furthermore, one-third of all cable operators' revenues were to be invested in new programming. Other restrictions on cable television transmission of films were similar to the ones imposed upon French broadcasters, including a minimum delay between theatrical and television release (Kuhn, 1985, pp. 50–66). The question of advertising over cable caused significant controversy because of the impact this would have on the revenue of powerful local newspapers. Their participation in local cable was possible, though their frequently conservative orientation raised political problems for the Socialists (Rozenblum, 1984a).

In 1987, PTT Minister Gérard Longuet limited the scope of the Plan Câble to the fifty largest cities; franchises would be awarded to private companies, which would construct and operate systems in uncabled cities. This meant that the cumbersome SLECs were no longer necessary.

The penetration rate of the original Plan Câble rapidly doubled as a result of this decision. But cable penetration in 1990 was still only 1 percent (400,000 subscribers), and only 2 million homes were passed, a fact attributable in part to the rapid expansion of Canal Plus, to the advent of new commercial channels (La Cinq, M6)—which gave households a larger over-the-air choice than that in most West European countries (TBI, 1990)—and high VCR penetration (about 45 percent in 1990). Providing initial cable service is not cheap ($20–$25). Until the recent shift in favor of a more traditional tree-and-branch coaxial cable system, a fiber-optic switched-star design was utilized. This technology, however, proved too complex and costly during the mid-1980s (Thierry Vedel, communication, 1990).

When the Socialists returned to power in 1988, the new government was not particularly actively involved in cable television policy. It gave France Télécom increased autonomy in its cable operations, but the latter's investment priorities were the digitalization of the public network.

In 1990, the Socialist government made two decisions affecting the French cable industry. First, it encouraged France Télécom to increase its commitment to cable television by becoming financially involved in the SLECs and to relax the financial and managerial criteria used to hire system operators. Second, it changed the procedure for the verification of cable programming schedules. Before this decision, cable operators had to obtain two separate approvals for each system—one from the local government regarding financial and technical requirements, and one from the CSA regarding the planned programs to be offered on the system. In the new procedure the CSA initially approves cable programs for national distribution, so that, after receiving approval for the system, the cable operator chooses its programming from a national menu (Yves Bertrand, communication, 1990).

By 1990, the French cable market was dominated by three major firms. Compagnie Générale des Eaux, a huge privately owned water utility with revenues of $12 billion, owned forty-five cable systems. Out of 2.65 million French TV homes passed, Générale's systems accounted for .9 million, and 132,000 subscribers, or about 33 percent. Compagnie Lyonnaise des Eaux, another water utility, owned eleven cable systems, passing 31 percent, or 710,000 of the French TV homes passed, with a 22 percent share, or 95,000 subscribers. Caisse des Dépots et Cosignations, a state bank, controlled through its subsidiary ComDev thirty cable systems that passed 17 percent of homes in their franchise area or 510,000, with a 30 percent market share, or 119,000 subscribers. The remainder, about 350,000 subscriptions, belong to the approximately ten small cable operators. Half of these are privately owned companies and the other half are owned by either federal or local governments and are independently operated (*Télécoms Magazine*, 1990). Overall penetration was still below 2 percent overall and below 17 percent of those households passed by cable. The three major cable operators all made efforts in program provision (Canal Plus; Havas; Canal Jimmy; Cine Cinema and Cine Cinefil (pay); Planete; Paris Premiere; and TV Sport).

France Télécom constructed all fifty-one French cable networks before 1986 and licensed available space to the three major cable firms. France Télécom still owns these systems. After that, forty-two more cable systems were constructed with only minor France Télécom involvement. By 1990 there were ninety-eight operational cable networks in France. France Télécom had partnership agreements and was responsible for the daily operation and technology of many. The only system it fully operated and programmed was Biarritz (*Télécoms Magazine*, 1990).

In 1988, Mission Câble changed its name to Agence Câble and became part of France's Ministry of Communication. Its main role is to provide information for Parliament and other organizations. It receives a share of the license fees from the INA and invests in projects proposed by private operators. For instance, it funds experimental cable projects in education and health and was involved in Eurocable, Educable, Canal Jimmy, and Canal Info (Yves Bertrand, communication, 1990).

Teletext and Videotex

For a time, information text service remained an area of contention between broadcast organizations and the telecommunication administration, DGT. Public television broadcasters and TDF initiated a one-way broadcast teletext under the name of Antiope,[5] and the DGT launched a technically related interactive videotex service Teletel (known more popularly as Minitel) on its network.

Under an executive order of 1984 the Ministry of Communications must authorize teletext service, whether offered free or for pay. Advertisements are permissible, but only the media, including television networks, may broadcast classified ads. With advertisements and subscription, Antiope makes it possible to provide genuine media services. The three broadcast networks—TF1, Antenne 2, and FR3—broadcast their own teletext magazines, close-captioned, nationally. Other information providers contribute text. Some teletext magazines are regional, whereas others, such as those of the National Weather Service and the Traffic Department, are national. One financial teletext company provides a magazine for approximately $90 per month, in addition to a second, free, stock market magazine. Several newspapers provide headline services, and a weekly classified magazine listing used car prices is also available. Similarly, farmers may subscribe to services providing daily agricultural prices and veterinary advice. The national French railway uses teletext as a directory for timetable information. On the whole, however, broadcast teletext does not compare in its significance in France with telephone-transmitted videotex.

8

United Kingdom

For more than thirty years Britain had a stable and effective broadcast duopoly. One of its elements was the accomplished BBC, arguably the world's flagship of public broadcasting. The other was a cartel of commercial firms providing independent television, often also of high quality. To be admitted to broadcasting, these private companies had to overcome high political barriers that kept subsequent entrants out. This system of profitable inside status for a few privileged firms was untenable in the long term. But because private television in Britain preceded that of most of the rest of Europe by a generation, pressures for change were less insistent; there was, after all, commercial television to serve the center and lower ends of the taste distribution, and the BBC itself was subject to daily rivalry that enhanced its responsiveness and sharpened its independence from a government that had kept elements of content control. Eventually, however, the limited television system was challenged from several directions: by the government's technology policy encouraging cable television and DBS; by the emergence of London as the European center for program supply; and by the aspirations of the free-market wing of the Conservative party for a more competitive economy. Britain moved, as the first European country after Italy, to the next stage in the opening of television.

History of the BBC

The development of wireless communications in Britain was particularly energetic because of its importance for naval and shipping use. Britannia set out to rule the airwaves through the Marconi Company, which held the major international radio patents. Legal control over the use of the wireless was firmly lodged in the Post Office through legislation passed in 1904. World War I created a core of trained military radio operators, and after demobilization, some of these men became enthusiastic radio amateurs. The airwaves began to be used in broadcastlike fashion by civilians. Early private broadcasting started when in 1919, the Post Office sanctioned the Marconi Company to set up an experimental station. At first, irregular transmissions were listened to by irregular listeners. June 15, 1920, was a milestone, when the famous soprano Dame Nellie Melba sang over the radio and was received by hundreds of listeners in Britain and as far off as Norway and Newfoundland (Briggs, 1961). The event received wide attention and put radio on the map. The government, however, was far less enthusiastic about the budding new mass medium. Criticism by the military (especially the Admiralty) and the Post Office about the use of radio as a "toy to amuse children" rather than a "servant of mankind" (*The Financier,* August 25, 1920, in Briggs, 1961, p. 49) and about the dangers of unauthorized reception and transmission led to the suspension of civilian broadcasts later that year; and they were not resumed until 1922, when news of the American radio boom, which had leapfrogged the earlier U.K. lead, reached Britain and led to much pressure by radio amateurs to participate in the new medium.

Marconi was not the only broadcaster, though it would have liked to replicate the tight control it had over radio telephony. Two other firms, Metropolitan-Vickers and Western Electric, also provided broadcasting. Subsequent applicants were told by the Post Office, at a time when only three stations were intermittently on the air, that "The ether is already full." Those firms holding a transmission permit had to comply with highly restrictive conditions. Initially, only speech was broadcast. For some reason, no music could be transmitted. Every seven minutes, three minutes of radio silence had to be maintained, during which the operator checked whether an official message to vacate the frequency was being sent out. Furthermore, no newspaper announcements of regular programs were permitted. Despite these restrictions, the Post Office was inundated by applications for transmission and reception. Unwilling to repeat the strained arrangement in radio telephony, where Marconi was the dominant force, and repelled by the chaos in the United States, the Post Office asked the several interested manufacturers in broadcasting to conceive a system for U.K. broadcasting.

The radio equipment industry, comprised of six firms, needed little prodding. Its interest was that of hardware manufacturers; broadcasting was merely a means to sell radio sets. Collaboration promised several advantages: avoidance of costly duplicative broadcast efforts; elimination of free-riding by manufacturers not contributing to the broadcast effort; pooling of patents; and cartel restrictions on equipment production and imports. The last point is essential. The Post Office agreed to approve only those radio receiving sets that were made by member firms of the British Broadcasting Company, and shares were allotted only to "genuine British manufacturers employing British labour." Even more important, the manufacturers needed the full cooperation of the Post Office to make broadcasting profitable: the economic linchpin would be a license fee on the use of receivers, which required governmental approval and enforcement. When the companies were on the verge of splitting into two rival groups, the chairman of the manufacturers' committee wrote that "It may be difficult to persuade the Post Office to approve these conditions, and any division among the manufacturers may well jeopardize the whole method of financing the broadcasting" (Sir Frank Gill in Briggs, 1961, p. 112). This admonition helped to form a single company. In 1923, this newly formed British Broadcasting Company received a monopoly for broadcasting in Britain from the Post Office. When the arrangement was disclosed to the public, it encountered much hostility. Some members of Parliament challenged its legality, and others criticized the impact on free trade. Postmaster-General Kellaway responded that it was "inconceivable" that "we should allow a new form of communication in this country to be exploited by foreign manufacturers" (*Hansard's Parliamentary Debates*, 1922). He countered the antimonopoly argument by insisting that every British manufacturer could join the BBC. "What you have to fear in this is not monopoly; it is more likely you will have cut-throat competition" (*Hansard's Parliamentary Debates*, 1923). This entirely missed the problem of monopoly broadcasting, as opposed to monopoly manufacturing.

Another interest group that needed placating by the government was the private publishers. They feared for their advertising and influence. A conference was held under government auspices, at which the representative of the press, Lord Riddell, demanded assurances that the BBC would not "lift" its property without payment, and that its interests "would not be negatively affected through the broadcasting of news" (Briggs, 1961, p. 131).

The BBC soon commenced operations, and tens of thousands bought officially stamped radios, manufactured by BBC companies. For the Post Office, the license fee became a windfall, which would not be equally available under a commercial system without user charges. But this system soon proved unstable: publishing interests attacked the monopoly system from the direction of program supply, radio set and component manufacturers undermined it from the hardware side, and many listeners ignored it altogether. For listeners, the loophole in the system was the possibility of obtaining an "experimental license" at greatly reduced rates. The official firms complained that many amateurs built their sets not for scientific reasons, but to avoid the more expensive BBC companies' radios. Moreover, inexpensive foreign radio components were being imported, primarily from the United States, that enabled even unskilled persons to assemble a set. Avoidance of the license fee became rampant. But a self-assembled set could not be licensed even if the owner wanted a license (Burns, 1977, p. 7). As the government was hectored by the BBC to crack down on unauthorized listening, some newspapers began taking up the amateurs' cause against monopoly and government control. A commission of inquiry was named in 1923 to look into the issues more carefully. This committee, chaired by Major General Sir Frederick Sykes, recommended that broadcasting be given greater independence from the manufacturers. By that time, John Reith had become the BBC's managing director. Reith, a charismatic Scotsman who had come to the job by responding to a published advertisement, began to view the interests of the broadcasting organization as separate from those of the parent manufacturers and to warm to the notion of a BBC free from both manufacturers and the Post Office. He began to conceive of a BBC that provided national, social, religious, and democratic integration in the service of ideas higher than entertainment and profit (Reith, 1924) and to articulate the idea of "public service broadcasting," which later became the BBC's guiding ethos. This concept was embraced by important segments of public opinion as the growing importance of radio raised new questions of control. Therefore, the government appointed in 1925 another committee, chaired by the Earl of Crawford, which proposed the establishment of a public corporation to take over private operations upon the expiration of the BBC license at the end of 1926. This was accepted and accomplished by a royal charter rather than by statute, with the granting of a ten-year license running from 1927. The new BBC, now called the British Broadcasting *Corporation* began operations, directed as before by John Reith. This second BBC held a monopoly over British broadcasting for more than a quarter century.

Given the far-flung colonial possessions of Britain, the BBC soon also provided overseas broadcasting over shortwave frequencies. It became Britain's voice in the propaganda war before and during World War II. Its Home Service, supervised by the Ministry of Information, was a beacon of hope and a source of information to hundreds of millions. Domestically, Winston Churchill's broadcasts to the nation became a significant element in morale building. The BBC also started a second channel, aimed at soldiers, which evolved eventually into the Light Programme. In 1946, a more serious Third Programme went on the air.

Britain also played a significant role in the development of television through John Logie Baird, who demonstrated in 1926 a semimechanical television set. In 1929, the BBC permitted his company to transmit experimentally. [TV broadcasts began in the United States in 1928, in Japan in 1931, in Germany and France in 1935, and in the Soviet Union in 1938 (Schubin, 1990, pp. 17–18).] A government commission recommended that the BBC be given authority over television. This was supported by the press, which had come to like the BBC because it was free of advertising. In 1936, the BBC introduced regular television service, transmitting two hours daily and alternating between the rival Baird and Marconi-EMI systems. The Selsdon Committee then recommended dropping the Baird system and expanding the BBC monopoly to television. By 1939, there were about 20,000 TV sets in Britain operating with relatively primitive 405–line VHF transmission (Central Office of Information, 1981, p. 237). When World War II broke out, television was suspended; it was resumed in 1946.

Over the years, the BBC grew into a huge institution. Its staff in 1987 totaled 30,000, plus countless free-lancers. Its TV production facility in London alone employs almost 10,000 people. Over 150,000 artists are under contract each year. It made use of more than 500 full-time musicians in 1980. Many of Britain's playwrights got their start on the BBC's radio drama, which commissions close to 800 scripts a year. (Stephen Hearst, communication).

The BBC is an extraordinarily successful institution in terms of its mission to produce quality programming, where it is second to none. It produces excellent and worthwhile programs. It also offers a large number of mediocre programs that do not fit the image as well.

The BBC staff is professional, experienced, and dedicated. For a long time, the leaders of the institution rose through production experience rather than management or politics. They constitute arguably the most impressive assembly of broadcasters in the world, and they, and not the board of governors, actually controlled the BBC in the past. However, some of these leaders have tended to equate the interests of their institution with that of British society and culture, and to view critics of this particular structural arrangement as advocates of philistinism.

From the beginning, some of the BBC's well-meaning supporters tended to go to great lengths in their willingness to protect the institution's exclusivity. In 1936, several of the Ullswater Committee members proposed that the BBC also control production of radio sets and even components. The arguments reveal the facile expansionism a public-interest argument can assume: "When a public service is established, it is, we think, necessary that the public interest should predominate throughout the whole range. If private profit is allowed a loophole, a proportion of the advantages of the system will be lost to the community. The weak spot of broadcasting is in the provision of receiving sets by private industry. . . . Evidence has been given that there is a combination in the manufacture of valves which keeps prices unnecessarily high" (*Report of the Broadcasting Committee*, 1935).

The collective influence of the BBC has been vast. A poll by *The Times* concluded that a "cross section of the elite, men and women listed in Who's Who" considered the BBC to be a more influential cultural institution than either Parliament or the church (Curran et al., 1977, p. 237). This also fits the BBC's self-perception. "The favorite image of the BBC during the 1930s was that of a great British institution, as British as the Bank of England, an institution which was different from other institutions, which took decisions that quite deliberately diverged from the decisions many—perhaps most—listeners would have taken" (Briggs, 1965, p. 12). There was a significant identification of the British elite with the BBC. Its governing boards have not been politicized by the parties as in many other European countries. Of the BBC's eighty-five governors during its first fifty years, forty were Oxford or Cambridge graduates and twenty attended Eton, Harrow, or Winchester (Briggs, 1979b, p. 30). Two-thirds of the BBC's governors who served in the period between 1955 and 1976 and attended university were either Cambridge or Oxford graduates (Paulu, 1981, p. 133).

News readers for a long time were expected to perform their task attired in dinner jackets and to speak quite formally, using the Southern Educated Standard, or "Received Pronunciation," the educated accent spoken by less than 5 percent of the population. To the other 95 percent, this became known (and not necessarily taken positively) as "BBC English" (Ducat, 1986). Over time, the sound of the BBC's broadcasts became more pluralistic, though the accent of its foreign broadcasts has remained resolutely traditional.

In its formative years the institution was shaped by what BBC veteran Stephen Hearst called the "puritan high priests." The BBC gave much time to religious broadcasts and established, under Reith's prodding, "closed periods" where no religious programs would be broadcast, in order to protect church attendance. Until 1959, no television was provided at all for an hour during Sunday evenings in order not to interfere with church services held at that time.

John Reith's personal style as the BBC's director general was distinctly autocratic, and in time led to a certain administrative ossification (Burns, 1977).

In 1934, after Hitler's "night of long knives," he wrote in his diary, "I really admire the way Hitler has cleaned up what looked like an incipient revolt against him by the Brown Shirt leaders. I admire the drastic actions taken which were obviously badly needed" (Reith, 1975, quoted in Paulu, 1981, p. 135).

In 1935 he told Marconi, "I had always admired Mussolini immensely and I had constantly hailed him as the outstanding example of accomplishing high democratic purpose by means which, though not democratic, were the only possible ones" (Reith, 1975, quoted in Paulu, 1981, pp. 135–36). This is not to suggest that Reith had totalitarian political sympathies, but rather to observe his respect for dominant leaders. Yet in the truly vital matter of war and peace, the BBC showed little comparable strength. Critics of the government were excluded from the air. "Sir John Reith saw to it that Churchill was seldom heard over the BBC and in that Reith had the full backing of the prime minister; twice in one week Horace Wilson (Chamberlain's right hand man) summoned Reith to No. 10 to warn him that Chamberlain disapproved of broadcasting excerpts from parlimentary speeches critical of the government" (Manchester, 1988, p. 245). Churchill had earlier written, in 1929, to Reith offering "£100 out of my own pocket for the right to speak of half an hour on Politics. How ashamed you will all be in a few years for having muzzled the broadcast!" Reith starchily responded that "the American plan . . . of allowing broadcasting to be available on a cash basis" operated "irrespective of any consideration of content or balance." To this Churchill replied that he preferred the American plan to "the present British methods of debarring public men from access to a public who wish to hear," and that the BBC should not let the political parties be its gatekeepers: "I was not aware that parties had a legal basis at all, or that they had been formally brought into your license" (in Briggs, 1965, p. 135). During the war, Reith served for a time as Minister of Information, using the BBC to support the war effort.

The BBC operates under conditions of its charter and of the periodic licensing agreements. These agreements give the government some powers of control, since it could theoretically revoke the operating license at its pleasure. Furthermore, the government can veto any program transmission, or, more accurately, require the BBC to refrain from broadcasting any specified matter, and any cabinet minister can demand that the BBC to undertake transmissions on issues of national importance. The agreements also require daily broadcast coverage of the proceedings of the Houses of Parliament, forbid subliminal advertising, and prohibit the BBC from expressing its opinion on current affairs or in matters of public policy outside of broadcasting. But most of the government's prerogatives remain unexercised and are probably too explosive to apply. Political advertising is not permitted on any channel. The various political parties have access rights to party broadcasts of their own making, which are allocated on the basis of voting strength in the previous election. The government ministers also have access rights for matters of public interest, and in some instances the opposition has a right of reply (Homet, 1979). Crises over government interference have occurred over coverage of the Suez crisis, the

Falkland Islands War, the Irish Revolutionary Army, and the U.S. bombing of Libya, among others.

For many years the BBC operated under the so-called fourteen-day rule, which prohibited broadcasts on all matters to be discussed in Parliament within the fortnight. This unusual rule allegedly was conceived by the BBC itself as a way to ease pressure from the government on its broadcasting. The Labour party, too, supported this rule. But in the 1950s the BBC grew restive under these shackles and, with the help of the National Council for Civil Liberties, succeeded in having the rule suspended.

The BBC is periodically scrutinized by committees of general or specific inquiry: the Sykes Committee, in 1923; Crawford, in 1925; Selsden, in 1935; Beveridge, in 1950; Pilkington, in 1962; Annan, in 1977; and Peacock, in 1986. Generally, these committees are convened every ten to fifteen years at some point before the BBC's charter expires in order to guide the legislation that will accompany the next charter. In 1962, the Pilkington Committee issued a report recommending that the BBC be strengthened by adding a second channel, moving to a 625-line standard, and adding color. BBC 2 was started in 1964, and in 1967 it became the first European network to operate in color.

The Home Secretary is responsible for law and order as well as for broadcasting, two tasks that can easily be in conflict. In 1985, the BBC was prepared to broadcast a profile of two Irish extremist leaders. Home Secretary Leon Brittan protested to the BBC's board of governors that it provided a forum for terrorists. Against the protests of the board of management, the BBC governors canceled the documentary, leading to a one-day strike by the BBC staff that blacked out domestic radio and television news broadcasts and BBC newscasts in the world. The program was later shown with minor additional footage. (David Webster, communication).

The BBC and Its Finances

Although the BBC's freedom from advertising provides independence from business, it also produces vulnerability to government pressure, because it must periodically appeal to the Home Secretary and to Parliament to increase the license fee. The government's prerogative to withhold or delay an increase in funds creates a reward and punishment mechanism. In the past, the BBC had less of a need to seek fee increases: the expansion in radio and television subscribers, and later in color sets, tended to generate annual revenue increases automatically. From 1927 until 1946, there were no fee increases. However, because 98 percent of all households now own a color television set, more money can be obtained only through changes in the license charges, through program sales abroad, and through miscellaneous ventures such as books, records, and cassettes.

Although the BBC is generally popular with the British public, its license fees of approximately $9 a month are not. It was estimated by the government that in 1985 about 1.5 million households were illegal viewers.

The license fee, as a fixed charge, is a regressive tax that virtually every household must pay regardless of income and BBC usage. A more equitable subsidy system would abolish the fee altogether, increase income tax rates slightly, and finance the BBC directly from this source. Although this arrangement would be socially fairer, it would eliminate the BBC's hold on an earmarked charge and could lead to a lowering of revenues and an increase in governmental control.

The BBC's revenues plateaued in the 1980s, but production costs continued to climb. Program costs rose between 1980 and 1985 from £34,000 to £52,000 per average hour. For drama, costs rose from £142,000 per hour to £278,000; for light entertainment, from £57,000 to £95,000; for current affairs, from £22,000 to £26,000; and for sports, from £17,000 to £25,000 (Nossiter, 1986, p. 42).[1] In 1985 the BBC showed a deficit of £80 million (Tracey, 1991, p. 9). The BBC's cost consciousness was enhanced by the government's pointedly managerial appointments to leadership positions. A signal was sent by the 1983 naming of Stuart Young, whose background was in accounting and business, as chairman of the board of governors. After Young's death, he was succeeded by Marmaduke Hussey, who had served as a director of Rupert Murdoch's newspaper operations. Shortly thereafter, Michael Checkland was named director general to succeed Alasdair Milne, who had been at odds with the Conservative government. Checkland's BBC background was in finance and accounting, not production, and he had made a name for himself as a cost cutter. He was chosen in preference to Jeremy Isaacs, who had produced some of the BBC's most noteworthy documentary series.

Advertising on television is, of course, an additional and major way to raise revenue, and one used by many public broadcasting institutions in Europe. In 1977, the 500-page Annan report considered advertising for the BBC, dismissing it in just sixteen lines. In the following decade, however, major changes and pressures emerged to raise the issue again. Simultaneously with the moderate increase in the license fee, the government appointed a committee headed by Professor Alan Peacock to reinvestigate the question of BBC advertising. The independent (i.e., commercial) broadcasters, in a curious but not surprising spectacle, argued eloquently for the importance of upholding BBC's commercial-free status as a guarantor of the latter's quality. The Adam Smith Institute, on the other hand, proposed that the BBC commercialize most of its activities, except for the news, since it was already filled with indirect advertisements such as talk shows with authors whose books had recently been published. The unpopularity of advertising on BBC tends to be exaggerated. A survey conducted by the BBC in 1980 indicated that almost 49 percent of total respondents (and 60 percent of working-class respondents) were in favor of advertising (O'Brian, 1980, p. 29). But of the upper classes only 25 percent preferred advertising.

Peacock, a strong believer in free markets, generally opposed government subsidies. His vision was broader than the question of BBC advertising. The committee recommended moving toward a television based on consumer choice and direct transactions in three phases. First, the BBC's license fee would be indexed; next, subscriptions would replace a portion of the license fee, and the remainder would be used to subsidize a public interest television under a Public Service Broadcasting Council; and finally, a full broadcasting market would emerge, in which a variety of transaction-based payment mechanisms—pay programs, pay channels, and so on—would coexist.

The Peacock Committee found that introducing advertising to the BBC would push the system away from a genuine consumer market because it would underrepresent minority interests and not measure intensity of preferences. This was good news for the BBC. The immediate outcome was that the license fee was indexed, thereby increasing the BBC's independence from the government. But one Conservative member of the committee, Samuel Brittan, wrote afterward about the "arrogance and complacency" of the BBC: "they do not realize how privileged and unusual their position is, and how much in need of continuing and detailed justification" (Brittan, 1986).

The Peacock Committee also recommended that the government auction off the ITV commercial television franchises in 1988 when their next franchise round was due. But there was no enthusiasm in the cabinet for some of the proposals. Douglas Hurd, as Home Secretary in charge of broadcast policy, asked for an immediate cabinet disavowal of the "underlying free market philosophy," and charged that the committee had gone beyond its terms of reference. On the other hand, Prime Minister Margaret Thatcher was disappointed that the report did not recommend advertising on BBC. In the end, the BBC got a moderate increase in the license fee, which was tied to the retail price index for three years. This removed some of its dependency, except that the RPI does not track the BBC's wages, which make up 70 percent of the BBC's costs. Together with the closing to the BBC of advertising as a source of revenue, this meant a continued dependence on government. Perhaps most important, the fierce debate over the BBC's finances revealed that the BBC could not command support as easily as in the past, and that fundamental questions about the BBC's role were being raised as never before.

The Creation of Independent Television

Because commercial television in Britain had more time to develop than anywhere else in Europe, it is important to trace its birth, growth, and maturity.

Anthony Smith (1983) observed that the BBC's monopoly structure goes back, in spirit, to the Stationers' Company monopoly on government printing in the Tudor period. For the BBC, the broadcast monopoly drew criticism almost from the beginning, as was discussed earlier in this chapter.

Once it was established, the BBC was ferocious in protecting its turf. Since in Britain it was assured a full monopoly, a breach in its exclusivity had to come from abroad; not surprisingly, commercial stations aimed at Britain soon began broadcasting from Luxembourg and the Normandy.

The BBC attempted various defensive strategies. First, it tried to bar the commercial stations from the wireline transmission operated by various private firms under license from the Post Office. It almost succeeded, but the Postmaster General demurred. Next, it sought the international outlawing of such programs. A resolution was adopted in 1933 by the International Broadcasting Union, at the BBC's behest, that the "systematic diffusion of the programmes or messages, which are specifically intended for listeners in another country and which have been the object of protest by the broadcasting organisation of that country, constitutes an 'inadmissible' act from the point of view of good international relations" (Briggs, 1965, p. 36). The BBC also engineered a refusal to grant Luxembourg's request for a long wave frequency. Radio Luxembourg went on the air anyway in 1933. The BBC then refused to publish the new stations' program schedules in its *World Radio* and saw to it that the Post Office refused telephone land lines to the station (Briggs, 1965). The publishing industry's interests were congruent, and led to similar opposition. When it became known that a newspaper, the *Sunday Referee,* was offering an advertising package for print and radio, it was expelled forthwith from the Newspaper Proprietors' Association.

World War II was the BBC's finest hour. But ironically, its success ultimately undermined its monopoly position. Many in society recognized broadcasting's strong influence on public opinion and questioned the appropriateness of its exclusivity. The new Labour government was quick to renew the BBC's charter and license in 1946 for five years, without setting up the usual Committee of Inquiry to investigate its future. Protest arose, this time from Winston Churchill and some of his allies, although opinions did not divide along party lines.

The government responded by promising a Committee of Inquiry. It began meeting under the chairmanship of Lord Beveridge in 1949. By that time influential Conservatives were lobbying their party to advocate a second and commercial television broadcasting service. Although the actions of some of these Tories were motivated by allied economic interests, the group included others who opposed monopoly on the basis of principle. Such opposition to the monopoly was also posed by groups representing writers, actors, musicians, the Fabian Society, the Liberal party, and even parts of the Labour party (Sendall, 1982). The Conservative party was split on the issue, as was the Beveridge Committee, with a majority advocating the maintenance of the monopoly and opposing the advent of commercial advertising, but with an influential and powerful minority represented by Selwyn Lloyd, a respected conservative politician. Even Reith's former successor as Director General of the BBC, F. Ogilvie, opposed the BBC monopoly (Burns, 1977, p. 46).

The Beveridge Committee issued its report in 1951, but late that year Labour was defeated in the general elections and the BBC charter was about to expire. This gave the new Conservative government an opportunity to reconsider its stance. In the following months discussion took place within the government and Parliament, with John Profumo, chairman of the Conservative party's broadcasting group, advocating the Conservative party's position in a lively debate in the House of Commons. [For a discussion of the politics involved, see Wilson (1961) and Briggs (1979).] The effort to establish an alternative to the BBC's monopoly centered on creating a majority for that position within the Conservative party. The strategy concentrated on television and ignored radio, which was regarded at the time as the more important medium and therefore harder to change.

Critics of the BBC monopoly outside of the Conservative Party pointed to the BBC's lack of enthusiasm about television. For example, in its 1955 handbook, the BBC devoted only three pages to television (though references to it were made elsewhere in the book); this was cited as a sign of BBC's technical conservatism. Successive heads of BBC television had expressed frustration over the lack of interest shown in television by the BBC's upper levels. One of them, Norman Collins, resigned from the BBC and was highly effective in promoting private broadcasting.

In 1952, the government's White Paper cautiously concluded that "provisions should be made to permit some element of competition" (Sendall, 1982, p. 13), with careful qualification accompanying the statement. Prime Minister Churchill was more adamant in his opposition to the BBC's broadcasting monopoly. Despite his masterful use of the BBC during the war, Churchill harbored long-standing resentments. He had neither forgiven nor forgotten having been denied access to the airwaves in the 1930s. His attitude was similar to that of France's Socialist President François Mitterrand, who, thirty years later, resented his earlier exclusion by the official broadcasters and, once in power, ended their monopoly.

A vigorous public discussion accompanied the government and Parliament's consideration of commercial television. Almost all of the country's newspapers were opposed to commercial television, partly on principle and partly on competitive grounds. Some of today's main commercial beneficiaries of private television were also critical: Granada Theatre, Thorn Electrical Industries, and even parts of the association of the advertisement agencies. A National Television Council was established to resist commercial television, boasting the support of several Lords. This organization was countered by the Popular Television Association, which included Rex Harrison, Somerset Maugham, and Malcolm Muggeridge among its supporters. The debate began to form along party lines, and the Conservatives were the majority party. The strategy of the opposition to commercial television therefore aimed at making the question one of a "free vote." However, former prime minister and Labour leader Clement Attlee hinted in a public speech that a future Labour government would repeal any legislation for commercial television. This transformed the matter into a party issue, making a "free" vote impossible.

In 1953, the government, again deeply divided, issued another White Paper that supported commercial television but aimed at protecting program standards from advertising's influence, and proposed the establishment of a controlling body. Parliament debated the proposal in late 1953. Allegedly, more peers attended the debate in the House of Lords than any other debate in a quarter of a century. Given some of the issues of that period—strikes, depression, royal abdication, world war, cold war—the control of television was obviously of overwhelming concern to the British elite. Even the Archbishop of Canterbury interrupted his vacation to oppose advertising on television. A strong voice for the opposition was Lord Reith, the legendary first director general of the BBC, who himself had headed the BBC when it was still a private commercial enterprise. In 1950, Reith had testified to the Beveridge Committee that "it was the brute force of monopoly that enabled the BBC to become what it did; and to do what it did; that made it possible for a policy of moral responsibility to be followed" (Wilson, 1961, p. 21). The unfortunate expression "brute monopoly" figured prominently in subsequent criticism of the BBC. But Reith was unrepentant: "Somebody introduced Christianity into England. And somebody introduced smallpox, bubonic plague and the Black Death. Somebody is minded now to introduce sponsored broadcasting" (Briggs, 1979a, p. 833). In the House of Commons, tensions ran equally high, and the opening speaker was interrupted more than thirty times. In the end, the motion against the government lost by a count of 87 to 157 votes.

After the government narrowly won the vote on the White Paper, the next step was the formulation of a television bill. The bill included safeguards that responded to the criticisms voiced in Parliament and stipulated that an Independent Television Authority be established as a supervisory institution. Many of today's restrictions on the independent television system can be traced back to those concessions and safeguards made to mollify critics and to persuade lukewarm supporters. The Parliamentary debate over the final bill was a long, drawn-out battle that included some strange lineups. One member, George Thomson, argued strongly for a free vote, which would have lost the vote. Later, as Lord Thomson of Monifieth, he became chairman of the IBA. Some Labour members, such as young Anthony Wedgewood-Benn (later known as Tony Benn, leader of the left wing of the Labour party), favored an end to the BBC monopoly, though not necessarily through advertising support (Sendall, 1982, p. 37). With some interruptions, the parliamentary debate lasted for four months, and included discussion of more than 200 amendments. Finally, on July 30, 1954, the bill was passed, thus ending more than two years of intense debate. The era of limited private television began in Britain.

The Institutions of Independent Television

During the year 1954–1955, the basic structure was set up that endured for many years. The ITA's first chairman was Sir Kenneth Clark, who, ironically, epitomizes for many Americans the BBC style. The first Director General was Sir Robert Fraser, an Australian who was almost elected in 1935 as a Labour member of Parliament.

The bill on independent television did not merely establish a second channel; it sought to encourage varied program suppliers. Fraser therefore initially sought the allocation of six channels for two or more full-coverage national independent networks and about fifty separate independent (ITV) stations. Alleged spectrum limitations, however, reduced this to one channel (though spectrum was later found for BBC-2 and Channel 4). The fear of too much commercial

TV too soon probably was the primary reason. The Authority therefore contemplated establishing competition by allocating a single channel in several ways, either by dividing broadcast time among different program providers or by dividing it according to geography. Fraser favored a system of rigorous competition among program suppliers, but the realities of power in the quickly established program companies resulted in regional monopolies or duopolies being carved up.

The Authority moved extraordinarily quickly to grant licenses. In August 1954, less than a month after the law had been passed, ITA members had already been appointed and had published invitations for license applications. In September, screening interviews were held, and in October, licenses were offered to six stations. By November, contracts were signed. In each of the first contract areas (London, Midlands, and Northern), the broadcasting time was split between weekend and weekdays and was awarded to different companies.

Two newspaper groups received licenses, and this generated criticism about the expansion of the powers of the press. Eventually, in 1963 amendments to the law, the cross-ownership of newspapers in broadcasting was restricted. Surprisingly, that matter had never come up in the parliamentary debates before the act was passed, even though almost everything else had been discussed (Sendall, 1982).

Another issue that was settled during the first months of the Authority was News provision. ITA and the initial program companies agreed to create a news subsidiary (ITN), with each program company owning a share.

The Authority also established rules about the "proper proportions" of programs of British origins, requiring negotiations with fourteen different organizations of creative talent headed by the British Actors Equity Association. A tacit agreement was reached under which an average of one hour per day of foreign-made film programs were permitted to be shown each week out of a total of fifty. This percentage (14 percent) has remained the rule since, though it is flexibly exercised.

The main technical function of the Independent Television Authority (ITA) was to provide technical transmission and broadcast facilities. Broadcast towers had to be erected, and their locations became highly significant, because they defined the range of the licensee's territory and hence audience and profits. Eventually, the BBC and the ITA became collaborators in the technical field. (All new UHF television stations share the same sites, for example.)

In September 1955, the first ITV programs were broadcast in London. In the Manchester and Liverpool regions, transmission began in mid-1956. In the following years, independent television spread across Britain. By 1962, fifteen companies had been licensed, and ITV reached most areas of the United Kingdom, except for northern Scotland and the heart of Wales, which were reached later.

Almost immediately, the ITV programs were successful in terms of audience. Five minutes after ITV's opening broadcast, the BBC recorded an audience share of 63 percent for ITV in London. One month after ITV commenced operation in Birmingham, a Gallup poll showed that 58 percent preferred ITV, whereas only 16 percent preferred the BBC. By 1957, ITV had over 70 percent of TV audiences. Of course, many responses were based on the novelty of ITV and on the satisfaction of seeing the mighty BBC forced into competition. As time passed, and following a major effort by the BBC, the percentages eventually became more even, though ITV tended to have a slightly larger audience.

Although the argument is frequently made that the introduction of commercial television reduces audiences for public broadcasters and hence contributes to their decline, the British example shows that the opposite can also be true in situations where the market is not saturated. After commercial television was introduced in 1955, the number of television households increased substantially (Heyn and Weiss, 1980, pp. 135–50). This increased the number of television set licenses, and thus the BBC's revenues grew faster than would otherwise have been the case.

Fifteen independent television program companies serve fourteen established television regions, with London, the most populous region, being shared by two companies. Of these fifteen regional stations, Thames, London Weekend, Central, Granada, and Yorkshire jointly provide most of the programming for the national TV schedule. TV-AM, the commercial venture broadcasting only in the morning, operates under a national franchise granted by the IBA in February 1983. The ITA limited influence in affecting the arrangements of program exchange. In the early 1960s, program companies increasingly formalized their policies, establishing in effect a program supply cartel, so that at any given time only one program was offered for network distribution. Furthermore, the agreements restricted regional companies from having their programs distributed over the network. Programs were also noncompetitively distributed by the program companies under identical terms, a practice that later became a subject of concern, and of reform in 1990.

When independent radio broadcasting was added in 1973 to the ITA's mandate, it was renamed the Independent Broadcasting Authority (IBA). The IBA had a staff of about 1500 employees, including technical personnel, and was run by a twelve-member board appointed by the Home Secretary. It operated transmitters for the fifteen regional television and radio program companies and was financed by payments from these companies. It also collected for the government the various charges and fees from the companies related to their profits.

The IBA possessed several regulatory tools. It could prohibit particular programs, temporarily suspend broadcasting, or cancel the license. In 1980, the license renewals of two ITV companies were denied without any specific explanations. Such criteria-less denials exerted pressure on the companies to stay within the good graces of the IBA. The entire license award system took place largely behind closed doors, and new entry was extremely difficult.

The IBA also established its authority to approve major ownership changes (above 5 percent) of the franchised companies, and in 1986 prevented Rank from making a hostile bid for Granada. Similarly, it prevented Thorn-EMI and BET from selling Thames TV to Carlton.

The IBA rules stipulated that no more than five feature films could be shown per week except during the Christmas season and that no more than four game shows with prizes could be shown per week during prime time. Sponsored programs were prohibited on ITV (though allowed on Channel 4). Advertising minutes were limited to an average of seven per clock hour on television, and nine minutes per hour on independent local radio. Advertisements were not allowed during the broadcasts of religious services, royal occasions, educational broadcasts, children's programs, or current affairs programs.

Advertising was censored before being broadcast and had to conform to an elaborate code of standards drawn up by the IBA in consultation with advisory committees and the Home Secretary. The Advertising Controls Division and a copy clearance office of the independent program companies associations carefully examined all advertisements. Political or religious advertisements were prohibited. Of the 12,000 advertising scripts reviewed annually, about 20 percent violated the code and were returned.

Although broadcast frequencies were available, the creation of a second commercial channel was stalled for a number of years, because of disputes among the BBC, the regional independent companies, independent producers (who desired a channel for their programs), the Welsh language minority, and the government. The Thatcher government fashioned in 1980 a compromise in which independent producers were encouraged to supply programs. Overall control over the channel, however, was given to a separately licensed entity without production capability, controlled by the IBA. Channel 4 is national rather than regional in structure. It is financed by the regional program companies, which could insert into it advertisements receivable within their region. This arrangement was significant because it maintains their regional monopoly over television advertising. In Wales, after much agitation, a separate authority runs a Welsh channel that includes ITV and BBC programs in Welsh.

Channel 4 was to provide experimental programming and to serve special audience interests. The company commissions and buys programs from ITV companies as well as from other sources, such as independents. It contributes to British moviemaking by cofunding a large number of theatrical feature films each year, thus providing a market for small independent film producers. The share of programming provided by independents has increased from one-third to one-half, with an average cost per hour of program production of initially about $40,000, extraordinarily low in comparison to those of the BBC and ITV/1 (*The Economist*, 1985b). With Channel 4's help, by 1988 there were more than 750 members in the Independent Programme Producers Association (IPPA), contributing to London's increasing importance as a center for video materials and a leading postproduction center in Europe. In the past, independent producers could not do much work for the ITV or BBC companies, because these had large in-house production operations. The Peacock report recommended that BBC and ITV carry 25 percent independent programs. Neither the BBC nor the ITV companies were happy about ceding production. The broadcasters convinced the government to exclude news and public affairs from the total amount for independent producers. The BBC lagged behind ITV in compliance and filled less than one-third of the narrowed goal in its 1991 schedule.

Private broadcasting downplays its commercial base. IBA's official brochure, "Independent Local Radio," did not refer even once, in twenty fact-filled pages, to advertisements, advertisers, or commercial operation. The preferred term is *independent* rather than *private, commercial,* or *for profit.* Despite such discretion, ITV profits are not understated in real life. In 1956, a House of Commons committee documented extraordinarily high returns. Responding to questions from the Pilkington Committee, the ITA reported in 1961 that on the average the program companies had a profit margin of 60 percent on revenues. These returns were based on the shared companies' monopoly over broadcast advertising. Such market power could have been greatly reduced by the licensing of additional alternate channels. Instead, the government, in search of revenue, preferred to become a participant in the monopoly rent and imposed an excise duty of 10 percent on all advertising revenues.

The terms of the levy changed several times since the early 1960s. Under an arrangement which came into force in January 1990, the aim is for three quarters of the levy yield to come from a 10 percent levy on net advertising revenue, and the remaining quarter from a 25 percent levy on domestic profits. Profits on overseas sales are exempt to encourage exports. There is a "free slice" on both elements of the levy: £15 million plus the equivalent of each contractor's Fourth Channel subscription on revenue, and £2 million on profits. The remaining profits are subject to a 35 percent corporation tax. This levy terminates at the end of 1992. From 1993 its role will be performed by the new competitive tender arrangements under which there will be payments for Channel 3 licences comprising a mixture of lump sums and annual payments related to income (advertising, subscription and sponsorship revenue). The changes in the levy structure contributed to an improvement in the efficiency of the ITV companies, including working practices, staffing levels and costs reductions (Tim Abraham, communication).

The past system reduced the incentives to companies to control their costs and has contributed to high expenditures and wage settlements. Within a short time, the BBC Staff Association was ousted at the program companies by the significantly more militant Association of Cinematograph and Allied Technicians (ACT, subsequently ACTT), setting in motion a sequence of significant labor strife.

Since profits from program exports were not part of the base for the levy, there was a strong incentive to push these activities. The system of levy on profits not only was economically inefficient in that it encourages wasteful ITV practices and salaries, but also undermined the BBC, which could not match these conditions. In 1988, the ITV companies' revenue was over £1 billion, whereas the BBC television budget was £800 million.

In 1962, the Pilkington Committee issued a report that sharply criticized ITV while praising the BBC's performance. It found the Authority to be passive and more often an advocate than a controller. It also criticized the independent companies' program quality (violence, stereotypes, etc.), the lack of balance between the smaller and larger companies in program resources, the preponderance of publisher involvement, and the absence of a proper control over advertising. The government accepted some of the recommendations and passed corrective legislation. But it did not restructure the entire system, as the report had recommended. The Television Act of 1963 strengthened ITA's control and established the "levy" on program company revenues. More informally, the program companies also took stock of their operations and modified some of their program offerings.

A decade later, in 1972, the Select Committee on Nationalized Industries issued a highly critical report about the ITA and its performance in the areas of programming, finance, and accountability. In 1977, another government report, this time by the Annan Committee, observed great improvements in IBA services, but it did not recommend that IBA supervise a fourth British television channel. Instead, it recommended that such a channel be run by a new "Open Broadcasting Authority" that would broadcast programs supplied by a variety of sources, including independent producers, education institutions, and ITV companies. The Annan report did, however, advise delaying the implementations of these proposals.

The emergence of commercial ITV programs did not lead the BBC to define its role as providing only those types of programs that commercial suppliers do not serve. In a speech to the General Assembly of the European Broadcasting Union, the BBC's then Director General, Alasdair Milne, was emphatic that it would never surrender the so-called popular areas of broadcasting to commercial competitors:

> We would regard such policy as a betrayal of the purpose for which the BBC was set up. The license fee would, were we to adopt such a course, come under intolerable political pressure, because many would be asked for services that only a few would use.
>
> The corporation would decline into insignificance and impotence. Only the memories of the good ol' days would remain. The most talented producers would all leave because we would neither reward their services adequately nor command comparable audiences to those of our competitors.
>
> We believe public service broadcasting must make the popular worthwhile and the worthwhile popular. We reject the notion that the popular is constant, and that we have as public service broadcasters any right to hand it over to men whose primary aim is to make money. Here we stand; we can do no other [Ball, 1984a, p. A12].

The reality of BBC programs, however, is more complex. The BBC's director of programs claimed that ratings are "of no great consequence." Yet how might one otherwise explain its importation of several Hollywood series which are silly even by the standards of American commercial TV? Could not a number of higher-quality U.S. series have been chosen? In surveys people tend to indicate that they prefer BBC programs over ITV, but actual viewing statistics show a somewhat greater ITV audience.[2]

The existence of rivalry between the BBC and ITV does not necessarily mean that the BBC was dragged down by its commercial rival. Between 1956 and 1976, the first two decades of competition between public and commercial television, the BBC's political coverage quadrupled. Its coverage of electoral events had been, originally, most reluctant. Anthony Smith, in observing that until the mid-1950s the BBC did not cover the influential annual conferences of the major parties, adds that "in its early days, the BBC actually prided itself for *not* covering the general elections" (1979, p. 28). The initiative was finally taken by the commercial IBA broadcasters.

Nor does the BBC always aim for the high end of the audience. When "breakfast television" was introduced in Britain, ITV's show, licensed as the separate operation TV-AM apart from the regional companies, began as loftier than the BBC's (Smith, 1983).

Non-British television audiences often incorrectly assume that any high quality programs with British accents are BBC productions. In fact, many quality programs from Britain originate with ITV companies. For example, both "Jewel in the Crown" and "Brideshead Revisited" were created by Granada Television, a broad-based media company known for its investigative journalism and its pioneering of the docudrama format (Nadelson, 1984, p. 26). In 1958, it caused a national controversy when it challenged the stuffy terms of a 1949 agreement that prohibited televising debates between political candidates and interviewing candidates on electoral issues.

The Establishment of Cable Television

The transmission of broadcasting signals over cable actually began before the introduction of British television. Radio relay by wire became popular in the 1920s because it often provided better sound quality and because users were able to avoid the greater expense of a regular receiver instead of simply a loudspeaker.

For a while, the BBC considered operating its own wire relays as an alternative form of distribution. Peter Eckersley, the BBC's first Chief Engineer and one of its visionary early figures, tried to persuade the BBC in 1925 to substitute wire for wireless. He argued that wire transmission solved spectrum scarcity. "It is not impossible to visualize, in say 20 years time, complete wire broadcasting, supplemented, it is true, but in minor part, by wireless broadcasting." [3] He even planned an experimental BBC exchange at Norwich, with wiring by the Post Office. But nothing came of it, partly because the Post Office would not promise to maintain the BBC monopoly in wireline transmission.

When the commercial Radio Luxembourg took to the air, the BBC tried to prevent its being carried on British wire relays. In 1937, "must-carry"-type rules were enacted that required the BBC to be carried, and relay companies were prohibited from originating programs.

By 1950, more than 1 million subscribers in urban areas received radio via wire networks (Dornan, 1984). Most systems were merely emerging cable TV upgrades of the earlier wire distribution of radio. Others were master antenna

television systems in housing developments aimed at preventing antenna for-
ests. One inhibiting factor for the growth of cable was the restriction on program channels other than BBC and ITV by restricting cable transmission to
simultaneous retransmission. At most, out-of-area regional ITV signals could
be imported. Because of improvements in broadcast transmission and reception
technology, the existing cable system actually declined in importance. Of the
relay cable systems, about one-half were operated by noncommercial operators
such as local authorities and housing associations. In 1982, there were 185
commercial operators (10 percent less than the year before and declining). Of
those operators, only a few had over 5000 customers. Commercial operators
served 1.36 million subscribers, and the 1566 noncommercial operators served
1.1 million subscribers (Veljanovski, 1984). In 1984, the three major systems
were Rediffusion (fifty-four franchised areas and 300,000–350,000 subscribers); Visionhire Cable (fifty-five systems and 300,000 subscribers); and Tele-
fusion (forty-two systems and 230,000 subscribers). Most systems had only a
four-channel capacity (McGhee, 1984, p. 41).

In 1972, the Conservative Heath government granted several limited experimental franchises that would have permitted additional programs. However, no
advertising, feature films, sponsor programs, or additional subscriber charges
were permitted. Only a few firms took advantages of this less-than-over-
whelming opportunity. In 1974, with the Labour party back in power, even
this modest development of cable was stopped.

But five years later, with the Conservatives' return, government policy changed.
The high-technology field was regarded as a key to Britain's recovery. And the
Labour party was consumed by internal struggles and did not pay much attention to cable television matters. In addition, the left wing of the Labour party
was hostile to the BBC and ITV.

A main catalyst for British cable was the 1982 report of the Information
Technology Advisory Panel (ITAP), a group consisting primarily of representatives of the technology sector rather than of the media and culture fields. The
report strongly supported the desirability of cable television on the grounds of
industrial development. These advantages could be secured without government
funds, merely by allowing entrance of the private sector.

> We suggested that (a) there would be a net employment generating effect, which
> could be substantial, (b) that insofar as manufacturing products are involved, these
> would at present . . . more likely be British made than if the same consumer
> expenditure were devoted to cars, video cassette recorders, etc., and (c) that the
> resulting stimulus to programme and information producers would result in prod-
> ucts that had significant international market, given the high reputation of U.K.
> broadcasting and information services [ITAP, 1982, pp. 28–29].

> [A decision to encourage cable systems would] therefore provide a large stimulus
> to developments in optical fiber technology as well as in the industries associated
> with consumer electronics and the supply of programme material [ITAP, 1982,
> p. 29].

The committee put pressure on the government's timing:

A delayed decision is, in this case, the same as a negative decision. There is a very limited time in which industrial capability and market opportunity will exist in the UK. Beyond this time, the chance of creating a strong UK presence in cable systems will have disappeared and with it some thousands of jobs and prospects of substantial export earnings [ITAP, 1982, p. 49].

On the day the ITAP report was issued, Home Secretary Whitelaw appointed a commission of inquiry chaired by Lord Hunt of Tanworth.[4] The committee was instructed,

to take as its frame of reference the Government's wish to secure the benefits for the United Kingdom which cable technology can offer and its willingness to consider an expansion of cable systems which could permit cable to carry a wider range of entertainment and other services . . . , but in a way consistent with a wider public interest, in particular the safeguarding of public service broadcasting [U.K. Home Office, 1982, p. 1].

In other words, the decision had already been made, without public debate, in favor of the expansion of cable television, and the Hunt Committee merely had to recommend the best way to achieve it.

When the Hunt Committee report was published, only six months later, it was termed by the *Financial Times* a "fiendishly clever web of British compromise, [that] appears to square every circle. . . ." The Hunt report agreed that multichannel cable not only was desirable, but could coexist with existing broadcasters without seriously harming them. This position was also held by the Department of Trade and Industry, which supported cable more strongly than the Home Office, the ministry in charge of supervising electronic media.[5] The report also stressed the importance of advanced service, a view that matched the government's.

The report distinguished between cable providers, cable operators, program or service providers, and program makers. The report recommended that only the cable providers and operators be regulated and licensed. It rejected a common carrier model with total separation between cable provider and cable operator, because it would discourage private capital, since the willingness to invest in the network infrastructure depended on control over the nature of the service offered to subscribers. Similarly, the Hunt report permitted the cable operator also to provide programs (i.e., be vertically integrated into program supply). An undesirable monopoly situation could be avoided by an "expectation of some channels to be available for lease use by persons having no connections with the cable operator" (U.K. Home Office, 1982, p. 8).

The then Director General of the BBC, Alasdair Milne, vehemently attacked the report: "The BBC does not . . . accept that cable operators should be licensed to interrupt the entertainment patterns of network television in order to finance a limited spread of cable in the United Kingdom" (*The Times,* Oct. 12, 1982).

Similar attacks were made by the chairman of the IBA, Lord Thomson, who said of the Hunt recommendations, "They could drive our broadcasting services—which have evolved over the years to be the highest quality in the world—

over a precipice, and break their back" (*Sunday Times,* Oct. 17, 1982, as quoted in Dornan, 1984, p. 30). Despite its own traumatic birth, the IBA clearly had no sympathy for the next generation of newcomers.

A government White Paper was published in April 1983 and took a more conciliatory line than the Hunt report: "the Government accepts that it has a responsibility to safeguard public service broadcasting" (U.K. Department of Trade and Industry and Home Office, 1983, pp. 38–39).

The White Paper recommended that a regulatory cable authority "use a light regulatory touch, and adopt a reactive rather than proactive style" in its franchise policies (U.K. Department of Trade and Industry and Home Office, 1983, p. 59).[6]

Importantly, the government encouraged the provisions of telecommunications services over cable. The exclusive right to interconnection of different local cable systems, however, would belong to British Telecom and Mercury. Moreover, cable operators would be able to provide voice telephone service only if they did so in partnership with BT or Mercury. Similarly, an association with one of those two companies would be necessary for a cable operator to provide data services in the five major business districts of the country.

On the same day that the government published the White Paper, it announced its intention to grant up to twelve interim cable licenses and emphasized testing advanced technology and interactive services. In selecting among the thirty-seven applicants, it generally favored technologically advanced systems.

Of the eleven interim franchises granted in 1983, eight were switched-star network configurations. British Telecom was involved in five of the consortia.[7]

In October 1984, the first of the initial real broadband cable systems to operate in Britain was opened in Swindon by a subsidiary of Thorn-EMI. The systems had a thirty-two-channel capacity and at first used thirteen channels, including the four TV broadcast channels, two out-of-area commercial ITV services, and the commercial satellite channels Music Box, ScreenSport, the Children's Channel, and Sky Channel. The pay channel Premiere was also offered. Also included was a local news program, teletext service, and stereo radio.

The Regulatory Framework of Cable Television

The Cable and Broadcasting Act 1984 that was passed following the White Paper provided a statutory framework for the new medium and established a Cable Authority to oversee it. The Authority granted and enforces franchises for new cable systems and establishes codes of program standards, advertising, sponsorship, and other content matter. The Authority also promotes the provision of all cable services, a point of potential conflict. As part of the Broadcasting Act 1990, the Authority became the Cable Division of the newly created Independent Television Commission.

Although the Cable Authority was appointed by the Home Secretary, it was an autonomous body. The first chairman was Richard Burton, retired chairman of the Gillette Razor Company. Appointed as the first Director General was Jon Davey, a former Home Office offical who had served as secretary to the Hunt Commission and had been instrumental in developing cable policy.

The Cable Authority announced the opening for bids to provide cable in areas where local interest for service has been expressed. Applications were then received and published, and public comments invited. In contrast to several countries having extensive cable systems—the United States, Canada, the Netherlands, Belgium, and Switzerland—cable franchises in the United Kingdom are awarded by a central rather than a local government authority, partly to avoid vetos by local councils dominated by the Labour party. Local input is only an informal influence.

A cable franchise operator requires two licenses: a program license from the Cable Division and a telecommunications license from the DTI. Of the two, the program license by the Cable Division is the significant hurdle, since the DTI tends not to stand in the way as long as technical requirements are fulfilled. By statute, the Division must consider certain specific points concerning applicants. These include their willingness to offer program materials originating in Britain and the E.C. countries; extension of assistance in the production of educational, local, and community access programs by local nonprofit organizations; assistance to the deaf; and provision of interactive services.

The Cable Division's mandate requires applicants to ensure decency, protection of children, news impartiality, and absence of political or religious bias. Code provisions govern the showing of violence and appeals for fund raising. The Division follows complaints and it samples programs to enforce standards.

Advertising on cable channels must accord with Division standards, which are similar to those of commercial broadcasting. There are fewer restrictions affecting the quantity and scheduling of these advertisements. Sponsored programs, which are prohibited on broadcasting, are also permitted.

The ITC has extensive powers. Under a Conservative government, it is unlikely that these powers would be exercised in a way that would hurt the cable industry during its early phases. But the standby powers nevertheless exist and could be applied in a less favorable political climate. For example, the ITC has the power to exclude certain organizations from holding shares in cable companies where it is "against the public interest." It can also change licenses after they have been granted and has the right to restrict the percentage of foreign language programs. Moreover, there is no forum for substantive appeal against the withdrawal of cable licenses.

Upon issuance of their licenses, license holders are charged a fee of £10,000 or more, depending on the number of homes passed. Additional fees are charged annually. The DTI also levies a license fee of £5,000 to £10,000, with annual renewal fees in the same range.

Companies and individuals that are not EC nationals or UK residents are restricted from holding a license. Also excluded are local authorities (to prevent hostile local government ownership, reminiscent of the early history of telephone service), political or religious bodies, and ITV commercial broadcasters in their franchise areas. The ITC has the power to judge whether granting licenses to companies with other media interests may lead to adverse results for the public interest and to disqualify those that do. Non-EC ownership is not completely excluded, as long as it is less than 50 percent of the voting shares. Where ownership is fragmented, non-EC participation must be less than 30 percent.

The licensing conditions set by the ITC and the Department of Trade and Industry reflect lessons from cable systems in other countries, particularly the United States. But some of the problems that have arisen in the context of American cable television were ignored. No provision exists for leased program access as a matter of right by those who supply video programming on a commercial basis.

On the other hand, the licensing requirements exhibit a progressive view of cable as an alternative form of local telecommunications distribution, beyond its role in video mass programs. A number of provisions deal with rights of interconnection, access charges, and equipment standards. These rules recognize that the second communications wire reaching British households can do more in the future than transmit television programs.[8]

The Problems of British Cable Television

The development of British cable program channels was more active than anywhere else in Europe. But the actual cabling of Britain has been very slow. Software was far ahead of hardware. Of the first eleven franchises awarded in 1984, several had not started any activities by 1987, whereas others were considerably delayed. Unlike Germany or France, where the telephone authorities are active in the construction of the cable networks and invest large sums of money, Britain tried to encourage private investors to assume this expense, but they have proved reluctant to do so.

Among the many reasons for the slow pace was a change in tax laws that reduced the ability to write off investments in cable and led to considerable ownership shifts in virtually all the systems. For various reasons the subscription rates for service ended up almost twice as high as initially anticipated, choking off subscriber demand. Only about 20 percent of homes passed actually subscribed. Also, the perceived risk for investors in cable television increased. DBS became a competitor, and the penetration of VCRs to two-thirds of all TV households reduced consumer demand for cable programs.

A casualty of the slow development was the switched-star system. Whereas in 1984 many systems had promised to offer such architecture, they subsequently moved to more conventional systems. British cabling policy, favoring a switched-star architecture and optical fiber, has been technologically more ambitious than that in other countries. Cable television, from the days of the ITAP Report, was considered a matter of industrial policy (Dyson and Humphreys, 1985). In contrast, the German Bundespost has been criticized for not being ambitious enough technologically and for not using fiber, the next generation of transmission. Thus, British cable policy was an uneasy mix of media policy, telecommunications policy, and industrial policy. It was wrought with multiple priorities and contradictions.

The technological requirements of a switched-star architecture is both the strongest and weakest part of the regulatory scheme. This distribution method reflects the leading edge of regulatory thinking about the role of cable transmission and its integration into the remainder of the telecommunications system. Yet these rules were not based on technological or economic reality; they set up a game for which no willing players turned out. Thus, the regulatory scheme pursued internally contradictory goals: encouraging competitiveness in telecommunications by establishing the next generation of cable transmission while at the same time espousing economic market principles.

No cable system offered true switched-star systems.[9] The emergence of switches that can handle the large capacity required for true broadband switches is only developing. Moreover, there is no evidence of present great need for switched, fully interactive services over cable, although it may well emerge in the future. Any need that does arise could be met mostly by traditional telephone systems without upgrading. In this area, however, the British government had a strong industrial policy goal in seeking a great leap forward in cable technology. This hazardous contradiction led to the emergence of cable television in economically fragile circumstances. In its first years, a cable operation requires large capital investments, and public acceptance is far from assured. A new media system has to set up an entire infrastructure consisting of program suppliers, advertisers, equipment manufacturers, and others. In the United States, this process took a substantial time. The various technical requirements of the systems, based on the desire to help British industry and high technology, complicate the development of commercially viable cable in its infancy.

To encourage switched systems, licenses were extended to twenty-three years (rather than fifteen) for cable operators who adopt the technology. An agreement on the technical specifications had to be entered with the DTI in advance.[10] Even operators installing tree and branch systems had to lay underground ducts in a configuration that would permit upgrading to a switched system without requiring the streets to be dug up again.

Cable operators were required to bury cable underground, which increases cost. Estimated construction of switched-star underground network for an area of 100,000 homes was £35 million, with a payback period of twenty years and a 10 percent return rate. An underground tree and branch system, on the other hand, cost about £26 million, with a payback period of fourteen years and a return rate of 17 percent. Still less expensive is an above-ground tree and branch system utilizing telephone poles, costing about £16 million with a payback period of twelve years and a return rate of 25 percent. The latter is the system typically used in the United States.

In 1985, the industry was shocked when the two largest firms, Rediffusion and Visionhire, departed from cable television within two days of each other, soon to be followed by Thorn-EMI. British Electric Traction sold Rediffusion, with 1.8 million homes passed, to Pergamon Press for $13.2 million, and was renamed British Cable Services (BCS). Pergamon is owned by the media magnate Robert Maxwell. Thus, as a traditional "technical" cable operator exited, a major publishing company entered. Robert Maxwell, who had arrived penniless from Czechoslovakia before World War II, started his publishing empire in 1951 from the base of five specialized trade publications that grew to over 350. His firm, the British Printing and Communications Corporation (BPCC), was a highly profitable printing, labeling, and publishing operation (Kerver, 1986). For a while, he served as a member of Parliament for the Labour party, until a financial controversy ended his political career. Maxwell, an increasingly significant presence in European and U.S. media, was also active in a videocassette magazine, in DBS, and in satellite program channels. He was creating an integrated media company: newspaper interests, cable network operations, and program channels, though the mix of these holdings kept changing toward a greater orientation to print and international involvements (Mirror Group; Pergamon; Macmillan; Collier; Berlitz; Official Airline Guide; New York *Daily News*; East European Publishers) and less television (divestiture of participations in Central Independent TV; TF1; MTV Europe; UK cable systems).

Another firm that left cable operations, Thorn, was engaged in appliance manufacturing, defense, entertainment, and music. In 1979, it acquired EMI, which owned record, film, and television productions, movie chains, and diverse copyrights. EMI also had experience in high-technology defense electronics and medical technologies and owned various dance halls, billiard and bingo halls, hotels, and restaurants. Together with Yorkshire-TV and Virgin Records, Thorn-EMI established the Music Box television channel. But in 1984–1985, Thorn-EMI profits declined, its chairman resigned, and it cut back many of its "new media" activities, including cable television.

In the face of this adversity, the government lowered its high-technology requirements. Going one step further, it also decided to support cable television financially by providing a subsidy to encourage R&D in interactive services and star-switched networks. These funds would go to cable operators to help demonstration projects for interactive services. The government also increasingly sought out the newly privatized British Telecom to play an active role in developing cable. Such reliance on BT was an acknowledgment that the private sector outside the telephone industry had difficulties in independently shouldering the large capital investments necessary for widespread cabling. To safeguard competition and prevent internal cross-subsidization, BT was required to keep its cable subsidiaries separate.[11] BT, however, eventually became more interested in upgrading its telecommunications network to broadband fiber and sought to exit cable altogether.

Next, the government encouraged foreign entry. Several dozen North American companies acquired equity interests in cable franchises. Investors include five of the regional Bell Holding Companies, and U.S. and Canadian cable firms. Although there are restrictions on the participation of non-EC interests in U.K. cable ownership, these can be bypassed by establishing British-controlled trusts (Glenn, 1990a, p. 4).

American interest in British cable stems both from the fact that the U.S.

cable market is largely cabled up, and that American Bell telephone companies can participate in Britain, in contrast to the restrictions placed on them in the United States.

Between 1983 and 1988, the Cable Authority issued thirty-one cable franchises; in 1989, it issued twenty-eight; and in 1990, it issued another twenty-five. But franchises and actual cable in the ground are two different matters. Only seventeen broadband systems were actually operational in 1990, but all franchises made available, save one, in major urban and suburban areas had been awarded. In January 1991, there were 150,000 subscribers and 670,000 homes passed, and the broadband penetration rate was a low 16 percent (*Cable Telco Report*, 1991, p. 9). In Aberdeen, only 11 percent of the 91,000 homes passed in 1990 chose to subscribe. There were fewer subscribers in the United Kingdom than in small countries, such as Austria, Finland, Norway, or Switzerland, not to mention Belgium or the Netherlands. The top cable companies in 1990, measured by population in the franchised areas and prorated by the equity share a company held in a consortium, showed a striking North American presence.

In most instances, the cable systems have not actually been constructed. But it suggests a future dominance of foreign firms in British cable, which is problematic for its long-term stability. If cable becomes the major distribution medium, as is the case in North America and parts of Europe, and as its financial and media power grows, the question of national sovereignty over communications will arise. This will be aggravated by the frictions with customers that unavoidably accumulate over the years. In a changed political environment, North American domination may not be acceptable. Thus, foreign investors may find themselves welcome when cable is lagging, but less popular when it becomes a success.

Many franchises did not speedily begin construction of their systems. In some instances, cable construction proceeded so slowly after the award of a franchise that the regulatory system took action. Oftel, the U.K.'s telecommunications regulatory agency in charge of enforcing the DTI's technical license, took action in 1991 against several franchises to speed up their construction. It also further announced, in a March 1991 White Paper, that telecommunication services could be provided by cable networks, and it restricted British Telecom from offering cable TV services for seven to ten years (DTI, 1991).

For all its efforts, British cable did not have much to show in terms of either technological performance or widespread presence as a distribution medium.

Cable Television Programming

In contrast to actual cable distribution network, the provision of program packaging has been very active. For nonbroadcast channels, no requirements exist for license or for carriage. A 1988 Cable Authority memorandum summarized the approach: "entry into this market is totally free: no license, contract, or official approval is required by anyone wishing in the UK to set up in business as a provider of programs to cable operators" (Home Office, 1988).

Of the new British channels, the most widespread in Europe is Sky Television, Rupert Murdoch's satellite program service, which has operated since 1982 and provides programs to several European countries.

The idea for Sky Television started with Brian Haynes, a former British television producer who had reported on the American cable boom and had the idea to set up a similar cable program distribution in Europe linking the various European cable islands. With access to an Intelsat transponder, Haynes secured credits and, together with publishers and insurance companies, founded Satellite Television (Biebl and Manthey, 1985).

The firm quickly ran into problems. First, it had to overcome a host of legal hurdles in different countries. In many instances the cable systems were operated by the domestic PTT and required time-consuming negotiations. Program copyrights did not necessarily cover all countries reached and led to legal and royalty expenses. Also, cable systems had not yet invested in satellite antennas that could connect the cable islands to each other. Haynes therefore needed to acquire and install the relatively costly dishes.

When Haynes ran out of money, Rupert Murdoch bought out the firm. Through his large involvement in Australian and American commercial broadcasting, he was also in a position to provide the ingredients for a European operation. Toward the same end, Murdoch was purchasing satellite distribution rights for much of Europe for many feature films. After 1984, Murdoch received access to the cable networks in Britain, Norway, Austria, Germany, and the Netherlands; he switched to the newer European ECS satellite and renamed the service "Sky Channel." Although audience interest was adequate and growing, Sky's problem was to attract advertising, of the kind that appeals across national boundaries.

Rupert Murdoch, the Australian media entrepreneur (he subsequently became an American citizen), is also one of the major figures in British media. Born in 1931 in Melbourne into a newspaper publisher family, he studied at Oxford and gained reporting experience in Birmingham. In 1952, he acquired the *Sunday Times* in Perth and made it into a success. It became a model for his operations, which later included over eighty newspapers and magazines with a combined circulation of more than 70 million. In the United States, Murdoch's media plans were not always successful; he failed in his attempts to acquire Warner Communications and the pay cable channel Showtime; he had to give up plans for a "Skyband" direct satellite broadcast system. Subsequently, he acquired American broadcast interests by purchasing six stations (in Chicago, New York, Washington, Dallas, Houston, and Boston) from Metromedia for $2.1 billion as well as the major Hollywood film studio and distributor 20th Century Fox. With these elements, he successfully structured a fourth network, Fox Television.[12]

In 1989, Murdoch expanded the single-channel Sky Channel, which operated on a low-power satellite, into the four-channel Sky Television—Sky One, Sky News (Britain's first 24-hours news channel), Sky Movies, and Eurosport—on the medium-power Luxembourg Astra satellite; there are also several radio channels (Sky Radio)

In 1990, a rival DBS system, British Satellite Broadcasting (BSB), launched its own multichannel program. BSB's channels, receivable directly over cable, were The Movie Channel (subscription movie), Now (leisure and women's programs), The Sports Channel, The Power Station (music videos), and Galaxy (drama and variety). It provided high-quality weekend arts programs. BSB's satellite system was its own, using two Hughes Communications satellites; it was incompatible with Sky. BSB's Marco Polo satellite signal was more powerful than Sky's and uses a square antenna, or "squarial." Three of its channels also had must-carry status on cable. (TBI, 1990). However, the high cost of BSB's investment required a large subscriber number to break even. Furthermore, BSB's D2-MAC standard required that subscribers purchase compatible decoders; there were manufacturing delays, and viewers experienced technical difficulties. Also, BSB's programming did not create a great demand. As a result, it did not do well financially, with less than 200,000 subscribers. Murdoch's Sky-TV, in contrast, expanded to about a million direct reception dishes in 1990, (plus many cable households) of which 70 percent subscribed to a pay-movie service. In 1990, Sky TV and BSB merged, having lost, respectively, $600 million and $900 million. The new company was named BSkyB and aimed at consolidating its nine channels to five and its two satellite systems to one carried on Astra and using PAL. Murdoch received a substantial cash payment that reduced his huge burden of debt, about $8–10 billion which was refinanced in 1990 subject to the requirements of some asset liquidation. British DBS is discussed further in the chapter on European DBS.

Other early satellite-delivered commercial channels were Music Box and ScreenSport. Cable News Network, from Atlanta, also entered the continental European market, first in large hotels and later on several U.K. cable channels. In 1987, the Super Channel was started as the satellite channel of fourteen ITV broadcasters, and with the major participation of Granada and Virgin. Eventually, it merged with Music Box and was owned by Italian investors (Marcucci) and then United Artists and Virgin. Another active participant in various program ventures was WH Smith, a retailing company.[13]

Another type of program provision is pay TV. In 1966, a firm by that name was established and provided service to about 10,000 subscribers in London and Sheffield. Two years later, the new Labour government decided to discontinue the experiment. Pay TV was reintroduced in 1981 when the Home Office designated a dozen two-year pilot projects by seven companies. Programs were supplied by a variety of sources, including the BBC and motion picture suppliers. None of the pilot projects could use advertisements, and all lost money, since only about 15 percent of cable households subscribed. A third effort began in 1985, this time with satellite-delivered pay channels. The first of these was The Entertainment Network (TEN), a movie channel set up by the British cable companies Rediffusion and Visionhire, the movie distributor Rank, and the equipment company Plessey. A major participant was UIP, the American joint venture of the major Hollywood studios MGM, United Artists, Universal, and Paramount for the foreign distribution of their films. TEN went out of business despite such backing because it could not attract enough viewers, and because the partners stalemated each other. The channel was replaced by Mirrorvision, established by Robert Maxwell, who at the time had acquired the Rediffusion cable company and had become one of the partners in TEN.

The second pay channel was Premiere, a joint project of Thorn-EMI, Goldcrest, several Hollywood distributors, HBO, and Showtime. Maxwell joined later after Thorn-EMI decided to divest itself of its film and cable interests and merged Mirrorvision into Premiere. These developments prompted British Telecom also to become active in program provision. BT had initiated a budget movie channel called Home Video Channel (HVC) that was distributed on cassettes to cable operators; it established Star Channel as the premium movie service and merged it in 1987 with Premiere (Jon Davey, communication).

Other video-type offerings available to British television viewers are teletext and videocassette recordings. Teletext is a text service delivered by broadcast or cable. In the early stages of teletext development, different standards were pursued by a variety of organizations. The IBA developed ORACLE, the BBC pursued CEEFAX; and the Post Office, then in control of the telephone service, developed Prestel, an interactive text (videotex) service on telephone lines. In 1974, these bodies cooperated for some common technical specifications by establishing a system of five "levels" of increasing graphic sophistication (McKenzie, 1983, pp. 4–10). On the whole, teletext has been more successful than telephone-delivered Prestel. Both CEEFAX and ORACLE were actively used and had several hundred pages.

Videocassette recorders (VCRs) are extraordinarily popular in Britain and are almost completely outside of governmental control. After Japan, Britain has the greatest concentration of VCRs of all major countries, yet no British manufacturer developed VCR equipment. In 1990, 66 percent of all households in Great Britain had VCRs (TBI, 1990).

The widespread use of VCRs encouraged the distribution of programs of sexually explicit and violent content. This development led to the imposition of some censorship via the Video Recordings Act 1984, which was supported by an unusual mix of Conservatives and feminists. The law goes beyond the existing censorship rules of the British Board of Film Censors (BBFC), which evaluates problematic scenes in the context of the entire work. Instead, the rules for videocassettes establish an index of prohibited acts that may not be shown. Though mainly directed against scenes of particularly obscene and violent content, the rules are sufficiently broad that they could be interpreted to include any realistic depiction of war. Although these rules apply only to videos sold for home viewing, they will invariably affect broadcasting and film production, since this programming is, in most cases, undertaken with a view to future home video distribution.

The Reformation of British Broadcasting

The Thatcher government had introduced far-reaching transformations in the telecommunications sector; it had also created an ambitious scheme for cable television. But for the broadcasting sector, the conservative government had taken few initiatives outside the attempt to keep the BBC's license fee down, and establishing Channel 4. This attitude changed in the late 1980s, when Margaret Thatcher herself chaired a top-level cabinet committee on broadcast reform. The committee concluded that ITV enjoyed excess profits from monopolistic advertising revenues ($2.3 billion in 1988) and that its protected status promoted poor management and union featherbedding.

Change began, as in continental Europe, in radio broadcasting. Here too a duopoly system existed. The BBC had a monopoly over national radio channels, with four national radio channels; regional service for Scotland, Wales, and Northern Ireland; and BBC local stations in England.[14] BBC Local Radio began in 1967 and was expanded in 1977. Local radio was also provided by the several dozen Independent (i.e., commercial) Local Radio (ILR) stations, regulated by the IBA.

In the 1960s, pirate radio stations from ships or other locations invaded Britain with low-budget commercial programs. A 1966 White Paper, still based on the law-and-order approach to broadcasting, had led to the outlawing of operation, supply, or advertising on pirate stations.

However, the pirates did not disappear, indicating that the public demand for diversity in radio was not filled. There were, at most times, at least half a dozen pirate radio stations on the air aiming at British audiences. In an attempt to undercut the pirates, the Home Office in 1985 announced its willingness to license twenty-one community radio stations, a new class of radio, for a two-year trial.[15] Eventually, the government's approach changed from suppressing commercial radio activities to channeling them into a market system.

In 1986, the Department of Trade and Industry recommended a market in radio spectrum, expanding on a 1983 report on radio spectrum policies and a more recent analysis advocating a market in radio spectrum (CSP International, 1987).

In February 1987, the government published a Green Paper concerning radio, entitled "Radio: Choices and Opportunities." The document provided for the establishment of three national private radio networks and hundreds of local and community radio stations during the 1990s. The government determined to open up the sector to competition and market forces. Specific standards were set up for local commercial radio, but within a context of general liberalization of regulations (both technical and in programming).

The debate of the future of British broadcasting came to a head with the October 1988 White Paper, *Broadcasting in the 1990's: Competition, Choices, and Quality,* the most significant expression of the planned deregulation of the British broadcasting system. It established a dramatic transition from the traditional system to a market-oriented model. It attempted to remove restrictions on the expansion of supply for the consumer, to strengthen the efficiency of the supplier, and to reduce the dualism of the public-private model. And it continued the Peacock Committee recommendations to infuse competition into the duopoly of the BBC and ITV firms (Home Office, 1988a).

The White Paper aimed at transforming ITV by competitive forces. The ITV franchises would be auctioned off in 1992 to groups offering both competitive bids and public service commitments (Lee, 1988). The proposals also included a new and fifth national channel and liberalized rules on sponsorship, advertising, and subscription fee rules. Also, an Independent Television Commission (ITC) would replace IBA and Cable Authority and regulate with a "light touch," which would lack the IBA's powers to restrict acquisitions. The ITC's licensing would follow a two-step test for programming quality and then the financial tender. Licenses would be for ten-year periods (Home Office, 1988, p. 22). Licensees would be taxed on revenues, not profits. Channel 4 would become fully independent of the ITV companies and able to enter the advertising and program markets directly, as a competitor; two additional DBS channels would be licensed by the IBA; and the BBC and others could raise revenues through subscription TV as fund-raising. The White Paper also commissioned a study of Multipoint-Video Distribution Systems (MVDS). Transmission (i.e., service delivery) would be separate from service provision (i.e., programming) (Home Office, 1988a, p. 39). Regionally based transmission systems, currently operated by BBC and IBA, would be private and competitive, except for certain common carrier obligations yet to be determined by the government. Broadcast standards and consumer protections would remain, prohibiting inaccurate reporting, offensive or violent programming, and requiring impartial coverage of religious or political issues. A Broadcasting Standards Council (BSC) was to be established on a statutory basis. One of the BBC's channels would be used by other broadcasters after midnight, and the second one would have to raise some income from subscription.

In addition, the traditional quota limit of 14 percent of American programming would be kept on BBC and ITV channels (Carter, 1989).

The White Paper's far-reaching proposals generated much controversy. Some 3000 parties offered formal comments on the White Paper. The BBC was relieved to find extensive criticism of ITV rather than of itself. The ITV firms, on the other hand, complained about the assault on their franchises, as well as its indirect threat of fostering cable and satellite competitors.

After public discussions, a more gentle Broadcasting Bill was presented by the government to Parliament and passed in 1990. Many Conservative party members concerned with traditional culture as well as the Labour party were opposed. The Act established the Independent Television Commission (ITC) as the new broadcasting and cable television regulator, with powers to grant broadcasting licenses to the highest bidder, with a strong consideration for quality standards that had to be shown first, and which could still overcome the highest bid at the end. (Bids would be for the first year; for the remaining nine years of a license, fees would be indexed.) ITV will be renamed Channel 3 (C3) in 1993, with a ten-year renewable license, and Channel 4 will be established as a separate corporation with the ability to sell its own airtime and a guaranteed minimum annual income of 14 percent of total television revenues; the Welsh Authority will continue broadcasting on S4C, with a guaranteed minimum of 3.2 percent of television revenues. The ITC will also award a national license for a fifth national channel (C5), and one or more news service providers for C3 and C5. At least 25 percent of programming time for all terrestrial licensees, the BBC and satellite service, will be filled by independent productions (though there is no provision dealing with the prices the independents could receive, as their after-rights, issues that led to chronic disputes in the United States).

The ITC also licenses domestic and nondomestic satellite services as well as program services provided via telecommunications networks for ten years. Local service licenses (for cable or microwave delivery of ITV, BBC, satellite, and radio) are licensed for fifteen years.

The bill, together with its amendments, also set stringent cross-ownership restrictions. Licenses, except for local delivery services and nondomestic satellite services, may be granted only to residents of the European Community. They may not be granted to political bodies, advertising agencies, and bodies with "undue influence." Terrestrial channels, domestic satellites services and national radio licenses cannot be owned by religious bodies. In general, ownership is limited to either two C3 regionals, one C3 national, one C5, one national radio, six local radio, or six restricted radio stations. Local or national newspaper owners cannot own more than 20 percent of a C3, C5, or national radio service. A local newspaper owner cannot hold more than 20 percent of a local radio or delivery system in its region. The same percentage restrictions hold true for C3, C5, or national radio stations owning newspapers. C3 licenses must provide children's, religious, news, and regional programs, and offer program diversity.

The bill strengthened quality safeguards for programming substantially compared with the White Paper. Incumbent ITV operators became more comfortable with the notion of an auction system, as long as it took quality into account, which they believed would favor them against the upstart rivals. This is partly wishful thinking, unless favoritism takes place in the bidding process. The ITV companies have high costs built into their operation (more than 14,000 employees alone for one channel), which should negatively affect their bids. They are unused to competing for advertising revenues, and their market share, given the entry of cable, satellite, and terrestrial rivals has nowhere to go but down. Under the Act, they must even help promote the programs of their now emancipated offspring, Channel 4, and fund some of its potential revenue shortfalls, while benefitting only little from its discriminating audience. Also, some of the incumbents formed alliances with each other and potential alternative bidders to reduce competition for the license.

Channel 5 was envisioned as a non-London based national broadcaster supported by advertising, and reaching those 70 percent of the population not located close to Ireland and France (whose interference prevents transmission).

Its frequency requires the retuning of most British VCRs and a new antenna. Its economic viability was uncertain in the short term.

There were also changes in radio broadcasting. The Broadcasting Act created a new Radio Authority that allocates, also by competitive tender, three new national radio stations and, in a gradual fashion, 200–300 new community stations. The three independent national radio (INR) stations would specialize, respectively, in pop music, non-pop, and news/speech programs. Licenses are based on sealed bid auctions. The local stations, on the other hand, are assigned according to diversity criteria and the discretion of the newly created Radio Authority (i.e., there is only limited competition within formats).

Transmission services provided by the IBA were moved into a private firm, National Transcommunications Ltd. C3 companies were required to use the same operator, most likely NTL. The company could also compete for the business of new broadcasters. The government also planned to permit competitive bidding for major sports events, removing a protection which had benefitted BBC and ITV. The bill was passed and received royal assent in November 1990. Britain had taken a major step in the direction of an open television system.

Conclusion

Britain's television had been stable for more than thirty years, based on the strong public BBC and the private ITV cartel. Because commercial television existed and served the center and lower ends of the taste distribution, there was less pressure for change than on the Continent. The British experience of stability within a limited mixed system may repeat itself in European countries after commercial television is instituted there, though it will be harder to maintain, given the proliferation of cable and satellite distribution and the increasingly open European frontiers. A pure public monopoly has certain arguments of principle in its favor; but there are few justifications for a limited private television except the flawed claims of spectrum scarcity, and the need for monopoly profits to support quality programs. Eventually, television was further opened in Britain. Several forces came together. The BBC's support had weakened in the British elite and could not be mustered in protection of the duopoly. The government also pursued high technology policies that encouraged cable television and domestic DBS satellites; and although neither distribution mode became successful in the 1980s, it sent signals to the programming part of the media system that change was on its way. This led to the perhaps strongest aspect of change: the emergence of London as the European center for program packaging and provision. This role was a natural one, given London's traditional role in information-based services, such as international trade and finance, shipping, and cultural productions from theater to film to publishing. The role was also a logical extension of London's gateway function between Europe and North America. These advantages were consciously strengthened by the British government's general economic liberalization policies. In television, it meant a great deal of freedom for satellite-delivered channels. In consequence, many of these channels originate in London.

British program channel supply thus raced far ahead of the available system of domestic distribution. They became integrated international firms. Sooner or later this forces distribution to move to a higher level; otherwise, the program end, lacking a home base, would miss critical stages in its release sequencing. In that sense, British media liberalization is software-driven, whereas in many other European countries it is hardware-driven, mainly by the construction of cable networks.

As the rest of Europe moved to the stage of limited private television, which Britain had reached more than a generation ago, the British government embarked on the next level of reform. Now the United Kingdom was on the road to establishing a market system in the private television field. The long-term significance of this is not just that a few more channels are likely to be available. Much more important is the fact that television moves beyond the stage of being a favor bestowed by the state. In that sense, Britain was moving, ahead of other European countries, from the television of privilege to the television of openness.

However, media policy in the United Kingdom was not based on a broad consensus. It was primarily supported by the free-market wing of the Conservative Party, with more American support and participation than elsewhere in Europe. A different constellation of power could modify this policy considerably.

9

Italy

Italian television provides less of a generally applicable precedent than a case study of what can happen if the political system is incapable of reform. On the one hand, Italy has had the most open broadcast system in Europe. There is little cable television, and few satellite channels are available, but hundreds of commercial television stations have broadcast since 1976. On the other hand, Italy's transformation was brought on largely by the initiatives of broadcast pirates, which were later sanctioned by the nation's courts. The Italian political system was unable to establish a policy on entry or regulation. Consequently, for more than a decade there had been almost no structural control of local private broadcasting. In its absence, Italian commercial TV has rapidly evolved into a highly concentrated industry dominated by Silvio Berlusconi, with strong elements of a public–private duopoly.

History

The early history of Italian broadcasting is closely linked with Mussolini's dictatorship. In 1924, the privately owned Union Radiofonica Italiana (URI) obtained a six-year, renewable monopolistic concession on broadcasting, subject to government censorship and financed by fees paid by radio set dealers.

Noting radio's popularity and power, the fascist government in 1929 transformed URI into Ente Italiano Audiozioni Radiofoniche (EIAR), a semigovernmental company, whose supervision it closely shared with local Fascist *vigilanza* organizations. After 1931, EIAR was put under the control of the Societa Idroelettrica Piemontese (SIP), then an electric utility and later the main state telephone company.

During World War II, government control was tightened still further. In 1944, RAI (originally Radio Audironi Italiane, later Radiotelevisione Italiane) was founded as a counteroperation to EIAR, which was still controlled by the Mussolini government. After 1945, RAI was left with exclusive broadcast rights. In 1952, ownership relations were reorganized, and SIP transferred 75 percent of its RAI ownership to the Instituto per la Ricostruzione Industriale (IRI), the government holding company for industrial enterprises. (In 1964, SIP sold its remaining interest in RAI to IRI.)

RAI's broadcasting activities were extended to television in 1952. Regular

TV transmission began in 1954, supported by license fees, and, since 1957, by advertising revenues (Rauen, 1980). Through the 1950s and 1960s, Italian television's popularity grew significantly.

The ruling Christian Democratic party used RAI extensively as a propaganda instrument. As a result of that Church-allied party's domination of Italian politics through the past decades of the postwar period, RAI's programs tended to be relatively straight-laced. This tradition partly explains the later success of sexually explicit programs on private television.

A few years after the onset of public television, a private consortium, Il Tempo, initiated a private broadcasting plan. But the Christian Democrats challenged and blocked these efforts (Sasson, 1985). In 1960, the Italian Constitutional Court upheld the legitimacy of the state monopoly, justifying its decision by pointing to the scarcity of broadcast frequencies. However, the court case and mounting public pressure demonstrated that more program diversity was desired. Consequently, a second channel, RAI-2, was launched in 1961 to provide a wider menu of programs.

Although it broadened the offerings available on Italian television, the Christian Democratic party maintained severe political control of RAI. It was not until 1963 that a leader of the Communist party, the country's second largest political grouping, appeared on an interview program. RAI's director general from 1961 to 1974, Ettore Bernabei, consolidated his power by providing broadcasting jobs to members of the Christian Democrats' new coalition partner, the Socialist party. He also coopted potentially critical intellectuals by a wide array of free-lance positions, consultancies, retainer relations, and other advantages.

But by the early 1970s the Christian Democrats and the government in general had lost much authority and stature. After protracted battles, supervision of RAI was transferred in 1975 from cabinet to parliamentary appointees. A body consisting of forty members of Parliament, appointed on the basis of their party's relative strength, began to look over RAI to assure political pluralism and diversity. The parliamentary overseers were also granted the power to appoint ten members to RAI's sixteen-man board of governors. The remaining six were appointed by RAI's shareholders; but because RAI was controlled by the state holding company IRI, these appointments were de facto by the government, too, thus ensuring the latter's control. Even so, the new arrangement gave a voice to the Communist party and other opposition parties.

An agreement between the Christian Democrats and the Socialists to divide control of the two RAI channels between themselves accompanied the Reform Law 103 of 1975. The first channel retained its distinctly Christian Democratic flavor, while the Socialists dominated RAI-2. A similar partisan division occurred among the various radio channels. Even more than before, most positions in Italian broadcasting, from top management and editorial positions to the most junior messengers, were political patronage jobs according to party affiliation. Every issue, every program question, every personnel question, and every management decision became rife with political ramifications (Cavazza, 1979).

According to a 1983 newspaper compilation, the party affiliations of editors of RAI-1 news programs were as follows: Christian Democrats, 63 percent; Socialists, 11 percent; and Communists, 7 percent. The party affiliations of editors of RAI-2 news programs were Socialists, 38 percent, Christian Democrats, 35 percent, and Communists, 19 percent. In voting in the early 1980s the Christian Democrats generally won the support of about 35 percent of the electorate, the Communists held about 30 percent and the Socialists won 10 to 15 percent. Thus, both Christian Democrats and Socialists were overrepresented in RAI (Grizaffi, 1983).

A third RAI channel, created in 1979 to provide regional programming, was dominated by the Communist party; in 1987, it became primarily a national channel. Its quality won respect, and its viewership increased.

Each of the RAI channels is oriented somewhat differently. Generally speaking, RAI 1, with 25 percent of the total audience share, provides information and entertainment programs to the broad public. RAI 2, with 17 percent of the audience, has more specialized programs for narrower audiences; and RAI 3, with 5.5 percent, broadcasts the most art and cultural programming, as well as national and local information and news (Mazzoleni, 1990, p. 118).

RAI also operates three national radio networks, regional stations, and German, French, and Slovene language programs.

The Demise of the RAI Monopoly

RAI's bureaucracy was legendary in Italy. In 1989, it employed 14,000 and had a $186 million deficit on an annual budget of $1.7 billion (Johnston et al., 1989). Yet for all of the resources, viewers were dissatisfied with the technical and content quality of service. Until 1977, for example, there was no color transmission.

RAI's staff, too, was unhappy about the lack of management professionalism. In one telling instance, the anchorman of a national news program and his entire news staff staged a walkout when their nightly current affairs show started thirty-two minutes late because the preceding program, a game show, had run over schedule. Over a stretch of fifty consecutive nights, the news program had been aired on schedule only eight times.

One study in the 1970s, commissioned by the Council of Europe and echoing the prevailing public sentiment, took the RAI monopoly to task: "Indeed, the most impartial observers say that such flagrant unscrupulousness is rarely displayed by any Western democracy as that witnessed in Italy in regard to the information broadcast by the RAI-TV" (Faenza, 1977).

In fairness, RAI also demonstrated an impressive record of self-produced programs, cultural events, and news broadcasts. Even so, the network had been so discredited and politicized that it could marshall only moderate support when its monopoly position began to be brazenly challenged.

The traditional alternatives to RAI lay across the border: Monaco's Tele-Monte Carlo, a private, primarily French-language broadcaster, and the Yugoslav Tele Capodistria with programs originally designed for Italian-language minorities in Yugoslavia. After a court ruling in 1974, these stations could be relayed into the heart of Italy. At the same time, the French government decided to establish a strong transmitter on Corsica that would also cover a large part of Italy. Domestic mavericks, too, began to challenge RAI's exclusivity. These alternatives, however, represented less than 10 percent of audience share.

In 1972, the tiny cable pirate Tele-Biella launched the first notable challenge, providing community programs to about 100 subscribers in the town of Biella near Turin. Its programs, not available over the air, were intended to "better inform" the local audience during elections and to counter the entrenched local political hierarchy from an independent leftist perspective. When the government attempted to close the system down, a local judge ruled in Tele-Biella's favor, finding that the station fulfilled a local information function that RAI had not addressed.

The Italian government, despite the ruling, moved to shut down Tele-Biella and what had by then become an association of eighteen similar cable stations. The case went before the Italian Constitutional Court, which in its 1973 Judgment 226 permitted the stations to continue operating.

After the Tele-Biella case, Italian Law 103 of 1975 liberalized private cable television and radio restrictions in extraordinary fashion. Every Italian or European Community citizen, after payment of a relatively minor fee, could provide local cable services, though rules against networking and interconnections were still very restrictive. Cable programmers, many part of the political left, were thus instrumental in ending the governmental monopoly. But cable's assertiveness ultimately undermined its foundation as a transmission medium. When unlicensed local broadcasters, learning from cable, went on the air, the need for the costlier cable transmission technology declined, and cable television played no further role in subsequent Italian television development.

In 1975, at least thirty-five private television and about 150 private radio stations began to broadcast without a license, opting to pay fines if necessary and appeal their cases to the courts. An avalanche of piracy began. A year later, hundreds of private commercial TV stations were on the air. Soon the courts spoke. In the historic 1976 Judgment Number 202, in a case involving a Florence station, the Italian Constitutional Court held that the RAI monopoly was unconstitutional with respect to local broadcasting. This ruling opened the floodgates immediately, and hundreds of small private broadcasters started low-power local operations.

Judgment 202 freed local broadcasting, and there was no subsequent legislation to establish a regulatory system or licensing. Throughout the 1970s and 1980s there was no mechanism or agency involved in the basic tasks of regulation. Yet this does not necessarily indicate an absence of policy, for the lack of government legislation indicated at least tacit agreement with unfolding events by several of the major political parties.

This was not surprising. The Christian Democrats supported the traditional governmental system as long as they controlled RAI; when their hold over the public network diminished—a process that began with the 1975 reform legislation—their interest shifted toward the private sector, where their position was much stronger (Silj, 1981). They regarded the emergence of private broadcasting favorably and were pleased when RAI's monopoly was declared unconstitutional. In 1982, for the first time since World War II, the Christian Democrats had to cede the prime minister's office to their Socialist coalition partner. Not surprisingly, this event brought home the fact that private interests might be more sympathetic to their concerns in the long run than a politicized broadcasting network subject to the uncertainties of electoral and coalition politics. And the smaller political parties viewed private broadcasting as their first opportunity to get their message on the airwaves.

The Socialist party at first launched an initiative to reform the broadcasting system by establishing a fourth RAI channel under the control of private publishers, following the British ITV model. Later, the party became a supporter of private TV, part of its strategy to become the voice of a professional and technically oriented middle class, and a defender of civil liberties (Sasson, 1985). Bettino Craxi, the Socialist leader and prime minister after 1982, developed close personal ties with Silvio Berlusconi, the emerging czar of Italian private television. The Socialists even opposed the application of antitrust legislation to broadcasting.

The Communist opposition to private broadcasting was also mild. The party's position on television was essentially reformist, and it introduced a regulatory proposal to extend private local broadcasting into regional networks, with licensing and antitrust provisions to limit the number of stations. They proposed to establish a regulatory authority and require that private stations self-produce at least 30 percent of their own programs; one private national news program could be broadcast. In northern Europe, where a more dogmatic stance in media issues was taken, such proposals—advanced in Italy by the Communist Party—was at the time a heresy even for moderate Social Democrats.

The Communist Party went on to operate its own network, Nuova Emittenza Televisiva (NET). Its program sources include, among others, Eastern Europe and the Soviet Union, and it carries advertising. It operated its own production facility, producing original TV films as well as current affairs programs (Rauen, 1980).

This is not to say that television became totally unrestricted in Italy. Networking, the electronic linkup of several stations, was not permitted because Judgment 202 referred specifically to local rather than national broadcasting. Private broadcasters were prohibited from showing national news programs, partly to prevent a private firm from establishing undue power over public opinion and partly to maintain political control over news distribution. In 1980, Rizzoli, the largest Italian publisher and owner of the prestigious Italian newspaper *Corriere della Sera* and of a TV network, began broadcasting hour-long news shows and rapidly attained a high viewing share. RAI went to court to prevent such live news broadcasting as a violation of the earlier judgment. In 1981, RAI won in the Italian Constitutional Court. This decision was peculiar. The state monopoly and its supporters for years disdainfully pointed to the frequently abysmal quality of private broadcasters, some of whose programs were violent or obscene. The court did not interfere with these programs; but when it came to news programs, the public had to be protected.

In 1976, there were ninety broadcast stations in Italy. By 1977, the number had grown to 264; by 1978, there were 305; and by 1979, 537 (*Media Perspektiven,* 1984). In 1983, there were 700 to 800 private TV and 6000 to 8000 private radio stations, according to RAI (Sasson, 1985). And in mid-1985 there were an astonishing 1319 private television stations in operation, 123 in Sicily, 160 in Lombardy, 83 in the Rome area, and 60 in Tuscany. With one television station per 10,000 households, Italy boasts the world's greatest density of broadcasters.[1]

About half of the Italian population is able to receive between seven and eleven television channels during most of the day. In most cities, program choices range up to twenty channels, with border areas also having access to broadcasts from adjacent countries.

There is great turnover in station ownership. In 1980 alone, almost one-third of the stations in Rome changed either ownership or political affiliation (Grizaffi, 1981). Six stopped broadcasting altogether, five new ones started up, and two merged.

Given this turbulence, it has never been possible to count television stations precisely. A 1980 census by the PTT Ministry found 972. However, many interested parties reported broadcasting activities simply to establish grandfather rights. The actual figure, according to a survey by the Friedrich Naumann Foundation/International Institute of Communications, was between 350 and 400 television stations (Silj, 1981). In 1988, RAI counted 941 stations, 701 of them without network affiliation (Mazzoleni, 1990, p. 114). The fluidity of numbers has often been cited by orderly minds as evidence for "chaos." Such a view assumes that simplicity in media is a virtue. Is it possible or necessary to state with any precision how many magazines there are in a country at any given time?

RAI faces the onslaught of thousands of private radio broadcasters too. In 1989, there were over 3000 private radio stations, according to the Italian PTT, of which about 1000 broadcast regularly (Mazzoleni, 1990, p. 119). Even the Catholic Church is a rival of sorts, through its official Radio Vatican, established in 1931. Radio Vatican broadcasts news and religious programs in thirty-four languages. Control lies in the hands of the Vatican secretary of state, sometimes in conflict with more liberal Jesuits (Riding, 1989, p. A4). Another peripheral broadcaster is Xandir Malta, the official Maltese TV and radio station, operated under the license of the Broadcasting Authority of the state of Malta.

As a result of private television, Italy has become by far the largest European market for television programs—whether from the United States or from other countries. Many of the programs shown in Italy are American and, increasingly, Brazilian films. Domestic production has picked up too. Because of the heavy television competition, Italy has also generated an increasingly strong production industry and has been active in international coproduction.

The Berlusconi Empire: Network Concentration Italian Style

The primary restriction on private broadcasting had been the prohibition of national networking among stations. The economic incentives for networking, however, proved too strong to be contained. Media entrepreneurs quickly undercut the network prohibition through the creation of de facto networks that broadcast prerecorded material simultaneously from their various stations across the country.

Three major private networks emerged from the fray: Canale-5, Italia-1, and Rete-4. Amazingly, all three became controlled by the industrialist Silvio Berlusconi and his Fininvest group. Canale-5 targets a general audience similar to that of RAI 1, although its news and information programs lack RAI's depth. Italia-1 and RETE-4 are geared toward a younger, female audience during most parts of the day. Smaller networks are Rete A, TMC (Globo Monte Carlo controlled by Brazil's TV Globo and the Italian chemical and agricultural firm Feruzzi), Odeon TV, Italia 7, and Orsini Pubblicita-Junior TV (TBI, 1990), some of which had program and advertising supply agreements with Fininvest.

In addition, there were also so-called *circuiti,* cooperative agreements among groups of broadcasters. A special role is played by so-called concessionarie, advertising companies that sell program packages, including preinserted commercials, to various stations.

Silvio Berlusconi is the son of a Milan bank director. At sixteen, he entered the world of entertainment as a part-time performer on a tourist ship. He studied law and wrote a doctoral dissertation on advertising. At twenty-five he began a construction company in Milan with support from a bank with which his father was affiliated.

Within fifteen years, he had become the leading construction entrepreneur in northern Italy; five years later, he had also established himself as the dominant force in Italian private television. The Berlusconi empire, controlled through the holding company Fininvest, includes hundreds of firms connected to each other in complex ways. Broadcasting activities account for more than half of Berlusconi's revenues. He also owned the conservative Milan newspaper *Il Giornale* and the largest television program guide magazine. These press holdings contributed to one critic's lament:

> The fourth estate does not exist in Italy as an independent power . . . journalism today has become a question of whether you are pro-Fiat, pro-de Benedetti or pro-Berlusconi (Cohen, 1990, p. 115).

Other media-related properties include a technical center; the advertising company Pubitalia, serving two-thirds of Italy's private TV; a financial firm; film production and distribution; music and records; the Milan soccer club; computer software houses; movie theater and department store chains, a transportation company; hotels; an insurance company; 25 percent of the private French

TV channel La Cinq; 20 percent of the German channel Tele-5; and part of Spain's Tele-5 (TBI, 1990). Evidently, Berlusconi's favorite number is 5, which he was making into a Europe-wide trademark. Berlusconi also signed a three-year contract to provide commercials to Gosteleradio, the Soviet state broadcasting company (*Broadcasting Abroad,* 1989, p. 6) and proposed private broadcast operation in Poland, Hungary, and Czechoslovakia. Fininvest group revenues were $8 billion in 1988 (Stuart, 1988b, p. 54).

For all his dominance, Berlusconi had not been a pioneer of Italian commercial television; he entered only after the tumultuous "wildcat" phase of private broadcasting had stabilized, leaving weakened competitors whom he managed to buy, hire, or outmaneuver. By 1982, almost one-half of the stations that had been active only three years earlier had been sold or closed down. Berlusconi entered broadcasting in 1980, setting up Canale-5 in Milan as his flagship operation, which he expanded by acquiring other stations and forming a national network. The other major networks at that time, held by various publishing houses, were Rete-Europa, owned by the Italian publishing house Rizzoli; Italia-1, owned by Rusconi; and Rete-4, owned by Mondadori.

From the start, Berlusconi's operation was marked by a free-spending vision. He put more money than others into stars and technology, and he paid independent antenna installers a bounty to ensure that the signals from his channels would be technically well received. He offered advertisers low rates and wooed viewers by offering fewer advertisements per hour than on competing channels.

Mondadori's Director General Piero Ottone describes how his network fell to Berlusconi: "The turning point in our venture, which had been successful that far, came when Rusconi (in the summer of 1982) decided that television was too risky for his company and offered (his network) Italia Uno to us. We were negotiating the deal (aiming to merge Rete Quattro and Italía Uno) when Berlusconi moved in and bought Italia Uno from Rusconi for a very good price. From that moment the fight became very uneven: two networks, Canale Cinque and Italia Uno, against one, Rete Quattro. That progressively weakened our position until we decided to sell Rete Quattro. Berlusconi bought it, thereby becoming practically the only private television in Italy. His surviving competitors are much smaller—and not doing well" (Piero Ottone, communication, 1986).

Ottone gives three reasons for the failure of Italian publishers in television: lack of television expertise, inability to interconnect, and inadequate financial resources. "Berlusconi has invested very lavishly, and partly raised his money by selling shares door to door, a very dubious procedure which we have always refused to adopt, and have fought against in our publications, because it gives investors no protection" (Piero Ottone, communication, 1986).

Thus, where four diversely owned networks had existed only a few years before, by 1983 three of them were owned and controlled by Silvio Berlusconi, and the fourth, Rete-Europe, was liquidated, with some of its stations going to Berlusconi. Berlusconi added to his program supply through Italia 7, Junior TV, and Capodistra Sport in 1988. (Stuart, 1988b, p. 52). Eventually, Tele-Monte Carlo was acquired by Brazil's TV Globo and established a national presence, providing some network competition. And there are hundreds of independent stations. But in terms of organized presence, nothing comes close to Berlusconi.

Berlusconi's influence grew enormously as he integrated horizontally and vertically. By 1986, his domestic production budget accounted for 60 percent of all Italian films and features (*Variety*, 1986, p. 146). Canale-5 first entered into public affairs coverage by reporting on local and regional elections. When the legal situation permitted (the independent network Rete A had begun an illegal news program), Berlusconi began moving into production of more regular national news, a necessary ingredient for respectability as a full-fledged broadcaster.

Berlusconi, though a business tycoon, is a close friend of Prime Minister Bettino Craxi, a Socialist. His Socialist political connections have also helped with the French and Spanish governments in launching new commercial channels in their countries. Ultimately, however, owners' political views make less difference in commercial television than is often believed, unless they are willing to subsidize them (as Axel Springer of Germany did in his flagship paper *Die Welt*). This is not to say that commercial television is not implicitly political; its underlying themes tend to encourage consumption and belief in simple and happy resolutions to problems. But this is independent of the personal politics of the owners, as long as the latter are commercially motivated. The main exception occurs when the political issue is the status of television itself. In any event, one should not exaggerate the commitment of any of the new media moguls to even the moderate left. In the final analysis, their allegiance is to their own economic interests.

Reform Legislation

Given the enormous concentration in Italian television, and the restrictions on private national networking of local stations, the government was increasingly pressured to establish a legal framework and resolve outstanding questions. In 1984, the Ministry of Post and Telecommunications prepared a bill that would make it legal for private television stations to broadcast the same program simultaneously throughout the country, that is, to create a network. Before this was permitted, program tapes had to be physically moved to stations. The bill still prohibited private national news programs, but allowed for local and regional news.

As the legislation inched its way through Parliament, outside events escalated. In 1984, judges and magistrates in three regions shut down Berlusconi's unofficial networks for violating a 1977 court ruling that gave RAI the exclusive right to transmit national network signals. This action, undertaken in the midst of the pre-Christmas advertising peak, infuriated many Italians, who were denied their accustomed programs. The government responded by approving an emergency decree overturning the magistrates' order. These actions raised significant constitutional issues about the role of the judiciary. In the meantime, the broadcasters operated under an emergency decree known as the *Decreto Berlusconi*.

By law, the initial decree had to be ratified by legislation within two months. But since this did not happen in time, the magistrates closed the stations again. This led to a second decree and a government promise to introduce and pass general broadcasting legislation.

There was much agitation within the government coalition and even within Prime Minister Craxi's Socialist party. Craxi had to ask for a vote of confidence, forcing the coalition to close ranks. Even so, the decree was approved only with the support of the neofascist opposition party, MSI.

To resolve these problems, the government proposed in 1985 a bill "for organic regulation of the broadcasting system." Two regulatory bodies were designed by the government's bill. The first is the National Private Broadcasting Supervisory Commission, whose three members are chosen from the disciplines of law, business, and economics. The commission assures the observance of regulations, independence, competition, and plurality. It can investigate the companies, request financial documents, and even control the measures for collecting audience ratings.

The second new institution is a National Broadcasting Committee within the PTT Ministry. It is composed of the minister, two ministry officials, appointees of the two chambers of the Italian Parliament, six members of the cabinet, and four of the Interregional Commission. The National Broadcasting Committee functions essentially as a licensing board, deciding on issuance and revocation of licenses. But all its decisions must be ratified by the PTT Ministry. It can undertake investigations of private broadcast stations. Its structure provides the government with solid control.

These bodies add to the existing Parliamentary Supervisory Commission, which formulates general guidelines on the management of RAI, establishes the maximum yearly revenue allowed from advertising for public broadcasting, and nominates RAI's board of management.

The law mandated certain production quotas: local stations must produce at least 10 percent of their programs; national concessions, (i.e., networks) must self-produce at least 20 percent; and the public corporation must self-produce at least 50 percent.

To protect movie theaters, films cannot be broadcast within a year of their first public theatrical showing in Italy. At least a quarter of the films must be of Italian or EC origin. The broadcasting of films banned for juveniles (under eighteen) can lead to a closing of the station for up to ten days.

For private broadcasters, licenses are not transferrable. Authorizations for local stations last nine years, and the concession for national networks is twelve years. To receive a concession for a nationwide television network, companies would need a minimum amount of capital. The National Broadcasting Committee publishes the number of concessions that can be issued, thus limiting the number of networks. However, concessions for simultaneous transmission of programs remain, permitting the previous type of informal networking.

Network concessions are based on applications that must specify the percentage of self-produced programs, the amount of Italian content, technical standards, and other criteria. The previous experience of the ownership group is an important factor.

A key provision affected Berlusconi. No individual can directly or indirectly control more than two such networks and no company with 20 percent or more total press volume can receive a license. In other words, Berlusconi must divest himself of one network, unless his lawyers can find a way around this provision.

Advertising on private stations cannot, according to the bill, exceed 16 percent of total broadcasting time on average, or 20 percent of any given hour. There are limitations on the share of network advertising in order to protect local stations' access to their own local markets. Stations can sell broadcast time for parties in election periods, but they cannot discriminate among parties and cannot allocate more than 20 percent of election transmission time to one party.

To prevent concentration, the bill also provides antimonopoly regulations, which the national Private Broadcasting Supervisory Commission monitors. The rules attempt to make transparent the ownership, intercorporate arrangements, and transfer of control. Fees for local television authorizations range between 5 million and 20 million lire annually; for national television concessions, they are 27 million lire for each "catchment" area.

Serious fines or confiscations of licenses could be levied for violations of their terms. And, importantly, RAI is assured adequate revenues (license fees and advertising) (Mazzoleni, 1990, p. 120).

The positions of the various Italian parties on the bill were mixed. Members of the governing coalition (Christian Democrats, Socialists, Republicans, Social Democrats, and Liberals) stressed the need for an antimonopoly provision. The Liberals called for restrictions on the state's role in managing RAI and for frequency allocations by a special judicial body. Both the opposition Communists and neo-Fascists also supported the mixed system. The Communists favored anti-trust regulation, limiting network interconnection to six hours a day, and restriction of advertising breaks.

There is, of course, a big difference between a bill and a law. It took five years for parts of a bill to be passed. Eventually, the backlash to Berlusconi's media empire led the Italian Senate to pass a media bill in 1990, in a highly unusual coalition of Communists and the defecting left wing of the Christian Democrats, and against the fierce opposition of the Socialists protecting Berlusconi.

When the bill reached the lower chamber of parliament, the government was so split that it almost collapsed. Voting took place by secret ballot. In the end, the "Mammi" law was passed in 1990 with provisions that restricted Berlusconi somewhat but opened important new opportunities to him. He had to divest his Milan daily paper *Il Giornale* to keep his three TV networks, but was permitted to interconnect his stations, thus permitting, for the first time, real-

time programs such as sports, news, and live events. There were some mild
restrictions on the quantity (18 percent of each hour) of advertising but stricter
ones were applied to RAI (12 percent per hour). Limits to the number of interruptions were set, but this actually liberalized a court decision which had prohibited them altogether. Berlusconi also had to end involvement in further networks beyond his three networks and 25 percent of frequency assignments, and
to stop selling advertising time on behalf of other networks. He also divested
himself of the new pay-TV channel Tele-piu (though it remained close to him),
the tiny networks Italia-7 and Junior TV, and radio stations. On the other hand,
he battled another major Italian industrialist, Carlo De Benedetti, for control
over the publisher Mondadori. The law also prohibits adult movies. Altogether,
Berlusconi was not seriously impacted, but was given the opportunity of ex-
tending the attractiveness of his three channels and operating in a more stable
legal environment.

In 1986, Berlusconi's three commercial networks together were about even
in viewership with RAI's three channels. In less than ten years, the monopoly
position of the state broadcast institution had vanished. Furthermore, many listeners—up to 25 percent by some estimates—had stopped paying their license
fee, thus reducing RAI's revenues (Mazzoleni, 1990, p. 116). But total television viewing increased: the prime-time adult audience in 1979 was 16 million; by 1983, it had grown to 18.6 million. And audiences watched longer.
During the RAI monopoly days, the average Italian household watched three
hours of TV a day; by 1984, viewing time had increased to five hours and ten
minutes. By 1986, it was five hours and forty-eight minutes, and even six hours
and eighteen minutes during peak holiday times (Mazzoleni, 1990, p. 117).

RAI, under pressure, reversed its downward slide. It improved its performance and won viewers back, especially through domestic Italian programs.
RAI-3, the channel in which the Communist party had been given a significant
role, led the RAI resurgence with ratings increasing from 2 percent to a temporary 14 percent in three years (Johnston, 1990a). RAI's overall ratings rose
to 47 percent by 1988, whereas Berlusconi's networks' combined audience share
was 38 percent. At prime time the gap was only 3 percent (Mazzoleni, 1990).
Although quality is hard to quantify, the view is widely shared that RAI's
programs have become better as a reaction to the erosion of its viewership.

But to do so was expensive. RAI faced heavy debts, and the government
initiated in 1990 a reorganization, which included the sale of RAI's transmission facilities to IRI, and moved towards some decentralization. Furthermore,
RAI went on the offensive and launched Italy's first pay-TV channel in July
1990

Italy's experience with commercial TV and the success of Berlusconi's empire is unlikely to be repeated in other European nations, where commercial
television is evolving at a slower and more controlled pace. But Berlusconi
himself, with ambitions to parlay his Italian stronghold into an international
media empire through inroads in France, Spain, and Germany, believes that
the Italian model may indeed find fertile ground across the continent. In his
words: ''The wind of commercial television blows now from Italy over all of

Europe. This is one of the few winds that blows from the south to the north''
(in Radke and Dilaurenzo, 1985, p. 128). But there is also another lesson from
Italy. The public institution RAI has not gone under, even in the face of massive challenge by private broadcasters. On the contrary, RAI is a better institution than it was when it could take its viewers for granted.

Television in the
Benelux and Alpine
Countries

10
Netherlands

Dutch broadcasting has often been idealized from a distance as a particularly pluralist and open system, but it could equally be described as the legacy of extraordinary past societal segregation. In the Netherlands the diversity in religious and political ideology resulted in a unique "pillarized" pluralism. But this system was eventually destabilized by several forces: the weakening hold of denominational and political elites on society; a loosening of collaboration among the ideological pillars; the entry of pirate broadcasters, who could be absorbed only for a while and whose influence on programming spread to the official broadcast associations; the evolution of European integration and opening of borders; and the substantial cabling of the country by municipalities and private firms. These forces overcame the considerable power of the traditional system that had integrated, for a long time, most of the relevant political and social currents of the country.

This is not to say that Dutch television is left without barriers. The entry of terrestrial broadcasters, for example, remained restricted. But the clear trend is toward a more open media system, with a continuing important role for public broadcasting and its traditional pillars.

History

Traditionally, four organized societal "pillars"—Protestantism, Catholicism, socialism, and liberalism—dominated Holland's political and social life, coexisiting with each other within marked separateness. In the early twentieth century, Protestant and Catholic political parties, though distrustful of each other, fought fierce battles with the liberal socialist forces in Dutch society. Religious hardliners believed that irreconcilable differences between the groups necessitated the establishment of institutions to insulate themselves (Cohen-Jehoram, 1981). For example, the Catholic "pillar" established over time official Catholic labor unions, employer organizations, schools, universities, sports clubs, and newspapers (Brants, 1985). As late as 1954, a bishop's decree prohibited Catholics from being members of the socialists' unions, reading their newspapers, or listening to the programs of their broadcasting organization. The Protestant and Socialist pillars were organized in similarly comprehensive fashion. In more recent times the high-ranking members of each pillar have been respectful of each other's domain, while controlling their own organizations. The Dutch broadcasting system emerged as merely another expression of the "pillarization." Radio broadcasting started in the Netherlands in 1919, with service provided by the Dutch radio pioneer Hanso Idzerda (van den Huevel, 1981). Despite appeals for contributions from audience members and radio enthusiasts in Holland and England, the service's continuing financial difficulties forced it into bankruptcy in 1924. In the meantime, the Netherlands Transmission Apparatus Factory (NSF), an electronic equipment and instruments manufacturer, began broadcasting in 1923 in order to create demand for its radios. Because of the expense of providing program services, NSF concentrated on transmission. However, because it needed programs to foster demand for its equipment, NSF helped organize the Hilversum broadcasting organization (HDO), a membership organization that produces and finances programs. Since the inception of Dutch broadcasting, the city of Hilversum has been its center.

HDO's neutral and national stance proved provocative in the pillarized Dutch society and encouraged Catholics and fundamentalist Protestants to form their own broadcast organizations, KRO and NCRV, in 1924. Liberal Protestants followed with VPRO, and Socialists followed with VARA soon thereafter. In 1928, the neutral-conservative AVRO was created as a successor to the original organization, HDO (Bos and van der Haak, 1982). Because of the organizations were directly or ideologically affiliated with a political party, the government's role was largely to ratify this system.

Subsequent government regulations required the licensing of broadcast organizations by the government rather than by private contract with the transmission company. Additionally, 1930 rules stipulated that the broadcasting organizations operate in the public interest and satisfy the cultural and religious needs of the population. These regulations provided a formula for the allocation of broadcast time among the major four broadcasting organizations, each of which received about one-quarter of air time. The associations were given substantial autonomy in their program production and selection. After 1935 all transmission facilities were incorporated in the mixed private-governmental Nazema organization.

World War II was not a particularly illustrious period for Dutch radio. Herman Wigbold, an authority on Dutch broadcasting who witnessed the war's effects on broadcasting, described the period as follows:

> The war seemed to deal the broadcasting system a death blow. The organizations emerged discredited. In some areas the Nazis were unopposed. AVRO, the politically neutral organization, had already dismissed the Jewish staff before the Germans demanded it. The Catholic broadcasting organization had been completely taken over by the Nazis before the Bishops, taking a firm stand, could intervene. The Socialist Broadcasting Organization bowed before the Nazis with the exception of one official, Broeks (later Chairman of the European Broadcasting Union). The history of broadcasting during the occupation is the history of collaboration. To maintain the institutions was more important than to stand by the principles on which they were founded [Wigbold, 1979, p. 195].

After the war there was a brief struggle for a nongovernmental national system, but the traditional ideological forces reasserted themselves and again divided the system among themselves according to the "pluriform" pillar model. In 1947, the Netherlands Radio Union (NRU) was created to provide technical support and coordination for the system. Its financing, originally through contributions to the broadcasting associations, was later supplemented by government funds from a radio receiver licensing fee.

Television broadcasting began in the Netherlands in 1951, again following the pillar model. In 1956, television was placed under the authority of the umbrella organization NTS, with the equipment manufacturer Philips playing an important role in this decision. Since no comprehensive broadcasting law existed, the prospect of a second television channel with possible commercial privileges created major battles over the status of television during the 1960s. The system became difficult to maintain once the official broadcasting organizations began actively competing with each other and once newcomers made claims for participation. In 1964, for example, the commercial station TV North Sea began broadcasts from a platform in international waters. The government quickly shut the station down despite its popularity. TV North Sea later became an official broadcast association, renamed TROS.

Some legislators advocated the introduction of commercial broadcasting modeled after Britain, while others feared the potential impact on culture and consumption. The ruling coalition was so severely split between liberal supporters of broadcast reform and Socialist and religious opponents that the government toppled in 1965. A new government eventually introduced a second television channel with limited advertising in 1967.

The 1967 Broadcasting Act also established a framework for adding new broadcasters to the pluralist model. Three categories for broadcasting organizations were defined, each entitled to air time in accordance with the organizations membership strength, usually measured by subscriptions to its program magazine. Category A required at least 450,000 "members," a somewhat peculiar number, which happened to cover the four large pillar organizations, each of which was allocated a weekly television broadcast quota of nine hours by 1987 (Logica, 1987, p. 406). Another category, B, applied to organizations with 300,000 to 450,000 members, which received five and one-half hours per week or programming time. A third category, C, required a minimum of 150,000 members and received two and one-half hours of broadcast time per week. "Aspirant" organizations are admitted into the system for a two-year trial period if they have more than 60,000 members. Importantly, candidacy for a prospective broadcasting organization depends on its contribution to greater diversity to the system. This vague requirement, by prohibiting the duplication of an existing broadcaster, protects the established organizations. The fledgling organizations, allotted a fairly meager one hour of weekly television broadcasting or three hours of radio time, must gain more than 150,000 members within three years to become regular organizations.

Since the 1967 Act, only three new associations have been added: the Protestant fundamentalist EO and the politically neutral and entertainment-orientated TROS and VOO. VOO grew out of the popular pirate station Veronica, and TROS originated from the illegal TV North Star, broadcasting from an offshore oil rig. In 1990, Veronica (VOO) had about 1 million members, ahead of the other two independent associations, AVRO (800,000) and TROS (700,000). Other associations were the Catholic KRO (650,000), the Protestant NCRV (550,000), the socialist VARA (530,000), the fundamentalist EO (330,000), and the liberal VPRO (337,000) (Versteeg and Stuart, 1989, p. 30).

Although the associations are supposed to be nonprofit membership organizations, TROS and Veronica muddied the noncommercial intent. Such organizations provided advertising and sponsorships in a variety of subtle forms. Moreover, the "paying membership" degenerated into a charade. Its primary basis were subscriptions sales to TV program magazines, over which the broadcast associations have substantial power ever since the party-written copyright law gave the rights to all publications of program listings. Anyone desiring schedule information thus became willy-nilly a "member" and was counted for purposes of time allocation. In one instance, AVRO, its membership declining, simply bought the one independent magazine that had challenged the system in court and added its subscribers to the AVRO head count (Cohen-Jehoram, 1981).

There is no necessary relation between allocated broadcasting time and viewership. The class A organization KRO had an average audience of 13 percent of its allocated eight and one-third hours per week in the 1980–1981 season, whereas at the same time, one class C organization had 19.5 percent of the audience during its allotted two and one-half hours.

All broadcasting organizations must try to provide programs that satisfy the cultural, religious, or spiritual needs of the population. In 1985 a media bill attempted to make such requirements specific by designating content quotas: at least 25 percent of a broadcast organization's program materials must be entertainment oriented; 25 percent informational; 20 percent cultural; and 5 percent educational (Hins and Hugenholtz, 1988). Moreover, organizational structure must permit members or contributors some influence over programming. In addition to programs produced by the various membership associations, "joint programs" such as sports and church broadcasts are provided by the umbrella organization NOS. All broadcast time is allocated with precision; Jews, for example, get one hour per year, as do Free Thinkers.

As societal identification with denominational or political associations weakened, the previously often cautious and partisan public affairs programs began to look beyond their own pillars. Their independence of perspective grew to the point that a Catholic party publication issued a warning to "its" broadcasters that a "broadcasting corporation which calls itself Catholic must have very strong reasons for publicly criticizing a political party which calls itself Catholic" (Brants, 1985).

In place of commercial advertising during their programs, organizations directly and indirectly promoted themselves, battled for viewership, and advised viewers on membership until this practice was restricted. Program magazines became general-interest publications, and promotions for subscriptions included gifts, travel, and discounts. Consequently, a competitive system emerged, but the result included some of the worst aspects of both commercial and nonprofit broadcasting. The quest for large audiences lowered production and programming standards—in what has been referred to as the "TROSsification" of Dutch television—but it did not generate sufficient revenues to finance a strong system of program production as would a commercial system.

Illegal television broadcasters returned in the early 1980s. After the end of the official evening broadcasts, pirate stations went on the air with films, adult programs, and advertising. In Amsterdam alone, there were in 1981 more than ten such illegal but highly popular television stations; some even published their own program guides (Bos and van der Haak, 1981). After courts ruled that these operations constituted copyright infringement, the government issued a decree criminalizing them. As a result, the pirate broadcasts eventually subsided.

There are five national radio prgrams on the AM and FM bands. In 1985, these stations were given more distinct formats, providing information offerings, classical or popular music. The broadcast associations divide airtime amoung themselves. In addition, there is some regional radio. Several FM radio stations and one television station serve foreign NATO forces, and intergovernmental agreements specify that their programs be noncommercial, mostly prerecorded, and broadcast at low power in order to affect Dutch audiences as little as possible. Commercial stations included Sky Radio (Murdoch) and Radio 10 (Italian-owned). Dutch owned commercial radio was legalized in 1991.

NOS

The 1967 Broadcasting Act created a strong umbrella organization, the Netherlands Broadcasting Corporation (NOS), to provide technical facilities and coordination, produce common programs such as news and sports, and service population segments not provided for by the broadcasting organizations. NOS provides teletext, a noncommercial text service, which can be received by many of the new television sets. The service is mainly used for sports, news, and weather but also offers subtitling of foreign-based satellite cable programs. The Dutch minister of culture appoints a chairman for the NOS, which is governed by a board representing the broadcast associations, various cultural and social organizations, and the government.

The 1985 bill was enacted in 1988. The law divided NOS into three new organizations, resulting in a structure that includes on branch for program provision, one for technical facilities, and a regulatory commission to supervise broadcasting and to license local cable broadcasting. The government reduced the time the broadcast organizations were required to use NOS's studios, sets, and other technical facilities to 75 percent of the total. It also established an independent audiovisual company to replace the NOS technical facilities department. The structure of the regulatory commission is similar to that of an independent regulatory agency and consists of five relatively independent commissioners.

The broadcasting organizations agreed to have NOS operate as their international agent in order to prevent price competition among themselves for foreign programs. Under this system, when NOS acquires a program in which several organizations are interested, a complex "claim system" is used to determine allocation. In 1984, about 30 percent of all programs were imported—almost 90 percent of television drama and over 60 percent of television sports programs.

The Dutch PTT plays an important role in the technical side of broadcast transmission. Based on a 1935 law, transmitters are operated by the Netherlands Broadcast Transmitter Company, Nozema, of which 59 percent of owned by the government and 40 percent is held by the various broadcasting organizations. The PTT installs and operates Nozema transmitters throughout the country. The 1988 Media Law permits community radio stations to transmit themselves, though Nozema has the first option on such new broadcasting.

Dutch broadcasting is financed primarily through one of Europe's lowest license fees, which was about $70 a year in 1988. This fee is set by the government and distributed to the broadcasting organizations. Advertising is permitted, but only through the separate public broadcast advertising organization STER, whose annual revenues fund about 60 percent of the broadcasting budget. Each year, STER also contributed between 5 and 10 percent of its revenues to support the press. (This, and the direct threat to their advertising revenues, contributed to the resistance of segments of the press toward television liberalization.) Total advertising time was limited to three hours per week, and advertisements were broadcast only before and after news programs.

In the early 1980s, pressures grew to expand the television system. A 1983 government White Paper on cable policy still precluded traditional broadcast organizations from offering pay-television programming. But the Christian Democrats, a major coalition partner, proposed establishing a third public broadcasting channel (Brants, 1985). The proposal was supported by the opposition Social Democratic party but opposed by the liberal-conservative coalition partner. In 1985, the government decided to go ahead with a third channel financed by an increase in advertising time. The law was eventually passed in 1988. As a result of the law and a major consultive study by McKinsey, the more Christian oriented associations moved to Netherlands 1, and the more independent A-category associations moved to the second channel (Bos and van Reenen, 1990, p. 155), and the third channel was filled by VARA, VPRO, and NOS. The smaller ideological associations rotate between the two channels.

Cable Television

Wire radio emerged in Holland before World War II to make foreign programs accessible to all Dutch listeners, not just those living near borders. During their occupation of Holland in World War II, the Germans, after unsuccessfully trying to prevent the population from listening to Allied broadcasts, ordered the confiscation of all private radio sets (Diller, 1980). This incident presents interesting evidence about the control potential of cable transmission.

During the late 1950s and 1960s, cable systems in Holland emerged as community antenna systems for radio and television. Until 1969, larger systems remained within the PTT monopoly. At that time, there were plans to unify the independent municipal systems into a national cable system under the PTT and the broadcasting system. In 1969, the law was changed to permit the minister of transport and public works to license "cable systems of a small size or special character" outside of the PTT. This led local governments and private interests to an ever-expanding interpretation of "small size," and large municipal cable networks were subsequently permitted. Many municipalities have since become license holders of cable television systems, although actual operation has often been carried out by private firms.

The cabling of Holland was greatly accelerated in the 1970s by the local governments' rules against private outdoor antennas. Ostensibly implemented for aesthetic reasons, the restriction yielded the convenient by-product of forcing television viewers to subscribe to the municipal cable networks. Responding to criticism concerning this strong-arm tactic, Parliament permitted such restrictions only if all over-the-air programs were carried by the cable systems (Hins and Hugenholtz, 1988), which in turn raised questions of interpretation. In one instance, an English teacher challenged this arrangement, claiming that for his job he needed to listen to English radio broadcasts, which were not carried over his cable system, and that he therefore needed his own roof antenna. Based on a violation of the European Convention, the court decided that the building ordinances were "stricter than necessary," though it upheld the right of municipalities, in principle, to restrict antennas.

Cable television density in Holland is between 70 and 90 percent, depending on whether the definition includes simple master antenna systems. The largest cable operator is Cosema BV, owned by the Dutch PTT, with over 570,000 subscribers. The largest network in all of Europe is KTA Amesterdam. In 1990, Holland was the second most heavily cabled nation in the world, behind Belgium (TBI, 1990, p. 71).

The availability of a multichannel transmission medium soon affected program offerings. In 1971, one municipality began to insert its own programs onto cable television, cleverly starting with its own council meetings. This created a major policy question, since it threatened to open broadcast programming to new participants. Evenutally, regulations were adopted that prohibited provision of any programs that were not available over-the-air, with the exception of experimental local programs and parliamentary meetings. In 1984, these rules were modified, liberalizing program access and permitting local programming, pay cable, cable text, and signals from telecommunications satellites. The 1988 Media Law overturned the earlier restriction on advertising on cable channels, which had been a key restriction. The advertising issue had arisen in 1979 when a bill authorizing the retransmission of distant broadcast signals through cable television was stopped just before passage because of fear that the bill would allow Luxembourg's CLT to provide Dutch-language commercial television delivered to Dutch cable systems via microwave. Dealing with this problem was complicated by various changes in government during the period.

After 1984, satellite-delivered channels were being carried on cable (e.g., Rupert Murdoch's Sky Channel and Music Box, which tripled its reach within a year to more than 1.5 million). The government, which viewed the tide of foreign commercial programs with some misgivings, proposed a bill to prohibit foreign commercial satellite programs on cable if the programs or advertisements were subtitled in Dutch or otherwise directed at Dutch audiences. These restrictions aroused protests, including those of the Commission of the European Communities, and led to litigation. The government was accused of illegally barricading the country from foreign media without justifying its interference in otherwise constitutionally protected expression (Cohen-Jehoram, 1981) and of violating the EEC treaty by restricting the flow of television programming within Europe. The government-appointed Boukema Committee concluded that the state had the right to make restrictions in the public interest. In 1984, the European Commission's Green Paper entitled "On the Establishment of the Common Market for Broadcasting, Especially by Satellite and Cable" also challenged the Dutch broadcasting's STER advertising monopoly under Article 90 of the EEC Treaty. In 1985, the Hague Appeals Court held that restriction of satellite television violated the freedom of expression section of the Dutch Constitution, but it ruled that the prohibition against advertising messages aimed at Dutch viewers was constitutional.

For a long time, no royalties were paid to foreign program suppliers. In 1984, the courts held that cable transmission was like a new publication, and therefore required royalty payments (Brants and Jankowski, 1985).

Cable television is provided by both private suppliers and municipalities. All networks are subject to local jurisdiction, and the linking of different cable networks across local lines is subject to the monopoly of the PTT. However, the minister of public welfare, health, and culture, not the minister in charge of the PTT, is responsible for cable television. Locally, the municipalities usually leave the installation and operation of the cable network to utilities or to a special nonprofit foundation, which typically includes representatives of major interest groups such as landlords, consumers, and the municipalities (Haverman, 1984).

Each municipality must have a local broadcasting organization in order to operate. Local cable programmers need a license from the minister for cultural affairs. Additional specialized organizations can operate under the local broadcasting organizations' overall supervision. Pay cable programs require licensing, and licenses cannot be denied if the applicant observes general regulations.

Cable television in Holland is regulated much more strictly than that in neighboring Belgium. The Dutch PTT specifies technical standards concerning hardware and network architecture. The primary architecture is the mini-star type, with eighteen subscribers per star; tree and branch systems can be used in low-density areas. Amplification and frequency range requirements increase the cost of providing a cable network in Holland to about $300 per subscriber, about twice the cost in Belgium. Most cable systems have a twelve- to thirty-channel capactiy. Some advanced systems, such as the Delta Cable Star system, have operated more than 100 channels experimentally.

In 1983, a government White Paper on cable policy proposed the introduction of pay TV as the exclusive province of the private sector. The proposed system had to operate on a subscription basis with no advertising. A reasonable proportion of its programming had to be Dutch, and the public broadccasting organization had the right of first refusal for certain programs (Nuyl, 1984).

The initial provider of pay television in Holland was Filnet, owned initially by the publisher's organization VNU, the Swedish Esselte, and United International Pictures, a consortium of Hollywood producers. Filmnet began operating in 1985, using a Belgian transponder on an ECS satellite. It charged subscribers about $12 per month and paid the cable systems a remarkably low $0.50 per month per customer.

The Dutch broadcast authority NOS entered the arena of satellite broadcasting by leasing a transponder on the European communications satellite ECS-1. The transponder was to operate in an inter-European broadcasting venture named Europa-TV. This venture brought together the German ARD, NOS, the Irish TVG, the Italian RAI, and the Portuguese RTP. By 1986, only NOS's financial infusions kept the channel alive, and it went off the air soon thereafter.

In 1986, the country's Media Council offered a proposal for two or three private and advertiser-supported program channels, primarily on cable. This was supported by a Liberal party and Christian Democrat coalition (Bos and van Reenen, 1990, p. 154). Independent associations such as Veronica and TROS were offered the possibility of creating their own commercial TV and radio channel and leaving the system. However, the proposal stipulated that advertising income and subscription fees for two public channels would not be received after eighteen months and that channels had to cooperate with other publishers. This deterred the interest of the existing associations (Bos and van Reenen, 1990). To avoid this burden, the country's major independent producer, Joop van den Ende, attempted to exploit a loophole in the law that gave advantages to foreign channels by broadcasting from a foreign satellite to the Dutch cable system. He named his station TV-10. But van den Ende was unable to convince the Media Council in 1989 that his TV-10 was foreign-owned. On the other hand, a rival, RTL-Veronique (owned by CLT and the electronics giant Philips among others), successfully navigated the legal barriers. It received a license and began sending Dutch-language programs via Luxembourg and the Astra satellite to Dutch cable systems. Van den Ende then provided programs to TRL-Veronique (Versteeg and Stuart, 1989, p. 34). The station is only indirectly related to the popular broadcast association VOO (Veronica) although the latter was fined (a seven-week suspension from broadcasting) for providing financial assistance and expertise. This was held to violate the non-commerciality of the official broadcast associations. RTL-Veronique changed its name to RTL-4. Thirty-eight percent of RTL-4 was acquired by Elsevier, a publisher, and VNU, a publishers association (Bos and van Reenen, 1990, p. 155). It quickly established stronger audience ratings than any other Dutch broadcast channel after its start in 1990. Thus, the first private Dutch broadcast television channel had been established. The new media law also opened television to other applicants, though their services had to be distributed over cable only.

Conclusion

The Netherlands has traditionally played an important role in international trade and commerce. It is therefore not surprising that its people were receptive to foreign radio and television. In a broader sense, the country was progressing in its role as a supplier of information and services. Its manufacturing too is strong in advanced electronics. On the other hand, Dutch broadcasting, for all of its pluralism, was an inward-looking affair. It accommodated most relevant internal forces, but in the age of information, that was not enough.

Television ceased to be territorial, and the Netherlands, traditionally an internationally oriented country and a strong advocate of European integration, could not keep its broadcasting apart. The traditional pluriform system provided greater program diversity (using the terminology of the model in Chapter 4) than that provided in other countries. Structure affects output. But the difference was not great enough since the traditional broadcast organizations differed along ideological and religious dimensions, but were similar in that each was controlled by its own hierarchy and responded to its expectations about appropriate programming. When this led to a fairly staid programming cartel, pirate broadcasters found ample room to place themselves at the center and lower parts of the quality spectrum. When the main pirates were legalized and integrated, they exerted competitive pressure on the traditional organizations to move toward the broad center. The contest for that center has been intensified by the satellite-delivered cable channels. But on the higher-quality end, too, Dutch public broadcasters had to contend with the programs of their sister public institutions from neighboring countries. Overall, Dutch viewers have gained in terms of choice, but the traditional broadcasters are under pressure.

11

Belgium

Belgium's complex electronic mass media system must be understood in the context of the tensions between its two language communities and their differing economic and political development. The other significant fact is the near-total penetration of cable television. The average Belgian household can view fifteen to twenty channels, making the country one of the largest multichannel environments outside of North America. The result is a loss of influence by the public broadcasters, for they must contend with many rivals, both private and public. Some of the largest private firms are active in cable television, including the country's major conglomerate, Société Generale de Belgique (SGB). But the large cable audience is not matched by equally strong domestic program production, though this may be changing through the efforts of the country's second largest conglomerate, Groupe Bruxelles Lambert (GBL), a part-owner of Luxembourg's CLT.

History

A government monopoly on wireless telegraphy was enacted in 1908. Upon King Albert's urging, regular transmissions to the Belgian Congo began in 1913, among the earliest in Europe (Clausse, 1941).

Early private broadcasting began in 1923 in the French language region by the private electrical manufacturer SBR and its subsidiary, Radio Bruxelles, soon renamed Radio Belgium (Herman Santy, communication). In 1928, Flemish radio (VNV) was started in Antwerp. In 1931, there were twenty-five private stations several of which represented societal pillars much like in the Netherlands. At that time, a set of laws was passed that created a public and national institution to provide a unifying force for the country and establish ample access rights for the government. This "Institute," INR/NIR, was subject to control by the PTT ministry (Hirsch, 1986, pp. E2–E5).

From the beginning, the institute did not allow advertisements. This became the major bone of contention in Belgian broadcasting well into the 1980s. The institute provided broadcast time to several independent groups (although not with the separation of the Dutch "pillar" system (Lange, 1987) and included Catholic, socialist, and liberal organizations of both language groups (Emery,

1969). About twenty private commercial stations received licenses from the RTT, the telecommunications monopoly administration that was created at the same time as INR/NIR.

During World War II, INR/NIR was taken over by the Germans. The private licenses were cancelled. A radio-in-exile (RNB) operated from the Congo, with offices in London. After the war, INR was resurrected. But it took until 1960 for a new broadcast law to be adopted. The private licenses, however, were not reactivated.

Television broadcasting was inaugurated in 1953, after a long debate along language lines, over which technical standards to adopt, the French 819 lines or the Dutch–German 625. In the end, both standards were chosen. But with the phasing out of France's standard, 625 lines became the norm.

Belgium's language split led in 1959 to a more general restructuring, which established a minister of cultural affairs to take over regulatory functions from the PTT ministry. In 1960, two separate institutions were created to replace INR/NIR. Radio Télévision Belge de la Communauté Française (RTBF) served the French cultural community, whereas Belgische Radio en Televisie (BRT) aimed at the Flemish one. Also established was an institute for common services in administrative, technical, financial, and international affairs, but it was dissolved in 1977. In addition, the small broadcast institution BRF was created in 1977 for the German-language minority (VerLommen, 1980). In 1971, the Belgian constitution was changed and decentralized, and broadcasting became subject to community parliamentary control. Advertising was prohibited, partly to help the ailing press.

The central government's role was to control commercial advertising and to retain some right of access for governmental purposes. In 1979, broadcast licensing laws were modified, and the legalization of the many pirate radio broadcasters was made possible. Television came under the supervision of the two regional governments, advised by the Conseil Supérieur de l'Audiovisuel (CSA).

The Evolution of Broadcasting

The two public broadcasters have long been mired in difficulties. They are pawns as well as instruments in the Belgian-language dispute. Furthermore, their position was severely undercut by cable television, which reaches 80 percent of Belgian homes and makes domestic broadcasting compete with foreign stations. This was particularly true for the French-language RTBF, which had to share its audience with a growing number of imported French stations and with the French-language Luxembourg RTL. For all practical purposes, RTL is a participant in Belgian broadcasting. Its French-language television program was geared toward Belgium; it accepted commercial advertisements aimed at Belgium, which its public rival RTBF could not do under the law; and it is partly owned by the well-connected Belgian giant conglomerate Groupe Bruxelles Lambert. Altogether, Belgian interests hold about 40 percent of RTL's parent company, CLT. RTL can be received over the air in large areas of French-speaking Belgium, and in others it is carried over cable.

Following additional revisions of the broadcast laws in 1977 and 1978, the BRT and RTBF have largely gone their own ways. Each operates two channels. The mixed region of Brussels adds further complexity. The French-speaking region is generally the more deregulated (Lange, 1987). Since 1976, there have been several nonprofit local cable channels, such as Canal Emploi, offered in Liège until 1989, which was aimed at the jobless. In 1985, the Walloons cable operators won the right to carry foreign satellite channels. For radio, liberalization goes back to the 1981 legalization of nonprofit pirates and the 1986 sanctioning of commercial pirates. This policy in the Walloons region is particularly interesting considering that until 1985 its government was to the left of the national and the Flemist governments.

In Flanders, a more regulated environment persisted. Local TV was not permitted, and local radio was slowly liberalized. Advertising by commercial entities is prohibited and commercial satellite channels are banned. Advertising by nonprofit organizations has been permitted since 1983 (François Pichault, 1987, communication).

After 1981, the Belgian government was for a long time a center-right coalition of CVP and PSC conservatives and PVV and PRL liberals. These parties were not especially supportive of the public broadcasters, regarding them as sympathetic to the left. In 1985, the government considered lifting the prohibition against commercial advertising by public stations and allowing the establishment of private broadcast stations. The government also wanted to open cable channels. A cabinet crisis and a parliamentary election put these plans on ice.

There is no legal monopoly for radio or television in Belgium. But there were no frequency allocations to private operators, although, as mentioned, twenty-five independent radio stations operated. Until 1931 several attempts to obtain licenses for new private stations did not succeed (Geerts, 1981). Pirate radio stations eventually emerged a few years later. These pirates included not only commercial entrepreneurs, but also local political activists promoting various causes. In Louvain-La-Neuve, a station went on the air in 1978 with the purpose of mobilizing community action. When the police attempted to close it down, 1500 sympathizers took to the streets to protect it. This situation opened a public debate about the exclusivity of broadcasting, causing the government to appoint a national audiovisual commission to study the possibility of legalizing local radio.

In 1978, the "free" stations Radio Eau Noire, named after a river whose damming was opposed by environmentalists, succeeded in stopping the construction project. Other underground stations followed, and they became collectively known as "handbill radio." Institutionalized and improved, it emerged as the "radio of animation." In time, there were more than one thousand private stations.

The political and commercial pirate stations did not coexist happily and developed into two rival associations. The political groups pressed the government to establish a legal framework for local radio stations. A 1981 Walloons decree legalized community radio and TV stations (Apeldoorn, 1985). The commercial pirates remained constrained, but they often simply continued broadcasting. This antagonized the community stations, which, ironically, now demanded that the government shut down their commerical rivals. A small radio war thus started. The public, on the other hand, looked with favor on the commercial stations. Most stations used advertisements to support themselves. They often combined into national networks, despite legal bans.

In 1984, RTBF, together with French, Canadian, and Swiss public television institutions, joined to create the satellite-delivered French-language channel TV5. In 1987, the Belgian Parliament passed significant legislation permitting TV advertisements by a single station (which could be the public regional station) in each language region, under conditions set by the cultural communities. By continuing to restrict advertising, the government hoped to protect newspapers from undue revenue losses.

The Luxembourg broadcaster RTL, owned by the holding company CLT, seized that opportunity, in agreement with Walloons publishers (Govaert and Lentzen, 1986). Together, they set up RTL-TVi (Télévision Indépendante)—the country's first commercial channel. Luxembourg's CLT held 66 percent and Walloon publishers, united in the group AudioPresse, had 34 percent. In 1986, RTL received a license to extend its Luxembourg transmissions into all of Wallonia. This came with a remarkable nine year monopoly on TV advertising for Wallonia. In return, it promised to support domestic film production. However, it did not subsequently fulfill all these conditions, claiming that advertising revenues were lower than expected. This, in turn, was caused by greater cross-border competition than had been anticipated, primarily from France's newly privatized TF1. Though elsewhere a champion of free transborder broadcasting, CLT now lobbied for protection from TF1's presence in Belgium, claiming it would turn Belgium into a French extension (Matthias, 1989, p. 24). TF1 proved popular with the public, as was the RTFB's second channel Télé 21. In 1989 TF1 had 20 percent of the French-region audience, and Télé 21 had 5 percent. RTL-TVi's audience dropped to 20 percent, it was allegedly losing money and it had to cut back on staff and programming in 1989 (Hirsch, 1990). Furthermore, the public RTFB itself, under its own financial pressures, began to demand the right to advertise. Soon the two rivals, RTL-TVi and RTBF, got together and negotiated a remarkable public-private cartel agreement called the Projet de Protocole d'Accord, under which they divided Walloon TV advertising among themselves. RTBF would be permitted some advertising after a change in the law. (It is noteworthy that a private foreign company could endeavor to make such promises to a domestic public institution.) Under a complex formula, RTL-TVi would get the rest, about four times as much as RTBF. To keep control, all advertising would be channeled through a joint agency, Television Belge. There would also be "coordination" in program acquisition, especially of sports events, and in program policy, whereby RTL-TVi would concentrate on entertainment and RTBF would deal with more serious fare (Hirsch, 1990).

The agreement was justified by the two parties as protecting Belgian culture and uniqueness. It demonstrates that foreign commercial broadcasters too can ride the national culture bandwagon when in need of arguments for protectionism.

The agreement was sharply criticized by the publishing industry, which sensed an opportunity to share in the cartel's profits. Arguing in the press that it would be harmed by the agreement's anticompetitiveness (though the opposite would also be equally plausible), they attacked the pact until they were assured an approved annual percentage of the two stations' advertising revenue in compensation. The weekly press, however, sued before the European Commission, charging anticompetitive practices.

The introduction of commercial television was much slower in Flanders, partly owing to socialist opposition, and it took from 1981, when the intent was announced, to 1989. First, the regional government considered creating a third and commercial Dutch-language television network or splitting the existing two public BRT channels and making them competitive with each other. An important political incentive was to provide an alternative news service to BRT, whose staff was considered by parts of the regional right-of-center government as too much in opposition. The government also wanted to halt the migration of advertising revenues to cable programmers in the Netherlands and Luxembourg.

In 1989, private broadcasting began when VTM went on the air. VTM (Vlaamse Televisie Maatschappij), similar to its Wallonian counterpart RTL-TVi, operates under an exclusive license. It is a consortium of nine of the major Flemish publishers, excluding only a few that participated in a rival bid. Its audience popularity was great with 38 percent of the audience as compared with 23 percent for BRT-1 and 9 percent for TV-2. It earned $87 million in its first year, half of BRT's budget (Nicholson et. al., 1990, p. 19). But like RTL-TVi, it faced competition, in this case from Netherlands-1,2 and 3, and the Dutch RTL-4.

Cable Television

While the political system agonized over the details of terrestrial broadcasting, significant changes were taking place in cable television. Rudimentary wire transmission preceded broadcasting in Belgium by many years. In the late nineteenth century several private firms used the telephone network to broadcast recordings of concerts. In 1901, Giuseppe Verdi won a lawsuit in Brussels for copyright infringement by the "telephone-casting" of portions of his "Rigoletto." This may well have been the world's first cable copyright case (Lange, 1987). Telephone broadcasting did not last, however. Twenty-five years later, radio broadcasting provided a significantly cheaper (and soon higher-quality) alternative.

Radio by cable spread during the 1930s, and regulations were set up in 1930, 1932, and 1934 that included a "must-carry" rule for the state radio system.

The first real cable network began operating in 1960 in Saint-Servais, in the region of Namur. The cities of Namur and Liége soon had cable networks as well; in 1964, Brussels followed. Most of the early facilities were in the French-speaking southern region of the country. In 1966, a royal decree estalished the legal foundation of cable television. In the local elections of 1970, the issue of cable television became important enough that many politicians campaigned with promises of such services. Although early cable companies were private, mixed private–local operations and pure municipal cable operations also sprang up (BFT Studiendienst, 1980). Within Belgium, many of the cable networks belong to subcompanies of the Société Générale de Belgique (SGB), the country's major conglomerate, which took control over one of the largest Walloon telecommunications equipment firms. SGB is also a participant in the huge merger of France's Alcatel and ITT's telecommunications interests.

The growth of cable in Belgium was rapid. In 1973, 11 percent of all households in the region of Flanders were connected to cable. By early 1980, this figure was 66 percent. By 1989, it was 93 percent (Poesmans, 1984, p. 2; Nicholson et al., 1990, p. 19).

Cable was not part of a national high-tech industrial policy aimed at creating an electronics or information industry. Technical standards and rules concerning installation were almost nonexistent, and this has helped the rapid cabling of the country. Cable systems almost invariably feature simple tree-and-branch architecture, and it may be installed above ground. Local operators can choose their technology and are responsible for its use. The role of the national telecommunications monopoly RTT is only to provide the network required for the importation of foreign television programs to the various cable head-ends within the country. Many of the cable networks are run by the electricity and gas utilities, which are therefore able to use their rights of way and utility poles, as well as their distribution and billing systems. Technologically, Belgian cable is not exciting, but is exists and prospers. Belgium has constructed the coaxial "facts on the ground," without much of the ideological or political turnmoil of other countries. This was possible for a variety of reasons, including Belgium's openness toward cultural offerings from its neighbors, a tradition strengthened by the sharp divisions between the two Belgian-language communities, which led to widespread watching of foreign broadcasts in their respective languages.

The local networks are licensed by the RTT, which also regulates maximum tariffs.[1] The carrying of advertisments was originally prohibited but was widely practiced. Enforcement of the prohibition would have required selective blacking out of neighboring countries' advertising spots. In theory, the distribution of commercial television programs over cable was prohibited, but enforcement of the law was lax, although its legality was confirmed in both 1979 by the European Court of Justice and 1980 by a Belgian court decision. Luxembourg's RTL became a major advertising presence in Belgium, well-protected by its public and private financial ties and its audience popularity.

Because the penetration of cable television in Belgium is the highest in the world, it is often viewed as an advanced media country. But this is not altogether correct. Belgium does indeed have a highly developed physical distribution system (although most systems carry only fifteen to twenty channels), but it plays virtually no direct role on the program side. Here British, French, Italian, German, and Luxembourgeois ventures abound, even though these are countries in which cable is much less prevalent.

In program provision the closest to an international role is played indirectly by Group Bruxelles Lambert (GBL), which owns a good-sized part of CLT, which in turn owns the private Luxembourg broadcast organization RTL. GBL is also involved in finance, oil, and media. In the 1980s, GBL became increasingly assertive in the operation of RTL, partly due to the absence of commercial broadcasting and the movie industry in Belgium (Hirsch, 1985). In 1985, GBL joined with Rupert Murdoch in a trans-European joint venture.

Two pay-cable ventures emerged. In Flanders, Filmnet was introduced, which involved Esselte of Sweden. Filmnet, which began operations in 1985, was also active in the Netherlands and in Scandinavia and claimed to be Europe's second-largest pay service. Monthly subscriptions were 145 BF ($23) (Epstein, 1989).

The introduction of pay TV was slower in Wallonia. A 1987 law permitted entry; seven applicants came forward. In the end, the license went in 1988 to Canal Plus Belgique, which brought together France's successful pay TV company of that name and the public broadcaster RTBF. Thus, the public RTBF managed to have a foot in the door of both of the channels that were supposed to compete with it: in the advertising-supported RTL-TVi, through its coordination pact, and in the pay-TV Canal Plus Belgique, through co-ownership.

Though Belgium had assumed the role of a key market for European cable programmers, because of its multilingual population and high penetration rate, controversy over the admission of foreign channels arose. The country lacked rules clarifying which foreign commercial programs delivered by satellite could be carried. The questions of whether and which such programs should be permitted entrance raised sensitive questions about commercial broadcasting in general, and about the balance between the two language communities.

A Belgium cable system was likely to carry four official Belgian channels (two Dutch, two French), two or three public and private programs from the Netherlands, three or four public and private channels from Germany, three to six from France, and RTL-TVi, and VTM. Some cable systems also carried the British BBC 1 and 2, ITV and Channel 4, as well as the Italian RAI, the French-language TV5, the British Sky television and Music Box, and the German SAT-1. Also often carried on cable are local and community television stations.

Cable operators pay a percentage of subscription revenues in exchange for permission to carry foreign programs. This policy came into effect in 1983 after a dispute with the British copyright organization and trade unions, which had demanded compensation for showing British programs over Belgian cable networks. Continental programs had been "imported" for free for years without similar claims. After extensive litigation, an agreement was reached, according to which every Belgian cable subscriber has to pay roughly $6 a year, or 15 percent more than before, to compensate most foreign program suppliers. This has provided incentives for additional foreign programmers to enter the market.

On the other hand, in 1990, the Flemish government allowed free negotiation between foreign commercial channels and cable networks on carriage. Some cable operators had asked program suppliers such as Rupert Murdoch's Sky Television to pay in order to have their channel programs carried. Operators thus assumed the role of gate-keepers, picking and choosing from among various channel providers and charging program providers for transmission. In such a situation, the public broadcasters—at least the non-Belgian ones—are likely to be under pressure. It does not make economic sense for a channel such as the BBC, which is advertisement-free and thus without economic incentives to be carried in Europe (except for the nominal copyright fees), to pay a private Belgian cable system to carry it. Hence, public channels such as the BBC may end up not being provided, unless audiences value them so much that enough would cancel their cable subscription if BBC were omitted. Otherwise, a substitution of private commercial stations for public channels could take place. Regulation of channel coverage and expansion of capacity could slow this process down but not eliminate it. Furthermore, it may be in violation of the EEC Treaty to favor the importation of government channels, most of which carry some advertising, over private ones.

Another unique feature in Belgian media policy is its special levy on foreign program providers. Since 1988, Wallonia required foreign program channels to contribute BFr 10 million, over $250,000, for each 100,000 viewers that are reachable. The money has to go toward Belgian film production, acquisition, or rental. However, investments undertaken in other countries of the European Council may be counted. Flanders adopted a similar though somewhat less restrictive rule. These provisions have been criticized as violating the European Treaty and as discriminating against the United States. Belgium had already been sued in 1987 before the EC by the Sky and Super Channels on a related restriction (Hirsch, 1990). In 1989, the European Commission advised Belgium to refrain from these actions.

Because of the strong move toward decentralization and separate language regions, teletext was started in two distinctly different experiments. In the French-language region, RTBF used the French Antiope system, whereas the Flemish BRT chose the British Ceefax. The Belgian "language war" was thus extended to the establishment of technological standards.

Belgian law prevents cable operators from distributing their own productions, including teletext services. In December 1988, Liéges' ALE-Teledis was forced to suspend a five-week-old public information service, which had been offered free of charge to 216,000 subscribers (*Media Monitor*, 1988).

Conclusion

Belgium is less centralized than most European countries, being deeply divided between its two major language groups. Public television, split into two major institutions, served as an instrument of regional cultural identity rather than of national integration. Given the country's centrifugalism, audiences watched the programs of neighboring countries more than anywhere else in Europe. Cable television emerged to facilitate that option. Once it had spread, the presence of commercial TV could not be excluded. Private over-the-air broadcasting exerted a similar presence. It had always existed de facto through the offerings of the nearby Luxembourg RTL station, in which Belgian interests had a large participation. RTL's success encouraged private and community pirates. Eventually, these broadcasters were legalized. Thus, in a highly confusing fashion, television media were partly liberalized. Restrictions remain, some supported by established private interests, but the overall trend is toward a mixed system of public, community, and private television, both domestic and international.

In this process, Belgian private media are becoming integrated with major national business conglomerate and with publishers. Multistage media firms are beginning to emerge and to form alliances across Europe. Few of these changes were technology-driven or caused by governmental industrial policy. Some changes were influenced by the opening of intra-European barriers; with Brussels the seat of the European community, and with Belgium itself culturally divided, a territorial television policy was increasingly irrelevant, and this is likely to continue into the future.

Thus, the future will likely include a smaller role for Belgian public broadcasters, even relative to those of most other European countries. But at least one of them, RTBF, has been adept in structuring a pragmatic alliance with its primary private rivals, and perhaps more generally foreshadowing future European attempts to create cooperative duopolies that restrict open entry. On the other hand, with Brussels becoming the administrative capital of Europe, high-information services will continue to make Belgium a supranational center, and the media should be no exception.

12

Luxembourg

Luxembourg's broadcast system has always been unusual in the European context as a private rather than public monopoly. It is operated by the entrepreneurial Radio Tèlèvision Luxemburgeois (RTL), itself owned by a parent firm, the Compagnie Luxemburgeois de Tèlèvision (CLT). CLT also controls or participates in broadcasting channels in several other countries: Belgium's RTL-TVi, France's M6 and RTL-Television, West Germany's RTL-Plus and Tele 5, and the Netherland's RTL-4.

Operating since 1924, Radio Luxembourg soon established a popular music program format in several languages and became known as the "station of the stars." Its emergence was strenuously resisted by monopoly broadcasters, especially the BBC, as well as many publishers. It was denied a long-wave frequency, but went on the air anyway (see the discussion on early U.K. broadcasting). With the ascendence of the National Socialists in Germany, Radio Luxembourg became a source of independent news. After the outbreak of World War II, however, the Luxembourg government ordered the station to stop broadcasting; it was soon taken over by the Germans, who used it for their own propaganda. Following the war, advertising income was initially so low that the station almost went bankrupt, and its recovery began with an international bank loan.

RTL's primary role was to broadcast music to audiences across Europe. Its pop-music format was highly popular with younger audiences and has made RTL into Western Euorpe's most listened to radio station. Never specifically geared to the Luxembourg market, RTL's program offering concentrated on nearby countries. "Hei Elei-Kuck Elei", long the only program in the Luxembourg language, was aired on Sunday afternoons. RTL was especially active in reaching Belgium, where broadcast advertising was long prohibited. In Germany, RTL's radio program had the highest rating for many years (Odenwald, 1985). All in all, RTL has been highly profitable for its owners and for the Grand Duchy of Luxembourg which franchises it.

RTL's success did not remain unnoticed, and entrepreneurs in other countries began imitating its breezy format of pop music and advertising. Most of these were pirate radio stations broadcasting from ships offshore without benefit of government licenses or copyright payments. Some of the pirate stations eventually achieved legal status, often in strange-bedfellow alliances with politically oriented community radio groups. Moving from local radio to local television was only a small step. RTL's role as the pathbreaker for commercial broadcasting thus had an impact far beyond its signal's reach.

Despite its private status, RTL is the official and sole Luxembourg radio and, since 1955, television broadcaster. It is a full member of the European Broadcasting Union (EBU) and has access to the European program organization Eurovision and its valuable international feed, which provides, in particular, major sports events.

In terms of organization, RTL is reputed to be unbureaucratic and flexible. In 1987, it employed only approximately 800 people. Its in-house program production and social mandates (such as the requirement to cover local affairs) institutions are, however, much smaller than those of other European broadcasting institutions.

RTL's advertising business is handled exclusively by the French company Information et Publicité (IP). The French government had an 80 percent stake in IP through Havas, which it owned for many years until its privatization by the Chirac government.

CLT is not Luxembourg owned. In a joint-stock ownership arrangement, virtually all its shares are held by French and Belgian interests. However, the concession contracts and the bylaws of the corporation require the majority of administrative board members and employees to be citizens and residents of Luxembourg. The main owner of the firm is the holding company Audiofina, which, directly and indirectly, through the holding company Fratel, controls 56.7 percent of CLT. Audiofina is owned, again directly and indirectly, by the Belgian Groupe Bruxelles Lambert (39 percent) and by Agence Havas (30 percent). Agence Havas was largely owned by the French government. Schlumberger, a firm with close personal and business connections to the Socialist French government, owned 13.4 percent of CLT through the Compagnie des Compteurs but later sold its interest to the French bank Paribas, which held an aggregate of 22.4 percent. (Opitz, 1990, p. D135).

France privatized Havas in 1987 as part of a broader denationalization program. This ended the strong direct control of the French government through its various ownership involvements, of which Havas was only one. The French influence had periodically led to fierce disputes between the French, the Luxembourgeois, and the more genuinely private Belgian shareholders. Directly and indirectly, French and Belgian interests each own about 40 percent of CLT. Luxembourg interests own less than 10 percent, but provide the swing vote for control.

In addition to owning various broadcasting operations, CLT controls the Luxembourg airline Luxair, several financial and insurance companies, advertising agencies, production studios, music publishing companies, and magazines. It is also a partner in a Canadian French-language pay-TV company.

CLT's administrative board included parliamentary leaders of the major parties. The Luxembourg government also appoints special commissioners to assure that CLT operates in the national interest. The government's influence was increased in 1973, when 70 percent of CLT shares became nontransferable without governmental consultation. The government can exercise a veto when the sovereignty and neutrality of CLT are affected (Dyson, 1990).

The French government has frequently tried to tie CLT to its own media policy (Hirsch, 1985) and has exerted its influence on a number of occasions when CLT projects would have been threatening to French media policy. At times, the French government has also tried to affect the content and leanings of the French-language programs of CLT.

CLT's close relations with the Luxembourg government function as a protective shield against France and other countries. Mindful of the need for political backing in Luxembourg, CLT appointed former Prime Minister Pierre Werner as president and chairman of the administrative board after 1985. At the same time, CLT appointed another former Luxembourg prime minister, Gaston Thorn, as vice chairman and general director with an assured right to succeed after Werner's retirement. Before being appointed to the CLT board, Thorn had been president of the European Commission in Brussels until 1985. Politically, this was a well-balanced ticket, with Thorn, a former leader of the liberal opposition party DP, and Werner, a former leader of the ruling Christian Socialist Party CSV.

CLT's television involvements take several forms. For Luxembourg, Belgium, and eastern France, it broadcasts RTL-Tèlèvision Luxembourg. For Germany it transmits RTL-Plus via satellite to most cable households. RTL-Plus, whose operations are mostly in Germany, also broadcasts terrestrially in other parts of Germany and has a transponder on the German DBS satellite TV-Sat. With its rival Sat-1, RTL-Plus also acquired a 25 percent interest in a German satellite channel Tele 5 from the Italian Silvio Berlusconi, who was left with 21 percent as a partner.

RTL-Plus is a venture of CLT (46 percent), the German publishing giant Bertelsmann/Ufa (39 percent), the major publishers WAZ (10 percent), FAZ (1 percent) and Burda (2 percent) (Schmidt, 1985). Bertelsmann became embattled with the other German publishing interests that were jointly negotiating to set up the unwieldy German publisher's satellite channel, SAT-1, and was forced to leave that venture. Thus, the major German publishing houses split into two camps: SAT-1 encompassed the huge firms Springer, Bauer, and Holtzbrinck, among others, whereas RTL-Plus involved Bertelsmann, the largest of them all, Burda, FAZ, and WAZ.

In 1985, RTL-Plus began satellite distribution into central Europe. Former German Chancellor Helmut Schmidt, no friend of television, had dreaded such an event as "more acute and dangerous than nuclear energy" (Odenwald, 1985). To undercut opposition, Bertelsmann picked Schmidt's protégé and head of his chancellory, and later his finance minister, Manfred Lahnstein, as its top man for new media issues.

In France, CLT had a 25 percent share in a joint venture M6, the sixth French terrestrial channel, covering two-thirds of the country. It received the license in 1987 after a conservative government came to power. Its control over M6 is larger then its ownership share, because CLT's French shareholders hold additionally more than 20 percent of M6. Of CLT's other French media ventures, most notable were its ceaseless efforts in gaining a franchise for access to the transponders of the French DBS satellite TDF-1. This is discussed in the chapters on French broadcasting and on DBS.

In Belgium, CLT's main broadcast entry is RTL-TVi (for *TV indépendante*), a joint advertising-supported venture in which it holds one-third and Belgian publishers two-thirds interests.

In the Netherlands, RTL has operated since 1989 as the first Dutch commercial cable channel (and possible future terrestrial channel, Netherland 4), under the name RTL-Véronique, later RTL-4, with Philips and the publishing interests Elsevier and VNU.

Cable television systems in Luxembourg are substantially unregulated. They are operated by private companies, municipalities, and local organizations. Most systems feature several public and commercial French, German, and Luxembourgeois channels. In 1990, penetration of households was estimated to be above 80 percent.

Another major Luxembourg broadcast effort, and the only one outside RTL/CLT, is the Société Européenne des Satellites (SES), which launched the Astra 1A satellite in 1988. Astra beams sixteen signals over Western Europe on a quasi-"common-carrier" basis. The SES venture was begun by the American-initiated GDL-Coronet. (For details see Chapters 7 and 28.)

Luxembourg's broadcast system has always been an anomaly in Europe, an American-style entertainment-oriented commercial station with very little public-interest content, aiming squarely for the broad center of audience taste. Yet it had several major advantages that most commercial broadcasters lack: a domestic monopoly; full international backing by the national government, which was a partner in its monopoly rent; and scarcity status within Europe, where it functioned as a rare commercial station. These enormous privileges required continued political protection by the Luxembourg government, which was a major beneficiary of its profitability. At the same time, the station's significance was such that the French government obtained substantial influence, and at times control, and interfered in the station's policies.

The high political stakes were based on RTL's uniqueness, which, in turn, depended on the restrictive broadcast regimes in the surrounding countries. But once these restrictions began to unravel, often pushed by pirates who were inspired by RTL's audience success, the Luxembourg station had to face competition for its core audience. Liberalization, however, also provided its parent CLT with fields of expansion. Moving in that direction, and based on Luxembourg's political backing and its own commercial track record, it began establishing itself as a prime model for future European commercial broadcasters: integrated horizontally with other media firms across Europe (in particular with Bertelsmann, Havas, and Benek publishers); integrated vertically across distribution and production modes; politically well connected; international in ownership; supranational in programming; with only modest service to its home turf's population; and ceaseless in its search for new opportunities.

And what of Luxembourg itself? To some extent the country benefits financially from its media star performer. But in terms of program provision, the country's need for programs of higher quality has largely been serviced by spill-ins from neighboring countries' public broadcasters. Unplanned by government, cable television has contributed to an opening of Luxembourg's commercial channels, and thus undercut RTL's domestic monopoly. In the future, though constrained by European harmonization, Luxembourg will have to decide whether it wishes to be more open to other stations—even becoming a broadcast "haven" similar to its role in other international services such as banking—or whether it sees itself as the home turf of a privileged national champion firm.

13

Switzerland

Broadcasting

After more than half a century of well-protected stability, Switzerland's broadcast monopoly was cautiously opened in the 1980s, and it is likely to erode further. Radio goes back to 1922 and amateur radio clubs that evolved into cooperatives and eventually into companies such as the "Utilitas" organization. By 1926, every private station was operated in five major cities by associations (Saxer, 1986). Newspaper publishers, alarmed by the potential competition, succeeded in imposing restrictions on radio news. In 1931, after several years in which the Swiss confederate tradition contended with the need for centralized frequency regulation, the Swiss Broadcasting Company (SBC, in German, SRG, and in French, SSR), was created as an umbrella organization for the regional companies, whose number eventually grew to nine. It is subject to regulation by the Ministry of Transport and Energy. The major broadcast transmitter in Beromunster was inaugurated in 1931. During World War II, the SBC license was suspended in favor of a government operation that took pains to assure Swiss broadcast neutrality. FM transmission began in 1952. Television went on the air experimentally in 1953 and permanently in 1958, with full coverage of second programs for each language by 1966. In 1967, color television was introduced. Actual transmission was undertaken by the PTT telecommunications administration.

Public broadcasting in Switzerland is private in strictly nominal terms. The federal government appoints the chairman and ten of the twenty-one member board of the SBC. There has been substantial questioning of the board's ability to supervise the organization. The SBC is a nonprofit association financed through a licensing fee that is collected by the PTT; the SBC receives 77 percent of these revenues; its 1990 budget was SFr 800 million. Since 1952, the SBC had monopoly status for both television and radio broadcasts. Before that time, the PTT could supply radio programs over its own wire lines as cable radio. The structure of the SBC is highly confederate, although the government has some influence over frequency assignments and technical facilities through the PTT. The SBC has three regional subcompanies, one for each of the three major language areas. CORSI broadcasts to the Italian-language population. The German-language company, RDRS, has six constituent companies of its own. Similarly, STRS, the French-language company, operates with two suborganizations. The operations of the regional companies include radio and television channels for each language group and an international shortwave program. The three television channels of these organizations are DRS (German), TSR (French), and TSI (Italian). SBC also supports programming in Romansh, a language spoken by about 1 percent of the population. Each regional company is run by membership associations, which elect a majority of the governing boards. There have traditionally been tensions between the regional companies and the SBC.

The SBC's programs must, according to its concession, "uphold and de- velop the cultural values of the country and contribute to the spiritual, moral, religious, civic, and artistic development" of listeners and viewers. They "must serve the interest of the country, reinforce national union and solidarity, and aid international understanding." The SBC tends to fulfill these mandates, but they do not necessarily make for interesting programs. In 1985, culture and religion received 19.6 percent of air time; news and information, 25.8 percent; film and drama, 19.6 percent; light entertainment, 8.1 percent; and sports, 16.1 percent (Jaques, 1987).

Legally, the Swiss Constitution provides, in its Article 36, that all post and telegraph issues fall under the jurisdiction of the Swiss confederation. It has been disputed, however, whether this provides full rights of control over program provision or applies only to transmission. Hence, the Swiss government has sought repeatedly to obtain more secure legal powers to control the program aspect of broadcasting. But in two referenda, in 1957 and 1976, the Swiss population voted against the government's proposals. This is remarkable in light of the broad political base of the long-standing Swiss government coalition (Noam, 1980). In 1981, because of various applications for local radio licenses and the emergence of satellite television and other new media, the government once again sought approval of a constitutional article that would establish its broadcast jurisdiction. This was accepted in 1984 by the Swiss electorate and adopted in the Federal Constitution in Article 55 *bis;* but by 1990 the legislation had still not been implemented.

Because of the absence of clear jurisdiction, federal regulations have largely been based on decrees and concessions. The two major legal structures of Swiss electronic media are the SBC Concession of 1964 and the Cablecasting Decree of 1977, as amended in 1982 to permit local broadcasting.

Much of Switzerland is in the broadcast range of some of its four neighbors. As their over-the-air television choice becomes more varied, so did that of Switzerland. Because the large neighboring countries' major channels are wealthier in resources than the Swiss ones, they pose the danger of relegating SBC to a regional channel. Swiss viewers also face a special problem in that they are caught in the no-man's-land of the rival color-TV standards PAL (the standard in Germany, Austria, and Italy) and SECAM (the standard in France). Switzerland has adopted PAL, but its French-language viewers, in particular, also yearn for French color programs. As a result, many color television sets can receive both standards. This makes the sets relatively expensive, but also helps protect the market against Asian imports.

For years, segments of the Swiss public and several of the political parties have called for alternatives to the SRG's broadcast monopoly. But they have faced a wide range of resistance. The opposition to commercial media spanned the political spectrum from the Social Democrats on the left, via the centrist press, to the traditional Christian Democratic People's Party (CVP). The head of the SBC in the mid-1980s, Leo Schurmann, was also an important CVP figure. He viewed the SBC as an essentially traditional organization (Frisch-knecht, 1981).

About 75 percent of broadcasting revenues comes from the annual tax on TV sets. The remainder is provided by advertising. Broadcast advertising was prohibited until 1965, largely due to the pressure of the newspaper publishers. The ban was lifted in order to finance color television. Many restrictions exist, such as on ads for tobacco, alcohol, drugs, banks, job listings, real estate, and used cars and classified advertisements. Even advertisements for most soap detergents are prohibited, allegedly for environmental reasons. There is little advertising time, limited to 2.2 percent of airtime (twenty-eight minutes per day), and rates are among the highest in Europe (*EBU Review,* 1989, p. 14). Sales are channeled through a special organization in which publishing interests hold almost 50 percent.

This restrictiveness is not surprising. A central feature of Swiss media is the cartelization of its advertising. Most Swiss newspapers cede all or much of their advertising space to an agency, which fills it (ECCMC, 1982). Four news-paper and magazine advertising agencies together control advertising access to most print media. Among these agencies, the firm Publicitas and its affiliates hold the predominant position, controlling the access to about two-thirds of advertisements in publications that appear more than once weekly. Publicitas, ASA, and a handful of smaller agencies are linked in an association formed in 1919 to "maintain the interest of the profession and the reputation of the sec-tor, as well as the maintenance of healthy business practices" (ECCMC, 1982, p. 124). Together they have kept advertising rates high, to their own benefit and that of the publisher given the inelasticity of demand. With such an indus-try structure, it is not surprising that opposition to advertising-supported com-mercial television was strong and well-organized within the traditional private media sector, too.

Challenges to the SBC from commercial media coincided with its financial crunch, similar to that experienced by other European public broadcast institu-tions, but exacerbated by the need to serve three and even four sets of radio and TV programs to the different language groups. The SBC managed to get its finances under control, although this required greater centralization (Alter, 1985). It also modified its programs to be more popular, sought cooperation with private publishers in teletext and pay TV, and joined several satellite proj-ects. These projects included ventures such as 3–SAT with the German ZDF and the Austrian ORF, 1–Plus with Germany's ARD, and TV-5 with French and Canadian public broadcasters. It also positioned itself as a general program provider for new private local radio stations and planned the same role for private regional television.

The SBC's monopoly ended in 1983, when private local radio was legalized after much public pressure. About forty stations were approved; many were organized as associations similar to the SBC, which was a compliment of sorts; but few were commercially successful during the initial phase (Haldimann, 1984). Because the 1982 regulations provided for a maximum of 10 kilometers of broadcast radius, broadcasters faced a restricted audience. Subsequently, advertising time was increased. These regulations were a compromise between the original government proposal and the views of opponents of commercialism. Three of the new local radio stations, the commercial stations Radio Z and Radio 24 and the noncommercial Radio LOR, were licensed in Zurich. Radio LOR is supported by a 3000-member radio club, volunteer workers, and donations. Radio 24 started out as an Italian station beaming into Switzerland and was almost the top station in its listening are in terms of audience (SRG Medienstudie, 1986).

Local private television licenses were granted experimentally after 1985. Broadcasting began in March 1986 when TV Verein Basel Regionalfernsehen (TV-VBR) was founded to produce programming for the city of Basel, which had no cable TV.

A national advertiser-supported independent television channel was proposed in 1990 to be considered in the 1922 Swiss Media Law.

Cable Television

Swiss private cable television is a pragmatic affair. It is locally controlled, modest in its ambitions, and technologically adequate. Nonetheless, 70 percent of Swiss households were passed by cable in 1989, and this was accomplished without the public fanfare and controversy that accompanied cable policy in neighboring countries. A wide diversity of organizational forms exist: many systems are owned and operated by municipalities, and others are cooperatives. Most important systems, however, are private. A typical network provides about a dozen television channels and up to eighteen stereo radio channels. In Zurich, where cable penetration exceeds 90 percent, some areas can receive twenty program channels. Older systems offer less variety, but newer ones have been developed that have a capacity of twenty-four television channels. The Swiss PTT leases duct space, where necessary, and approves the technical standards. Local communities grant operating permits and can, in theory, even grant multiple franchises. Franchise agreements require universal service and include some local voice in rates and program changes (Hoepli, 1984).

The advent of private wire radio service in the 1930s greatly facilitated the later introduction of cable television. The mountainous Swiss terrain often required the provision of radio by wire. In addition, in those days of economic crisis, cable wire manufacturers were interested in developing new uses for their products. In 1931, the first concession for wire radio was given to the Rediffusion company, which has subsequently become the largest Swiss cable television operator. (It is not related to the British cable firm of the same name.) By 1980, Rediffusion had about 300,000 subscribers in five major regions. The majority of these subscribers were in Zurich. Another factor in the development of cable television was the multilingual character of Switzerland. It was desirable for all three language programs to be attainable anywhere in Switzerland, but this often proved to be impossible with over-the-air broadcasts. In addition, cable television made it possible to carry various programs from the neighboring countries with which the three major language groups have close cultural affinities.

However, there were restrictions on the programming side. TV advertising was limited to SRG, which slowed the introduction of commercial media, or at least their ability to finance themselves through advertising.

In 1978, the Swiss government appointed a commission to study the Swiss media environment. The commission, chaired by Dr. Hans W. Kopp, included some of the best-known Swiss experts in communications and media. A report, issued in 1982, recommended broader experimentation with cable systems and proposed temporary advertising (ECCMC, 1982). Eventually, the government in 1983 approved pay television. Two companies, Pay Sat and Telecine Romandie (TCR), were formed. Pay Sat aimed at the German-speaking regions and brought together Rediffusion (40 percent), the SBC (15 percent), the Kirch Group's Beta-Taurus (a dominant German film distributor), and other interests. In an organizational setup that exhibited the characteristic complexity of European commercial media ventures, Pay Sat functioned as the operating company, Teleclub (owned 60 percent by Rediffusion and 40 percent by Kirch) supplied programming, and Eutelsat provided the transponder. (Teleclub had offered local pay television on the Rediffusion cable network in Zurich since 1982.) Pay television in the French-speaking part of Switzerland started with some financial difficulties in 1985 under the name of Telecine Romandie.

Furthermore, several advertiser-supported channels began to be carried over cable, including Sky and Super Channels from Britain, the German Sat-1 and RTL-Plus, and the French TV5 and La Sept.

The first Swiss-based advertiser-supported satellite channels is the European Business Channel. EBC began broadcasting in 1988. It was funded by a consortium of Swiss banks and others, including Thames TV, Blackbox, the Luxembourg CLT, Swiss publisher Jean Frey, and industrialist Leo Tischer. EBC's telecasts were produced in both English and German. Both EBC and Teleclub were permitted in 1989 to carry advertising, but EBC folded in 1990 for lack of revenues.

In addition to the established cable and pay television broadcasts, there were also plans for a Swiss DBS satellite, Helvesat. Helvesat was a joint venture of the Swiss PTT, the SBC, the newspaper publishing associations, chambers of commerce, national industry associations, and the Swiss Federal Transportation, Communications, and Energy Department.

Another example of restrictiveness against new media options were the PTT-imposed charges for using satellite antennas, which were a draconian $760 per year; in consequence, hardly any private antennas existed, at least legally. In 1987, the PTT Ministry reduced the fees to a more reasonable $64 per year.

Conclusion

The Swiss broadcasting system reflects the decentralization of the country and the coexistence of its three major language groups. The public institution has operated reasonably well and is supplemented by widely available channels from neighboring countries. The legal foundations for this system have never been completely resolved and provide uncertainty as the government struggles to define its role while the target is moving. Cable television exists widely due to the mountainous topography and desire to receive neighboring countries' programs. Foreign media entrepreneurs have seen Switzerland as a springboard to the rest of Europe, and domestic firms have become interested in local and regional broadcasting. Swiss viewers have also benefited from their neighbors' liberalization. Yet both the political right and left have been reluctant to support change, and the liberal center has not made it a priority. As in other countries, the print publishers and advertising agencies (the latter more heavily centralized in Switzerland than anywhere else in Europe) were for a time part of the opposition to television liberalization. But, eventually, parts of the press acquired new media interests.

As these changes take place, they add to the traditionally very limited, decent but not especially exciting, and politically extremely cautious fare of Swiss public television. In the process, Switzerland, historically an exporter of information-intensive products and services, may strengthen its presently weak international position in program production and channel packaging. But for a long time to come, the twin Swiss traditions of internationalism and localism will continue to be at tension with each other when it comes to television.

14

Austria

Broadcasting

Austria, among several other countries, claims to be the site of the world's first radio transmission, an experimental broadcast that took place in Graz in 1904 (Signitzer and Luger, 1984). In 1924, radio broadcasting was begun by the concessionary monopoly Radio-Verkehrs Aktien Gesellschaft (RAVAG), a collaboration between government and private industry that joined the Ministry of Commerce and Transportation with banks, advertising companies, and radio set manufacturers (Fabris et al., 1982). Though intended to be nonpartisan, RAVAG became an instrument of the government in its disputes with the left and extreme right during the first Austrian Republic. It was opposed by an active workers radio listeners movement, which promoted greater freedom of radio. RAVAG supported the government in its 1934 suppression of the Social Democrats, a lesson not forgotten. When Austria was absorbed by Germany in 1938, RAVAG was acquired by the German state broadcasting system RRG and the German Reichspost. The resulting Reichssender Wien was reduced to providing music and regional programs. After 1945, the Allies exerted considerable influence over the further development of radio. The most influential concept promoted during the Occupation was the BBC's model for a publicly chartered broadcasting organization.

In 1955, the Allied stations were transferred to the new Austrian broadcasting service operating under governmental control. RAVAG was not reconstructed. Two years later, a more independent structure was established through the Austrian Broadcasting Company, which also began television broadcasting that year. In the following years, there was much public dissatisfaction with radio and television, largely due to the extreme partisanship imposed on broadcasting by the great coalition of the Conservative People's party and the Socialist party. The two were divided by the fear of the other's control, but unlimited in seeking prestigious jobs for their supporters. Following a great deal of negative publicity stirred up by the daily and weekly press, which saw the broadcast media as infringing on their audience and advertising, 832,000 people signed a petition demanding the liberation of broadcasting from the two major parties and the establishment of journalistic professionalism. The first plebiscite of postwar Austria took place in 1964 on that issue. Accordingly, broadcasting was restructured in 1966 with the provision for three radio and two television channels. The broadcast institution was renamed Österrei-chischer Rundfunk (ORF), and significant program and management powers were given to the Director General, the *Generalindendant*.

In 1974, the then Socialist government implemented a second broadcast reform. Two laws, declaring independent broadcasting to be a public right, transformed ORF into a public corporation with monopoly status. They also attempted unsuccessfully to weaken the role of the Generalindendant, Gerd Bacher, who was not a Social Democrat.

In 1984, a third broadcast reform reorganized ORF again, creating several functional directors general to supervise specific television functions such as programming and information. The reform was designed to improve coordination between the two television channels and to prevent incipient competition between them by centralizing programming.

The ORF's governing board consists of thirty-five representatives of the lower house of Parliament (6), provincial governments (9), the federal governments (9), subscriber associations (6), and employees (5). Listeners and audiences are also represented on another board, which has no direct power. A special commission in the federal chancellor's office, comprised mainly of judges, determines whether violations of the broadcast law have occurred.

ORF is a multimedia institution. It has more than 3000 regular employees, including a full-fledged symphony orchestra, and 10,000 part-timers and accounts for 46 percent of the entire advertising revenue of the country (ORF, communication, 1990). It provides teletext service (Nidetzky, 1981) and is a partner with the German ZDF and the Swiss SRG in the joint satellite channel 3-SAT. It operates some 1400 transmitters because of the mountainous character of the country. About half of its budget is financed from subscriber fees, and 40 percent comes from advertising.

With a minor exception, ORF is the only domestic broadcaster in Austria. In each of the nine federal regions, a local radio program (Ö2) broadcasts nine hours a day. Each of the relatively independent regional studios provides its own transmission. There are two major national radio channels, one oriented toward cultural programs (Ö1), the other toward entertainment (Ö3). Radio Austria, a radio-telephone outfit, which originated in 1922 as a Marconi private company, has been owned by the government since 1955. It is not a broadcaster. The "Blue Danube" station (Ö3 International), which dates back to the U.S. forces after the war, broadcasts in English and French, serving primarily the personnel of the international organizations in Vienna but becoming a nationwide station in the process.

The three German channels are accessible to about a quarter of the population. Several private Italian stations are specifically aimed at an Austrian audience. The advertising rates of these Italian stations are substantially lower than those charged by the ORF. In 1989, the private Austrian Pannonia Media Corporation set up radio transmission from within Hungary, then still Communist-governed, but within reach of half of the Austrian audience.

An unusually large percentage of ORF television programs (54 percent in

1990) is produced in Austria (Wolf, 1985). Most of these programs are produced in-house rather than by independent producers. In 1989, ORF came to the aid of the Austrian film industry by supporting a fund for the advancement of film.

Discussion about commercial television in Austria dates back to 1972, when Chancellor Bruno Kreisky proposed an additional channel to be cooperatively operated by the Austrian publishers. Despite support from the chancellor, the journalists' unions, and eventually the opposition ÖVP, the plan collapsed because the publishers feared that the economics of the planned enterprise were inadequate.

In 1985, ORF and the publishers reached an agreement that restricted advertising competition between the two media. The agreement, which was sponsored by the federal chancellor and the Socialist party as a way to strengthen ORF, gave the latter more advertising time; in return it prohibited another FM radio channel and advertising on any future regional television channels. The agreement profited newspaper publishers while strengthening the revenues of the ORF and its broadcast exclusivity.

Nevertheless, several of the largest of the publishers did not stop eyeing commercial television. The *Neue Kronenzeitung,* a newspaper read by an extraordinary 42 percent of all adult Austrians, explored the prospects and became involved in an Italian station that broadcast in German (Luger, 1983). The large Kurier publishing group also became active. To preempt these efforts, ORF proposed a third television channel in eventual collaboration with newspaper publishers, describing this channel as a new step toward regional and local coverage. The proposed channel would not, however, be allowed to impinge upon ORF's advertising monopoly.

ORF's continuing resistance to incursions upon its monopolistic status began to draw criticism. In 1986, the government indicated its intention to loosen the monopoly and to consider private local radio. This led to a 1989 agreement between ORF and the publishers' association to begin regional pilot projects under the ORF umbrella. Such collaborative arrangements would begin to replace the public monopoly with a shared monopoly of ORF and the publishers. The two signatories desired legislation to ratify their agreement, but the exclusion of all but established publishers appeared to make its constitutionality suspect. These maneuvers led to public criticism (Fabris et al., 1990).

But when, in 1989, the liberal opposition party, FPÖ, called a referendum on broadcast liberalization, public response was minuscule. Only 120,000 people (from a population of over 7.5 million eligible voters) showed up to vote for greater viewing choice (TBI, 1990, p. 24), despite polls suggesting that the majority of Austrians would welcome the opportunity to subject ORF to competition (Ahrens, 1989, p. 26). The electoral threat gone, ORF proposed two further collaborative models with the publishers: The first, nicknamed "Radio-Print," would provide technical assistance to newspaper publishers involved in commercial radio; and this would be in exchange for a pledge not to introduce commercial TV for five years. The second suggestion involved launching a partly commercial third ORF channel (FS3) in which private interests would hold 49 percent. After the 1990 election, the government announced its willingness to permit private regional radio based on local publishers.

Cable Television

Given Austria's mountainous topography and desire to receive programs from neighboring countries, cable television spread at a steady pace. Like several other small European countries, Austria was cabled in the absence of an official policy. In 1979, Chancellor Kreisky appointed a commission to examine cable television legislation, but it never even met. The successor government similarly failed to establish a direction. This situation resulted partly from ORF's aggressive defense of its monopoly and its skillful and preemptive use of technology (Fabris et al., 1986).

Since 1977, the provision of cable television has been considered a "free economic activity," requiring no licensing, only a permit by the telephone administration, PTV. In 1989, about 40 percent of the 2.5 million television households were provided with cable television by the 200 cable companies operating in Austria with varying degrees of private, local, and electric utility involvement. (About half of these are MATV systems.) The Vienna Telekabel, 95 percent owned by the Dutch electronics giant Philips, was one of Europe's largest networks and accounted for almost half of Austria's subscribers. The PTV could not construct its own cable networks because it experienced capacity and financing problems while expanding telephone service in the late 1970s (Bauer and Latzer, 1987). Cable program rules are fairly restrictive. The broadcasting law of 1974 allowed the cable systems to provide service to the two public Austrian ORF channels and foreign channels over the air or by satellite but barred them from introducing new Austrian channels (Wolf, 1984). The law was designed to limit advertising that was aimed at Austrians and thus to protect the Austrian publishers and the ORF. The law stipulated that foreign programs be carried simultaneously and unchanged. As a result, Austrian cable television viewers began to receive programs from a number of foreign countries but were severely limited in getting additional Austrian programs beyond what the two state-run channels offered (Haas, 1989).

Foreign cable programs were first offered in 1984 with the introduction of the Sky Channel and later RTL-Plus and the noncommercial 3-SAT. The preferential treatment given to foreign program providers was insupportable in the long run.

One special problem of Austrian cable television policy is its copyright law, which established a compulsory license for foreign programs, with rates set by mediation if necessary. A mediation board soon established copyright contributions to a general fund at extremely low rates. Foreign copyright holders protested that this was expropriation, and even the Generalintendant of the ORF concurred, referring to this law assisting his program competitors as a "scandal, cold expropriation . . ." (Wolf, 1984).

In 1985, the government presented a draft of a media television bill that allowed the carrying by cable of programs from the public broadcast authorities of adjacent states and from foreign private satellite programs, and still stipulated simultaneous and unaltered distribution in Austria (i.e., without Austrian advertising). Government licensing is required for these channels. Pay TV is permissible, but only without advertising.

Conclusion

Austria's public broadcast system, ORF, has been remarkably resilient and politically well connected in preventing or preempting potential entry. Exercising an extraordinarily powerful presence in a culturally active country, it has provided qualitatively good but limited television. Nevertheless, ORF has not been able to prevent a gradual opening centered around the evolution of cable television. This development was based less on policy initiations and more on the mountainous character of the country and the desire to receive German and Swiss stations.

ORF has also been effective in reaching accommodations with the powerful print publishing industry. This alliance of two interest groups has been effective in slowing down the evolution of the media environment, but it will not be able to stop it. With cable distribution increasingly available and foreign commercial channels available, the emergence of their Austrian counterparts seem inevitable. The days of exclusivity for one of Europe's last broadcast monopolists therefore seem numbered, though the transition phase may be controlled by a duopoly of the public broadcaster and the publishing industry.

Broadcasting in
Scandinavia and the
North Atlantic Countries

15

Sweden

Through much of the broadcast era Sweden has been run by a state apparatus aiming at bettering society. Broadcasting has been an important element in this effort. The semi-independent state monopoly, Sveriges Radio, exerted a strong hold over broadcasting, though somewhat softened by a pluralistic ownership model. This structure has resulted in high quality but limited diversity. The monopoly caused growing dissatisfaction and led to an opening to local radio broadcasting during the brief tenure of an opposition-dominated government. Likewise, the introduction of cable television destabilized the monopoly by introducing foreign and then Swedish satellite-delivered channels and by bringing in other economic interests, including the telephone administration, Televerket.

History

Experimental radio broadcasting began in Sweden in 1923. By 1924, broadcasting was structured so that technical transmission services were in the hands of the telephone monopoly, while programming was developed by the newly formed AB Radiotjanst. AB Radiotjanst was a nonprofit company, in which the Swedish News Agency (a publishers organization) and the press held two-thirds interest and the Swedish radio set industry held the remainder. From the beginning, it derived its revenues from government-imposed license fees on radio sets. Advertising was prohibited. Transmission was through the telephone administration. The government was represented on the company's board of governors and set guidelines for its activities and objectives. Radiotjanst was required to broadcast only news provided by the Swedish News Agency, and the two companies were led by the same managing director for many years. The strong control of the newspaper publishers is not surprising, given their political influence and integration with the important paper mill industry. The publishers' economic interest was in restricting the potential broadcast rival, and they maintained this position for a very long time.

In 1927, the government attempted to expand its authority through a short-lived state program council. A parliamentary inquiry commission recommended nationalization in 1933, but the government opted instead to increase its representation on Radiotjanst's board. In 1943, a parliamentary proposal for a second radio channel was dropped in favor of expanding the distribution network. Subsequent proposals in the early 1950s culminated in the adoption of a second radio channel in 1955 (Ploman, 1976).

Thus, the richest nation of Europe—a country with long winters, a dispersed rural population, and comparatively few neighboring states' radio programs within listening-range—permitted itself only one radio channel during an entire generation. Only later, under the pressure from pirate stations, did Swedish broadcasting add a popular music channel in 1962 and one for light music in 1964.

The introduction of television in Sweden proceeded at a similarly stately and controlled pace; experimental transmission began in 1948. By 1950, the electronics industry recognized the manufacture and sale of television sets as a potential boon. But Radiotjanst was not particularly interested, and the government turned to a committee for a long-term study. In 1954, a Swedish film producer generated significant public interest in television when he was permitted to broadcast advertising-supported programs for one week. In the same year, a parliamentary commission finally recommended the introduction of television, but without advertising. Legislation followed in 1957 and 1958 (Gustafsson, 1982). Despite the many years it had dedicated to studying the issues, the government relied in the end on essentially the same organizational structure for television as it had used for radio. Radiotjanst again served as broadcaster, under the new name Sveriges Radio AB. Sixty percent of its shares were reallocated to "popular movements," spanning an array of economic and ideological interests.

In the early 1960s, fifty Swedish companies formed the consortium Telepromotion to advance the establishment of an advertiser-supported second channel. Although they were not successful, the initiative resulted in 1969 in the creation of a second public channel, also part of Sveriges Radio AB. The two channels have considerable internal autonomy in finances, management, and programming, and a limited rivalry. Allocations for broadcast time were agreed upon for certain major program categories. In addition, they had, at least for a time, a common news-gathering department and sports desk. Rival bidding was eliminated through coordinated purchasing of films and contracts with artists.

In 1978, under a brief non-socialist democrat period of government, Sveriges Radio AB was reorganized by a new and non-Socialist government, the first in forty years, into several program companies: one for the three national radio channels, one for the two television channels, and one each for local radio and educational radio and television (Hedebro, 1983). Though each was still under the umbrella of Sveriges Radio, the government was directed to reach agreements (the basic guidelines) with the various companies rather than with the parent organization, as had been the case in the past. Any cooperation between the subsidiaries was based on agreements among themselves. The parent was primarily responsible for long-term planning of broadcasting as a whole, as well as for distribution of funds and general guidelines. It also provided some overhead services, technical television services, and centralized research and development facilities.

This complicated institutional setup, in which five separate but interrelated entities collaborated with each other, was a result of pressure in the late 1960s and early 1970s for the decentralization of Swedish broadcasting. The goal was to separate issues of economic management from program scheduling and production. At the same time there was another, contradictory goal of reducing excessive management overhead. The 1978 reorganization provided a limited rivalry between the two television channels, but it also resulted in further administrative duplication.

Legally, Sveriges Radio AB is a private company, of whose shares 20 percent are held by the Swedish press (which initially controlled the broadcasting monopoly), 20 percent by other private trade and business organizations, and 60 percent by so-called popular movements (Soderstrom, 1981). The last group includes labor unions, consumer groups, farmers' associations, adult education bodies, churches, and even temperance groups. The government participates indirectly in the running of Sveriges Radio through supportive organizations and more directly through its appointees to the governing board. Social Democrats, who traditionally dominate the government, exercise indirect influence on Sveriges Radio through the labor unions' representatives. Of the fifteen members on the board of governors, seven plus the chair are government appointees, though opposition members must be included. Additional political influence can be exerted through the budgetary process and the setting of the viewer's license fee. This is not to suggest that Sveriges Radio is a mouthpiece for the government; it has a tradition of significant autonomy. But neither is its governance fully independent from the government and its supporting groups.

The framework of Swedish broadcasting is established in the Swedish Radio Act, a document of commendable brevity (five typewritten pages). A second fundamental document, the agreement between the government and Sveriges Radio, is a mere two and one half typewritten pages. Similar agreements exist between the program companies and the government (twenty-three paragraphs). These agreements list relatively general programming principles such as accessibility and diversity and establish several obligations, including those to "stimulate debate on important social and cultural issues" and to "scrutinize authorities, organizations and private enterprises that exert influence over decisions that concern the citizenry and to monitor activities in these and other organizations" (Sec. 11, Radio Agreements). The broadcast companies are required to "promote the basic principles of democratic government, the principles of the equality of man and the liberty and dignity of the individual" (Sec. 6, Radio Act).

Legal protection for the press and for free expression in Sweden goes far back. The articles of the 1766 Press Law subsequently became part of the Swedish Constitution and are included in the Radio Responsibility Act. There is also a strong freedom of information provision in the Constitution as well as traditional protection of privacy. Section 8 of the Radio Act prohibits government censorship of programs. An appointed independent Radio Council supervises broadcasting and evaluates complaints against programs that have been broadcast. If the Radio Council finds a violation of the Swedish Radio Act, it can, in theory, recommend that the government withdraw Sveriges Radio's transmitting license. Libel provisions are also applicable to broadcasting; each program has a "program supervisor" who is held solely responsible for defamatory content.

A strong proponent of broadcast independence was Olof Palme, minister of communications, and later a dominant prime minister until his assassination in 1986. Palme declared in 1966 that "we must safeguard, uncompromisingly and with a steadfastness bordering on passion, the right of television to make open criticism of society, of the authorities, and the private interests" (Ortmark, 1979).[1] He did not endorse, however, a more diversified television structure.

Television Programming

Swedish television programming is rooted in the public-service tradition. It is less party dominated than most European broadcasters. Programs are often of a very high quality. Dissatisfaction centers on the absence of choice. Swedish viewers were willing to spend extra for more diverse programming (Wachtmeister, 1990).

According to one anecdote, when the Swedish king died in 1973, the television channels immediately looked at their program schedules to determine whether to omit light programs. But since the regular programming was already serious, few changes were required (Soderstrom, 1981). (In fairness, this was not the situation at the time of a later tragedy, the Palme assassination in 1986.)

When the second television channel was introduced in 1969, it was found that audiences for news programs dropped by one-half as viewers chose alternatives to the news. The two channels, therefore, scheduled specialized programs against each others' news programs to prevent audience defection from the news. An official of another Swedish near-monopoly institution, the telecommunications administration, Televerket (which has an interest in cable television), writes,

> Swedish TV households are accustomed to very little choice in the selection of TV programs. During the last three years, almost half-a-million video recorders have been sold in Sweden. Such a dynamic growth in sales of video recorders shows that the Swedish public are not in fact satisfied with such a narrow range of programmes. . . . It will be of great interest to see how people choose when they have the freedom of choice [Aronsson, 1983].

As this quote illustrates, videocassette recorders have disturbed the status quo. One half of Swedish televison households own VCRs. To deal with side effects, Parliament passed a law in 1981 prohibiting the rental and showing of cassettes portraying violence to humans or animals to children under fifteen years of age and restricting adult access to cassettes with brutal or sadistic violence.

Finances and Advertising

Television revenues, in the absence of advertising, are almost exclusively derived from license fees paid by television set owners. License fee revenues do not, however, go automatically to Sveriges Radio but are allocated by Parliament annually. Television license fees are not cheap; in 1990, it cost SK 1100, or $170, per year to receive the two channels in color. This figure is comparable to what many American cable subscribers pay for a package of several dozen commercial and nonprofit channels.

Of European countries, none is as opposed to advertising as Sweden. Yet even in Sweden, financial pressures have forced a reevaluation. These pressures have mounted from two directions. First, TV-set license fees were determined to be insufficient to provide future needed revenue. In Sweden, as in other European countries, the steady increase in subscriber revenues, which in the past had seemed almost a law of nature, petered out as soon as most of the country's households had color sets. Increasing the fees proved to be difficult as more and more viewers evaded them after increases of 19 percent in 1980 and 17 percent in 1981 (Gustafsson, 1982). Even though, in real terms, license fees were lower in the 1980s than they were in the 1970s, politicians were willing to make them an issue. Second, whereas foreign broadcast signals with TV advertising had long covered small parts of Sweden, the emergence of satellite-delivered programs increased such spillovers to cover the entire country, undermining the government's policy and making it possible for foreign products to be advertised in Sweden, whereas Swedish products could not.

The government responded by commissioning a report, completed in 1986, to analyze this situation. The report concluded that advertisements could be permitted on the existing two television channels, or a third, advertiser-supported channel could be started. But the commission dedicated much attention to the impact of the introduction of advertising into Swedish television on the newspaper industry, which strenuously resisted it. Traditionally, Sweden has had a remarkably large number of daily newspapers with significant political influence and with close ties to the important paper mill industry. One-fifth to one-third of Swedish newspapers exist only with state subsidies, including low-interest loans and direct grants, which account for about 5 percent of total press revenues. Even larger, more profitable newspapers have been under pressure to reduce their costs and introduce new production technologies (Svard, 1982). The commission report on TV advertising thus ended up largely discussing the effects of TV advertisements on the newspaper industry.

The proposal to introduce advertising to Swedish television drew varied responses. The Social Democrats opposed advertising, though by the end of the 1980s they had become split into three factions. The moderate and liberal parties were joined by the Federation of Swedish Industries in support of a third, independent channel. The liberal and conservative parties opposed the existing broadcast monopoly. The newspaper publishing industry, which was initially skeptical of broadcast reform, increasingly embraced it as it realized that it could benefit from the new opportunities. The Bonnier family, which controls the largest publishing group in Sweden, led this industry realignment by acquiring in 1980 the film company Svensk Filmindustri. This prompted the government to launch a study of media concentration.

Ironically, while Parliament debated what it would do about advertising, pay-television channels drew some support from opponents of advertising. Having given priority to creating equal income distribution in its society, the Swedish government, paradoxically, allowed the emergence of pay TV, which differentiates access to video programs according to one's ability to pay. In the United States, the partial substitution of pay TV for free commercial television has raised fears about the emergence of an "information-poor" class. Yet in Sweden, pay TV was considered, curiously, by some as part of a progressive communications policy as long as it kept advertising off television. There was much criticism about the viability of a pay-channel. The director of the Swedish Film Institute, Klas Olofsson, contended with a pessimism reminiscent of Sweden's earlier debates on a second radio channel that "there doesn't seem to be enough creative resources for our present two [TV] channels, so why start a third?" (Ahlen, 1984, p. 12). At the same time, the supporters of pay TV often did not recognize that one cannot freeze "free" television, keeping it as it once was, while adding another program layer, as if no dynamic interaction existed between the two. In 1990, Sveriges Radio adopted a further refinement on the payment scheme, by planning for a pay-per-view channel.

Breaches in the Radio Monopoly

As in several other countries, the Swedish communications monopoly was first challenged in radio broadcasting. The main public radio broadcaster, Sveriges Riksradio (not to be confused with the similarly named parent company Sveriges Radio), provided three national channels (including production from ten regional centers) and one overseas channel. A fourth national network linked regional radio. Transmission services were operated by Televerket. The first channel broadcast news, lectures, and theater, primarily to an educated or older audience. Channel 2 carried classical music, minority services, and educational programs. Because of its serious nature, Channel 2 attracted only a very small percentage of the listening audience (Soderstrom, 1981). Channel 3 primarily broadcasts light music and news headlines. Its original mandate was to regain the audience lost to the active and popular commercial pirate stations.

There have always been pressures to open radio to private groups. In the 1950s, several religious groups applied unsuccessfully for licenses and began shortwave transmissions from other countries (Svard, 1982). Pressures for a more flexible radio system built up, partly reflecting the communications aspirations of community groups and of regions outside the capital. A parliamentary commission eventually recommended the opening of local "access" radio, to be independent of the national channels and self-financed. This proposal was rejected by the Social Democrats on the grounds that it would favor the rich (Browne, 1984).

In 1973, another committee recommended three options to Parliament for providing decentralized regional (referred to as local) radio, but the Social Democrats remained largely unconvinced and opposed independent stations outside the existing Sveriges Radio system. They favored, instead, local subsidiaries of SR. But Sveriges Radio was unenthusiastic about the creation of new broadcast outlets with which it would have to share its revenues. In 1975, Parliament nevertheless approved such a structure, which reduced the broadcaster's powers; regional radio began in 1977, with one regional station for each of Sweden's twenty-four administrative regions. These subdivisions made sense in regions with historic, social, and geographic cohesion, but were less suitable where regional boundaries had become arbitrary. Public access demands persisted though, fueled by the desire to decentralize state power (Hultén, 1988).

Even though it was confined to relatively short windows within the third national radio channel (three times daily, for a total of two to three hours during prime listening times), local (i.e., regional) radio became reasonably successful, attracting between 36 and 64 percent of the potential audiences. Once the novelty wore off, however, its audiences declined. In 1986, it was decided that a fourth FM network should be created for the regional stations, with full coverage by 1990. Over time, local radio grew less local in focus. By 1983–84, of an average of twenty-two weekly district productions, only six had a specific relation to their region (Audience and Programme Research, 1985).

In addition to official local radio, a particularly interesting form of community access radio emerged in Sweden. A government commission on neighborhood radio, set up in 1981, found that local broadcasting needs were not being provided for, despite the availability of frequencies that could serve about 200 low-power stations. The commission thus recommended that experimental local radio stations be established. The government, having just changed hands and therefore being less wedded to the status quo in broadcasting than its predecessors had been, approved such an experiment. Närradio was established as an independent radio service, open for radio broadcasts by outside groups. The term Närradio refers to "near" or "neighborhood." These broadcasts did not have to be impartial, as did the regular radio channels. In 1982, as one of its final acts, the center-right government passed legislation making community radio permanent by a one-vote majority. Sixteen locations were chosen, and more than 500 organizations applied for access licenses. Although the majority of licenses went to churches and political parties, other participants were migrant-worker groups, sports clubs, trade unions, educational associations, tenant organizations, environmentalists, and motor clubs. Their programs generated a lively interest among the listening populations. The Social Democrats, in media issues the traditionalists, had opposed the experiment, arguing that only economically powerful groups could afford to participate. But the groups chosen were diverse; in Stockholm there were about 100 Närradio groups sharing the two transmitters. Another thirty-six transmitters across the country served about 150 other groups with various involvements in politics, religion, ecology, and ethnic activities. Moreover, the predicted financial barriers to entry turned out to be very small; transmitter time provided by Televerket was cheap. The rental rate for a full-time transmitter in 1986 was roughly $1600 per year, and was divisible among groups sharing the same transmitter. The feared social divisiveness of unbalanced programs did not materialize, although there were some instances of racist broadcasts. In 1982, after complaints about a program that urged the expulsion of "alien" people, access rules were tightened. När-radio users were required to have an existence and identity beyond broadcasting. A local radio office was set up to grant licenses. Advertising of party propaganda was prohibited (though unpaid partisanship was not).

When the Social Democrats returned to power, the future of Närradio seemed uncertain, but it was soon evident that the concept of public access radio had taken hold. A wide variety of groups was using and supporting it, and its popularity—if not its audience—was considerable. Närradio was thus left intact. Sweden had acquired a vigorous and diverse radio system over the opposition of its major media institution and dominant political party. Whereas as late as 1955 it was argued that even a second radio channel would be beyond the creative and economic capabilities of the country, in 1988 there were 110 transmitting stations run by over 2000 organizations, broadcasting 16,000 hours annually, with the help of 15,000 volunteers.

Cable Television

A major impetus for the opening of television has been cable television. Over 33 percent, or 1.1 million, of Swedish households in 1990 were connected to cable systems, mostly MATV systems. Although some systems initially carried only the two Swedish channels, others, particularly in border areas, have always offered Danish, Norwegian, and Finnish programs. MATV systems are frequently owned by housing associations, but they also let private contractors operate and upgrade them to a greater channel capacity.

More advanced cable television networks were slower in construction. They were promoted by the Swedish Telecommunications Administration, along with housing cooperatives and local newspapers (Engelhart, 1988). Municipal and nonprofit organizations exert some control over cable television via their ownership of a large part of apartment stock. They have clashed with Televerket over its charges for technical cable system services (Hultén, 1986). Sveriges Radio, for its part, decided early not to participate in actual cabling, but to be a program provider.

In contrast, Televerket initially requested permission to connect two-thirds of the country by linking master antenna systems in the larger cities and towns. The cost of this first stage of development was estimated at $20 billion (Swedish Telecom, 1983). The second stage, to connect the last third of the country, would have cost another $20 billion. Televerket's schedule included trial networks in Lund and Stockholm by 1984, trunk networks throughout the country by 1988, fiber trunks to smaller networks by 1992, a national fiber network by 1995, and a fiber MATV network by the year 2000.

Televerket's large-scale pilot cable system in Lund provided nearly 4000 households with twenty TV and twenty radio channels. At first, it offered only nine TV channels, all of which were "safe" public broadcasters from Sweden, West Germany, and Denmark, as well as East German channels. Eventually, Televerket began to carry a local channel (mandatory under the Swedish broadcasting legislation), plus the satellite-delivered Sky Channel and Music Box from the UK, TV5 from France, and the Russian programs carried on the Gorizont satellites.

The conservative government established a parliamentary commission of inquiry on cable television in 1982, but its instructions were revised when the Social Democrats returned to power and were framed so as to discourage advertising. The commission's ultimate report in 1984 on the advancement of cable television warned of the costs of both cabling Sweden and producing programs (Hultén, 1984). It recommended that private rather than public funds be used for cable network development and that all have the right to build cable networks at their own financial risk—including Televerket, if it did not use public funds. The state should retain the right to regulate programming and license programmers. On the issue of who should receive program licenses, the commission split along ideological lines, with the Social Democrats favoring greater restrictions than the liberals and conservatives. The commission argued that pricing and construction be left to cable owners but that the government's cable authority monitor the market and recommend governmental actions against monopoly abusers. In each licensing area, the cable system would (but need not) be a monopoly. (Networks for less than 100 households would be outside of these regulations.) Public-access channels would be available at no charge, and under the control of a local programming entity. Local entities and cable owners alike could apply for a license to retransmit satellite-delivered programs. Local entities could originate programs on stations other than the local access channels and can become the primary or sole program provider for a system, with private systems providing only transmission. Private firms, meanwhile, could obtain a license to fill a channel, and could include the operators of the cable system themselves, including Televerket.

Under the rules, licenses are issued by the cable authority for three years and may not be transferred or sold. Local systems require formal approval by local authorities and no local system may network into other communities. Pornography and violence in programming and advertising and sponsorship in general are also prohibited. Under temporary legislation in 1984, Televerket was permitted to distribute satellite programs on its cable networks. Subsequent legislation in 1986 established a Cable Television Authority as a regulatory and license-granting body pursuant to the commission's recommendation.

Under the 1986 legislation, MATV system operators of more than 100 homes require licenses. Systems may carry foreign channels, including those with advertising, as long as the advertising does not specifically target Swedish audiences.

By 1988, Televerket had connected about 200,000 homes. It also experimented with optical fiber as a video transmission medium. Other major cable operators include Finvik, Stjärn TV Natet, and Kabelvision (TBI, 1990).

Another form of television distribution is through the Nordic DBS Satellite Tele-X, which was launched and operated since 1989. In 1990, a channel on that satellite, TV4 Nordisk Television, became the first commercial broadcaster to originate from *within* Sweden, thus breaking this particular barrier. Advertising on over-the-air broadcast channels was still prohibited, making Sweden West Europe's last holdout. Audiences were miniscule. But TV4 also maneuvered to obtain a commericial television license as Sweden's third channel (Wachtmeister, 1990).

For a time, advertiser-supported satellite channels were carried on Swedish cable systems as long as they were foreign and did not directly address the Swedish market. This created an untenable restriction against potential Swedish entrants. A major turning point occurred in 1988, when the program channel TV3 began to be distributed in Scandinavia. The channel, though based in London, is owned by the Swedish company Kinnevik, which is part of the growing media activities of Jan Stenbeck. Stenbeck, from a major industrialist family, was engaged in steel, coal, and other businesses. His strategy was to invest in telecommunications services with an eye toward their deregulation. Thus, Stenbeck owned Comvik, which ran Sweden's second cellular telephone service and expanded to other services, including long-distance telephone service. His TV3 channel was transmitted via the Astra satellite, in which he was also a part owner. He also owned the pay service TV1000 and cable distribution networks (Finvik). Through his diversified communications holdings, Stenbeck positioned himself to be the Nordic equivalent of Berlusconi, Murdoch, Maxwell, and Kirch. As these developments took place, the resistance to commercial television weakened. The raising of new revenues became necessary to offset SR's increasing costs, and advertising as a source began to draw support from the Social Democrats and other parties. Furthermore, moderates and liberals favored a third national television channel independent of SR (Svärd, 1990, p. 6). TV3's legality was evaluated by the Swedish cable authority, which determined that the scope of the advertising transmitted to Sweden was not illegal (Hultén, 1990, p. 198). Stenbeck was also a candidate for a Swedish terrestrial channel, and manuevered to get an advantage for his proposed Rikstelevision against TV4, a venture backed by another Swedish industrial dynasty, the Wallenbergs (Saab-Scania).

Pay channels in Sweden include TV-Plus (which failed) and FilmNet, owned by Esselte, a leader in Scandinavian and Benelux subscription television, and the second largest pay-TV service in Europe after Canal Plus. In 1990 it was offered for sale and became a target for Kinnevik, Murdoch, Berlusconi, Springer, and Canal Plus. SF Succé, jointly owned by Svensk Filmindustri, the large publishing firm Bonnier, and Warner, is another pay television entrant (Nicholson, 1990). In 1991, Social Democrats and the opposition reached agreement on the introduction of commercial TV.

Conclusion

By 1991 even Sweden, arguably the strictest proponent of the traditional public broadcasting monopoly, had not been able to hold the line. Cable television was in the process of replacing over-the-air broadcasting as the primary form of distribution. This marked a shift from television as a purely public good to a more mixed system, with cable operators and commercial channel providers filling a growing role. Their emergence was not surprising. Perhaps no European broadcast system had been more resistant to opening up than had the Swedish one. Even relatively simple steps such as a second or third public radio program or a first or second public TV channel had to be forced by the threat of private entry. Yet when audiences were offered choice by pirates or videocassettes, they indicated that the broadcasting system ignored important segments of viewers. In time, these unserved segments found willing suppliers. The conservatism of the traditional system was not aimed solely at commercial offerings; it opposed even opening broadcasting to community groups. Yet this dike was breached and the remarkable Närradio system emerged.

In addition to demand-side pressures, media liberalization received impetus from the supply side. The near monopoly in telecommunications, Televerket, and other companies were pursuing the cabling of the country. Important segments of the electronic industry advanced an ambitious direct broadcast satellite project. And important parts of the influential newspaper publishing industry reversed their opposition to commercial broadcasting and began a strategy of becoming integrated information firms.

16

Finland

Finland's electronic mass media are characterized by a duality of public and private institutions, with overlapping roles that are separate in most other European countries. The dividing line between telephony and television is also fluid. And telephony itself is divided between public- and private-service operators. Similarly, cable television involves multiple interests. Finland's rival communications institutions have learned to cooperate almost too well, establishing in the process a duopoly in television. But in the process, a media system has been created that promises more dynamism and variety than the small population of the country would lead one to expect.

History

The first experimental broadcast was attempted by amateurs in 1921 and soon became regularized through the Finnish Amateur Radio League and the Finnish broadcasting association. By 1924, a large total of 1254 private local radio stations had been started, many by newspaper and news agencies. Soon there were also eleven national broadcasting stations (Mäkinen, 1990, p. D35).

To establish coordination, a radio commission was founded by the journalist organization of Helsinki. It proposed that transmission stations be constructed and operated by the state and that program production be left to a single private monopoly. As a result, in 1926, the national broadcasting company YLE (Yleisradio) was founded by various banks, newspapers, and radio stations. YLE was to produce and transmit programs in the two official languages, Finnish and Swedish. Later, in 1934, Parliament made YLE a state-owned company.

The subsequent 1927 Radio Act became the legal foundation of broadcasting, giving the Ministry of Communications and Public Works the authority to grant broadcasting licenses.

The national telecommunications administration P&T has not been involved in direct radio or television broadcasting since 1934, when it was forced to sell its broadcasting facilities to YLE as part of a general restructuring of telecommunications (Howkins, 1982). It maintains, however, limited involvement in cable transmission.

Regular television broadcasting was also started as a public-private mix when a private license was extended to the Foundation of Technology in 1957. Under its license, TV operations began in Helsinki (Tesvisio) and Tampere (Tamvisio). The major commercial broadcasting company MTV initiated regular operations jointly with YLE in 1958. In 1964, YLE acquired Tesvisio and Tamvisio's stock and formed TV-2 from their licensed channels (Bruce et al., 1985).

The YLE and MTV Duopoly

No legal monopoly exists for broadcast program provision, and as a rule, the new private local radio stations broadcast their own programs. Although it does have some private stockholders, YLE is overwhelmingly (99.9 percent) government owned. Parliament selects the twenty-one members of its governing board, and the government sets the license fees for television sets. These fees account for about three-quarters of YLE's income. Since 1934, YLE has owned transmission facilities.

MTV has maintained a leasing agreement with YLE for broadcast time and transmission. In effect, the two broadcasting organizations have shared channels, although they are entirely separate organizationally and are financed differently (YLE by license fees and payments from MTV, and MTV by advertisements). This arrangement is an illustration of the fairly undogmatic way in which public and private telecommunications services cooperate in Finland. MTV's programs are subject, to some extent, to YLE's influence regarding quality and content; also, MTV could not address news-related topics except on its 10 o'clock news program. To establish even that newscast involved a long fight, and the approval was linked to an increase in MTV's fee, payable to YLE.

Under the co-op arrangement, MTV's share of total broadcasting time is about 20 percent; but its part of the prime evening and weekend time is at least 40 percent. In 1982, MTV paid YLE almost two-thirds of its gross revenue from advertising sales to pay for broadcast time. This amounted to almost one-quarter of YLE's total revenues. Thus, YLE enjoys the best of both worlds; it maintains the aura of freedom from commercial involvement, but is heavily, if indirectly, supported by advertising revenues (Mäkinen, 1984). MTV, on the other hand, pays a very stiff de facto license fee of two-thirds of its revenues.

The Liberalization of Radio

In 1990, YLE was restructured and a third network was allocated to begin service in 1993 (Sorämaki, 1990, p. 4). YLE operates several national radio channels. In 1968, it added a regional radio service, but regional air time was very limited (Browne, 1984). Since 1975, YLE has also operated local radio under its control in Helsinki, and after 1982 in Tampere, Turku, and several other locations.

In time, pressures built to permit private and community radio stations. A parliamentary Committee on Radio and Television Broadcasting was set up in 1979, and in 1984 it recommended introducing private local radio broadcasting. Licenses for such broadcasters would be granted and supervised by a Media Council. This would require a constitutional amendment. Initially, no advertisements would be included (Soramaki, 1984).

Even before the committee submitted its report, fifty-three local publishing houses founded an advocacy group and submitted nearly 100 license applications (Finnish Local Radio Association, 1987). Twenty-two licenses were awarded, many to joint ventures sharing air time. Most licenses were given to newspaper publishers, many of which were affiliated with political parties; seven national dailies were granted a joint license and twelve regional or local papers received licenses. Large newspaper publishers also diversified into cable television and videotex, and multimedia firms emerged. The remaining licenses were allocated among trade union organizations, a student union, private companies, and a small municipality (Paldan, 1985). Transmission range varies from 30 to 50 kilometers. Private radio reached 19 percent of the listening audience in 1989. The airing of advertisements became possible except where the leading local newspaper received the license.

The positions of the various political parties on the liberalization of broadcasting varied. The two major socialist parties, the Social Democratic Party and the Finnish People's League, did not oppose new media in principle but wanted the local stations to meet certain national and social goals and to be controlled by YLE, leaving only a limited role for commercial interests (Mäkinen, 1984). On the conservative side, the National Coalition Party sought an open media system and a guarantee of freedom of expression, whereas the Christian League of Finland emphasized a more constructive societal role for media.

Opponents pointed to the precarious financial positions of most stations. But the popularity of the stations grew with their exposure, and their financial difficulties gradually diminished. As local stations approached and at times even surpassed the audience share of YLE broadcasts, they applied for extended licenses. Eventually, after the 1987 elections, the new government moved local radio from an experimental phase into regularized operation (Finnish Local Radio Association, 1987). In 1989, for example, twenty-five new local radio stations were granted licenses.

Television

Given the mixed nature of the television system, it is not surprising that its programming was varied (Nordenstreng, 1969; Wilo, 1980). In the past, YLE and MTV generally coordinated their program buying (Humphreys, 1990 p. 37). Foreign programming filled 37 percent of YLE and 52 percent of MTV offerings in 1981, supplied mostly by the United States (28 percent), the United Kingdom (20 percent), and Sweden (12 percent). YLE was more likely to use Nordic programs, whereas MTV was the largest importer of U.S. and U.K.

products (Sarkkinen, 1983). Defying the stereotype of American programs consisting solely of entertainment and serials, 12 percent of all YLE-imported documentaries were of American origin. On MTV, the American share of documentaries was 36 percent (Sarkkinen, 1983). American imports represent 17 percent of children's programming, the second highest (Erholm and Oksanen, 1982).

Of the top ten most popular programs in 1985 on Channel 1, eight were by MTV and two were by YLE (the top two, both national song contests). On Channel 2, MTV had three of the top five (MTV, 1985). YLE-TV was thought to broadcast most often low quality or political programs, but was viewed as reliable and not overly commercial. YLE Radio was by far the leader in regional programming, but was also often seen as political (Oksanen, 1985).

The liberalization of terrestrial television was far more cautious than that of radio, where the stakes are lower. When the opening of radio broadcasting proved popular and demonstrated that the sky did not fall in, the government approved the creation of a third television channel. This was not a major step, since it primarily involved expansion among the traditional participants. The channel was licensed in 1986 on a temporary basis to Kolmostelevisio, owned by YLE (50 percent), MTV (35 percent) and Nokia, the country's largest electronics firm (15 percent). In 1988, its first year of operation, Channel Three broadcast 2000 hours of programming, almost double that of MTV. Channel Three had 17 percent of the total audience in areas it could be received. It operated with only 40 employees compared with 600 at MTV and 4800 at YLE. Under 1989 legislation, by 1993, MTV will transfer all of its programming to the third channel and control it (65 percent), with the remainder held by YLE and Noika. The transfer will leave TV-1 and TV-2 free from advertisements; that is, MTV will be free from competition in the television advertising market. In return, MTV will still pay a substantial license fee and "public-service" charges, thus supporting YLE's finances. MTV's program output will have to double much of its air time; 35 percent must be domestically produced. (Paavela and Miettinen, 1990, p. 5).

Cable Television and New Media

Cable television started as a community antenna system to counter poor broadcast reception in some locations. The desire to receive Swedish-language television in the western part of the country, where a substantial Swedish-language minority lives, was an added factor. The basic Radio Act of 1927 provided little guidance. The number of entrepreneurial players, coupled with the lack of clear legislation, allowed Finnish cable television to forge ahead rapidly; Finland was the second country, after the United States, to have pay cable.

The first genuine cable company was formed in 1973 in Helsinki with the participation of the Helsinki Telephone Company, which owned part of the network. In the distinct Finnish arrangement, that telephone company, like many others, itself is controlled by its subscribers, who elect the board of directors.

Cable transmission began in 1975 under the name Helsinki Television (HTV). YLE, MTV, and several publishers were offered participation but declined. During the period from 1975 to 1980, HTV produced its own programs for cable, but production was suspended for economic reasons (Soramaki and Osterlund, 1983). It was acquired by Finland's largest newspaper publisher, Sanoma Oy. The cable system in Tampere, Finland's second largest city, is owned by the city, the local telephone cooperative, a leading newspaper, and MTV.

HTV's income derives from basic service fees (40 percent), pay television (33 percent), and advertisements (18 percent) (YLE Research Department, 1986).

The two major state telecommunications organizations, the broadcasting authority YLE and the telephone administration P&T, joined their cable efforts in 1982 with a plan under which the P&T would become involved in basic and pay cable transmission. This alliance made the local independent telephone companies nervous, because YLE's reach was national, in contrast to P&T's local distribution, which was mostly limited to rural areas. Hence, they feared P&T construction and operation of cable networks in their own areas of local telephone operations.

Of still greater sensitivity was the question of program channels. Until 1987, there was no regulatory system for the reception and distribution of distant signals (Bruce, et al., 1985). In 1981, a parliamentary committee on radio and television proposed a framework for program provision. Advertising could not exceed 7.5 percent of total program time. YLE's two channels would have to be carried, and YLE could also operate its own cable activities. A counterproposal by the publishing house Sanoma was to have the telephone companies construct cable networks and lease them to a cable operator who would function as a common carrier (Howkins, 1982).

A Cable Television Act was submitted in 1985 and was approved by Parliament in 1987. It provided that every Finnish citizen could receive a concession to cable-cast; that a cable network must reserve channels for outside programmers on equal terms; that locally originated programming must be at least 15% Finnish; and that advertisements must be limited to 11 percent of programming time. (Hannuksela, 1987; Castren, 1987). By 1989 the government had issued 187 licenses to 206 communities, with 71 going to the PTT, 41 to local telephone companies and 21 to cable firms.

In 1982, several cable television systems had begun distributing the satellite-delivered Sky Channel and Music Box from Britain. By 1990, dozens of cable networks carried satellite programs. Offerings are quite varied: Eurosport; Super Channel; MTV Europe; TV5; FilmNet; Moscow 1; Moscow 2; CNN; BBC; Children's Channel; Lifestyle; Screen Sport; Discovery (Jaakko Hannuksela, communication). Other offerings include three of HTV's own: the Entertainment Channel (a pay-TV channel with eight hours of mostly American, British, and German programming, as well as music and sports); the Helsinki Channel, with a limited menu of serials and Finnish programs; and the Information Channel, with news and light music around the clock.

Direct competition to MTV has increased since 1990 through PTV, a Finnish commercial cable channel owned by Sanoma, Turun Sanomat, some publishers, and the Helsinki, Tampere, and Turku cable companies (Humphreys, 1990, p. 34). PTV also sought a broadcast license under a law establishing microwave (MMDS) broadcasting.

In 1989, cable television subscriptions reached about one-third of households.

Finland was initially a participant in the Scandinavian Nordsat DBS system, but its interest waned considerably as the costs and other problems of coordination became apparent. When the Nordsat project dissolved, Sweden promoted Tele-X as an alternative, with a view to assisting the Swedish electronic industry. Other Nordic countries were invited to participate. Finland's share in this project is about 5 percent.

Since 1981, YLE has distributed a teletext information service on both of its channels, using the Ceefax standard and the vertical blanking interval of television transmission during its own, as well as during MTV's, broadcasting time.

Videocassette recorders have increased rapidly in popularity. The heaviest use was among viewers fifteen to twenty-four years old (Oksanen, 1986). With the emergence of such viewing, concerns grew about the impact of certain programs. Under the initiative of the Ministry of Education, a censorship proposal was passed in 1984 that prohibits the selling, renting, and loaning of video recordings with crude and violent content (Kalkkinen, 1984; see also Varis, 1970).

Conclusion

Despite its small population, peripheral location, and distinct language, Finland's opening to a more diversified media environment has been smoother than that of almost any other European country. Communications have long been provided by a mixed private and public system in Finland, a legacy of the czarist days, when the country was a reluctant Russian province that established its own institutions outside of the state. A pragmatic approach has permeated Finnish telephone and broadcast communications since then. Even the political parties of the left are more tolerant toward regulated private television than those in many other countries. The public broadcaster YLE reached an arrangement that appeared ideal from its point of view: one-quarter of its revenues derive from the private broadcaster MTV's fees to it. It can maintain good quality in its program approach, ceding the popular broad center to MTV, while being subsidized by the latter. Commercial television is not the enemy of public broadcasting but its funding base. On the other hand, MTV holds a privileged position in private broadcasting, and the industry structure through the 1980's can be characterized as a duopoly.

A second important characteristic of Finnish media is their integration. In Finland print publishers, including strictly local ones, have become more involved in broadcasting than anywhere in Europe, on both national and regional levels. Electronic equipment manufacturers and the telephone industry are also actively involved in media issues. And competitive entry began with radio and will continue into terrestrial television, where change has been slow, thus reducing MTV dominance in that field. Finland has been an early active participant in cable television. Program provision on cable is fairly open and will lead to further liberalization. Microwave broadcasting is likely to be a next step. As this evolution takes place it makes Finland a surprisingly strong media presence.

17

Norway

In Norway, pluralism and localism combined to break up the state broadcast monopoly in radio and television. For a long time, this institution, Norsk Rikskringkasting (NRK), offered Norwegians high-quality but limited fare on one channel of each medium, both largely centralized in Oslo. Diversification began in 1981 with the licensing of noncommercial local broadcasting operations. At the same time, private cable operators started to carry more foreign satellite-delivered commercial channels. Challenged from two directions, broadcasting was opened. NRK remains by far the major broadcast institution, but without its past exclusivity.

History

Broadcast reception in Norway began with British signals, which generated much amateur radio enthusiasm and led to experimental Norwegian broadcasting in 1923. In 1925, the government issued broadcast licenses to private companies in Oslo, Bergen, and two other cities. The state telegraph and telephone administration provided technical transmission services. In contrast to today's situation, advertising was permitted, but it did not comprise a significant part of the budget (Roloff and Köhne, 1990, p. D160). The first private license was given to Kringskastingselkapet in Oslo. By 1929, there were thirteen stations in the country, one of which was the most powerful in Europe (Emery, 1969). In 1933, with radio growing increasingly popular, the Norwegian parliament established NRK, a public monopoly that absorbed the private firms.

During World War II, the German occupiers confiscated most radio sets and made listening to the BBC a capital offense. When the Germans withdrew, they demolished the new broadcasting building. After the war, radio penetration increased dramatically, although only one radio channel was provided until 1984, when a second radio channel was established.

Television was introduced late to Norway—in 1960, eight years after it had been proposed in the parliament. In 1972, color broadcasting was added. (In 1983, teletext service was introduced.) Despite the leisurely pace of the authorities, which disregarded foreign experience and underestimated the public's interest in television, penetration was almost complete within a few years.

NRK and the State

NRK is controlled by the Ministry of Culture and Sciences and is governed by a supervisory board of seven members. Two of the board members are staff representatives, and the other five, including one "technical expert," are appointed by the king, that is, the government. Programming and administration are controlled by a director general, who is appointed directly by the government for an eight-year term. The government also appoints the program directors for radio and television. A broadcast council designated by the government and parliament advises on program issues.

The Norwegian parliament, the Storting, directly influences NRK by approving its annual budgets and by setting the vital license fees. NRK also includes regional broadcast program councils and a complaint commission for rectification of incorrect statements. To fulfill its mandate to reach one-hundred percent of the population, NRK maintains an extensive transmission network. NRK is reputed to be a slow-moving institution. It was centralized in Oslo until the 1980s. In recent years, a remarkable change in the status of the NRK has occured. A decision in the parliament and the concurrence of the NRK gave it the status of a foundation, starting May 1, 1988, in order to guarantee its independence from the state (Roloff and Köhne, 1990, p. D164).

Regional radio broadcasting was introduced by NRK in 1957. At that time, limited regional coverage existed for the Bergen and Lapp regions. Nineteen regional radio services have since been established (Browne, 1984).

One peculiarity of Norwegian broadcasting is the existence of two official Norwegian dialects. Since 1970, a very generous 25 percent of NRK programming has been in the minority dialect, Nynorsk, and it is often in foreign film subtitles. Radio broadcast time is also allotted to the Finnish-related language spoken by ethnic minorities in the north.

Nærradio and the Diversification of Broadcast Sources

In 1980, the law establishing NRK dating to 1933 was amended to affirm NRK's monopoly, but it also permitted some exceptions. In 1982, Minister of Culture Lars Roar Langslet therefore freed the concept of local, or "near," radio (Nærradio). In 1984, under the conservative government of Kaare Willoch, who had promised to reduce the scope of NRK's monopoly, the broadcasting law was modified to permit the creation of more local stations. Forty areas were designated to allow advertising-free local television broadcasts (Logica, 1987). The government received almost 750 applications for permission to provide local broadcasting and licensed 119 local television and 380 local radio operations. The licenses represented a variety of interests (Nyheim, 1984); one-third were newspaper publishers. In 1985, Oslo had thirty-six Nærradio stations, which shared three channels, and twenty-three licensed local television stations, though only a few of them were actually operational. In Bergen, there

were one television and twenty-four radio stations. At the end of 1987, another
128 TV and 381 local radio units had received permission to operate. A survey
conducted in February 1989 showed that three-quarters of the population was
reached by the new local stations, and 22 percent by new TV stations. Among
those questioned, 14 percent listened to local radio daily (Roloff and Köhne,
1990, p. D163).

Since advertising was forbidden, small operations were soon in financial
trouble. In many instances, small stations were operated by groups such as
local governments and political, religious, community, or trade groups. Without advertising, only the wealthier, larger, or most resourceful of these groups
could afford to carry a broadcasting operation. Hence, most of the groups argued to permit advertising. The Christian Peoples' party supported them.

Cable Television and Satellites

As in other small-population European countries, cable television has been important to Norway as a source for diversification. In 1990, 30 percent of the
country's households were cabled (Nicholson, 1990); this percentage was even
higher in the cities.

Cable distribution operations are undertaken by both private firms and the
Televerket telephone authority. In 1990, over 200 cable operators and 480 cable
systems existed in Norway (TBI, 1990). Most cable networks had very low
capacity, but they were being upgraded. The largest cable company in the country,
Janco TV, began operating in the early 1970s. By 1984, it delivered five channels, including its own Jancovision associated with Norway's second-largest
newspaper, Dagbladet, to approximately 135,000 subscribers in the Oslo area.
Hoping to expand its offerings, Janco asked for government permission to start
a pay-TV service (Engelhart, 1988).

In 1984, a cable authority, Kabelnettkontrollen, was established under the
Ministry of Transport and Communications. Its responsibility was to regulate
the physical development of cable networks in Norway by licensing and standard setting. Although some smaller systems still had to be registered, licenses
were not required for systems of less than ten buildings and/or 100 subscribers.
All new or modernized networks must have at least a twenty-four channel capacity, and subscriber networks must be in star or mini-star configurations. A
government commission also recommended local licensing of videocassette distributors, registration of all titles, and censorship to protect minors and prevent
pirating.

Programs typically delivered are the Norwegian, Finnish, and Swedish public channels; commercial satellite channels include Sweden's TV-3 (broadcast
from England). Norway has also begun to develop its own program packaging.
In 1989, two Norwegian channels, TV-1 and TV Norge (the latter backed by
Sweden's Esselte), began operating, the latter of which is essentially aimed at
providing sports and foreign serials (Roloff and Köhne, 1990, p. D165). In

1990, NRK also allowed its local stations to carry one commercial satellite channel in each coverage area (TBI, 1990).

Norway was one of the first two countries to permit the distribution of the British Sky Channel, which was then called Satellite Television, and thus helped to establish the principle of European distribution. Although Sky Channel programs are in English, they received much audience attention as a new program choice. The conservative government was relatively open to private broadcasting. It believed it could not prohibit citizens from watching television programs and that, given the government's financial situation, only commercial television would permit expansion of Norwegian television options.

In 1987, the minister of cultural affairs permitted cable networks to retransmit two additional satellite channels, the Superchannel and the Arts Channel, in addition to the previously approved Sky Channel.

In 1987, the Ministry of Culture granted temporary permission to thirty-three of sixty-eight pay-TV applicants (mostly local broadcasters with need for revenue) for a two-year trial period. A year later, the trial phase was extended to 1991 (Roloff and Köhne, 1990, p. D165).

Norway was also involved in Nordsat, the direct broadcast satellite project of the Nordic countries. The system proved to be too costly, however, and encountered political obstacles. It was replaced by a second joint DBS project, Tele-X, largely under Swedish control and financing, and with a small Norwegian participation. After the 1989 launch, NRK used Tele-X for its radio and television programming to remote locales and some regional operators.

The Opening of Commercial Television Broadcasting

NRK (which became an independent foundation in 1988) operates without advertising revenues; income is obtained primarily from license fees. In 1989, NRK derived NKr 1.6 billion (about $250 million) from 1.46 million license holders, supplying 82 percent of its funds. Sixteen percent comes from a television set tax. Advertising is a thorny issue in domestic Norwegian politics. The left is opposed to advertising and is joined by parts of the Conservative party, whereas the Liberals are in favor of it, at least for additional television channels. All parties agree, however, that proposed advertising should be carried on the private channels.

In 1984, NRK considered providing pay television but was criticized because the majority of the programs it would offer were of foreign origin. As an alternative, the government commission proposed in 1985 that a second national broadcast channel be created outside of NRK. The commission recommended that some advertising be allowed on this new channel so that Norway's broadcasting system could be expanded to a second channel and could also develop local broadcasting, DBS, cable television, and videotex from the revenues. It proposed that advertising be restricted to twenty minutes per channel during weekdays so as to maintain editorial integrity.

Once local TV and commercial satellite channels were widely available, it was difficult to deny the establishment of additional national channels. In 1990, a national terrestrial private television channel was opened for license application. It was structured with rules for ownership, national coverage, and programming. Limited foreign investing is allowed, and no single organization can own more than 20 percent of the company. (TBI, 1990).

Conclusion

The evolution of television in Norway was slow, due partly to geography and demographics and partly to the reluctance of the government to open electronic media to publishing interests and decentralize the system. In return, Norway had some of Europe's strictest rules against advertising on public television. In time, however, pirates (who had also been instrumental in the early beginning of radio) began providing broadcasting to unserved segments of the audience. Community and local stations were licensed when a conservative government came to power.

Opportunities for an opening to commercial television also came from the emergence of cable distribution, which led to the carrying of foreign commercial channels, among the first in Europe outside their country of origin, thus setting a continent-wide precedent. During this evolution, integrated media firms began to emerge that cover broadcasting, pay-TV program packaging, and cable distribution. Program diversity has increased, although barriers are still considerable.

18

Denmark

The Scandinavian tradition of social and cultural concern characterized the development of broadcasting in Denmark. A state monopoly dominated broadcasting throughout most of its history; but broad citizen participation and foreign broadcast spill-ins have tempered its power. In the 1980s, the previously highly constricted one-channel television system was opened significantly through the creation of community radio and television, cable television, and satellite-delivered channels.

History

The regulation of Danish radio began in 1907 with the enactment of a law giving the minister of public works the authority to grant licenses for wireless communication. Soon, many radio clubs operated informally by broadcasting over governmental and military transmitters (Prehn, 1986), with a certain amount of disorganization. These private operations were closed down by the government in 1925 and replaced with the passage of a broadcast law by the state radio authority, Statsradiofonien. Although the minister of public works still maintained some regulatory capacity over radio, Statsradiofonien received all radio control previously held by private interests. Over the next quarter century, the public monopolist developed a national network of radio stations financed by listening fees.

In 1951, Statsradiofonien added two AM and two FM stations and established a second network. In 1963, under pressure because of the popularity of broadcast pirates, a third network was added that specialized in entertainment and popular music. In 1951, Denmark became the first Nordic country to introduce a national television channel.

In 1959, a new broadcasting law was passed that provided for the establishment of an independent public institution with a monopoly over both television and radio broadcasts. This institution, which replaced Statsradiofonien, was named Danmarks Radio. Until 1964, the government had the right of advance censorship over Danmarks Radio, and advertising was prohibited.

The Radio and Television Broadcasting Act of 1973 and its subsequent amendments established various bodies for the control of broadcasting. The governing board of Danmarks Radio consists of eleven members, with the chairman appointed by Danmarks Radio and the remaining members appointed by parliament. It became highly politicized, and reform proposals recommended a smaller and less political body. As a result of the push for reform, the composition and jurisdiction of the governing board changed; it can no longer address programming matters and members of the parliament can no longer sit on the board (GEAR, 1988).

There is also a General Program Advisory Committee, appointed by the minister for communications, as well as a County Program Advisory Committee. Separate local commissions are in charge of granting three-year radio and five-year television broadcasting licenses to nonprofit and independent companies and associations. The minister for communications appoints a committee to distribute transmitter stations, handle complaints about licensees' operations, and revoke licenses when necessary. The minister also established a Broadcasting Complaints Commission, which can order broadcasting stations to correct misrepresentation of facts, and a TV Advertising Advisory Committee, which offers advice about the content of television commercials and which also has the authority to order the correction of misrepresentation.

Because Denmark is a small country and because no advertising is allowed on the national channel, DR's broadcast budget is limited. This situation necessitated a substantial importation of programs, which in turn caused domestic criticism. The result was a focus on domestic production and a domestic content of 51 percent in 1983, increasing to 60 percent in 1990.

The Opening of Broadcasting

Pressures for diversity and change came first from pirate radio stations. In 1958, Radio Mercur began broadcasting from international waters and rapidly gained popularity. To prevent such pirate broadcasting, the Telecommunication by Radio Act of 1949 had legislated that, ''The setting up of, operation of, or use of broadcasting stations on the open sea or in the air space above it shall not be permitted.'' On that basis, Radio Mercur was shut down by the government in 1963. The message of its audience appeal, however, was not lost, and a similar program mix on the third official channel was introduced. Some of the pirate radio's disc jockeys were even included in the staff of the new channel. Soon the new third channel became highly popular. In 1987, 73 percent of listeners tuned to the third channel and only 17 percent to the first channel, which maintained talk and serious programming. Even more striking, the first channel attracted listeners for only eleven minutes per day, compared to ninety-two minutes for the third channel. A proposed fourth channel was postponed for economic reasons.

In 1983, local radio became a policy priority again under pressure from the pirates, this time mostly land-based, small community groups. The second channel was transformed to serve regional broadcasting, through nine regional radio stations. Also established at that time were radio workshops in which community groups were taught how to use radio. These local radio operators either transmitted over a low-power station or distributed their programs over cable television. State and local subsidies were provided and additional income was contributed from other sources, but advertising was not permitted. In late 1985, a permanent legal structure that would regularize local radio broadcasting was proposed to Parliament (Prehn, 1986). Act 589 of December 19, 1985, amended the 1973 law to standardize transmission facilities and licensing for local radio (Danmarks Radio, 1987). The 1987 amendments to Part IIa of the Act cemented the local, noncommercial status of broadcasters and allowed local authorities to hold licenses as providers of production and transmission facilities. As a result, the minister of communications or local councils was empowered to force licensees to broadcast public affairs programming.

In 1983, the Ministry of Culture granted a total of ninety-two operating licenses to local radio stations for a three-year trial period accompanied by scientific research. By 1986, 300 organizations had applied for licenses and 108 local radio and 43 television projects had been licensed. Of the newly licensed projects, 24 percent were community groups; 6 percent, religious organizations; 12 percent, newspaper publishers and journalists; 18 percent, labor unions and adult education organizations; 6 percent, municipalities; and 26 percent, citizens groups (Prehn, 1986). As they became more established, the community stations increased their broadcasting time to about six hours per day in 1988 (Petersen et al., 1988).

The low wattage of their transmitters limited the range of community radio to about 10 kilometers (Petersen et al., 1988). Networking too was technically prohibited, but economic and political imperatives overcame these prohibitions. The variety of new radio stations was great, ranging from one-person operations that aired a few hours a day, to stations operated by religious organizations or unions, and catering to their members especially. Eight local television stations are operated by the trade union, which is the closest to a network that the government will allow without a license. However, these stations required a substantial union subsidy. There were also citizen radio stations that aimed at "total plurality." Radio Aarhus, located in the second largest city in Denmark, was probably the most extreme of such operators. It was founded by 120 Aarhus organizations and clubs, and each of these, no matter how large, has at most thirty minutes of weekly programming. Twenty-five percent of weekly air time is kept open. Radio Aarhus claims to run without any hierarchy or censorship, and all citizens can air their announcements. Most of the fixed costs of rent and technical operations are covered by the municipality, but much of the money is provided by the Association of Radio Aarhus' friends and listeners. In 1985, 45 percent of the population listened to community radio; by 1987, this number had grown to 55 percent. Danmarks Radio attracted listeners for 828 minutes per week in 1985, compared to 281 for community radio, but its popularity slipped, and by 1987, it drew listeners for 788 minutes compared to 409 for community radio (GEAR, 1988).

By 1989, there were 277 local radio stations authorized and operating. Advertisements were permitted after 1989.

Although official broadcast television policy limits Danes to only two channels, much of the country can receive at least one foreign TV channel, and most Danes supplemented their spartan one-channel choice with the German and Swedish public channels. About half of the households can receive all three German public channels, and Sweden's two channels are similarly watched by half of the viewing population. Others could receive East Germany or Norway. One study shows that households receiving only the Danish channel watch sixteen hours per week, whereas those that can receive five additional channels from Germany and Sweden watch five hours more. Of those Danish households that have a choice, 29 percent watch a German rather than the Danish channel (Prehn, 1986).

The political left and right were split over the issue of private television (Henriksen and Schmidt, 1980). The left was not prepared to relinquish the idea of broadcasting as a forum for public education, and the right was against a state broadcasting monopoly. Since the opponents had almost equal representation in parliament, much influence fell to a small center party.

From 1983 to 1985, an experiment with regional television was conducted in southern Denmark (TV-Syd). In addition, community television was begun in 1983, with thirty-four stations using low-power transmission or cable. The experiment was made permanent in 1987. About fifteen public stations operate. Although commercial organizations were technically excluded, some of the local organizations were, or became, covers for commercial interests. Weekend Television in Copenhagen, for example, started as a genuine community effort but eventually was operated by large newspaper publishers and Denmark's largest film company. Another Copenhagen channel started with amateurs and volunteers but eventually became a pay-television channel owned by the Swedish company Esselte, the largest producer of videocassettes in Scandinavia and a major participant in Dutch pay cable.

In 1991, there were 174 radio stations, with an audience of about one quarter of the listening population. Forty radio and eight local TV stations are operated by the trade union movement. These stations have collaborated with local publishers in advertising and have even attempted, in association with Esselte Film and Nordiske Film, to introduce pay TV (Prehn, 1990, p. D25). However, the union stations' financial losses mounted, and they were partly sold to Lifacto, a multinational company that owned Copenhagen's Kanal 2.

In Denmark, as in Norway, a discussion of new commercial media was linked with the question of advertising. Traditionally, the Nordic countries, with the exception of Finland and Iceland, have not permitted advertising. Reception of foreign commercial broadcast signals with advertising was accelerated by the emergence of satellite-delivered programs distributed to 35 percent of the households in Denmark over cable. Satellite transmissions made foreign advertising possible, but domestic advertising was still banned, thus disadvantaging Danish industry in its own country. Since 1988, advertising has been allowed.

In 1980, a media commission was appointed by the Social Democratic government to recommend policy. After five years, the commission published a report that recommended, among other things, the establishment of a second television channel. TV2 was set up as an independent public channel, with a dual national and regional structure, and began broadcasting in 1988. It is financed largely by advertising but is not a commercial channel. TV-Syd, one of the experimental TV stations, was converted into an independent TV station and became the first part of the new network. TV2 is governed by an eight-member central board, with five members appointed by the minister for communications, two appointed by regional boards and one by labor unions. Each of its eight regional enterprises, to be phased into operation by 1991, is similarly overseen by a regional board.

TV2 encourages independent TV production; the idea is that, for the first time, Danes will have a choice of outlets for domestically produced programming. It is hoped that Danish viewers who were disinterested in DR's schedule will turn to other Danish programming rather than to foreign networks.

TV2 is permitted to include advertisements, handled by the separate state-owned corporation TV-Reklame. Commercials for alcohol or tobacco are not permitted, and ads may not interrupt programming (Danmarks Radio, 1987). Advertising revenues supply about 70 percent of the station's budget. The other 30 percent comes from license fees of about $200 annually for color sets.

TV2 broadcasts in-house productions during 30 percent of its air time; 50 percent of its programming originated in Denmark and Norway. By 1989, TV2 had achieved viewing parity with DR (TBI, 1990).

In 1990, a fully commercial national channel, P4, was proposed.

Cable Television

The emergence of cable television as a driving force for media reform was unplanned. Until the 1980s, there was no clear governmental policy on cable television. Apartment complexes established master antennas to avoid a forest of individual ones. In time, they amplified weak signals from West German and Swedish stations (and sometimes East German and Norwegian signals). By 1983, almost 60 percent of all Danish households were connected to one of the 8000 master antenna (MATV) systems that are usually run by local housing associations. Most systems had six channels and less than 100 subscribers. However, some were much larger (Qvortrup, 1984). The Royal Danish Committee on Mass Media reported that eight MATV systems had more than 10,000 subscribers. Connection charge per subscriber was $300 to $400, plus an annual subscription charge of $20 to $35. The housing associations that operate the systems became an important independent force for media liberalization, since they represent viewers' interests.

In 1985, the Social Democrats and the Conservatives passed a new media law permitting the cabling of Copenhagen for satellite reception and cable TV and allowing the cable distribution of foreign television programs (*Medium,* 1985). This was a major step in liberalization. Under this law, however, the nonlocal distribution monopoly would still belong to the PTT. Only the PTT and the regional Danish telephone companies could receive satellite programs and distribute them.

This was based on a decade-old concept. In 1974, the established Danish cable manufacturer NKT had developed plans to link up with the Jutland Telephone Company, one of the Danish regional telephone organizations, in order to provide an integrated fiber-optic broadband network. This led to innovative network planning, and in 1980, details of the project were taking shape. The driving forces behind this project were the PTT and the four regional telephone companies (then independent), all of which were concerned about loss of control over satellite reception. In 1983, the Royal Commission on Mass Media proposed a "hybrid" solution, with an integrated national broadband network that would provide both television and telephone linkages. The PTT, however, preferred to separate telephony from broadband services in order to pursue the ISDN (integrated services digital network) route for telephony while linking the many MATV systems by a nationwide microwave network to the PTT-operated satellite earth stations. The regional telephone companies, on the other hand, were more eager for a nationwide integrated broadband communications system partly because an expansion to broadband service would free them from restrictions imposed by old agreements with the PTT (Qvortrup, 1984). And the influential housing associations had a still different perspective; they desired satellite programs received directly through their MATV systems without having to go through the telephone carriers at all. The most aggressive private cable network operator, Finvik, part of the larger Swedish firm Kennevik, took a similar position. Thus, the issue of a broadband network was shaped by the relative power relations between the PTT, the regional telephone companies, and the housing associations.

In 1986, the ruling center-left coalition and the Social Democratic opposition came to an agreement about a national broadband cable system. They approved the innovative Digital Optical CATV Trunk (DOCAT) system as a hybrid (digital/fiber, analog/coax) trunk system connecting the cable systems with satellite receiving stations and other sources of programming. The system is run by the PTT and the regional telephone companies and feeds television and radio channels to the local cable networks, which select and distribute them to households. DOCAT is viewed as a step toward an integrated broadband network.

Yet DOCAT met with strong resistance from influential local housing associates and cable companies, because it established a high-priced monopoly over satellite telephone and program importation. Many associations began to bypass the telephone companies and receive satellite signals directly and more cheaply.

Eventually, satellite reception was liberalized in 1987. The telephone organizations thus must work harder to make their investment in DOCAT worthwhile, and this creates an incentive for them to provide the seed money for many channels.

In 1991, 30 percent of the country was interconnected by DOCAT. Over 50 percent of Denmark (about 600,000 households) was effectively cabled and some 25 percent of all homes received satellite programming. Forty-eight percent of the TV audience regularly viewed Swedish stations and 31 percent watched West German stations. Yet over 80 percent of the viewers were watching Danish television, equally split between DR and TV2, showing a stable interest in national programs.

Conclusion

At the end of a decade's evolution, Danish television looked much changed. Where there once had been a sole public channel with limited appeal and supplemented by foreign spill-ins, there was now more diversity. These changes were the result of public preferences (evidenced by the popularity of pirate broadcasters), the wish of community groups to be heard and seen over the air, the desire of commercial interests for a national advertising outlet, and the emergence of numerous cable systems carrying a variety of imported channels. Although cable television began in an unplanned fashion, often at the initiative of housing associations, it soon became an industrial policy and prestige project for government and the telephone industry. The investments in the national cable interconnection are likely to create pressures for the transmission of further satellite programs and Danish channels. Barriers still exist, but further liberalization, including continued international and domestic integration, is likely.

19

Iceland

Despite Iceland's tiny population, which suggests a natural monopoly, Iceland's broadcasting system was also opened in the 1980s. This occurred when a conservative coalition came to power and found it popular as well as politically useful to provide a private alternative to the traditional one-channel public system.

Public broadcasting in Iceland dates back to 1930, when the Icelandic State Broadcasting Service (RUV-Rikisutvarpith) was formed. RUV is state-owned and is governed by a council whose thirteen members are elected by the Althing, the Icelandic parliament. Until the 1986 Broadcasting Act, RUV had a monopoly over broadcasting for both radio and television. The PTT installs and maintains radio and television transmitters and supplies fiber-optic links between studios and transmitters. Since the mid-1960s, the PTT has operated a high-powered transmitting station as a navigational service, with a 470 m-high antenna, the largest of its kind in the world (Post and Telecommunications Administration, 1987).

Television was introduced in 1966. Until October 1986, when it began operating every day of the week, RUV's television station operated only six days a week and was closed on Thursdays.

The inescapable realities of Iceland are its tiny population of 251,000, its remote location, and its distinct language. Diseconomies of scale abound. The cost of broadcasting is high, and revenues are minuscule. For a time, RUV even tried to derive income from the sale and repair of radio sets. Advertising revenues comprised 33 percent of total revenues (and declined after the second channel was introduced). Annual license fees for radio and television sets were a fairly high $187 in 1988. Total income of the RUV in 1988 was $31 million, which may be high per household but cannot buy many mobile studios. License fee revenue was supplemented by the Broadcasting Stations' Cultural Fund, established in the 1986 Act. The fund consists of a 10 percent levy on all broadcast advertisements (Gunnarsdottir, 1988, p. 21). On its budget, RUV had to operate one television and two radio channels, uphold Icelandic traditions and culture, support 25 percent of the Iceland Symphony Orchestra, provide a window to the world, and educate, inform, and entertain. Its network of foreign correspondents consists of one reporter permanently stationed in Copenhagen. For financial reasons, the 1984 Olympics were not shown live.

Unavoidably, most programs broadcast by RUV are imported (approximately

60 percent in 1990). If one subtracts news, current affairs, religious programs, and local sports from total broadcast time, the percentage of foreign imports is considerably higher. Of the imports, the great bulk is from the United Kingdom and the United States, which together comprise 67 percent. Despite the historical, cultural, and language affinities that Iceland shares with other Nordic countries, imports from these countries amount to less than 10 percent. Partly to protect Icelandic language traditions, all imports must be subtitled. American military forces stationed at the Keflavik Airbase provide limited low-power television broadcasting, which reaches the nearby region.

Despite (or perhaps because of) the broadcasting services' efforts, RUV was not uniformly popular in Iceland. It was criticized particularly by the young for a certain paternalism in matters of culture and language. Conservatives felt that it leaned too far left in its coverage. In 1983, a right-center coalition came to power, and with support from the Social Democrats and opposition from the People's Alliance party, ended the RUV monopoly. At the same time that it liberalized broadcast policy, the conservative government also put pressure on RUV's alleged leftists, in effect silencing several journalists. In 1983, a second radio channel went on the air, and included advertising. Since 1986, several other commercial radio stations began broadcasting, including Bylgjan (popular music), Ljosvakinn (light classical music), and Stjarnan (youth music and news). Ljosvakinn folded in 1987 and was replaced by Radio Alfa, a religious station. It too soon closed because of financial problems (Gunnarsdottir, 1990).

In 1985, the Althing passed a Broadcast Act that permitted, after 1986, private and municipal/regional television with license approval by a broadcasting committee elected by the Althing (RUV, 1985). Only Icelandic interests, however, were allowed to participate in this liberalization.

In 1986, Stod 2, a second television station, was inaugurated by the private ITC (Icelandic Television Corporation). ITC was originally owned by two dozen stockholders. Its unscrambled broadcasts (20 percent of the total) include news. A decoder is required to receive its pay programs. Pay-TV is not cheap. A subscription costs $38 per month plus $400 for a decoder. There is also advertising (TBI, 1990).

In 1990, Stod 2 was suffering financial difficulties, mostly because of the cost of producing its own programming. Its ownership changed. A rival national station, TV One, was created, owned by a former executive of Stod 2. It too is a pay service, with charges of $30 a month. A merger between the two pay services was likely. Stod 2 and TV One also petitioned the government to prohibit advertising on RUV (Nicholson, 1990).

By 1990, Iceland had a greater television diversity than its small population would have led one to expect. The explanations for the opening of the public broadcasting monopoly lie not in any technology push or European integrative force, but mainly in RUV's leaving a substantial share of its audience unserviced as it earnestly pursued a cultural mission. Extension of RUV's operations to a second and more entertainment-oriented channel might have been a logical solution, but the public institution had become identified with only part of the political environment, making it desirable for the opposition to establish commercial broadcasting as a counterweight, once it was in power. RUV's dual role as a cultural producer and distributor put it into constant financial pressures and at the mercy of the political system's willingness to approve high license fees on viewers. In the end, RUV's narrow identification prevented it from becoming broader, and the provision of programs serving centrist quality became privatized while the cultural mission remained public.

There is very little cable television in Iceland. Hence, satellite-delivered international program channels from Europe and North America are not yet distributed. But their arrival is likely, and will provide, together with DBS channels (e.g., from the Nordic Tele-X satellite) a considerable addition to Iceland's television choices, and more pressure on the public broadcasting system.

20

Ireland

Since its inception, the national broadcasting authority was faced with the challenge of treading its way through Ireland's various conflicts: the problems of Irish unification; the religious conflict; the question of the identity of the new state; the tensions between supporters of the English and Gaelic languages; the differences between city and country and between east and west.

Radio and Television

During the Irish Easter rising of 1916, revolutionaries occupied the General Post Office and the School of Telegraphy, proclaiming the Irish Free State by sending out telegraph communiques in a broadcastlike fashion (Bell, 1985). The revolutionaries also used a ship transmitter for their communiques. Neither constituted, however, the world's first broadcasting, as is sometimes erroneously claimed. In 1926, four years after the establishment of the Irish Free State, the implementation of radio broadcasting was accelerated by the fear that British Marconi interests were attempting to establish a broadcasting operation in Ireland. Broadcasting's role was to strengthen the national identity of the new country and to heal its wounds.

This task was not made easier by the politics that have always been part of the Irish broadcast environment. A participant remembers the beginnings of state radio:

> When proposals began to take shape for the setting up of a station the protectors of the nation were in like a ton of bricks, and every moralist on two legs was buzzing with concern for the dangers to our Irish way of life, whatever that might be. A commission of inquiry was appointed and the outcome was that broadcasting was established under the safe, paternal umbrella of the Department of Posts and Telegraphs, as the department in charge of communications [Kelly, 1976, pp. 17–18].

With the Wireless Telegraphy Act of 1926, broadcasting became a state concern operated by the postal ministry. Financial support was obtained through license fees. Advertising yielded hardly any revenue, and advertisements aimed at Britain were restricted (Richard Pine, communication). Broadcasting grew slowly. By 1933, full national coverage was achieved, but there were still fewer than 30,000 licensed sets. The government viewed broadcasting primarily as a tool for promoting a sense of national identity rather than as an independent professional operation. It also starved the broadcasting system of funds (these were needed for more urgent infrastructural tasks—roadbuilding, power plant construction, and so forth), and denied it the ability to accept advertising freely. When international shortwave broadcasting was resumed after World War II, the government finally became supportive of Irish broadcasting.

The Broadcasting Act of 1960 established the radio authority Radio Eireann, which was renamed *Radio Telefis Eireann* (RTE) with the introduction of television. Television arrived in Ireland relatively late (1962), prompted once again by the wide availability of British broadcasts. A governmental television commission had been instituted in 1958 that prohibited the accrual of television costs to the government. Although a commercial operation had been briefly contemplated, television went on to operate as a public institution, with television studios allegedly located on the grounds of the family home of Marconi's mother, Annie Jameson.

The progressive impact of TV on Irish society cannot be overestimated. TV entered during the 1960s, providing a vehicle for broadcasting controversial debate, and was met by opposition from conservative governmental groups (Murphy, 1990).

The importance of Irish content was stressed from the inception of RTE television. For a young service in a small country, the proportion of domestically produced programs was large: during the mid-1960s, more than 60 percent of its output was domestically produced. This percentage has since declined to 40 percent, partly because of an increase in the total number of broadcast hours and partly for financial reasons. Gaelic-language programs account for 4 percent of total broadcast time. RTE has encouraged independent production, and Irish independents held a 45 percent share in its programs in 1988 (Rohan, 1988).

RTE is an independent public authority, operates its own transmission system, and is governed by a nine-member board appointed by the government. Former employees and critics of the organization have accused it of being full of the "self-censorship of senior officials, in a poor, small country which is notorious for its preoccupation with job-security" (Doolan et al., 1969, p. 363).

During the late 1960s, with unrest in Ulster creating problems in the Republic, the government imposed direct censorship over broadcast news and current affairs coverage. When RTE interviewed a spokesman for the Provisional IRA in 1972, the government dismissed the entire broadcasting authority and appointed a new board.

A special radio service to the Gaeltacht (the Gaelic speaking region) was authorized in 1970 and started in 1972. By 1987 Raidio na Gaeltachta had expanded to become a national service that broadcast fifty-three hours weekly of news, public affairs, sports, and traditional singing (Raidio na Gaeltachta, 1987).

In 1978, a second RTE television channel commenced broadcasting. This followed a long and bitter dispute over whether the British BBC service should simply be relayed to those parts of Ireland not already receiving it or whether a second Irish channel should be provided. The government initially supported the idea of more comprehensive distribution of programming but then took a public survey of viewer preferences. An emotional political campaign followed that registered preferences for an Irish channel over the BBC service by a margin of two to one. Government financing did not increase to support the new channel, however, and advertising revenues and license fees remained relatively stagnant. RTE 2, renamed Network 2, is designed to offer complementary programming to RTE 1.

The largest problem faced by RTE is financial. Advertising produced slightly more than half of the organization's revenues in the late 1970s, although this has increased to about two-thirds in the last few years. Advertising rates must be government approved. License fees are also controlled by the government, which has only grudgingly increased these fees over the years (RTE, 1983). RTE also suffers from what it refers to as the "scandal of evasion" of license fees. According to its Annual Report of 1983, Ireland has the highest European rate of license fee nonpayment.

RTE was affected by the numerous illegal radio stations in the country. Despite occasional raids, these stations operated, especially between 1975 and 1988, with relative impunity, causing serious losses in audience and revenues for RTE. The pirate radio broadcasters operated on unauthorized frequencies and occasionally used material from the public broadcast stations in their newscasts (Bell, 1985). Major political figures were connected with some of these stations. In 1981, the government introduced a Local Radio Authority bill, which would have provided private commercial local radio services separate from those of RTE. The legislature was dissolved, however, before acting on the bill. New legislation was proposed in 1985 to establish CORA, a community broadcasting authority to license and regulate private local broadcasters. This legislation failed due to opposition by the small Labour party (Pine and Thomas, 1986). Labour was to remain RTE's staunchest political supporter throughout the mid-1980s as pressures for media liberalization rapidly increased.

Another Local Radio Bill submitted late in 1986 by the Minister for Communications was unsuccessful in yet another attempt to thwart the activities of lucrative pirate stations. The bill proposed that local radio broadcasting in Dublin and Cork, the largest metropolitan areas, be controlled by RTE, which would also fund a supervisory body, the Local Radio Commission. The licensing of a new private station serving the Dublin region was also recommended.

In 1987 the government changed. The conservative Fianna Fáil party assumed power; Labour joined the Fine Gael group (liberal-conservative) in opposition. The Progressive Democrats, a splinter group from Fianna Fáil, proposed radical modernization and privatization within the public sector. This catalyzed the shift toward broadcast deregulation and commercialization, ultimately ending RTE's legal monopoly (Murphy, 1990).

The new government introduced a Broadcasting and Wireless Telegraphy Bill in late 1987, which sought to establish independent radio operations and legalize many of the pirates. It was in part a response to British pressure for elimination of pirate stations, many of which aimed at the U.K. market. In 1988, the newly founded Independent Radio and Television Commission (IRTC) was charged with the responsibility of distributing twenty-five broadcast radio licenses. The initial offering drew eighty-three applicants, despite advertising restrictions (maximum 15 percent of air time) and a 20 percent news programming requirement. This measure effectively eliminated the pirate stations, at least in the short term.

The IRTC's other primary responsibility was to issue a nationwide radio franchise. This was awarded to Century Communications in 1989.

The legislation instituting the IRTC provided also for a third public TV station. Particularly significant was a relaxation of the requirement that at least 40 percent of programming carried on the channel must be domestically produced. Instead, it was required that an "appropriate amount" of material originate in the EC. The new independent commercial channel TV3, launched in 1990, is run by an Irish consortium (the Windmill Lane Group) representing major forces in the country's television, film, and video industry. Twenty-five percent is held by the Smurfit Group, Ireland's largest company. Distribution is through the existing cable network as well as through microwave (MMDS). The MMDS system, to be newly constructed according to government blueprint, will involve twenty-nine transmitter units, each serving about 10,000 potential subscribers within a twenty-mile radius and offering twelve channels. Cost to subscribers was estimated at $280 per year, twice as high as that for cable. But the high level of cable penetration in Dublin (eighty-three percent in 1990) indicates a substantial market demand throughout much of the rest of the country for multichannel television (Rohan, 1989). Nevertheless, it is a risky proposition for the new commercial channel TV3 to be dependent on the success of a fairly new transmission mode that has not been successful (e.g., in the United States), and therefore access to UHF broadcasting was grudgingly added by the 1990 Broadcasting Act.

Like Britain's Channel Four, the new station will subcontract most program production (apart from news and current affairs) to independents. Fifteen percent of its airtime (an anticipated 75 hours per week) may be used for advertising, compared with 10 percent for the two RTE channels.

RTE's financial prospects have been subject to attack through political pressure to abolish its rights to advertising. The Broadcasting Act of 1990 limited RTE's advertising to 7.5 percent of air time while allowing twice as much for IRTC licenses. The bill placed a cap of IR £55 million ($88 million) on RTE's advertising revenues and diverted 25% of license fees to independent TV and radio firms (Rohan, 1990, p. 7). Lost revenues were expected to force significant cutbacks at RTE. It made it less likely to ensure that 25 percent of programming was produced domestically. The Act also gave the minister powers to establish broadcast standards and strengthened the Broadcasting Complaints Commission (Kenny, 1990, p. 6).

Cable and Satellite Television

With more than fifty licensed operators, Ireland is fairly extensively cabled, particularly on its eastern shore.

About one-third of all households are passed by cable, of which more than three-quarters are subscribers. This high penetration ratio is comparable to that of Holland and Belgium. Each of these countries is relatively small, and its viewers desire programs of larger neighboring countries. Network capacity is limited to nine to ten channels throughout most of the country. Cork and Limerick have systems with potentially over twenty channels (Logica, 1987). In the past, Irish cable was restricted to carrying the two Irish and four British broadcast channels. Only Cork had a local channel as well. Cable operators varied this official menu subsequently by offering pay TV. In 1986, it became permissible to carry international satellite-delivered programs on Irish cable channels. This policy was opposed by RTE, since it introduced further competition for its broadcasts. The non-RTE cable systems, in contrast, were solidly in favor of permitting cable satellite-delivered channels in order to make their product more attractive. The rules remained restrictive, with only two satellite channels for the older systems and a maximum of four for the newer ones. Furthermore, cable operators could not charge for the new services. Most cable operators added Superchannel and Sky.

The Wireless Telegraphy Act of 1974 established regulations for cable television by setting a 15 percent charge on cable subscription revenue, to be paid to RTE. Since 1970, RTE has also operated its own cable system distribution networks. These were originally named RTE Relays and then renamed Cablelink in 1988. Cablelink acquired several private cable operators; many of these were concentrated in the Dublin area, where, with approximately 250,000 subscribers, it had a virtual monopoly.

In 1991, Cablelink served 290,000 homes with nine program channels. In 1988, RTE offered its 80 percent share for sale and an open tender process was established. The national PTT Telecom Eireann bought half of the RTE stake, as well as the remaining 20 percent held by financier Allied Combined Trust (O'Carroll, 1990).

In 1983, the government appointed a cable television committee chaired by Communications Minister James Mitchell, and mandated an examination of national telecommunications policy, including the issues of DBS and data transmission. In 1985, the committee recommended that cable television distribution be expanded, that cable operations be privately financed in a method similar to Britain's, and that cable operators be given latitude in program selection. The committee report provided for a governmental role to encourage two-way cable service if private interests fail to do so, and a national distribution network for cable programming under the aegis of the telecommunications authority Bord Telecom Eireann (TE). Furthermore, the Department of Communications would regulate and license cable systems, replacing prior licenses with new ones. Licenses would run for twenty years for systems with interactive capability and ten years for those without. RTE would receive up to 15 percent of subscription fees as compensation for income loss due to congestion from cable television. Cable operators would not be obligated to provide programs for special interest viewing and would be loosely supervised by a consultative council.

Direct Satellite Broadcasting

After the collapse of the British DBS project Unisat in 1985, interest grew in an Irish DBS system that could broadcast programs to Britain and continental Europe. The government granted a license to Atlantic Satellites, a company founded by the Irish businessman James Stafford. The American firm Hughes Communications, owned by General Motors, won Irish governmental approval in 1986 to launch a DBS project and bought 80 percent of Atlantic Satellite (Multichannel News, 1986, p. 17). The project was similar to the Luxembourg Coronet venture in which Hughes was comparably involved, and which failed after fierce French and general European PTT opposition.

A rival DBS consortium, WestSat, comprising the two national authorities, RTE (broadcast) and TE (telecommunications), as well as Irish commercial interests, was also formed. The government, however, rejected its application, because it did not want governmental organizations to enter into a high-risk DBS venture.

Conclusion

The fundamental contradiction experienced by Irish broadcasters is that the government (and many of those it represents) expects it to play a key role in fostering the country's cultural identity, yet is unwilling to adequately pay for this function. While RTE struggles, cable televison is becoming widespread, providing greater program diversity and program spread than in the past. In time, an integration of the various distribution modes with film production is likely to take hold, and Ireland could become an exporter of programs and production activities.

Television in the
Mediterranean Countries
and Eastern Europe

21

Spain

Spain is one of Europe's largest countries, but its many problems during this century have kept it out of the mainstream of European politics and economics. The democratic governments that followed the Franco dictatorship inherited an unusually varied broadcast structure. After a phase of centralizing government control, Spanish television, even without cable distribution, is beginning to open up and join the evolution in the rest of Europe.

History

Radio was initiated in Spain by Antonio de Castilla in 1917 with the establishment of the private Iberian Telecommunications Company for radio sets (Emery, 1969). Experimental broadcasts were begun in 1918. In 1923, the government decreed a code for radio regulation, establishing a state monopoly, but with the possibility for private licenses, placing it under the supervision of the Ministry of Interior. Radio Barcelona, the first private station, began transmissions in 1924. After some consolidation, Radio Iberia emerged as the primary station, and other stations were rapidly granted licenses. Low-power stations were also approved and networks soon emerged. In 1929, a state radio system was proposed, and in 1934, the law establishing the system was passed. At the outbreak of the Civil War in 1936, there were sixty-eight radio stations, the most important of which were Union Radio and its successor, the Sociedad Española de Radiodiffusión (SER) (Lopez-Escobar and Faus-Belau, 1985).

In 1937, the Franco rebels established the Radio Nacional de España (RNE), which became the official government station after their Civil War victory in 1939. It was awarded a monopoly over radio news, and all other stations were required to carry its news broadcasts exclusively. This state monopoly of news dissemination was later extended to television and led to its low credibility.

The Spanish Broadcasting Authority was created in February 1942 and placed under the control of the National Ministry of Education three years later. After 1945, the Franco regime granted licenses for several new radio stations and chains to its various supporters, which included the Church, the official national labor union, the Falange party, certain business interests, and the provincial branches of the Franco party (Franuquet, 1986; Gorostiaga, 1976; Ezcurra,

1984). It did so outside the allocations of the international frequency system, from which it had been excluded as an illegitimate regime.

The regime later permitted the establishment of low-power local stations. By 1962 there were about 1300 such radio transmitters in the country! The state loosened its tight restrictions on news coverage in 1964, allowing the nongovernmental radio stations to begin carrying some local news in addition to the official RNE menu. But only the SER stations did so; the others cautiously abstained (Faus-Belau, 1990). During the 1960s, however, most of the small local stations were shut down and others were required to upgrade their equipment. By the time of Franco's death in 1975, there were 210 stations still operating (Lopez-Escobar and Faus-Belau, 1985).

Television service began with a single channel in 1956 provided by the government authority Televisión Española. A second channel was added in 1965, and color broadcasting began in 1969 (de Moragas et al., 1986). In contrast to radio, television operated from the beginning as a state monopoly. Unlike common European practice, TVE exists without license fee financing and, until 1984, relied on a budgetary allocation by the state and advertising revenue. Until 1977, the Ministry of Information made certain that television news content adhered to the official line.

By the end of the Franco regime, several radio networks had emerged, including the private SER system, which was owned primarily by two families and the newspaper *El País* and which controlled fifty-four AM stations. The country's other large networks included the following: the Franco-controlled REM/CAR, with forty-seven stations; the Church's COPE, network with forty-four; CES, run by the official trade union movement, with twenty-seven; and RNE, the official governmental system, with twenty-one. Two smaller private networks, CRI and RATO, were also operating in 1985.

Regulation and Reform

A former member of Franco's regime characterized the governmental broadcast system that the Generalissimo left behind in 1975 as being "industrially obsolete, economically extravagant and intellectually reactionary" (Howkins, 1983, p. 22). By the time of the dictator's death in 1975, it had become obvious that change was necessary. But the new government did not want to relinquish its influence over broadcasting. In 1977, the first of Prime Minister Adolfo Suarez's broadcasting reforms went into effect, with a royal decree proclaiming freedom of speech over radio. Yet the government also kept a 25 percent ownership in larger private broadcasting operations. Soon thereafter, several of the Church and labor organization stations were integrated into the state RCE system, which must be distinguished from the advertising-free governmental RNE network that remained. RCE, RNE, and RTE were put under a holding organization RTVE, the central institution of Spanish broadcasting. Thus, the state broadcasting apparatus created by the fascist dictatorship was preserved and strengthened even though it was now run by a democratic regime.

Two years later, however, the Suarez government opened up FM radio to new private entrants by initiating a two-phase process for the issuance of 300 new licenses for low-power and local broadcasting. More than 2000 applications for the stations were received from a variety of groups, including private firms, political parties, local governments, publishers, and labor unions. Most of the first group of licenses went to established broadcasters and publishing firms.

Two networks emerged from among the new stations: Antenna-3, a system of stations run by private newspapers, and Radio 80. Competition from these new networks reinvigorated the private SER and the Church-run COPE networks. Private radio networks included SER (140 stations), COPE (98), RR (37), Antena 3/Radio BU (50), and Cadena 13 (13) (de Moragas et al., 1986).

The Suarez government also authorized regional governments to allocate broadcast licenses. This new policy led to the proliferation of public municipal FM stations, which often operated without any license or authorization, and to the growth of the pirate "radios libres." In 1988, there were an estimated 640 unauthorized radio stations in operation. The local and regional governments' ability to run their own public radio stations encouraged the creation of official broadcasting organizations on a variety of government levels, since each desired a direct access to the population.

The Socialist government that followed accelerated the trend toward official radio. The plan gave 31 percent of the 1856 new FM stations to the state broadcasting system, 8 percent to regional governments, and 42 percent to local authorities. Only 18 percent went to private broadcasters, whose stations were also often restricted to much lower signal strength than official stations. Of the private licenses, many went to individuals and firms supporting the Socialists, and they quickly announced plans to organize into a national network dubbed the "Rose Network." The governmental RCE and RNE also received twenty-two additional licenses and were merged into one radio organization, RNE. Despite the enormous allocation to official stations, they have only 20 percent of the audience, whereas 80 percent listen to private stations (Faus-Belau, 1990).

RTVE consists of three separate divisions: TVE (Televisión España) and the two radio networks RNE (Radio Nacional de España), and RCE (Radio Cadena Española). RTVE conducts broadcast transmission and provides the links between its various transmitters rather than employing the telephone monopoly Telefónica. It is controlled by a board of governors appointed by the two chambers of Parliament (i.e., by the major political parties). RTVE's director general is appointed directly by the government and not by the board. The director general, in turn, appoints the directors of the television and radio companies and their regional representatives. Because RTVE's high administrative officers depend on political appointments, changes in the composition of the governmental bodies lead to turnover at the top of RTVE.

The first director general, Fernando Castedo, a member of the centrist Democratic Union, resigned after only six months in office. His resignation was the result of pressure from narrow-minded conservative politicians who charged him with giving the opposition too much influence over broadcasting by encouraging independent broadcasting. His successor, Robles Piquer, was related to the leader of the conservatives, and his appointment was thus a response to criticism that the RTVE had become too liberal. These moves damaged the RTVE's embryonic neutral image. The changes also triggered heated confrontations within the television staff, and hundreds of members signed petitions for and against various policies of the authority.

In 1982, the Socialist party received an absolute electoral majority. Like the UCD before it, the Socialists found it difficult to permit truly independent broadcasting, and the government of Prime Minister Felipe Gonzalez exerted strong control over both television and radio. It increased the number of government radio stations by incorporating a number of private stations into the public RCE network and in the process gave the state, for the first time, control over a majority of Spanish radio stations. The government also blocked the introduction of private television broadcasting, which was on the brink of realization. Partly as a result of the politicization of the broadcast institutions, the listenership of RNE stations dropped precipitously.

In 1983, the Socialists enacted their own reform of the broadcasting charter and brought RTVE under the direction of a new government department, the Ministry of the Presidency. Only one-half of RTVE's administrative board would be elected by the two chambers of Parliament; the rest of its members would represent cultural, educational, and economic interests. Through the exercise of powers accorded to the government under a constitutional court decision, RTVE's monopoly was extended into all forms of broadcasting and transmission, including cable and satellites.

The government also passed a law permitting the establishment of a third television channel under state control. In addition, it provided for broadcast concessions to be granted to autonomous regions such as that of the Basques, who wanted to operate their own programs. The Basques and Catalans advocacy of provisions for regionally controlled broadcasting came to fruition with the creation of a third RTVE channel designed to feature regionally provided programming. Although this station was placed under the control of the central government, elements of decentralization were built into its organizational structure. When the new channel was introduced, the ruling Socialist party was not in power in either of these regions, and thus its locally provided programming supplied a measure of political contrast to the fare provided by RTVE's national stations. For that reason, the Socialists were not very enthusiastic about regional TV.

Because the Spanish constitution guarantees the freedom of expression through the media, those seeking the liberalization of broadcasting brought a number of cases before the constitutional court. The first case was argued in 1980, when an applicant for a private television channel sued the government to force it to act upon requests it had previously ignored. The court ruled that although private television broadcasting was not prohibited by the Spanish constitution, the right to allow it was a political matter and thus the prerogative of the government.

In 1982, the second case resulted in a temporary liberalization of television similar to the landmark decision of the Italian constitutional court a decade earlier. The suit was a challenge to state television monopoly brought by Antena-3, a venture of several large publishers. Referring to the constitutional principle of free speech, the court found no basis in the Spanish constitution for the existence of such a governmental monopoly. Until Parliament succeeded in passing a law specifically outlawing it, private broadcasting was thus permissible (Howkins, 1983). Eight companies announced their interest in television licenses, including one company that was already operating SER, the country's largest private radio network. Among the others were a left-wing newspaper, various Catholic organizations, and Basque, Catalan, and Valencian interests. The political center and right were in favor of this liberalization, but the Socialist party opposed it.

In 1984, the publishing group *El País,* a newspaper close to the government, acquired control of the private radio network SER, thus bringing the largest private broadcast network in Europe into the government's orbit. Allegedly, the government exerted pressure on the stock owners of SER to sell to *El País.* The government owned 25 percent of SER since the end of the Franco regime.

An important attempt to reorganize overall Spanish telecommunications and media was made with the decision of the proposed Communications Ordinance Decree (LOC) in 1985, which aimed to integrate the various telecommunications authorities. This attempt at broad reform was stalled, however, by a government crisis, leading instead to the introduction of several narrower reform bills.

Under the provisions of the television reform, RTVE was to begin sharing its authority with three regional television operations, one for each of the three major Spanish regions, but all three operated under state or community government control. These regional organizations would be supervised by administrative committees appointed by either regional legislators or the Spanish Parliament, with the membership of each reflecting the strength of the various political parties (de Moragas et al., forthcoming).

In 1986, the Socialist government published a bill for the legalization of private television and the establishment of three private networks. It was criticized as requiring several years for actual implementation and as providing inadequate assurances of renewal in case of a change of government. It specified that 40 percent of the programs on the new private channels would be of Spanish origin and that advertising would be permitted for up to ten minutes per hour. Foreign investment would be allowed up to 25 percent of total ownership, provided it came from other EC countries and Latin America (i.e., not from the United States). The law was enacted in 1988, and the government began granting licenses in 1989. Transmission facilities were transferred to a new state agency, Retevisión (Magdaleno, 1989).

The most successful of the new regional television channels was Telemadrid, which gained over 40 percent of the audience in Madrid in a short time. Others were TV3 and Canal 33 (Barcelona stations in Catalan language), TV Galicia,

Televisión Valencia, Canal Sur (Andalucia), and Euskal Telebista (Basque). These regional stations formed the Association of Autonomous Television Stations. In many instances, they are dependent on their regional governments.

Cable television came to Spain in 1970, with the government's extension of cable rights to RTVE. Two years later, RTVE entered into an agreement with the telecommunications administration CTNE (also known as Telefónica) for the construction of pilot networks in Madrid and Barcelona. Trunk lines were laid for these networks, but for a variety of reasons, no households were ever connected to them.

Subsequently, cable service existed only on a very small scale. Although Telefónica had a general interest in its development, the administration was not given legislative support and had to abandon a Madrid development. There were only a few municipal pilots projects in place and two tiny private systems. In 1986, however, the Catalan regional government initiated a project for Barcelona, as part of modernizing for the 1992 Olympic Games. Telefónica also began to plan for a Madrid system as a core of national cable distribution. In 1991, the government announced plans to award franchises in five large cities.

In 1989, the government awarded three licenses for national commercial networks to Antena 3, Canal Plus, and Tele-5. Charges of political favoritism were made when two other broadcast groups, Canal C and Grupo Zeta, the latter backed by Rupert Murdoch, were denied licenses. Each channel must offer at least 40 percent domestic programming. Antena 3, a consortium of 24 newspaper publishers, several radio stations, and foreign investors (20 percent) was the first to begin broadcasting in 1989, after the October 1989 elections, with a fairly domestic and family-oriented programming. Canal Plus is a pay channel owned by the French company of the same name (25 percent), the dailies *El País* (25 percent), Prisa (20 percent), an ex-minister of the Socialist government, and others. Tele-5 is owned by the Italian Silvio Berlusconi, the publisher Anaya, and the semiofficial Spanish Institute for the Blind. In just six months, with imported programming, Tele-5 won a 27 percent audience rating and $90 million in revenues for 1990. Tele-5 reached 34 percent of Spanish viewers concentrated in major urban areas, and planned national coverage by 1994. Indirectly, the government has some influence over Canal Plus and Tele-5.

Conclusion

Broadcasting in the Iberian Peninsula was for a long time distinct from the rest of Europe, since the fascist government's attitude toward private participation was ambiguous. On the one hand, the strong state required state broadcasting as a means of propaganda. But on the other hand, it rewarded private supporters, and its corporatist ideology permitted broadcasting by the Church, official labor organizations, and municipalities. The system inherited by the new democratic regime was thus mixed, at least for radio, and susceptible to opening, especially given the left's relative tolerance of a mixed system. At first, radio was liberalized, though with a strong emphasis on official radio. The radio model was continued into television, in which more publishers participate and international media firms actively participate. The strong regional diversity of the country also led to autonomous public and private broadcast institutions.

Spain is only beginning to evolve into an information society, but the trend is unmistakable and will lead in time to a greater diversity of content, as well as role in production, especially for Latin America, in the way that it already does in the very active telephone sector.

Broadcasting in Gibraltar

Gibraltar is located at the southern tip of the Iberian Peninsula and has been a British possession since 1704. Its relations with neighboring Spain have been strained, since Spain claims it as its own. In 1958, government radio broadcasting began in Gibraltar. Four years later, a private local broadcast operation with connections to the Thomson organization started its own service. In 1963, the two were merged to create the independent Gibraltar Broadcasting Corporation (GibBC), which was managed by Thomson television until 1978 (Black, 1980).

GibBC is formally run by a board of eight members who answer to the governor-in-council. The board is responsible for broadcasting standards and practices and maintains editorial independence from the government. The government supports GibBC through subsidies because advertising revenues, given the area's small population, are not adequate. Additional financing comes from license fees. GibBC Radio broadcasts a fair amount of Spanish-language programming, but television is available only in English. A second radio service was started in the early 1980s on the VHF band.

22
Portugal

Portugal's broadcast system has traditionally been an instrument of influence used by those holding or seeking political power: first the fascist dictatorship then the various factions in the struggles that followed the revolution. With the eventual calming of domestic turmoil, the broadcast system too slowly began to become more independent.

Early radio broadcasting can be dated back to 1914 and the amateur-operated Radio Hertz in Lisbon. Other short-lived experiments followed until 1925, when CTIAA began regular transmission (Erhardt, 1990, p. D188). This and other stations came under governmental control in 1930, followed by the formation of a state-run operation, the Emissora Nacional de Radiodifusaõ (ENR), in 1933. ENR was originally commercial-free, but accepted advertisements after 1950. Throughout the fascist dictatorship, its popularity was continually low in comparison to the private regional stations that had predated it (Optenhoegel, 1986). ENR provided three national radio channels and five regional programs, including service to the islands of Madeira and the Azores. Among the private stations, the main presence was Rádio Clube Português, which began in 1928, supported by private members and advertising revenue. In the late 1930s smaller private broadcasters combined into the transmission group Emissores Associados de Lisboa. A similar unification occurred in Oporto in 1941, with the formation of the Emissores do Norte Reunidos. Another important station was Radio Renascença, which has been run by the Catholic Church since 1936.

It is interesting to note that the world's first book on television was published in Portugal, as early as 1880 (TBI, 1990)! In 1955, Radio-Televisáo Portuguesa (RTP) was established by the government, separate from ENR, as the national company for television broadcasting. RTP was owned jointly by the state (60 percent), private radio broadcasters (20 percent), and the public through representation by several banks (20 percent). RTP started broadcasting in 1957 and expanded both domestically and abroad, adding a second channel in 1968 and servicing the several Portuguese colonies existing at the time.

Of the two state-run television channels, RTP-1 broadcasts to all of Portugal and RTP-2, for a long time, to only about one-half of the country. RTP-2 in 1991 reached 80 percent of the country. Each receives over half of its income from advertising under a system whereby commercial time is limited to eight minutes per hour, but the limits are often not reached. The selling of advertisements is assigned to a separate advertising agency which is an RTP subsidiary.

TV penetration in Portugal is the lowest in Western Europe. Many sets, however, are undeclared. Similarly, most videocassette recorders in use in Portugal were imported illegally to avoid high tariffs and thus were outside of official statistics.

The various Portuguese broadcasting institutions all played important parts in the 1974 revolution. It was a private radio station that signaled members of the armed forces over the airwaves to start their uprising, by playing an agreed upon revolutionary song. Almost immediately, the rebels occupied the other radio and television transmitters. RTP played a major role in the political discussions that opened as a result of the revolution, and its lively programs initially epitomized the freedom of expression that had been won.

But just as the broadcasters had a major influence over the course of the revolt, the various political factions taking part in it sought to extend their own control over the broadcasters. Both RTP and ENR came under the control of the communist sympathizers and the wing of the military with which it was affiliated. In 1975, Rádio Renascença was occupied for several months by a Maoist workers' group that used its facilities to publicize its own messages. Programs from the USSR, Poland and Bulgaria were aired. Extreme leftist control over broadcasting was reduced only at the end of 1975, when democratic forces prevailed.

In that year, nearly all private radio stations were nationalized and, in a wide-reaching move, merged with ENR into the new public broadcasting authority Radiodifusao Portuguesa (RDP). There were, however, several exceptions to this sweeping nationalization, including Radio Renascença, which was returned to Church control. At the same time, the government assumed sole ownership of the television authority RTP.

These changes did not end the disputes over control of broadcast institutions. Politicization contributed to an enormous turnover in the membership of the various boards controlling RDP; institutional continuity was reduced and party affiliation was emphasized in the sixteen changes of government, many provisional, that followed the revolution. This led to considerable organizational chaos, which was in turn complicated by financial problems. The revolution was also followed by eleven democratic governments, but several were led by the same prime ministers.

The broadcast institutions are regulated by a media council whose members are appointed by Parliament to assure pluralistic control. The Constitution also provides for the right of political parties, professional associations, and trade unions to receive access to an amount of broadcast time proportional to their size. The guarantees of independence enshrined in the 1974 constitution have been ineffectual, however, and the broadcast institutions have suffered through great uncertainty. In 1980, the governmental control over broadcasting was extended to cable television, though none had been introduced to Portugal at that time.

The popularity of the public channels, much of which consists of subtitled foreign offerings, is modest (Specht, 1986).

Foreign shows account for about 40 percent of total programming. Particularly influential are American films and the Brazilian-inspired soap operas known as *telenovelas,* which have had an impact on social customs. Also available to a number of viewers are several channels from Spain, which reach about one-quarter of the Portuguese population and capture 15 percent of the audience. Critics argue that RTP should aim at creating more Portuguese programming (Torres, 1989, p. 14).

Pressures for the introduction of private media existed in Portugal for some time. In the 1970s, a pirate television station began operating openly in Oporto, Portugal's second largest city, but it was soon shut down by the government. In 1988, there were an estimated 600 radio pirates on the air, which could be licensed after the government capitulated and began to legalize them. In an effort to satisfy the demand for a wider selection of television programming, Portugal joined the pan-European satellite channel Europa-TV with the intention of using its own RTP-2 channel to rebroadcast the satellite programs terrestrially. However, Europa-TV closed its operations in 1986. This led to the consideration of commercial television. The 1976 and 1982 constitutions and subsequent broadcasting law stated that television should not be private property. Radio licenses were possible after a July 1988 law. However, this restrictive article was dropped from the revised 1989 Constitution. Broadcasting licenses for TV could therefore be subsequently issued, and the previous media council was replaced by a media regulatory authority to monitor the independence of communications media (Ehrhardt, 1990, p. D191).

During the presidential election campaign of 1985, the right-of-center Social Democratic party promised to reduce the government's role in broadcasting by eventually privatizing the RTP-2 television channel, two radio stations, and a dozen newspapers. Regionalized private television was also favored, since regional transmitters built in Lisbon or Oporto could reach the majority of the country's population (Torres, 1989, p. 13).

Eventually, the government decided to license two private stations, with operations to start in 1991. Contenders were independent associations, politically connected media companies, and European media firms. They included Sociedade Independente de Comunicacao (SIC) and TV Nova. SIC was led by former Prime Minister Francisco Pinto Balsemao (who holds magazine interests in *Expresso*), and Granada Television, with links to Canal Plus, Hachette, and Brazil's TV-Globo. TV Nova was led by SONEA, Portugal's largest consortium, and has ties with France's TF-1 (*Screen Finance,* 1990). Another consortium involved another major publisher. Silvio Berlusconi of Italy was also a participant in the process. A particular complication was that the Social Democrats had pledged in the past to give a license to Radio Renascença. Yet the 1989 broadcast law outlining private television denied preferential treatment for the Church, suggesting that Church involvement would be unconstitutional. More likely was that Renascença would share time in RPT-2. The law also required 50 percent of programs to be in Portuguese, with 10 percent of the programming produced domestically (Torres, 1990, p. 10). These production quotas are difficult to meet, and Portugal may thus become dependent upon Brazilian imports. The Constitution also requires access to RTP by various social and political movements, and a right of reply (Ehrhardt, 1990). These provisions will help transform RTP into a more independent broadcaster, though the government was first actively putting its own partisans into control in the time-honored tradition of RTP. The introduction of cable television was also proposed, and was awaiting legal clarification of the channels it could carry. There are also several thousand satellite receiving antennas in Portugal, serving the unsatisfied demand for program diversity. Liberalizing legislation was expected that would not require any franchise.

As Portugal moves into the European mainstream, so will its broadcasting media move from a politicized spoils system to a more open system. At the beginning of the 1990s, the viewing options available to the public were still more limited than anywhere else in Western Europe, but the 1989 Constitution made change likely.

23
Turkey

Despite several attempts to reduce the government's influence, the development of Turkish broadcasting has often been strictly controlled by a series of autocratic regimes. As a result, the Turkish broadcast institution has periodically functioned with a general at its head, and broadcast policy has been characterized by restrictiveness and censorship, with slow opening arriving only recently.

Historically, Turkish rulers have been extraordinarily wary of communications. For a long time, printing was outlawed. The first printer, a Hebrew press, was permitted in 1493 but was prohibited from printing Turkish and Arabic books (Karpat, 1964, p. 255). Turkish-language printing did not begin until 1727! By 1830, only 100 books had been printed.

The first newspapers were started by French and British citizens. The foreign-owned press was protected by special treaties imposed on Turkey, and foreign publications were at times more numerous than Turkish papers. In 1908, only three Turkish newspapers had survived, with a combined circulation of 29,000. But this changed with the ascent of the Young Turks that year. Within five years there were 161 Turkish-language papers alone, many of which were highly political. This situation was curbed during World War I, but liberalized again under Mustafa Kemal Ataturk, when the sultanate was abolished in 1922.

Broadcasting control was lodged in the Telecommunication and Postal Authority by a law enacted in 1924, one of the first of the Turkish Republic. In 1926, the Turkish Telephones and Telegraphs Ltd. received a broadcast concession from the postal authority, which was a part owner (Ansay, 1986). Since 1936, broadcasting has been under tight government control. In 1940, the Directorate General of the Press assumed supervision of broadcasting. In 1935, fewer than 8000 receivers existed in the entire country, and in 1942, there was still less than one-half set per 100 population, most of them in Istanbul and Ankara.

After World War II, there was agitation to open broadcasting to the ruling Republic People's Party's (RPP) new opposition, but it did not prevail. Even though its victory had been well supported by the press, the autocratic Democratic Party (DP) regime that followed after 1950 shut out the RPP and thoroughly dominated the airwaves. Following the overthrow of the Menderes regime and his DP party, the democratic constitution of 1961 provided for an independent public broadcast authority. Menderes was tried and accused, among other acts, of abusing the state radio. A 1963 law established an independent and impartial broadcast institution, TRT. TRT was launched, after some back and forth negotiations, in 1968 with a monopoly over radio and television broadcasting. At that time, radio transmission still reached less than half the population. Although legislative attempts were made to provide for lack of bias, the government managed to retain a strong influence.

Within two years, Menderes' spiritual successor Demirel and his Justice party came to power, and had little sympathy for the liberal reforms (Salin, 1981). This created constant conflicts, with the government trying to pressure TRT by freezing the license fee. In 1971, the military forced Demirel to resign and declared martial law. Control of TRT was given to a general. The new constitution had an authoritarian bent, which also affected broadcasting. Instead of speaking of TRT as "autonomous," the Constitution now read "impartial," a term not of structure but of attitude. The liberal experience of an autonomous broadcast institution had been unable to survive the deep divisions of Turkish society, and broadcasting once again became state-dominated.

Throughout the 1970s, directors general came and went, and the staff was periodically shaken up as leadership of the government shifted between the conservative Justice party of Demirel and the moderately left RPP of Ecevit. Domestic clashes, which included more than 2000 political killings in 1980, led to a new military coup, and TRT once again found itself with a general at its head.

In the 1982 Constitution and in 1983 legislation, attempts were made to reduce governmental control. A High Authority for radio and television was established whose members were appointed largely by the president of the republic. That body in turn appoints the administrative council and the director general of the broadcast institution. The High Authority establishes program policy guidelines for broadcasting but can control programs only after their airing. It notifies governmental authorities of breaches in the conditions under which TRT operates, makes recommendations on the establishment of new broadcast stations, and grants licenses for non-public and cable television for educational purposes or tourism.

The High Commission is reputed to be a body with high standards. All members are required to hold a university degree, and eight of twelve members must be noted personalities in broadcasting. Three of the members are appointed directly by the president of the republic. The president also selects two members out of four candidates recommended by the Higher Education Council from the fields of electronics and law, and three of six candidates nominated by the High Institution for Culture, Language, and History. The government appoints three members, and the National Security Council appoints one member. In practice, the president of the republic tends to sympathize with the government, and thus the commission has a substantial partisan coloration despite all of its educational credentials.

The government additionally has the right to present a monthly half-hour of programs directly under its control. It can also ban programs or news items for security reasons (Besiroglu, 1986, p. 30). The law provides for a right of reply to broadcasts affecting the "dignity and honor" of a person.

Programs operate in accordance with the principles of the Constitution, which charges TRT with promoting the values of country, unity, republic, public order, harmony, and welfare and to strengthen the principles of Kemal Ataturk's reforms. Failure to adhere to these guidelines can lead to trouble. In late 1989, for example, TRT came under fire for broadcasting programs that supported Islamic fundamentalism, an ideology long anathema to the country's secularly oriented republican governments, and the resulting shakeup led to the resignation of the agency's director general.

The 1983 law permitted broadcast advertising, subject to certain restrictions. In 1985, the license fee for receivers was abolished, partly because it had proved difficult to enforce. Instead, the government established a system of tax "banderoles," which must be attached to TV sets, radios, and VCRs by the commercial sellers of such equipment. Owners of existing equipment must buy the banderoles. An extra 50 percent fee was levied on previously undeclared sets. Government-provided subsidies supplement the TRT's funding.

TRT television broadcasts began in 1968. In 1984, color television was introduced, and in 1986, a second channel was added. Two additional channels have since been added—TV3 in the main cities since 1989, and GAP for the southeast region, transmitting twenty-eight and forty-nine hours a week, respectively. A fifth public channel, TRT-International, was introduced early in 1990. Although there were 6 to 8 million people speaking Kurdish, there were no broadcasts in that language.

Regulations on cable and closed-circuit television were established in 1985 for applications in education, tourism, and security. The regulations permit the licensed and limited private provision of cable service; advertising, however, is prohibited (Besiroglu, 1986).

There are about 2.5 million VCRs in Turkey, most of them unregistered. VCRs could even be found on public buses until a severe accident led to an outlaw of the practice (Ogan, 1986). Thousands of video distributors dot the country, and program piracy is their normal practice. Illegal commercial copying of tapes is prevalent on several levels of the distribution chain, negatively affecting foreign as well as domestic films. In 1986, a more restrictive copying law was passed.

In 1990, as part of a general governmental policy of privatization, the introduction of private television was being planned. Actively interested parties included Ulusal TV, partly owned by the press group Huriyet, in which the U.K.'s Robert Maxwell held 49 percent at the time. Among the other applicants, perhaps the most active was Magic Box, run by the TRT's former director general, and enjoying backing inside the government (TBI, 1990).

Turkey has not yet become an information society, still struggling to overcome the legacy of centuries of conscious anti-information policy by government. Broadcasting, when it emerged, became an instrument of the state, partly for modernization, partly for consolidation of partisan control. As independence and professional standards improve and as the widespread availability of videocassette recorders increases the public taste for program choice, greater broadcast diversity is forthcoming.

24

Israel

Israel's broadcasting system has been strongly shaped by its use as an instrument of social and cultural integration in a heterogeneous society in the midst of periodic warfare. The government has been reluctant to loosen its control, whether by expansion of channels or by liberalization of entry. However, alternative media options such as pirate cable television, Arab countries' TV stations, and VCRs forced a change. The consequence was the establishment of cable television and of a second broadcast channel, with the likelihood of satellite program activities. These developments have paved the way to a more diverse television landscape in Israel.

Broadcasting

Broadcasting developed fairly slowly in British Palestine and later in Israel. Radio broadcasting began with the Palestine Broadcasting Service (PBS) in 1936, operated by the British mandatory government, in English, Arabic, and Hebrew. Despite its British roots, this operation possessed neither the liberal spirit nor the credibility of the BBC. During World War II, illegal Jewish programs were broadcast primarily by the underground military. When the British mandate came to an end in 1948, the "Kol Israel," or Voice of Israel, broadcasting authority was created. Its first program was the proclamation of the state's independence.

For political reasons, the government kept tight control over broadcasting. Until 1965, it was a branch of the prime minister's office. In 1965, the Israel Broadcasting Authority (IBA) was established with an independent status, but the prime minister's office maintained its control. The armed forces operate a second and separate broadcast operation (IBA, 1986). Public television became part of the IBA after 1968. The IBA is governed by a thirty-one-member Plenum; one member is appointed by the Jewish Agency; and the remaining thirty are appointed by the country's president, though based on governmental recommendations, which tend to require a lengthy consultative process among the parties. Seven members of the Plenum are appointed by the government to make up the board of governors and supervise operations. Administrative responsibility lies with the director general, a government appointee whose term lasts five years. The government also designates a cabinet minister to be responsible for implementing the broadcast law. Although the minister has in theory no involvement with broadcast content itself, he often plays a policy role and bears ministerial responsibility for the authority's operation. Bezeq, the government-owned telecommunications carrier, operates and maintains the actual transmission network.

Of the IBA's budget, about 75 percent comes from license fees, 12 percent from radio commercials, 10 percent from public service announcements and program sponsorships, and 7 percent from the Jewish Agency and Israel Foreign Ministry to cover international broadcasts. (In the past, the government had contributed as much as 40 percent of the IBA's budget, but this was cut back considerably.) IBA has a staff of about 1500, including a symphony and an Arab music orchestra. Of the radio channels, Network A is the "serious" station, with talk, education, drama, art, and public service programming, some in the native languages of Israel's immigrants, as well as several religious programs. It also operates an additional FM channel, the Voice of Music, which, according to the IBA, is the only noncommercial FM station in Europe or the Middle East completely devoted to classical music. Many of its programs are live. It also boasts an active system of recognizing new Israeli performing artists. Network B broadcasts light music and covers news, sports, and talk shows. Network C is the most popular music station. Network D is the Arab-language channel, which is regularly listened to in neighboring Arab countries for news items about the Arab world that may not be available otherwise. Network E is an overseas channel. Starting as the Voice of Zion to the Diaspora in 1948, it became Israel Radio International. It broadcasts in sixteen languages, but its primary target is the Jewish population in the Soviet Union. In 1970, the Soviet Union effectively jammed the Israeli broadcasts. Consequently, new shortwave broadcast operations commenced with powerful 300-, 100-, and 50-kilowatt transmitters.

Television was introduced fairly late in Israel. The socialists who dominated the government in its first decades regarded American entertainment as a negative influence. Prime Minister David Ben Gurion opposed television as improper for the "people of the book." There were also economic arguments against television, especially for its impact on the considerable balance-of-trade deficit.

In 1961, the Israeli government solicited advice about the establishment of television from Henry Cassirer, a television expert with the United Nations. Positive recommendations led to a commission chaired by the director general of the Education Ministry, which initiated the notions of a noncommercial public system (Gil, 1986). Since the government was slow in moving, the Rothschild Foundation was persuaded in 1962 to support educational television as an interim step toward more general public television. However, the existing radio broadcast organization and in particular its unionized employees were adamantly opposed to this move and had to be reassured that the Rothschild system was only an interim arrangement. Despite the support of Israel Galili, an influential inner member of the cabinet from a small leftist party, the development of television was stalled for several more years.

In 1966, the Rothschild Foundation provided grant money for the first small step, the introduction of instructional television. As Arab Israelis had done for some time, Jewish Israelis started to buy television sets to watch broadcasts from adjoining Arab countries, as well as programs for secondary schools. When Israel occupied West Bank and Gaza territories in March of 1967, it found it necessary to provide Arab-language TV programs to counteract Jordanian programs. The government decided formally to establish a general television system, but only after the general election of 1969 and within the framework of a broadcast authority that would also include the radio services. Galili at first wanted to appoint a trusted retired general as the head of the interim organization that would set up television; but when he became unavailable, he chose an internationally respected communications scholar, Professor Elihu Katz of the Hebrew University. Suddenly, after years of go-slow policy, the government was in a hurry. The government hoped that Arab-language Israeli broadcasts would establish a more friendly cooperation. Through the Katz appointment the government was able to present television as outside of direct government control.

Katz tried to establish professionalism by bringing in television experts from abroad, mostly from the United States and France, as well as Israelis who had studied the subject abroad. Others came from the existing broadcast system. Katz, despite or because of his American origins, opposed an Americanization of the broadcasting system and cooperated reluctantly only with the American CBS network for the provision of technical support. Broadcasts started in May of 1968 and the early programs were hastily assembled. Viewership was extraordinarily high from the beginning and has remained so. The main daily news show is watched by more than 60 percent of all Israeli households every day (Avnerre, 1981).

Soon after it was formed, the board of the broadcasting authority, a politically complex body, tried to establish control over day-to-day decisions, rather than setting broad policy guidelines. It forced Katz, in one instance, to provide a list of potential invitees for an interview program, remove some names and add others. One of the people crossed off the list was the head of the Port Authority, which was soon engaged in a very difficult strike with its employees. The issue led to much public dispute and put Katz in an adversarial situation with the board. Soon broadcasting became an integral part of the new broadcasting authority, IBA, and the interim organization headed by Katz was terminated (Gil, 1986).

This did not change the basic conflicts between broadcasters and the government. One issue in question was broadcasting on the Sabbath, which was vigorously opposed by the religious parties. Although a large majority of the government supported the broadcasts, they were also engaged in discussions over the formation of a coalition and hoped the issue could be postponed until after the 1969 elections. This stalling was opposed by the IBA's board despite heavy government pressures. However, opponents to Sabbath broadcasting were able to block such broadcasts procedurally. At the last moment, an enterprising young attorney went to the home of a member of Israel's Supreme Court and obtained a staying order for the nonbroadcasting and the first Sabbath broadcast was aired. Programming on the Sabbath was not challenged again. Beyond the issue in question, this episode brought the public and the government to realize that, for the first time, the new broadcast authority had some measure of independence.

Another example of grudging acceptance of television was the introduction of color television. For a long time, in contrast to its neighbors, Israeli television was black and white. Some people bought color television sets to watch Jordanian color broadcasts. They also found that with proper equipment they could restore the color to some Israeli transmissions. Calls for introduction of color television were countered again with arguments about the impact on the balance of trade, but color broadcasting began in 1983.

Forty percent of all television programs are domestically produced. Most imports are subtitled in both Hebrew and Arabic and many of the imported children's programs have Hebrew dubbing. There are broadcasts of Arab-language television for fifteen hours a week. Since 1990 there are also English-language news broadcasts.

Although there have been many attempts at government interference, Israeli broadcasting has over time established some independence and even contentiousness among its journalists, though not always among its managers. The independence of Israeli television was demonstrated in the coverage of the Israeli invasion of Lebanon, where the government did not succeed in achieving the kind of coverage it preferred. The broadcasting authority has also been criticized by the government for presenting unfavorable economic news.

Expansion of the System

Through 1988, there was only one full-service channel; a second channel has operated since 1986 on a limited basis. That main channel therefore had to serve the impossible demands of the Jewish population, with its heterogeneity of origin and language, political diversity, municipal tasks, and split between the religious and the secular; of the Arab Israeli population, which is equally complex in its stratification; of the Arabs in the occupied Gaza and West Bank territories; and lastly, of the populations of the neighboring Arab countries. IBA also shared its channel with the Ministry of Education and Culture which broadcasts educational programs during the daytime.

A pirate radio station, "Voice of Peace" operated from offshore by the peace activist Abie Nathan.

The establishment of a second channel, recommended in 1978 by the Kubersky Committee, was stalled by bitter political fighting between the IBA and the Ministry of Communications. The IBA became enmeshed in controversy as it revealed a $95 million development fund surplus after frequent pleas of poverty.

Channel 2 commenced operations in 1986 as a national television service under the auspices of a special committee established by the Ministry of Communications. It operated for over three years outside the existing legal framework: official recognition required overturning the law mandating that all national broadcasters be controlled by the Israeli Broadcasting Authority (IBA).

A new law, the Second Television Channel and Private Radio Law, was passed in 1990 and provided, as an interim measure, for Channel 2's continued operation by the Ministry of Communications. Also due to the formation of a rightist government in 1990, authority was shifted to the prime minister's office. But an Independent Broadcasting Authority was established to process applications for regional private radio broadcast licenses according to an open tender process.

In addition, franchises were issued to independent televison companies that together operate a second and private national TV network. This was expected to operate similarly to the model of Britain's independent television network. Regulatory oversight is provided by the Independent Broadcasting Authority, which is funded by proportional contributions from the member companies and which assigns responsibility for various components of the national daily and weekly broadcast schedules. TV2 quickly achieved a substantial share of viewers. A third channel was officially approved in the law for the future. Thus, Israel was on the way to commercial television.

Cable television emerged also, though through the back door. In 1980, the minister of communications published a tender for the construction and operation of cable systems. However, the attorney general deemed such a tender to be without proper legal basis. In 1981, the government appointed a committee, under the chairmanship of Yoram Barsela, to study cable television. In 1982, the committee recommended the immediate introduction of cable television to be installed by private firms and regulated by a government board (State of Israel, 1983). The alternative, it argued, would be to have the country covered by haphazard unlicensed systems with poor standards of technology and safety, creating a chaotic situation (State of Israel, 1983, p. 7). It recommended that a board of public and private participants, responsible to either the minister of communications or the minister of education and culture be appointed to supervise, control, and license private cable systems. Through Israeli citizens, foreign partners would be permitted up to one quarter participation. The committee recommended that the country be divided into units of about 100,000 households; any operator could own one franchise, with special exceptions possible. Systems would be constructed on the basis of technical specifications set by the board, providing maximum transmission capacity based upon current technology. Systems would provide approximately forty to fifty channels, be convertible to two-way systems, and be interconnected.

Community and locally originated programming, including Arab-language programming, was stressed by the committee. Faced with the prospect of hostile Arab programs from adjoining countries over Israeli cable television, the commission recommended that systems carry such programs but enforce propaganda restrictions. Israel has been tolerant of the widespread availability and viewership of television from Arab countries. The programs of Jordanian TV, many of which are English-language films, had become an unofficial second channel for Israel. On the other hand, it is a more politically sensitive matter to retransmit on a cable television network programs which call for the destruction of one's country.

Of the total transmission capacity, the commission recommended that up to 60 percent be used for television programs or other nonentertainment services the operator wishes to provide, that 20 percent be available to the government for its purposes, and that the remaining 20 percent be made available to other private parties for transmission of programs under licenses granted by the board. In other words, a right of access for licensed program suppliers would be established for that 20 percent. Israeli television and radio broadcasts would be carried at no charge. Foreign television programs, including those of neighboring Arab countries, would be permissible, as would local and new programs, but political and party propaganda would be forbidden. The board would fix subscriber rates and the proposed license fee would be 3 percent of gross revenues.

The Barsela Commission report was very far-reaching, given the government's traditional reluctance to expand television. The report aimed to change the landscape of Israeli television. Where there were one or two channels, it proposed up to twenty-five. Where government provision of telecommunications services was the rule, it proposed private supply. And where programming content was aimed at the integration of the disparate elements of Israeli society, it opened the door wide to "narrowcasting" programs. For the political parties, this was more change than they could handle. Hence the proposals were shelved. However, actual "facts on the ground" did not wait for the cabinet.

Cable television developed very rapidly in a pirate fashion. By 1986, there were an estimated 700 pirate cable systems, some of which were operated by criminal elements. Enforcement proved difficult. Several political groups were using illegal cable for electoral propaganda. To establish a legal framework for cable, Minister of Communications Amnon Rubinstein initially proposed passage of a comprehensive bill that would have considered the multiple and interrelated segments of the electronic mass media. But it is in the nature of comprehensive legislation to be long delayed. Instead, a law to move private television forward was brought to a vote, proposed by a member of the Knesset who was himself mayor of a small town. By linking it to the increase of media availability in development towns, it gained a wider political support and passed Parliament. The law divides the country into thirty-one franchise districts of about 40,000 inhabitants each. Licenses will not be granted to individuals with direct political affiliations or criminal records. Licensed operations are permitted to carry daily local news, which had been a major selling point for private cablers. The government pledged to make cable available to all residents by the middle of the 1990s (Bainerman, 1990a, p. 39). In 1989, it awarded cable franchises serving 750,000 of its 1.1 million homes to a number of firms, including Gvanim, Tevel, ICS, and CSM. Several of these were supported by foreign companies. These investors, primarily from the United States, the United Kingdom, France, and Switzerland, were limited by Israeli law to a maximum of 49 percent ownership in cable stations. Investors included United Cable, Southwestern Bell, Malarkey-Taylor, the Swiss Rediffusion, and the British Westminster Cable. They were attracted to the emerging industry by hopes that a high level of penetration (about 70 percent) could be achieved, given the limited media alternatives. Systems were required to support themselves by subscriptions. Because of the well-organized opposition of publishers, advertising was prohibited until at least 1991.

Actual service began in 1990. Programming was required to include the state-run IBA and educational channels, in addition to limited news, community access, and Arab programs (Greenberg, 1989: p. 59). A large share of the programming was to be supplied by the newly formed Israel Cable Programming (ICP) organization, created by the country's four major cable operators. It planned four cable channels for movies, sports, children, and family programming and considered three additional channels for documentaries, arts, and science. Eighty percent of ICP's planned programs were expected to be American imports, a fact that led to talk about the need for cultural protection. Meanwhile, the existing pirate cable stations had not gone away, and cable companies, worried about competition, sought harsher penalties for offenders (Bainerman, 1989), especially after their equipment was sabotaged by pirates.

The national telecommunication organization Bezeq offered its infrastructure facilities on a commercial basis to the regional cable operators, and was accepted in more than 60 percent of the cable systems.

Regulatory oversight over cable operations is carried out by the Israeli Council for Cable TV Broadcasts, a committee of eleven members, five of which are government appointees, two from the ministry of communications. The remaining six are divided evenly among representatives of local authorities and consumers. A department was created in the Ministry of Communications for control of program and engineering standards.

Cable television was also utilized outside the private sector. Some of the socialist collective kibbutz settlements introduced community video (Stoney, 1984). To harness new technology for the kibbutz ideal, some settlements began to produce their own video programs and exchange them with one another (Viorst, 1981). The government also addressed in 1990 the question of satellite pay TV. Bids for a seven-year franchise were accepted from several companies, which were required to be majority owned by Israelis. The new service would have to provide 30 percent domestic programming. A further requirement was adherence to a 1985 must-carry rule imposed on existing cable systems, which effectively cut down on demand for direct satellite-to-home reception. Opposition to this statute came from International Superstar TV (ISTV), which planned to circumvent the law by transmitting into Cyprus and then retransmitting into Israel (TBI, 1990).

Israel also became active in communications satellites, as part of a high-technology policy. Already, a good number of satellite antennas exist in the country, often used to receive Russian or Arabic language programs. Ofeq-1 was launched as the precursor to the more advanced Amos, a joint venture between Israel Aircraft Industries, Bezeq, General Satellite Corporation (Israel), and French and German partners. Given Israel's activities in the construction and launch of satellites, it is likely that a wider role in program transmission, including services to Europe, will emerge.

Conclusion

Israel's broadcast system reflects the great political diversity and heterogeneity of the country and its military struggles. In its first decades, radio broadcasting was an instrument for societal integration, and the introduction of television was consciously delayed by the government as potentially disruptive. Later, questions of control over broadcasting led to conflicts and growing independence. Liberalization was long resisted, and was forced on the government, as in the case of cable television, by viewers' access to private commercial providers. Subsequently, official multichannel cable television was introduced and commercial television was licensed.

25

Greece

Greek modern history has been convulsed by dictatorships, wars, occupation, and a civil war. As a society, Greece is characterized by strong political divisions between the left and the right. Partly in consequence, the common thread in broadcast policy running throughout this tumultuous period has been government use of broadcasting in a highly partisan fashion. The broadcast monopolist has been subservient to whomever happened to be in power. About one-half of the population at any given time considers public television to be the despised mouthpiece of its opponents, whereas the other half is likely to see it as a valuable, though not necessarily respected, political tool. Thus, the credibility of Greece's public broadcast system is low. Throughout West Europe, it is difficult to find a state broadcasting system more discredited, which helps explain the changes toward private television after 1987.

History of Broadcasting

Both radio and television came late to Greece, and each appeared at the beginning of a period of dictatorship. Early radio transmission was initiated in 1924 by a technical college, and in 1928 by Christopher Tsigirdis in Thessaloniki. A year later, a broadcasting law was ratified that assigned the regulation of broadcasting to the Ministry of the Navy and later to the PTT (Emery, 1969). Subsequently, the government also awarded a concession for radio service to another firm. When General Metaxas took power in 1936, the government decided to set up its own radio operations and established a state system. The German company Telefunken was placed in charge of technical operations for the new state system. Regular broadcasting commenced in 1938. After World War II and the German occupation, the national broadcasting corporation EIR was established. But because of the civil war that was raging, broadcasting operated without a firm legal foundation for the next several years. Eventually, with some political stability restored, a law was issued in 1953 that gave EIR, in effect, a monopoly status. Private broadcasting was permissible, but private stations were never licensed. This system prevailed until the end of the colonels' military dictatorship in 1974, when the national radio system was reorganized (Katsoudas, 1985).

Experimental television broadcasting began after 1960, and regular programs commenced in 1970. Its tardy introduction was partly caused by the political power of the movie theater owners; at the time there were 500 theater screens in the Athens area alone. The spread of TV was further slowed by the difficulty and the expense of covering the mountainous country and its many islands with transmitters; transmission coverage was still incomplete in the mid-1980s. The impetus to inaugurate television came from the military regime's desire to establish a propaganda tool. Nevertheless, the number of people owning a television set increased dramatically. By 1974, there were already 1.2 million, and in 1982, 2.8 million, or 93 percent of all households (Heretakis, 1986). FM radio transmission was also introduced in 1971. With the introduction of television, EIR changed its name to EIRT.

From the beginning, state broadcasting was structured to protect and expand the power of the government. The director general was a government appointee and the Board of Governors had only limited power. There was no tradition of an independent civil service or journalism. Furthermore, a 1953 decree stipulated the right of a cabinet member (the minister to the prime minister) to have the text of any program submitted to him for approval. These controls later served the colonels' dictatorship well in its efforts to maintain control over state broadcasting. In addition, the government ran the unique system of national military broadcasting, which had been established in 1951 to "boost the national morale." During the dictatorship, the military broadcast system YENED was controlled by the Ministry of National Defense. YENED provided programs that catered to popular tastes and also accepted advertising. The audience for the military television channel, in fact, eclipsed at times that of the state channel.

With the restoration of democracy, the Constitution of 1975 established guarantees of freedom of the press. At the same time, however, it also stipulated in Article 15(2) that "radio and television shall be under the immediate control of the state and their purpose shall be the objective, and on equal terms, transmission of news and information as well as works of literature and arts . . ." This reflected a fundamental unease with independence in broadcasting. The former director general of the BBC, Hugh Greene, played an important role in postdictatorship reform of EIRT, just as he had in the establishment of postwar German broadcasting, but with much less success. Greene recommended that ERT be transformed from a state enterprise subject to arcane bureaucratic rule to a private limited company owned by the government. He also recommended considerably more independent status for the broadcasting organization. Despite positive public reaction to the Greene report, the government preferred to maintain control. A limited-stock company under state ownership was established under the name ERT (Greek Radio and Television) and the government announced its intention to merge it with the military's YENED. The government established an ostensibly pluralistic governing body for ERT, but kept control over the director general, board of governors, and general assembly. The broadcasting Law 230, anchored in Article 15 of the Constitution, is cast in the often meaningless phraseology of such enactments; it pointedly states that "ERT broadcasting shall be permeated by the democratic spirit, a feeling of cultural responsibility, humanism, and objectivity, and they shall be adjusted to Greek reality'' (Katsoudas, 1985, p. 145). The board of governors could not even elect its own chairman and vice-chairman, and board members could be replaced by the government at any time. ERT was a source for patronage jobs. The General Assembly that had been proposed by Greene as a further insulating mechanism was filled with governmental appointees such as university presidents and the director of the Bank of Greece. In a country of close elections, only a handful of members represented the opposition. The director general was given considerable power within the broadcast organization, but was ultimately totally dependent upon the government. Those filling the post came and went in rapid succession. The first director general resigned a few months before a general election in disagreement with government policy on the coverage of the contest.

Financial control over ERT rests with the government. The authority finances its operations through a special charge on every Greek household that is connected to electricity. Until Greece's highest court struck the policy down, one had to pay the TV fee whether or not one had a TV set. For all the anticommercial rhetoric, Greek television depended heavily on advertising revenues, which contributed over 40 percent of ERT's income. Advertising was not permitted during the main religious holidays and there were some restrictions on the interruption of programs and on tobacco advertising normally limited to five to ten minutes during such programs. On ERT-2, there can be as many as seventeen minutes of advertisements during programs more than one hour in length. Interestingly, almost one-half of all advertising revenue in Greece went to television, an extremely high percentage, though it was still a relatively small figure as a percentage of GNP (Dimitras and Doulkeri, 1986).

The minister to the prime minister has the power to "stop or postpone any program under exceptional circumstances." Furthermore, "ERT is obliged to broadcast all government press releases, whenever the Minister to the Prime Minister requests it" (Dimitras and Doulkeri, 1986, p. 139). He can also assume control over ERT's administration during national emergencies. Whether or not the government can maintain this kind of control is an important issue for the future of Greek broadcasting because of the arrival of satellite-delivered channels.

Already strong under the conservative government, the politicization of broadcasting intensified under the socialist PASOK government, which came to power on a promise of liberalizing society. Although campaign posters for the 1981 election proclaimed that "PASOK wants to and can liberalize television" (Katsoudas, 1985, p. 149), little of that was remembered after the election victory. In fairness, it should be noted that the opposition subsequently received more air time than it had before. Greek television and the four national radio and twenty-two regional stations were more liberal in allowing access during electoral periods than previously. However, even pro-government newspapers became critical of television's more general obsequiousness to the government (Katsoudas, 1985).

YENED, which was to be abolished under provisions of the 1975 broadcasting reform, had continued to exist until 1982, when the newly elected PASOK government placed it under the authority of a board controlled by the minister to the prime minister and renamed the channel ERT-2. The new authority was to be organizationally independent, but its bias was pro-government and pro-party. In 1987, it was merged with ERT. One of ERT's more positive priorities became to increase domestic production and to diversify import sources.

In 1985, there was a short-lived attempt at installing a more neutral ERT regime. But after only two months, Prime Minister Papandreou declared: "Those responsible for ERT were covering in an exaggerated way marginal phenomena in activities of . . . [a] destabilizing nature. . . . Whoever is appointed to manage the television must implement the government's and not his own policy." One former ERT news director revealed that a few days before an election for the European Parliament, he was forced to include in his newscast a list of the cities that various ministers would visit on election day, but was not permitted until later to report on a train accident that would have been negatively received by the public. In August 1985, when a Chinese aircraft pilot defected to South Korea on the same day that a Bulgarian helicopter pilot escaped to Greece, only the story about the Chinese aircraft could be reported. Another ERT news director was fired by order of Prime Minister Papandreou because an opposition leader's statement on a political assassination had been broadcast without waiting for a governmental reply (Dimitras and Doulkeri, 1986). As one critic noted of the political manipulation of media: "tight government control has doomed even the most capable and good-willed to failure. It is not only the vast bureaucracy, the over-manning, the lack of expertise and the occasional technological backwardness that the Director General has to face, but also the lack of any infrastructure to secure his reputation" (Papathanasso-poulos, 1989a, p. 29).

Governmental meddling in Greek broadcasting was so pervasive that it even extended into the presentation of the foreign programs that still made up much of the fare offered on Greek television. Subtitles were misleadingly translated or scenes omitted for political reasons. In one instance, the government of Sweden protested that 17 minutes of the film "Wallenberg" had been cut when it was run on Greek television. The omitted scenes showed how the Swedish humanitarian hero was mistreated by Russians and subsequently disappeared (Dimitras and Doulkeri, 1986).

In 1986, the conservative, then opposition party, Nea Demokratia, having been part of the problem when it was itself in power, introduced a reform bill providing for a governing council and a five-member general assembly to oversee the broadcast media (Lazos, 1986). The governing council was meant to provide broad popular representation: the government would have one seat on it, the parties nine, and others were to be reserved for "social partners" and "popular representatives" such as the medical association and the program producers.

Also in 1986, the government presented its own new broadcasting bill, which provided for the merger of ERT and ERT-2, forming a new and centralized broadcast authority. The structure of the broadcast authority resembled the system that resulted from a 1970s media reorganization in France in which President Giscard D'Estaing similarly undertook a promised reform while maintaining full governmental control. Five new subsidiaries of ERT were created: ET1 and ET2 for television, ERA for four radio networks, a television program production and marketing division, and an Institute for Audiovisual Media. The law also included a provision for the establishment of a third television channel, ET3, whose transmissions were initially only to the major cities. All these subsidiaries were run by government-appointed directors, as was the umbrella ERT organization. Even so, the minister to the prime minister retained substantial powers to override board decisions. There was also an advisory Radio-Television council.

Cable television exists experimentally. Since the existing basic telephone network still requires major investments, the telephone administration was in no position to play a role in cable. Furthermore, the implications to the ERT monopoly of a multichannel system were clear. (The PTT, itself highly politicized, had restricted the interconnection of opposition broadcasts during the 1989 election period.) Here the socialist government was opposed by the mayors of Athens, Piraeus, and Thessaloniki, who announced cable plans. The mayors promised, perhaps too optimistically, that cable service would be available free of charge.

The Beginnings of Liberalization

Government overreach caused the first cracks in the high monopoly system. Disputes between the government and candidates campaigning for the 1986 municipal elections led to the establishment of municipal radio stations by opposition parties. Prior to the elections, many candidates requested television and radio air time to represent their views. The government rejected the proposal, claiming that even a debate between candidates running for office in Athens would be of little interest to the general population. The opposition parties criticized the government decision and accused it of trying to protect the pro-government mayors of the three largest cities. The government announced the intention to permit new stations, but dragged its feet. Candidates who promised to create municipal networks were subsequently elected in the three cities, and they moved forward immediately to break the central government's monopoly, arguing that municipal stations were possible under the constitution. The first municipal radio stations opened in May 1987 in Athens, Piraeus, and Thessaloniki (Papathanassopoulos, 1989a). These stations derived their revenues from advertising and municipal allocations (Dimitras, 1986). Others followed, including a communist local station in the Athens region, since they too had been restricted from ERT. Fighting back, the government at last issued a presidential decree to restrain the stations.

Several large publishing groups also became interested in private broadcasting, alerted by a videocassette recorder penetration of almost 40 percent. Pirates proliferated. In 1988, the government bent to the inevitable and legalized private local radio by decree, after its referencing in a 1987 law. But it was a case of too little, too late. Even as radio licenses were issued, more stations went on the air illegally. By 1989, 120 stations had been licensed, and another 400 pirate stations were operating. Municipal stations, run by local boards, were excused by the Commission on Local Radio Broadcasting, as were private radio stations.

The next step was television. Here the mayor of Thessaloniki began television broadcasts in 1988 through the station TV-100, after one year of retransmitting European satellite channels. Piraeus and Athens followed, forcing the government to promise the licensing of a third and private channel to one of the three publisher groups. A 1989 law on private TV began partial opening; it limited the individual ownership of a station to 25 percent and created a National Broadcasting Council.

In Athens, Mega Channel, the first of three private channels backed by powerful publishers, began broadcasts in 1989. In its first week, Megachannel had a 31 percent share of the audience. A third government channel, ET3, was hastily launched to compete with Thessaloniki's TV-100. ET1 and 2 also made rate and schedule concessions to advertisers to deter competitors, but both lost half their audience to new pirate channels. In addition, Prime Minister Papandreou allowed for the retransmission of European satellite services. It was generally considered that these were pre-election moves against the mayors (Papathanassopoulus, 1989b).

After the April 1990 voting, the new conservative government, which had come to power after several inconclusive and bitter elections, and whose majority was very narrow, issued a statement regarding future broadcasting policy. It supported private sector efforts and promised to modernize and streamline the ERT system, that is to replace its leadership. But it did not indicate a readiness to make ERT an independent institution, such as those existing in most European countries. In the private sector, however, the transition to commercial competition was rapid. Two stations, Mega Channel, owned by the large publishers Teletypos, and New Channel, owned by another group of Athens publishers, were awarded provisional licenses in March 1990. Other stations went on the air without waiting for licenses. They included Antenna TV, Kanali 29 (Kouris Publishing), TV Plus, and Seven X TV. The latter two are partly pay channels.

Despite its illegal status, Antenna TV's primary owner, Minos Kyriakou, who also runs a radio station, spent approximately $20 million to launch the channel, with the support of the international media czars Rupert Murdoch and Leo Kirch (Stuart, 1990). Soon, Mega Channel and Antenna TV surpassed ET1 in audience ratings, and depressed ERT's advertising revenues.

The competition added to ERT's problems, which were political, qualitative, and financial. Its debt had accrued to over $250 million (Papathanassopoulos, 1990). This has even spurred discussion over privatization of either ET2 or ET3. The government also considered a new private national channel, or regional private channels. A research committee recommended to the National Broadcasting Council that the Athens area alone could technically support 13 channels. However, given the tumultuous environment and the absence of a clear licensing policy and the will to enforce it, it appears that events were not easy to plan and control.

Conclusion

Until 1990, Greece represented the earliest stage of broadcasting, and one that most of West Europe has long surpassed: broadcasting as a propaganda instrument of the government in power. This "spoils system" model of broadcasting had been replaced almost everywhere else by a public system of some independence and a certain integration, within it, of the major political and social forces. Because the divisions in Greek society ran too deep for this, pluralism eventually began not by bending but by breaking: by opposition politicians starting partisan rival local systems. Their facts on the ground (and in the air) were supplemented by entrepreneurial efforts, whose illegal nature was acceptable since the official system did not possess public legitimacy. Technological change had little to do with broadcast liberalization; nor did the telephone administration play a role. There is little cable distribution, and hence access to foreign commercial channels is limited to satellite reception. Whether ERT will become an independent institution is not certain. When it comes to broadcast freedom and diversity, the cradle of democracy still has a long way to go.

26
Television in Eastern Europe

Introduction[1]

This book's focus is the dynamic change of media from tight control to diversity. Until 1989, this excluded the eastern part of the continent, where broadcasting was rigorously frozen. After 1989, changes began to occur at a revolutionary pace and the opposite problem arose: Developments were moving so rapidly that no book treatment could avoid being outdated. Given these circumstances, the following chapter is only a brief survey.

Although originally there was much commonality in the East, with the disintegration of the Soviet Bloc, Eastern European broadcasting began to return to the European mainstream, but along distinct paths, reflecting a combination of varying historical circumstances and economic and political exigencies.

Eastern Europe's broadcasting institutions shared many basic features during the communist period; Among them, the most important was that television and radio were subordinated to the pursuit of state control over society. The basic structure of broadcasting in prereform Eastern Europe (as in Western Europe) established broadcasting as a state monopoly institution, and rigorously nonindependent. State broadcasting committees subject to party control directed programming content, and the ministries of communications controlled transmission (Paulu, 1974). In various ways, the ministries of education, culture, and propaganda or information, as well as the Communist Party directly, also influenced programming content. Radio and television institutions generally operated in parallel; their programming emphasized political propaganda, educational material for children, sports, classical and folk music and politically correct imports.

An important, if unofficial, part of the prereform media environment in Eastern Europe was the unsanctioned reception of broadcast signals from the West (Head, 1985, p. 361f). Eastern Europeans could often receive Western information sources from bordering Western countries, such as West Germany and Austria. In addition, many Eastern Europeans received broadcast services specially formatted and transmitted for worldwide distribution, such as the BBC's World Service and the Voice of America. Finally, some Western services were specifically beamed at Eastern countries as part of the West's Cold War efforts to counter domestic news and information in Eastern bloc countries. (Indeed, in their earliest forms, these stations often advocated violent resistance to the

Communist leadership; they later moderated their approach.) The United States operates two such services. Perhaps the best known, Radio Free Europe, was aimed at audiences in Poland, Hungary, Czechoslovakia, Bulgaria, and Romania, Radio Liberty provided a similar service aimed directly at the U.S.S.R. For twenty years these broadcasts were secretly funded by the Central Intelligence Agency. Once that became known in the United States, Congress decided to put both services under the direction of a nonprofit organization, the Board for International Broadcasting, whose board of directors is appointed by the president, and to fund them directly. These transborder broadcasts encouraged change.

Most of the initial reform in Eastern European countries' broadcasting was in the liberalization of content. But, soon the introduction of private broadcasting was discussed to operate alongside the public broadcasting media whose credibility was badly tarnished. Reform of the structure of public broadcasting institutions came about only slowly. With the exception of the elimination of party and propaganda ministry control over programming fare, the basic structure of public broadcasting did not change drastically in the early postreform era.

As countries began to shift from state monopoly broadcasting to more pluralistic forms, they encountered some of the same issues as their Western European counterparts. Development priorities were the upgrading of outmoded equipment and the creation of more diverse programs. The lack of strong consumer markets made advertising insufficient as a financial source for private channels and discouraged potential foreign commercial investments. At the same time, the lack of hard currency made it difficult to acquire Western programming or equipment.

Other impediments to change were the vast and conservative radio and television bureaucracies, mostly Communist Party staffed, that remained even after reform. Heavy-handed direct government censorship had been mostly unnecessary under the communist rule because the broadcasting employees avoided critical or controversial topics unless clear guidelines had been set from above. Now, with reform everywhere, the broadcast media institutions were rarely at the forefront of media institution change. For example, even though Czechoslovakia's state-run TV monopoly Czeskoslovenska Televize (CST) boldly supported the Czech reform movement in November 1989, it experienced internal controversy over attempts to remove old-line employees.

Adding to the complexities was spectrum allocation. With expanding private interests, as well as the burgeoning number of political parties competing for airtime, East European reform governments experienced for the first time the need to allocate and manage their broadcast airwaves.

As the initial euphoria of change subsided, the early scenario of freedom in broadcasting began to be framed more cautiously. Just as in Western Europe in the post-World War II period, internal politics in East Europe were unsettled and tumultuous; different groups jockeyed for power and policy influence; centrifugalism tested the cohesion of the state; new values of democracy and economic enterprise had to be conveyed; employment opportunities for supporters were needed. In short, all the pressures that led to the early creation of West European broadcast institutions were present, plus that of organizational self-preservation. On the other hand, there was more hostility to government control and greater willingness to accept some private presence. Hence, the most likely model for Eastern Europe are large national or regional public stations, along the Western model, with some independence but considerable influence of political parties, supplemented by a limited number of private stations awarded to influential figures close to the government, and often operating with the collaboration of foreign media companies.

The Soviet Union

Change in the Soviet Union's broadcast system was much more cautious than in most of Eastern Europe, mirroring its relative pace of political evolution. With its vast geographic size, the U.S.S.R. has always faced a unique challenge in establishing a national broadcasting system. The desire for political control over a country that spanned eleven time zones was behind the creation of early broadcasting (Michel, 1990). As early as 1918, Lenin, who understood the power of the new medium to communicate with the nation's vast illiterate population, called for a national construction program for radio broadcasting stations, with messages originating in Moscow. Lenin believed "the matter is *of gigantic importance*," and foresaw that "all Russia will hear a newspaper read in Moscow" (Guback and Hill, 1972). These goals led the Soviet government to make radio and later television a high priority and to put significant resources into it. As a result, the U.S.S.R. was able to achieve very high penetration comparatively quickly (Campbell, 1988). In 1922, the strongest radio transmitter in the world, broadcasting with 12,000 watts of power, was put into service in Moscow (Paulu, 1974, p. 35). Later, the U.S.S.R. established in 1965 the world's first satellite distribution of television broadcasts.

Broadcasting in the U.S.S.R. is controlled by several different governmental organizations. The Commissariat of Posts and Telegraphs assumed initial responsibility for construction in 1921, with political control being held by the Radio Commission of the Communist Party's Central Committee. In 1931, control shifted to the All-Union Radio Committee, within the People's Commission for Education. The committee instituted an annual license fee. In 1962, the annual fee was replaced by an excise tax on each radio receiver sold in the U.S.S.R.

Control shifted again in 1957, when the Committee for Radio and Television was created at the Cabinet Council of the U.S.S.R. The committee delegated many responsibilities to similar committees on the regional level. Multichannel systems were expanded after World War II, reaching 200 cities by 1971 and 520 by 1976 (Campbell, 1988, p. 122)

This arrangement was reorganized in 1970 into the All Union State Committee for Television and Radio Broadcasting (Gostelradio), which is responsible for radio and television programming. With the acquisition of better transmission technology, national control over programming was more tightly centralized and local broadcasters were treated with less tolerance. However, each of the fifteen Soviet Republics has its own broadcasting ministry to oversee TV and radio, and regional, district, and local Soviets also maintain some input into the system. Local broadcast committees are responsible to both the local government and the broadcast committee above it. Until the recent reforms, the Communist Party maintained political control over program decisions, and the local government committees provided funding and administrative guidance (Remington, 1988).

Gostelradio consists of a hierarchy of a chairman, several deputy chairmen, and a board overseeing functional areas.[2] Since the reforms introduced in 1988 and 1989, the Supreme Soviet (parliament) confirms the Gostelradio chairman. The first appointee under this system was Michail F. Nenaschew, who approached change with caution.

Gostelradio employs approximately 83,000 employees and runs on a budget of 2 billion rubles annually. Contrary to many other European countries, funding comes not from subscriber fees but from the national budget, with some additional revenue furnished by the sale of advertising.[3]

While Gostelradio is responsible for programming, the broadcast facilities for transmitting programs are built and operated by the Ministry of Communications, or "Minsviaz." Minsviaz has broad authority over telecommunications and the postal system as well (Campbell, 1988, p. 12). Gostelradio leases transmission facilities from Minsviaz, which is also supported by the government's broadcast budget.

The Soviet Union claims that radio technology was invented by Alexander Stephanovitch Popov, independently of Marconi. May 7 is celebrated as Radio Day to commemorate Popov's 1895 discovery. Popov followed the 1895 radio telegraph with a radio telephone in 1904. In the years following the 1917 revolutions, radio stations began to spring up all over the U.S.S.R., with national programming in Russian and local and regional broadcasts in over half of the U.S.S.R.'s 100 separate languages. World War II spurred the growth of radio; even though the German invasion destroyed nearly half of the country's broadcast facilities, the amount of programming increased over the course of the war.

Programming was originally distributed through a largely wireline network, with a central receiver or head-end wired to many loudspeakers in people's homes as well as in public places. At first this arrangement was used to broadcast one program over the system's one channel, which all listeners received at the same time. There are still more households served by the 100 million wire receivers than by regular radios (Campbell, 1988, p. 122). The wire system prevented listening to unauthorized stations. But it also strengthened a local rather than centralized production of programs.

Over-the-air broadcasting utilized short-wave and medium-wave frequencies for many years, although today shortwave broadcasting within the U.S.S.R. has been mostly replaced by medium- and long-wave broadcasting, except for certain isolated areas. A greater emphasis on FM developed in the 1960s and stereo broadcasts did not begin until 1972 because of the limitations of the wired system. Stereo reached 40 percent of the population in 1987. International radio broadcasts began in 1929, and by the late 1980s, the Soviet Foreign Radio service was available worldwide in more than seventy languages.

Two general-interest national radio channels from Moscow reach more than 85 percent of the population; a third channel reaches perhaps 45 percent of the country, and there are many more local and regional broadcasts. Gostelradio produces fourteen channels of programming, although much of it is either regional or for special groups, such as programming for sailors and fishermen at sea. (Androunas, communication). The national radio network also includes 176 radio stations that develop their own programming and broadcast it in their areas, and 5000 local "editorial offices" that create programming for local audiences. There were also pirate broadcasts ("radio hooligans"), whose programs cover the range from Voice of America recordings, popular music, and religious messages to political comments, accounts of dance performances, and reports on the intimate lives of radio announcers (Paulu, 1974, p. 48, 49).

Experiments in television began in 1931. In 1938, the Moscow television center opened, and regular broadcasts began in Moscow and Leningrad, available to an estimated 2000–3000 people. Development was halted during the war, but was quickly renewed in 1945, with twice-weekly broadcasts. The Moscow television center was rebuilt, and in 1949, a 625-line standard was adopted. Moscow's central TV studio was opened in 1951. Over the following twenty years, over 120 cities built their own television studios, although in 1962 the Communist Party decreed that the Moscow First Program would become a national program as part of its efforts to centralize control. Educational television began broadcasting in January 1955. In 1967, a modified version of France's SECAM color system was adopted. By 1978, all the U.S.S.R.'s central TV production was in color, and all TV broadcasting has been in color since early 1986. After demand for smuggled tapes and VCRs grew, the Soviets copied a Western technology to produce one VCR model in 1985, the Elektronika VM-12 (Campbell, 1988, p. 132, 135).

By the early 1980s, when the party decreed that the second channel of central TV would join the educational and principal channel as all-union programs, Soviet television offered programming daily in sixty-eight languages, reaching 80 percent of Soviet citizens. This was accomplished through a complicated network of satellites, ground lines, and 130 broadcasting stations, each broadcasting several different channels. The satellite systems include the Orbita network, which uses four Molniya satellites in a polar orbit, the Ekran, which was put into geostationary orbit in 1976, and, since 1980, Moskva, which uses the non-stationary Gorizont satellites (Michel, 1990). Later government efforts seem aimed at using more high-powered satellites to transmit to smaller dishes serving smaller areas, including settlements and apartment complexes (Remington, 1988, p. 258). Eighty percent of households get two programs and one-third get three or more programs. In Moscow, five programs are available: three national programs, plus the local programs from Moscow and Leningrad.

Most Soviet republics have their own TV channel; the larger republics also have regional programming. The system has 122 television programming centers with their own studios. Local efforts are pushing into the traditionally top–down hierarchy as part of reforms sweeping the country. For example, following unrest in Armenia, the Central Committee promised that the Nagorno–Karabakh area would get access to the central, all-union program. Several republics reportedly refused to broadcast the central programming and used the channel time to broadcast their own programming.

A dramatic confrontation occurred in Russia, the largest republic and, paradoxically, the only one without its own channel. The Russian parliament created its own Committee on Television and Radio, and an All Russian Television and Radio Company was formed. The Russian Republican government bid to take over one of the two all-union channels for its own use, but President Mikhail Gorbachev refused. In July 1990, President Gorbachev signed a decree, "On the Democratization and Development of Television and Radio Broadcasting in the U.S.S.R.," that reiterated the importance of preserving the national system of television and radio and called "illegitimate" any attempt by republic or regional bodies to restructure broadcasting without central approval. As a compromise, Russia was given two hours per day on each of the two all-union channels, and an agreement was struck between Gostelradio and the Russian government for technical assistance.

The Soviet government introduced a commercial television station geared toward business and other informational programming. The channel remains under the control of Gostelradio. In addition, Soviet entrepreneur Nikolai Lutsenko created the first independent television company in the U.S.S.R., Nika TV, at first only available in Moscow (Zeidenberg, 1990b).

The first independent radio service in the Soviet Union appeared in Vilnius, Lithuania, in 1990. The FM service, Youth Radio MI, operates independently of the government and broadcasts popular music as well as advertisements. The station is mostly supported by business interests, a political association, and a West German regional broadcaster.

Other available video media include an estimated 2.2 million VCRs and 15,000 satellite antennas. Further liberalization of government controls on private ownership of satellite antennas was also expected.

Poland

Broadcasting began in Poland in the 1920s, when a handful of private broadcasters started operating radio transmitters. The Polskie Radio Company began regular broadcasting in 1926. Soon thereafter, broadcasting was centralized into a state-run enterprise. After World War II, radio transmission resumed. Television was introduced in the 1950s. In 1960, the Committee for Radio and Television was created as the central authority that controls broadcasting, with the Ministry of Communications overseeing spectrum allocation.

Broadcasting is operated by Polskie Radio i Telewizja (PRT) with a budget partially supplemented by license fees and limited advertising. Poland has two national television channels serving 10 million television households. Channel

One programs news, films, and serials; Channel Two airs more cultural and regional programming. The two channels share one news department (Dennis and vanden Heuvel, 1990). In addition, Poland has eight regional television stations that remain under the supervision of the central authorities; it also receives signals from other East Bloc countries. Advertising was capped at eight minutes per hour.

For Poland, the prereform era meant a build-up of the Polish military, tightening of local political repression, no economic reforms, and liberalization in the areas of culture and mass media. The result was a plethora of underground mass media enterprises: illegal radio, underground books and newspapers, often ideologically in line with the Solidarity labor movement. Unable to crack down on such widespread dissent, and unsupported by the new, increasingly liberal U.S.S.R. regime, Polish authorities had to reform their mass communications policies quickly if they were to keep any hold on the younger generation of Poles. The highly centralized Committee for Radio and Television, which had controlled even the details of national and regional programming, could no longer maintain control (Gajlewicz, 1990).

With reform, the restructuring of Poland's broadcasting system moved toward a dual public–private system. Oversight and regulation was to be exercised by a board composed of members of parliament and key executive branch officials. The public system was to be financed by advertising and license fees (Jakubowicz, 1990). But the backlash against state institutions hurt efforts to establish strong public broadcasting along the Western European model. Popular pressures in favor of private solutions were strong. Late in 1989, Solidarity's radio committee drafted a law that would allow independent, advertiser-supported radio stations throughout the country.

Discussions about restructuring began in June 1989 (Gajlewicz, 1990). Within months the opposition had access to the airwaves. Among the first private radio stations was an internal effort called Radio-Market, operating in Gdansk in November of 1989. In Warsaw, Radio Solidarity began broadcasting Western pop music with some call-in talk shows and rebroadcasts of the BBC's World Service. Radio Malopolska Fun, a private broadcaster, aired French programs in Cracow, and a private religious station was planned there. A private television channel, ITI, is available in Warsaw, and in Wroclaw, a local TV broadcaster uses a private transmitter to broadcast "TV Echo" to a small local audience. In 1990, the government turned its second channel into a commercial venture and signed an exclusive agreement with Conduit Internationale Film to supply programming, including U.S. television series.

The first cable operation, Polska Telewizja Kablowa (PTK), was launched in December 1989 as a cooperative effort between the U.S.-based Chase Enterprises and four Polish state entities, with the aim of cabling of 1.8 million homes. Construction centered on Warsaw and Cracow (Dziadul, 1990). Plans were to offer about twenty channels.

There were about 1 million VCRs in 1990, with many VCR tapes brought from West Germany being sold on the black market. Reportedly, 18,000 satellite dishes were in use (Zeidenberg, 1990d).

More significant than technological improvements were the political reforms being discussed, including the offering of accurate news, presentation of diverse political opinions, and introduction of the media in a watchdog role. Lech Walesa, among others, campaigned on this issue when running for president. The reformers wanted independent stations, but traditionalists would offer only isolated, independently produced alternative programs on the state-owned stations for thirty to sixty minutes per week. Applications for private licenses were submitted by more than 250 interests; but only one national and several regional channels were expected.

Czechoslovakia

Radio began in Czechoslovakia in 1923, developing innovative types of journalism and radio plays until it was repressed by Hitler's occupying forces in 1938. Broadcasts from Moscow and London kept Czechs informed during World War II. As a Soviet satellite, Czechoslovakia adopted a centralized ministry of media. Experiments with television began in the 1920s, and by 1934, an inventor demonstrated transmissions with a 30-line definition. Television broadcasting began in 1953 and was concentrated in 1958 under the Radio Ministry and in 1959 under its own ministry.

The government maintained strict controls over news and information. During the political liberalization of the Prague Spring of 1968, many restrictions gave way. Independent broadcasts continued in the days after the Soviet invasion.

The state television authority, Csekoslovenskie Televize (CST), broadcasts programming in both Czech and Slovak on its three channels. Channel 1 is the federal station that broadcasts across the country. Channel 2 is the "national" channel, which means it broadcasts Czech programming in the Czech region and Slovak programming in the country's Slovak area. Channel 3 programs international material. In 1990, Slovakian TV received a more clearly separate identity. Program decisions are made by a program director, who is a government employee, and a twelve member board. The system is supported by viewers, who pay a monthly license fee.

The 1989 "velvet revolution," was encouraged by some television journalists' courageous coverage. The first commercial broadcast venture was Masseba 10, which produced instructional economic and managerial programming to support emerging private enterprise (U.S. Department of State, 1990). The government accumulated over twenty applications for possibly three independent station licenses. The applicants included the foreign media entrepreneurs Maxwell, Berlusconi, and Murdoch. Channel 3, which had been used primarily for the Soviet military, became an informal "open channel." For all these steps, however, there were also countermoves in the direction of state control.

Four radio stations broadcast nationwide, two of which are general-interest broadcasts; the other two air mostly music. In addition, there are ten regional stations. Czechoslovak Radio and France's Europe 1 began an FM service, Europe 2, as a joint venture, and Radio Free Europe will be available through an AM transmitter in Prague. A new broadcasting law is being drafted.

Known for its fine film making, Czech TV coproduced some programs with foreign companies. Bratislava has a cable television venture through a firm called Videoton. Estimates for 1990 were that Czechoslovakia had 800,000 VCRs and 30,000 satellite antennas.

Bulgaria

Professional radio began in Bulgaria in 1929. In 1935 all radio became part of a state-owned monopoly. In 1944, radio was placed under the Ministry of Information and Propaganda, and in 1946, a second radio station was introduced. Experiments with television began in 1954, with regular programs in 1959 on the anniversary of the Russian Revolution. One national and three regional television stations went on the air from 1962 to 1973. A second TV channel was added in 1975. By 1985, there were also six local stations (Popova and Ivanova, 1990).

Bulgaria was the U.S.S.R.'s most loyal ally; its broadcasting was among the most propagandistic in the Eastern bloc. Its quality was improved by an institute for experimental TV. In the reform era, the various emergent political parties benefited from liberalization by receiving TV airtime.

In 1990, Bulgaria had 3.9 million television households and 550,000 VCRs. Satellite dishes were rare; only about 1000 were estimated to be in use (Zeidenberg, 1990d).

Romania

Under the Ceaucescu regime, Romania maintained a somewhat distant stance vis-à-vis Soviet political and cultural influence (Popa, 1986). Its broadcasting system, however, was typical of Eastern Europe, with a state monopoly in charge of programming while a ministry of posts and telecommunications handles transmission. The state broadcaster Radio Televiziunea Romania (RTR) played a key role in the revolution of 1989 and continued after the revolution with full reportage of the trials of former Ceaucescu regime officials.

Although no commercial broadcasting was developed in the months following the revolution, RTR (renamed RTRL for "Libera") began programming eighteen hours per day on two channels, compared to as little as two hours per day on a single channel at the time of the revolution. Approximately 4.1 million TV sets were in use (Posner, 1990).

As in many Eastern European countries, RTRL had been supported by the state, which assessed licensing fees on receivers. However, those fees, did not cover the RTRL's expenses. In 1990, the government announced that it would stop subsidizing RTRL. RTRL was forced to appeal directly to its viewers to support what was expected to be a significant increase in the viewer fee. There were four separate radio channels. Since the revolution, several pirate radio ventures were launched, one of which, "Radio Fun," began broadcasting from a university building in Bucharest, and received some funding from a French commercial broadcasting group (U.S. Department of State, 1990).

Romania was among the first Eastern bloc countries to join Eutelsat. Home satellite dishes remain almost unknown. But there are several hundred thousand VCRs in the country.

Yugoslavia

Yugoslavia had been described as "a state with six republics, five South Slav peoples, four languages, three religions, two alphabets, and one political party" (Campbell, 1972). The first radio station of Yugoslavia was founded in Zagreb in 1926 and followed by others in 1927 and 1929. A foreign-oriented station began in 1936 on a fourth channel. However, all these stations were destroyed during World War II, leaving only an underground station, Free Yugoslavia, operating from Moscow. After the war, that station became the nucleus for the national system. Yugoslavia created eight regional radio stations, one for each republic or region, and the national station Free Yugoslavia for international service with radio and television organizations in Belgrade, Zagreb, Ljubljana, Sarajevo, Skpoje, Titograd, Novisad, and Priština.

Historically the most independent broadcaster in Eastern Europe, Jugoslovenska Radio Televizija (JRT) varied from the typical centralized organizational structure of Eastern Europe. Its federated studio system reflected the country's republics (Nihailovic and Sinobad, 1986). Although membership in the JRT was nominally voluntary, all eight of the republic's broadcasting institutions participated. JRT's council board, in contrast to a centralized ministry, is responsible for the cooperation of the various stations, technological development, cooperation on the international level including representing Yugoslav broadcasting abroad, and programming policies. Since 1989, JRT's structure and reality have been subjected to the general centrifugalism in the Yugoslav federation. Above this organization stood the Socialist Alliance, which had the final word on policies and on the naming of directors and editors-in-chief. As in most other Eastern European countries, broadcasting was supported by a combination of license fees and advertising. Each republic sets its own license fees and could supplement income by producing and selling its own programming. Each station, furthermore, can regulate the amount of advertising it sells. In 1991, violent unrest in the country focused on the party's control over television, and led to its greater independence and diversity. As the country's cohesion was breaking up, so did the broadcast system.

The first three TV stations were founded in 1956 and the last in 1958. By 1973, one station existed for each republic. In time, the Republics had two or three channels, supplemented by regional program windows. Care was taken that stations not program so as to compete for viewers but complement each other. The eight RTV centers program in ten different languages, including their mostly English-language imports.

Plans for development of cable television included installation of cable networks and a Yugoslav satellite (Reuter, 1990). Master antenna systems already feed 200,000 apartments, and 30,000 Yugoslavs have satellites dishes. In addition, Yugoslavia had 2 million VCRs in 1990 (Zeidenberg, 1990d). While Yugoslavia traditionally imposed fewer restrictions on content than its Eastern European neighbors, some limits were in effect: one could not directly criticize the Communist system, encourage ethnic dissension, attack the Soviet Union, or challenge Marshall Tito (Paulu, 1974).

Albania

Albania, traditionally in self-imposed isolation, remained most impervious to institutional change. As an ally of China since the 1960s, the state broadcast monopoly Radiotelevizioni Shqiptar transmitted the Chinese and its own viewpoints worldwide through the high-powered Radio Tirana. Domestically, Shqiptar operates four regional stations. With the upheavals in 1991 and the first free elections, broadcasting's propaganda stance was loosened.

Hungary

Hungary was at the forefront of broadcasting reform in Eastern Europe. Even during the prereform period, Hungarian broadcasting was the most liberal in Eastern Europe. For example, church services were broadcast, and the Voice of America was not jammed.

Wired broadcasting was allegedly invented by a Hungarian, Tivadan Puskás, who demonstrated the "tele-phonograph" at the Paris World Exhibition of 1881. This system was put into operation the following year in Budapest and carried news and live music. The first radio transmissions in Hungary began in 1914, and operated throughout World War I. The Hungarian Telegraph Agency took over control of radio and telegraph transmission in 1922, and in 1924 it began transmitting experimental programs.

In 1925, a communications law established government control over all radio transmission in Hungary and gave the postal service exclusive authority to operate a transmitter. Within weeks, the Hungarian Telediffusion and Radio Corporation was set up to build studios and provide programming, using post office transmitters and equipment, as a licensee under the regulatory control of the Ministries of Trade and Postal Service. Programming was overseen by an interministerial committee, and the government ordered that all programming be submitted to the committee for approval a week before airtime (Szendrey, 1988).

A system of broadcast towers was constructed in the 1930s to replace what had originally been principally a wireline transmission network. Listener subscriptions increased rapidly. A musical advisory committee and a literary program section were created, and a steady flow of educational programming was brought directly into Hungarian schools.

While Hungarian radio operated throughout most of Second World War, the retreating German army decimated most of the system. In May 1945, two small transmitters went back on the air for six hours per day. The Hungarian Central Broadcasting Corporation was formed to replace Hungarian Telediffusion and Radio.

As the Communist Party established control in the immediate postwar years, Central Broadcasting was among the first industries to be nationalized, and broadcasting was operated directly by the government rather than through a licensee (Szendrey, 1988). Two AM networks were transmitting: the Kossuth, which was the main national service, and the Petöfi, which carried special programming for various interest groups as well as entertainment and news. With the onset of Stalinism, the state made so-called "people's radios" available that could receive only these two signals. In the 1960s, a third network, called Bartok, was created on the FM band (Horvat, Communication, 1990). In 1980, the government dropped the subscription requirement.

The first and perhaps most successful early commercial broadcasting project in Eastern Europe was Radio Danubius. In 1986, Magyar Radio, the state-run radio monopoly, launched this advertiser-supported channel containing light music and news programming for tourists, and it proved highly successful (Jakab, 1990). The station enjoyed high audience ratings and expanded its schedule. But its true commercial strength remains open to question, since it is housed in a government office and probably received preferential financial treatment from the PTT (U.S. Department of State, 1990).

Hungary's first experiments with television began in 1953. As a consequence of the Hungarian uprising in 1956, the Hungarian Television Company was dissolved in September of that year, and TV was put under the control of the Department of Hungarian Radio in early 1957. Subsequently, Hungarian Radio and Television was organized as a single organization with one chairman. Regular transmissions began in 1958. Color broadcasts began in 1969.

By 1972, a second TV channel was in place, and the coverage reached between 80 and 87 percent of the national territory. The following year, Hungarian Radio and TV was split and Magyar Televizio (MTV) was created as the national television system. Regional studios were added to the system. In 1976, MTV opened a studio in Pécs that produces programs in Romanian, Serbo-Croatian, and German. A regional studio was also put in Szeged to produce Slovakian and Romanian language programming.

The exclusivity of Hungary's national channel, MTV, was broken by the TV signals from foreign countries, especially from Austria. By 1987, Hungarians were allowed to receive Western satellite programming such as Sky Channel (Jakab, 1990); a third of the population watched such programs at least occasionally.

Even under communist rule, several reforms liberalized electronic media.

When a free election for parliament was held in 1990, the electronic media fulfilled the role of political watchdog. Just as the media affected political change in Hungary, so the new government's economic reforms—privatization, deregulation, and the encouragement of foreign investment—greatly influenced electronic media. Under the new government, the Bureau for Agitation and Propaganda was dismantled and censorship laws and other regulations governing the national press were essentially abandoned. Because the transformation of both the electronic and the print media was so publicly visible, it became a symbol of the snowballing reform movement in Hungary. In this free-market reformism, the view of electronic media as fulfilling certain public service functions such as cultural education and information was subordinated. The new view was that mass media must not be restricted with regard to freedom of the press; the result was the birth of advertiser-supported independent radio and television (Jakab, 1990).

Moreover, by the late 1980s it was clear that the over $50 million annual government subsidies did not adequately support the broadcasting infrastructure. Although some commercial advertising on the radio and TV networks had long been permitted, there was no government fee on radio receivers.

Like many of its neighbors, Hungary had a two-part broadcasting bureaucracy. Magyar Radio (MR) and Magyar Televizio (MTV) produced programming, while the PTT maintained absolute control over all transmission towers and facilities. The chairmen of MTV and MR are nominated by the prime minister and appointed by the president.

In 1989, the Hungarian Post was divided into three administrations, one of which is the Program Transmitting Company for radio, television, and other transmission functions. Although it remains a government corporation, it is run for profit (Jänos Horvat, communication).

In 1989, the government received seventeen applications to operate private stations and accepted four. New services included Radio Juventus Balaton, a music and news station; Radio Bridge, serving a business audience; and Calypso, a Budapest-area joint venture with Magyar Radio that programmed news, music, and "police information."

Additional local stations sprang up. Local broadcast stations were operated by city councils. Other local stations were carried on cable systems (Horvat, communication, 1990). Local cable systems were allowed to produce as well as broadcast their own programs since 1983, when they broke MTV's monopoly on program production.

The first commercial television station in Eastern Europe, the Siofok Channel (TV-S, also known as the Balaton channel), began broadcasting in Hungary's Lake Balaton district in 1989, with supplementary programming during the tourist season targeted toward Austrian and German visitors. Nap-TV, a joint venture among several Hungarian commercial interests and including the best-selling daily tabloid *Mai-Nap*, followed. (Rupert Murdoch had a stake.) In keeping with the Program Transmission Company's control of the airwaves, even these private broadcasters used the government broadcast facilities.

The government received scores of applications for new licenses but set a moratorium on frequency allocations pending the enactment of the new media law. Among the most important issues to be resolved were those of cross-ownership and foreign ownership.

Hungary has more cable television than many of its Western European neighbors. The first cable systems were built by the PTT, but in time most cable systems became privately owned or municipal. Hungarian private cable was launched in 1980 by Hungarian entrepreneur Robert Zimmerman, who carried the two national Hungarian channels as well as programming from Czechoslovakia, Yugoslavia, and Austria to 18,000 homes in the Lake Balaton area. Although one of Zimmerman's foreign channels was jammed by the disapproving PTT, he was later allowed to expand his service. At least forty-two cable systems are reported in operation (Jakab, 1990, p. D252). Master antenna television service connects 250,000 homes in twenty-five communities. These systems carry some western satellite services, such as Sky Channel and TV-5 (Scott, 1988, p. 11).

About 20 percent of Hungarian homes had a videorecorder in 1989, and over 10,000 had satellite dishes.

III

THE EVOLUTION OF EUROPEAN BROADCASTING

27

Three Efforts at European Integration

The Administration of a Cartel: The European Broadcasting Union

From the beginning, European broadcasters collaborated with each other. In 1925, at the BBC's initiative, the International Broadcasting Union (IBU) was established. One of the early functions of the Geneva-based organization was to draft a frequency allocation plan. It also tried, unsuccessfully, to reduce commercial as well as propaganda broadcasting across national frontiers and initiated a program exchange, mostly of concerts (Eugster, 1983). During World War II, the IBU was largely dormant, but it was revived afterward along with a new organization, the International Broadcasting Organization (OIR) (Briggs, 1979). The OIR, however, was soon abandoned by the West European countries. It was renamed OIRT with the advent of television and headquartered in Prague. The West European broadcasters established in 1950 the European Broadcasting Union (EBU), to which broadcasters from middle-Eastern and North African countries were soon added. The EBU domiciled itself in Geneva and shortly thereafter absorbed the IBU. With the demise of the Eastern Bloc after 1989, it seemed likely that the EBU would absorb the OIRT.

The EBU is an association of thirty-nine European and Mediterranean broadcasting organizations, not of governments. There are fifty-five associate members in thirty-three other countries across the globe. Nineteen national languages are spoken in the active member countries. There are an estimated 168 million television households in the active member nations (Michael Type, communication). Commercial stations are not excluded in principle, but members must provide a national service, and regional broadcasters are not eligible. This therefore excludes Italian private stations or the various ITV companies, but the private Luxembourg RTL was an EBU member from the beginning (though the latter's predecessor, IBU, had tried to suppress it). After much resistance by the BBC, which had not reconciled itself to the loss of its exclusivity, the United Kingdom's independent broadcast authority (IBA) was eventually admitted.

The EBU established a program exchange through its Eurovision system. Eurovision has provided transmission for programs since 1954, with a technical coordination center in Lille, France, and a control center in Brussels. The guiding spirit behind its creation was Marcel Bezençon of Switzerland. The system was seen as a way of protecting public broadcasting from commercial television by providing particularly the smaller public broadcasters with programs from other countries. The EBU also finances a fund that supports multilingual productions. (European Task Force, 1988) By a wide margin, sports events are the staple of Eurovision programming (80 percent); cultural programs trail far behind. Eurovision also provides an exchange of news footage. Its Eastern European equivalent is Intervision, and the two systems transmit programs to each other, though the eastward flow was vastly larger than the reverse flow, even before the democratic revolutions.

As discussed in Chapter 2, the EBU was used from the beginning to establish a common bargaining position against copyright holders such as music publishers. There are two main elements to the cartel powers of the EBU. First, it is the sole representative of all its members in international purchase negotiations for sports and other events. Second, it controls program distribution between member organizations. An example of its first power is provided by the bidding for the 1984 Summer Olympics games in Los Angeles. After competition among the three major networks for the American rights ABC paid $1.67 per household, whereas the EBU, having no competition, acquired the rights for $0.17 per household (Cryan et al., 1987).

EBU also requires that if one sells an event to one member country, one must deal only with EBU members in the other countries. The provisions of exclusivity were somewhat loosened in 1986 (European Task Force, 1988, p. 75).

These policies meant that the EBU could limit bidding for events and squeeze out potential buyers who sought rights for one country only. It was also able to limit the payment to the owner of the events.

The advent of cable television and satellite-transmitted channels undercut the need for Eurovision, because its program exchange functions could easily be undertaken by a satellite channel. Commercial television channels also raised again the difficult question of the admittance of multiple representation from countries. The EBU's problem is that it must either integrate the new program providers into its organization or be threatened by the emergence of a rival organization of commercial program providers. Many EBU members opposed admitting new categories of members who they believed would affect their "public service" orientation (and create competition in bidding for broadcast rights) (European Task Force, 1988, p. 66). Eventually, after broadcasters such as Berlusconi and Sat-1 were denied membership, the commercial broadcasters founded the Association of Commercial Television (ACT) in 1989. The EBU's program buying power began to weaken in the face of strong commercial competition. In 1989 the EBU for the first time lost the rights to broadcast the Wimbledon tennis tournament when a West German agent outbid them (Scharf, 1990). But it has continued to hold technical advantages when it comes to covering complex events such as the Olympics and the soccer World Cup.

The EBU also set up the satellite-delivered sports channel, co-owned by seventeen of its members and Murdoch's Sky TV. This arrangement continued EBU's preferential access and control over sports programming. It was challenged by a rival channel, Sports Screen (owned by WH Smith 75% and ESPN 25%), and was struck down by the European Common as anti-competitive.

1992 and Television Without Frontiers

In the past the limited reach of electromagnetic signals allowed a state to regulate most of the television that could be received in its territory. Later advances in broadcast technology did not greatly affect national control because additional power did not increase range by much, and transmission tower height had its structural limits. In border regions, however, viewers were able to circumvent state control and receive programs from abroad.

The European Community does not include a number of states, such as Switzerland, Austria, Sweden, Norway, Iceland, and Finland. Yet broadcasting does not respect national frontiers. The Council of Europe, a broader grouping, is therefore often thought to be the geographically appropriate forum for European media policy. On the other hand, and in contrast to the EC, it has no executive powers and acts through "recommendations." In 1988 it passed a Broadcast Convention for member states' adoption, similar to the EC directive in that both consider the originating country's rules to be the binding law in transfrontier transmission. The convention's program standards and specific product advertising rules are more rigorous than those of the EC's directive. Both require the right of reply, but the convention does not address copyright or advise on quotas for European programs.

Perhaps most controversial in the EC's directive was the requirement that at least 51 percent of entertainment programming be of European origin. Although not formally aimed at any specific country, it was fairly obviously a measure to restrict Hollywood imports. Opposition by the United States was vociferous and was generated on several fronts. Several measures were proposed by Congress, including a retaliatory plan prohibiting the Corporation for Public Broadcasting (CPB) from buying European programs. The U.S. Commerce Department also filed a complaint with the GATT arguing that the directive was protectionist (Cate, 1990, p. 4).

The United Kingdom, Italy, Spain, West Germany, Denmark, and Belgium were also opposed, as were many members of the Association for Commercial Television (ACT) (Glenn, 1989). The Bavarian government challenged the EC's right to promulgate cultural laws, and other countries were uneasy about EC interference in cultural affairs. At first the French strongly supported the quotas. But eventually, French Minister of Culture Jack Lang proposed instead that the broadcasters devote a fixed percentage of revenues to domestic production.

In the face of this opposition, the EC Council of Ministers pulled somewhat back (Cate, 1990, p. 5) and adopted a vague, nonbinding clause recommending that European majority quotas should be met after 1992 "where practicable." Member states could thus practice their own policies. But those had frequently been restrictive. At the same time the EC approved $270 million in subsidies for domestic film production (Greenhouse, 1989, p. A1).

The concept of formal film quotas was also rejected in the Council of Europe's 1989 Broadcast Convention (Margolies, 1989). But the reality was a different matter. Even in the U.K., the Independent Television Commission proposed a minimum of 75 percent European programming for Channel 3 licensees.

In 1986, the Commission established BABEL—Broadcasting Across the Barriers of European Language—a noncommercial association for promoting pan-European multilingual broadcasts. It is comprised of the E.C. Commission's media group, the EBU, and the Alliance Européenne pour la Télévision et la Culture. BABEL supported dubbing and subtitling.

In 1990, an "Action Programme to Promote the Development of the European AudioVisual Industry," known as the "Media" plan, was passed; it sought to develop three critical areas of European broadcasting: programming, regulation and market structure, and technology ("Europe," 1989, pp. 13–14).

To enhance market structure, the commission recommended that future national regulations take into account better than before the new European media industry. The commission recommended greater support of independent producers, especially in facilitating their access to major broadcasters as competition intensified for air time. A five-year, $260 million plan was approved. (Papathanassopoulos, 1990)

The EC also set a goal of introduction of high definition television by 1992 and recommended pushing the European-developed Eureka standard. It also tried unseccessfully to require the use of the D2-MAC standard on all European broadcast satellites.

Such varied activities and initiatives, in the aggregate, increasingly establish Brussels as a major regulatory presence in television.

Technological Nationalism: The Struggle Over TV Standards

Technological nationalism is an important force retarding European integration. Color television standards provide a good historical illustration. The French color television system SECAM (Séquential à Mémoire) was promoted in the late 1950s by Henri de France (Crane, 1979). Patent rights were acquired by a joint venture between CSF and the glass manufacturer Saint Gobain, later joined by the conglomerate Floréat and the French government itself. A rival German system, PAL (Phase Alternation by Line), was developed by AEG-Telefunken in the early 1960s. PAL, like the North American National Television Subcommittee Standard (NTSC), uses AM modulation for the color subcarrier, whereas SECAM uses FM modulation. All three systems require three signals for color transmission, luminance, and chrominance information. Their sequencing, however, differs. PAL and SECAM both have 625 line pictures, as opposed to the 525-lines of the older (NTSC) standard used in the United States, Canada, Japan, Korea, and several other countries.

France traditionally maintained a policy of promoting "national champion" projects of high visibility, such as the first supersonic transport aircraft (with the United Kingdom), the first tidal power plant, and the largest solar energy furnace. *Le Monde* dubbed these projects the "new cathedrals." When SECAM was developed, the French broadcast institution ORTF gave it only a lukewarm reception. Its engineers viewed Henri de France as an outsider, and they stressed the importance of international compatibility and of selecting the most effective system. Soon, however, ORTF received orders from the "very highest levels" of the French government to support the SECAM system, whatever the comparative test results. Once this political decision had been made, the French government embarked on an international offensive. Its strategy included discrediting the American NTSC technology as inferior and presenting SECAM as a way of reducing European dependence on America. Unfortunately for the French, the German PAL could just as easily play this European role. AEG-Telefunken had orginally approached the French SCF with a proposal for cross-licensing patents to make it possible for the German firm to produce SECAM equipment. German public opinion was strongly in favor of a European solution, but the French declared the German terms for licensing unreasonable. Hence, the German company went ahead with its development of PAL, led by Walter Bruch.

The debate about which system to choose quickly became heated, with the French charging that NTSC stood for "never twice the same color," while Americans dubbed SECAM as the "supreme effort contra-America" (Crane, 1979, p. 53). It is difficult to rank the technical merits of the three systems, because each has some advantages and some disadvantages. Studies by the European Broadcasting Union concluded that no system was consistently superior to its competitors and that the average viewer could find little difference among them. PAL incorporated several of the features of both its rivals.

Some of the smaller European countries refused to be coerced by de Gaulle— a problem going far beyond television standards at the time—and France, therefore, forged a technological alliance with the Eastern European countries. If the Soviet Union adopted SECAM, surely the rest of Eastern Europe, particularly East Germany, would follow. Then, West Germany, sensitive to the ability to broadcast to East Germans, would fall into line. Furthermore, with both Soviet and French backing, SECAM would be adopted by many Third World countries.

Because the Soviet Union was reluctant, for political reasons, to adopt American or West German technology, the French plan was attractive. The French also offered economic incentives. In 1965 an agreement was reached. The Soviets were permitted to refer to SECAM as a Franco-Soviet development, in spite of their negligible contributions, which amounted to the addition of a few circuits. The French, while calling the Soviet modifications unnecessary, permitted the Soviets to use SECAM without royalty and to take out patent rights entitling them to royalties payments from East European licensees. This was ironic, because it was France's initial intransigence with German manufacturers on the issue of royalties that encouraged PAL as a rival. The

Franco–Soviet agreement was hailed by both countries as a great victory. Alain Peyrefitte, the French Minister of Information, called it a "glorious day for the human race" (Crane, 1979, p. 73).

But the joy did not last long. Most of the countries assembled for the subsequent CCIR (the International Consultative Committee on Radio) meeting in Vienna wanted to come to an agreement on standards. The Franco–Soviet accord, in effect, indicated that the French- and Soviet-influenced parts of Europe would proceed with SECAM regardless of the outcome of the CCIR conference. Yet even the French ORTF representatives preferred a single European standard to a specifically French technology. The Franco–Soviet agreement led to a counteralliance between PAL and NTSC backers. At the Vienna meeting, SECAM obtained twenty-one country votes, whereas the German–American coalition had eighteen. But the SECAM votes included the economically less important countries of Eastern Europe and several former French African colonies that had no television at all. Most of Western Europe preferred the PAL system. The conference ended in an impasse. A year later, in Oslo, a similar stalemate occurred. In the end, each country went its own way. French industry did not succeed in establishing international or European standards, but it had given some protection to its own market from imports.

Following the development of PAL and SECAM in the 1960s, engineering improvements overcame some of the systems' initial technical problems. A remaining weakness was that both interweave color information with brightness information, causing a shimmering effect known as "cross-color" on finely detailed picture areas.

Audio signal quality was another shortcoming of the existing systems, and one becoming increasingly irritating to users accustomed to high-quality stereo sound. As satellite transmission of television emerged, sound tracks in different languages became important. Similarly, capability for data transmission, teletex, and subtitles also became desirable. All this suggested the need for updated television transmission standards that would incorporate advances in signal processing. Beyond the technical reasons, the introduction of new, Europe-wide standards was sought partly to reconstitute the protection that the PAL and SECAM patents had provided to West European television set manufacturers from cheaper Asian imports. The expiration of those patents created an incentive for a new patent round (Snoddy, 1986, p. 15). In the United Kingdom, for example, the loss of the PAL patent threatened 20,000 jobs in color television manufacturing (Dornan, 1984, p. 24). A British government commission report acknowledged that more sophisticated sets featuring decoders for videotex, teletex, cable, and direct brocast satellites (DBS) would be particularly useful in protecting British television set manufacturers against cheap imports (ITAP, 1982). During the discussions of a new standard, several variants of so-called MAC (Multiplexed Analog Components) were considered. One variant of MAC (C-MAC) provides a "group" sound system using the EBU specifications.[1]

C-MAC requires greater bandwidth than some of its alternatives. A variant, D2–MAC, achieves compression of the bandwidth at the cost of some picture clarity and a smaller number of sound channels, though the compressed bandwidth enables programs to be broadcast in the four major West European languages. To transform the D2–MAC signal into a signal compatible with existing PAL television sets, a converter is necessary, costing some $300 when produced in quantity.

In 1984 several European manufacturers, including Philips and Thompson, advocated a version of C-MAC as a standard. However, the German and French governments, whose direct broadcast satellites TDF-1 and TV-SAT were the first scheduled for launch, agreed among themselves in 1985 instead to support D2-MAC (with HD-MAC for future high definition) and furthermore to use initially their own PAL and SECAM standards in their respective satellites. The British, on the other hand, supported C-MAC partly because its independent broadcasting authority and several British companies had been active in the development of the chip technology for C-MAC. This threatened to result in four different satellite broadcast standards in Western Europe alone. Eventually, negotiations led to a 1985 agreement in which EBU declared C-MAC as its preference but also approved D2-MAC.

In 1988, the British direct broadcast satellite operation BSB agreed to employ the D2-MAC. Thus, it seemed that this standard had been generally agreed upon. However, D2-MAC did not attain the success expected in the marketplace. Political decisions could not substitute for consumer decisions. Also, there were coordination problems. Terrestrial broadcasters had little use for the new transmission standards. TV-SAT's broadcasters refused to pay the German Bundespost Telecom's rental fee because of the absence of viewers. For them, improved and compatible variants (e.g., "Super-PAL") were quite enough. Television equipment manufacturers, who had to develop conversion devices and entirely new receivers, were slow in their R&D and blamed many of their problems on an even slower chip manufacturing industry. In 1989, when the first direct broadcasts were becoming operational (TV-SAT 1 had failed in 1987 TDF 1 and 2 were ailing), D2-MAC reception equipment was just being introduced, retarding the standard's evolution and shifting users to the German PAL-satellite Copernicus (with low-power transmission). Also, the success of the Astra satellite and its PAL transmissions proved to both public and private broadcasters that D2-MAC was not worth waiting for. Consumers were not familiar with D2-MAC devices and the D2-MAC television sets were quite expensive. Cable systems, a primary distributor of satellite signals, were also not yet D2-MAC compatible.

Support from France and Germany began to wane. The French government chose to put pay-TV services, including Canal Plus over its TDF-1 satellite, instead of using it for general broadcasts, thus reducing the audience for D2-MAC transmissions. This sharply reduced French demand for any D2-MAC devices. In West Germany sales of the expensive D2-MAC receivers were minimal, and concern rose about the difficulty of supplying German audiences. By 1990, both German and French officials who supported D2-MAC were beginning to mourn its death, although many were still promoting the development of a future high definition standard (HD-MAC) (*Funkschau*, 1990, pp. 24–26).

Peter Glotz, the media spokesman of the German Social Democrats, pronounced "D2-MAC is dead." The European Commission tried hard to make the standard a requirement for satellites.

A related standards battle was waged over high-definition television (HDTV). The Japanese broadcasting authority, NHK, supervised the development of the Japanese "MUSE" HDTV standard with 1125 lines. Several other MUSE variants were also offered. Europeans, however, were reluctant to agree with that standard, and in the 1986 CCIR meeting they managed to postpone decisions for four years. European manufacturers feared that if the Japanese standards were adopted, they would be without protection against the lower-priced and often higher-quality Asian products. Therefore, they decided to develop HDTV with the MAC-packet standard as the basis for various forms of television transmission.

Europe (and similarly the United States) was unprepared for HDTV, and sought delays when it realized the potential commercial implications of the Japanese standards. In Europe the primary focus for HDTV has been DBS, not terrestrial broadcasting. HDTV development began on a pan-European scale in 1986 with the Eureka project. It involves thirty-three companies from nine European countries, including non-EC countries. The main industrial participants are Bosch, Philips, Thompson, and Thorn-EMI. The EC's RACE Program (Research and Development in Advanced Communications Technologies in Europe) also conducted research on HDTV standards development, especially on digital HDTV technology and the transmission of signals through integrated fiber-optic broadband networks. HD-MAC broadcasts were expected by 1994 (OTA, 1990).

Thus, for all the national and supranational efforts, European standards setting was in disarray. The early PAL versus SECAM controversy involved questions of national prestige that could not be overcome. But even when, in the next standards round, Germany and France reached agreement at the highest levels of government, its viability was challenged in the marketplace. This demonstrates the difficulty of creating standards by fiat, when the industry is composed of several heterogenous segments (broadcasters satellite operators consumer electronics manufacturers and component makers) resident in several countries. In the United States, the HDTV trend was to an all-digital format, which would permit a greater openness to variation, and reduce the need for complex agreements.

28

Direct Satellite Broadcasting

Introduction to DBS

One form of broadcasting that threatens to overcome national boundaries is high-powered direct broadcast satellites (DBS). DBS as a concept goes back to 1977, when a World Administrative Radio Conference (WARC), in a contentious meeting pitting the United States against the rest of the world, established the basic framework (Pool, 1991). At the time, European officials saw DBS as imminent. They regarded it as a wide-open field where no country had yet achieved technological dominance and where the potential existed to develop domestic electronic strength. It was also viewed as a way to establish the traditional national broadcast institutions in space, since DBS's large power requirements permitted only a small number of channels, thus causing little disruption to the existing national systems. To achieve high-power beam required a small "footprint" of coverage; thus, the scarcity of channels in the sky would match the scarcity of channels on the ground.

Despite these early hopes, DBS soon ran into problems. Cost estimates rapidly escalated. A typical DBS plan included three satellites of great complexity and expense: two in the sky, one of which served primarily as a standby, and one spare on the ground. Without the redundancy, a small malfunction in a vital component of this expensive technology could cause tens of millions of subscribers to be stranded for a year or more. Thus, the cost estimate for the space segment alone climbed to well above $500 million, and because the life expectancy of a satellite is only about ten years or less, the annual anticipated cost of space hardware was enormous. Launch and insurance costs also mounted, as several telecommunications satellites were lost in highly publicized rocket mishaps. On top of that, there were the considerable expenses of ground stations, program supply, marketing, administration, and subscriber services.

As the projects were considered, technological progress changed the discussion; the need for high-powered satellites was increasingly questioned in favor of medium-powered ones. When DBS was originally conceived in 1977, WARC agreed on a necessary signal power of 230 watts, requiring a receiving antenna of 0.9 meters. To transmit with such power required new and untested technology. (In comparison, regular low-power telecommunications satellites reach around 10 watts of power.)

However, the efficiency of antennas soon improved rapidly. At the 1977

WARC, it was still assumed that antennas would have a so-called merit factor of 6 decibels (per degree Kelvin). By 1985, antennas of 30 db/K were readily available. Since an increase of 3 db/K nearly doubles reception power, many wondered whether high-power transmission was really necessary. Similarly, the attenuation of signals by rain proved to be a much less severe problem than was originally feared. Thus, it became possible to use medium-powered satellites that could provide more program channels and require smaller antennas than had previously been imagined.

In addition to technical dilemmas, the logic behind the use of DBS by established public broadcasting institutions remained unclear. After all, traditional broadcasters typically reach the entire population of their countries through terrestrial broadcasting and have no real ambition to reach the rest of Europe. To add one or two program channels would be simpler and much less expensive by using additional terrestrial frequencies, and this would also involve less interference from one country to another. One rationale for public broadcasters' DBS plans was a desire to preempt private entrants; however, the enormous cost of DBS had already created major entry barriers for private firms. There was also the question of whether audiences for Europe-wide programs were large enough. According to one school of thought, there were only two such categories of viewers: adolescents interested in music and managers interested in economic news. Both groups are light television watchers and may not provide an adequate audience base.

Language barriers also undermine pan-European satellite TV. There is less bilingualism than is often believed. Although many viewers claim an "excellent" command of English, actual knowledge is much more modest. Furthermore, dismal foreign-language TV ratings in Europe reveal that even viewers who understand English shy away from English language channels (Evans et al., 1990, p. 76).

Further, the number of products that would permit Europe-wide advertising is not large. The example usually given is Coca-Cola. Even a multinational company such as Unilever, the soap and food giant, has only twenty Europe-wide brand names out of 2000 that are used throughout Europe (McCartney, 1985). Advertising approaches differ greatly in various countries, and a strategy that fits them all may be difficult to find. Most European companies are structured along national lines and their accounts do not have Europe-wide advertising budgets. Of course, many organizational constraints can be changed, but this would take time and in the meantime the infant satellite channels would be in difficulty.

The differing rules on advertising within European countries provide an additional hindrance to pan-European channels. For example, in Italy RAI was prohibited from carrying advertisements for furs, boats, pet foods, automobiles, and newspapers. In Holland, advertising for sweets and correspondence courses was prohibited. In France, margarine, newspapers, real estate, and alcoholic beverages could not be advertised (*Connections*, 1985). This is being changed through the harmonization efforts of the EC Commission and the Council of Europe. Since the early 1970s, there have been experimental DBS ventures, as well as commercial failures; the U.S. ventures, USCI, failed because of technical problems. Since then, there have been attempts at DBS in India (ATS6), Canada (CTS), USSR (Statsionar 1), France (TDF 1,2), Germany (TV-SAT), Scandinavia (Tele-X), and Luxembourg (Coronet/Astra).

The case of the DBS medium-power project Coronet, pitting broadcast interests in Luxembourg, France, Germany, and the United States against each other, illustrates the complex scenario of European direct broadcast satellites.

Luxembourg and the Saga of Coronet

Luxembourg, situated physically and culturally in the heart of Europe, was well placed to host a satellite venture. The country has traditionally benefited from playing the maverick in a number of economic activities, including broadcasting. A first plan was LuxSat. That concept united the West Germans and French in opposition and encouraged the two countries to pursue collaborative development and production of their TDF-1 and TV-SAT satellite projects. In 1983, the French government used its indirect controlling interest in CLT, the parent company of Luxembourg's national broadcasting firm, to block the LuxSat project. Pierre Werner, the prime minister of Luxembourg, therefore sought authorization for another plan, the Coronet project (*Neue Medien,* 1984).

Coronet was the brainchild of the American entrepreneur Clay T. Whitehead, who had formerly headed the Office for Telecommunications Policy (OTP) in the Nixon White House, and later managed the satellite manufacturer Hughes Communications. Whitehead proposed a satellite with intermediate power of about 50 watts located between telecommunications and DBS signal strength. A second part of Whitehead's concept was for the satellite to serve as a transmission facility rather than as a program provider. It would lease its sixteen transponders to interested parties as a common carrier. In 1983, Whitehead convinced Prime Minister Werner of the advantages of the satellite project, which was christened GDL-Coronet (*GDL* for "Grand Duchy of Luxembourg"). Whitehead began recruiting potential investors and users, including the American program provider HBO and the investment bank Salomon Brothers acted as advisor.

The French government opposed the Coronet project because it did not control it as it did CLT. It viewed GDL-Coronet as a threat not only to its own cable and satellite projects but to French sovereignty. France therefore led opposition to the project in Eutelsat, the European telecommunications satellite organization, by pointing to the precedent this project represented: the provision of telecommunications services for hire by a carrier outside of PTT control.

The French government also renewed its commitment to its own TDF-1 project. To ensure usage of that satellite and to draw Luxembourg's CLT into its orbit, it agreed in principle to lease two of the four channels to CLT and offered attractive terms to CLT for commercial television broadcasting in the French language in France, as long as no competitive satellite service was established. French pressure on Luxembourg grew massively, and the major French shareholders in CLT, most either owned by or close to the government, threatened not to approve any further investment in CLT if Coronet proceeded.

Meanwhile, the disagreement between CLT and the Luxembourg government quickly escalated into a legal confrontation. CLT claimed a contractual monopoly for Luxembourg broadcasting, while the government of Luxembourg countered that no such monopoly existed because GDL-Coronet was a telecommunications satellite and was providing service for which CLT had no exclusivity.

CLT and the French government relied on the solidarity among the European PTTs against the intruder. Of course, very little encouragement was needed to generate PTT opposition to a potential competitor, especially a private system with American backing. Through their coordinating organizations CEPT and Eutelsat, the PTTs agreed to resist cooperation with Coronet. Eutelsat objected to Coronet's orbital position and frequency use; later, its secretary general Andrea Caruso recommended that member states bar any telecommunication access to Coronet. Eutelsat ignored assurances that Luxembourg would maintain control over Coronet and that American program channels would be prohibited.

By 1984 the GDL-Coronet project became an issue in the Luxembourg parliamentary election, with the Socialist opposition arguing against provoking France. French PTT minister Mexandeau stated, "If the American businessmen attempt to test our abilities to accept their challenge, then we answer them: impossible in a European framework. In any case, we are not willing to let the Coca-Cola satellites undermine our linguistic and cultural identity" (*Neue Medien*, 1984).[1]

The call to European solidarity against the American invasion convinced Germany to join the opposition to the project. In a meeting with Prime Minister Werner of Luxembourg, German Chancellor Kohl made it clear that Germany would give priority to the industrial collaboration with France. In addition, the German Bundespost concluded that a DBS system such as Coronet could threaten its own massive cabling projects and its own TV-SAT DBS project. Consequently, the Dresdner Bank, the venture's main banker replacing the American Salomon Brothers, became cautious about proceeding with the project.

In an attempt to bolster European credibility, Coronet tried to further de-Americanize itself by promising to use the French Ariane rocket for launching, by including many European components in the satellite, and by reducing Clay Whitehead's participation from 20 to 10 percent.

However, the unified opposition proved insurmountable. Coronet suffered a major setback when Werner, its principal governmental supporter, retired after the 1984 election and was replaced by Jacques Santer. The government then decided to form an alternative satellite organization, Société Européenne des Satellites (SES) to replace Coronet. In effect, the American interests were expelled but the business plan and the satellite were kept. SES was partly owned by two Luxembourg government banks, as well as by other firms from Luxembourg, Belgium, Sweden, and Denmark. Later, the British ITV firm Thames Television joined. SES assumed for all practical purposes the GDL-Coronet position, and Whitehead received some compensation. SES also took over the contract for an RCA 4000 satellite.

Once Coronet had been eliminated, the French government modified the arrangement with CLT. By permitting commercial terrestrial broadcasting within France by two other consortia, the French government eliminated the exclusivity to the French language commercial broadcasting market with which it had lured CLT. It also demanded high rates from CLT for the use of the TDF satellite. When the TDF-1 project developed technical problems and fell far behind schedule, CLT found itself undercut and without a satellite for its own European ambitions.

SES, too, met strong opposition from France and Eutelsat. The Luxembourg government fought with Eutelsat over the question of whether SES was proposing "a public telecommunications service." Ironically, the Luxembourg position was mildly favored by several other countries such as West Germany and France, which otherwise staunchly endorsed PTT exclusivity, but which were establishing their own national satellite systems whose use could be restricted by Intelsat with similar arguments.

In 1988 SES successfully launched its satellite, Astra 1A. Soon, all of its 16 transponders were leased, and served about 15 million European homes. Astra was used for Rupert Murdoch's four Sky Television channels and 12 other primarily English and German stations, including Sat-1, RTL Plus, Screen Sport, Lifestyle, MTV Europe, and The Children's Channel. Astra claimed a third of the British direct-to-home viewing audience (Glenn, 1989a: p. 9). But most of the audience to Astra transmissions are cable subscribers via the head-end of their cable network.

A second Astra satellite was launched in 1990. A third satellite was to follow, all operating from the same orbital positions and offering together 48 channels. According to Astra, 16 million European cable households could receive it. Astra was becoming a huge success.

France

In France the development of both cable television and direct broadcast satellites (DBS) was primarily a hardware-oriented and political question, leaving the programming use of new distribution channels to be determined later. Decisions on program transponder allocation for the DBS satellite project TDF-1, were made almost on the eve of the launch, years after the allocation of investments, and have since changed repeatedly. Similarly, multibillion dollar cable television investment plans were pursued with only vague program planning.

The electronics and space industries and their allied government ministries viewed a DBS project as a promising source of demand for expensive satellites, millions of ground antennas, and upgraded TV sets, while creating much export potential. DBS also presented an opportunity to expand the reach of French broadcasting and culture to other countries. Moreover, it provided a vehicle for collaboration with West Germany. In 1980 the two countries signed an agreement for a three-satellite system, each with three transponders (later expanded to four and then five) of 250 watts, and costing FFr 1.1 billion. Later, a Nordic consortium headed by Sweden joined in the agreement. The German project, called TV-SAT, was scheduled for launch in April 1985, followed shortly thereafter by the French TDF-1 and a spare satellite. As the French satellite's name implies, it was at the time under the control of the broadcasting administration, TDF, rather than that of its long-standing telecommunications rival, the telecommunications monopoly administration, DGT.

This Eurosatellite consortium included the German firms MBB and AEG-Telefunken, as well as the French companies SNIAS, Thomson, and Aérospatiale (Vedel, 1987). Germany and France agreed on the D2-MAC transmission standard.

The Socialist government, which came to power soon thereafter, scrutinized the project. The DGT, by now actively lobbying for cable, argued that high-powered satellites were unproven as a technology and would be made obsolete as a transmission concept. The TDF-1 satellite had only five broadcast transponders, in contrast to the two dozen or more stations available with cable transmission. The costs inherent in the satellites, including subscriber equipment, antennas, amplifiers, and decoders, as well as environmental limitations (e.g., unsightly antennae, need for a clear southern exposure, and problems in maintaining signal quality in the event of rain or snow) provided strong arguments against DBS. The DGT advocated the use of medium-power satellites with more channels, or, preferably, reliance on the DGT's own low-power telecommunications satellite project together with its terrestrial cable transmission.

In the face of powerful but conflicting interests, the new Socialist government of François Mitterrand compromised by adopting both cable and DBS, declaring them complementary. Ridiculed at the time, this view is nevertheless correct, particularly if it would combine cable with multichannel, medium-power satellites. Cable offers advantages to most urban and suburban viewers, whereas satellites could cover less densely populated regions and feed the cable systems in other areas.

The government also had to face the task of allocating the transponders. The minister of communications, Georges Fillioud, discarded the original allocation in favor of new channels. He assigned one channel to the French public broadcasters, and a second to a French-language European channel, and he dangled a third and fourth channel before Luxembourg's CLT to lure it away from pursuing its own LuxSat. CLT could contribute its popularity as a program provider, and because various French state companies owned large blocks of its shares, it was viewed as controllable by the French government.

An agreement was reached for two CLT channels on TDF-1, one each in French and German, for FFr 90 million per transponder per year (Vedel, 1987). But after Luxembourg ended its Coronet involvement, CLT was dropped. In the meantime, TDF-1 launching dates fell behind schedule, disputes over transmission standards erupted, and costs rose to over FFr 3.5 billion. Despite the setbacks and rising costs, the largest threat to the project was the introduction of commercial terrestrial television, which undermined the market for DBS and made the main argument for the costly satellite concept, the absence of suitable terrestrial television frequencies, seem disingenuous. The negotiations unraveled: CLT now wanted one of the two terrestrial channels, while terrestrial applicants wanted also to be carried on TDF-1 to increase their reach.

Télévision par Satellites, a company that had foreign participation, was established to operate the satellite; the French government held 34 percent, and together with other government-linked French companies such as Aérospatiale and the bank Crédit Agricole, it had majority ownership. Foreign participants included Robert Maxwell, the British media mogul (then-owner of the Mirror newspaper group and of the largest British cable system, who held 20 percent), Luxembourg financial institutions (17 percent), Berlusconi (8 percent), and the Dutch company Philips (5 percent).

When a conservative French government assumed power in 1986, it questioned the concept, and even more the transponder assignments. Both the terrestrial stations awarded to La Cinq and M6 and their transponders on TDF-1 were at first rescinded. CNCL, the new media regulatory agency, reassigned the transponders, one to the modified La Cinq group of Berlusconi, Seydoux, and Hersant, and the other to the new holders of M6, CLT and Lyonnaise des Eaux. By that time, project cost had risen to FFr 2 billion for one satellite, almost six times the original cost, not counting inflation. But the industry interests lobbied furiously to save the project, using scare scenarios about British, Japanese, Luxembourgeois, and other satellite projects relegating France to the role of a second-rate power. Meanwhile, corresponding interests in other countries were lobbying their own governments, using similar arguments.

TDF-1 was launched in April 1988, shortly after its German counterpart, TV-Sat, was unsuccessfully put into orbit. TDF-2 followed in 1990.

The French satellites were hampered by serious technical difficulties, including the permanent breakdown of several channels. Because TDF-1 was the first satellite to use the D2-MAC transmission standard, consumers had to purchase new reception devices that were in short supply and expensive. Luxembourg's Astra satellite which uses PAL also proved to be a formidable competitor.

In 1990, the new French–German public channel La Sept was the only unencrypted television broadcaster operating on TDF-1 that could reach all French homes, and it was neither well known nor popular. The other transponders are allocated to the pay-TV channel Canal Plus which has no full terrestrial coverage, Sports 2/3, Canal Enfants (a children's channel in which Canal Plus holds a stake), and Euromusique. Three radio stations—Hector, Victor, and Radio France Internationale—were also using the satellite. Few French were willing to invest in a satellite dish for so few DBS program channels, while terrestrial broadcast options were expanding. To give the program channels on TDF a boost, the French regulatory agency CSA decided in 1990 that all cable networks must carry these channels.

Germany

German involvement with satellite broadcasting began in the late 1960s when the Ministry for Research and Technology ordered two competing private consortia to develop and analyze the feasibility of direct satellite broadcasting. West Germany later joined the European Space Agency (ESA) and assumed a share of the cost of the agency's European Communications Satellite (ECS) project. The two countries agreed in 1979 to develop and produce the nearly identical German TV-SAT and the French TDF-1 satellites, with 54 percent of production costs assumed by Germany and 46 percent by France (Scherer, 1985). In 1982, the German states declared that they wanted to play a part in the decisions concerning satellite use (Bullinger, 1985). Several years and many debates later, the states' prime ministers decided to allot two of TV-SAT's five transponders to the established public broadcast institutions ARD and ZDF for their satellite channels 1-Plus and 3-Sat and to allocate the three other transponders to private program providers. Two of the private channels would be SAT-1 and RTL-Plus, both preferred in states dominated by the Christian Democratic Party, and the third private channel was left to the discretion of states dominated by the Social Democratic Party (Müller-Romer, 1988).

In 1984 France and Germany began the development of a new 130 watt broadcast satellite generation with ten transponders, to be operated jointly by the two countries.[2] Germany developed a purely national telecommunications satellite project called DFS-1 Kopernikus which serves as a backup for TV-SAT-2 in reaching cable head-ends.[3]

TV-SAT-1 was launched into orbit in late 1987. However, a defective solar panel immediately made the project a failure. TV-SAT-2, launched two years later, utilizes the D2-MAC transmission standard. It experienced problems in acceptance: Terrestial broadcasters preferred improved and compatible PAL standard (e.g., Super-PAL), reception equipment was slow to reach the market and very expensive, and consumers chose to view channels on Kopernikus (with low-power transmission) or the medium power Astra, both of which use PAL (*Funkschau*, 1990, pp. 24–26).

Scandinavia

In the early 1970s the Scandinavian countries began negotiating for NORD-SAT, a joint high-power satellite program intended to carry the national channels of all five Nordic countries on seven TV and eleven radio transponders, thus giving each country access to the others' programs. However, the participant countries soon fell to bickering about the financial burden and the adjustment of different national regulations. For example, since Finnish television carries advertisements, Sweden argued that its firms would be at a disadvantage if Finnish programs were freely available in Sweden. The NORDSAT project was eventually shelved, but Swedish high-technology firms sought to rescue their project through the creation of an alternative government-supported satellite program, and in 1982 proposed the less ambitious Tele-X project.

Tele-X is associated with the joint French–German TDF-1/TV-Sat project. Ericsson supplies the antennae and communications modules and is the primary contractor for the earth station. Saab-Scania provides high-powered television and transponders.

The Tele-X satellite itself cost about $88 million, and total system costs reached over $200 million. Of these costs, more than 80 percent were borne by Sweden, with Norway and Finland accounting for the remainder. Work on Tele-X is managed by the Swedish Board of Space activities. The Swedish and Norwegian telecommunication administrations set up the Nordic Telecommunication Satellite Corporation (Notelsat) to be responsible for Tele-X experiments and operation of broadcasting and commercial services, but Finland and Denmark withdrew from Notelsat, and Norway reduced its role.

Tele-X faces several difficulties. The satellite's orbital slot is not a good one, and its capacity is limited to five transponders. It faces competition from established satellites of Eutelsat, Intelsat, and Astra, and from proposed projects that include the Eutelsat II generation. In 1990, TV-4—Sweden's first commercial network—became the first television channel to use the Tele-X satellite (Nicholson, 1990, p. 28).

United Kingdom

The British aerospace and electronic industries were the initial driving forces behind DBS in the United Kingdom. The Home Office let it be known that the government would not provide financial support for the establishment of DBS. The BBC was interested and wanted to assure its presence in new technology. The ITV companies, however, were not supportive because they did not want competition with their monopoly over television commercials. In 1982, Home Secretary William Whitelaw announced the beginning of a DBS project. The BBC would be licensed to lease two transponders on a planned high-power satellite Unisat, which would be built by a private consortium that included British Aerospace, British Telecom, GEC-Marconi, and the Rothschild Bank. The two BBC DBS channels would carry pay TV and BBC highlights from past years, together with quality international television.

In its preference for British development, the government demonstrated the tension between aspirations for high technology and for media liberalization. As in cable television, the government backed a British high-tech solution, thereby jeopardizing the development of a new medium.

The BBC negotiated with the consortium for British design and construction of the satellite. When it became evident that costs would be substantial, the BBC received governmental authority to go beyond its borrowing limits, though there was no increase in the license fee to finance this. Furthermore, the government also proposed including two ITV channels in order to decrease the BBC's financial burden. The remaining shares would go to other firms. These were Thorn-EMI, Granada, Virgin (a record, film, and airline firm), S. Pearson (a conglomerate with publishing and entertainment interests), and Consolidated Satellite Broadcasting (an entity with a complicated structure involving the Luxembourg CLT and British independent producers).

In 1984, the consortium faced new cost projections that went far beyond what the participants were willing to bear. For several months the consortium explored the possibility of dropping the expensive British satellite and going with a cheaper American one that would cost only half as much ($46.8 million a year for five RCA transponders versus $96 million a year for three Unisat transponders). This, however, would have run counter to the government's aim of launching a British-made satellite.

The situation became even more complicated when the BBC engaged in negotiations with the government to link its license fee increases with its contribution to the DBS venture. In the end, the government approved rates of only £58, significantly below the rate for which the BBC applied. This made the fate of the DBS venture dependent on an unobtainable major government subsidy and led to the BBC's withdrawal and the shelving of the Unisat project.

But the demise of Unisat did not put DBS to rest. For a while British Telecom (BT), the telephone near-monopolist, considered launching its own satellite system. But it decided to join with the other public PTTs and to bet on their Eutelsat II satellite generation, with the request that the satellites be modified to provide for eight transponders of 50- to 60-watt strength, which BT would lease.

In 1986, the Independent Broadcasting Authority (IBA) rekindled an interest in a British DBS project, but this time without requiring a British-built satellite. It invited programmers' bids for DBS transmission of three television channels. It permitted the participation of existing ITV companies, but limited them to holdings of 15 percent in order to bring in new interests. The government again established its position that it would not provide financial support for the project.

After some vigorous jockeying, a fifteen-year franchise for British DBS was awarded in 1986 to the consortium BSB (British Satellite Broadcasting), whose initial partners were Anglia, Amstrad, Granada, Pearson, and Virgin. These participants were later joined by Bond, Chargeurs, Invest International, and London Merchant Securities; others dropped out. After a six-month delay, the BSB satellite, built by Hughes Communications, a subsidiary of General Motors, was launched and began broadcasts in April 1990. A month after its launch, 25,000 receivers had been sold. Its dish receiver kit sold for almost $600 and rented for $36 a month. In 1990 BSB began marketing a squarial—a flat antenna. Although the size has been increased from 25 to 40 cm, the squarial is still small enough to hang out a window. The receiver package, which includes the antenna, decoder, and remote controller, sold for $540 (*EBU Review*, 1989). BSB's biggest advantage, however, may be its fifteen-year official franchise, which also gave it a must-carry status on British cable systems. Unlike most European DBS projects, BSB was more than a satellite hardware project serving other providers, since it provided its own program channels, offering movies (Screen), sports and news (Now), children's programs (Zig Zag), and general entertainment (Galaxy) (Glenn, 1990a, p. 8) and rock music (Power Station). The service had access to $2.4 billion in capital and spent $500 million on program libraries and film rights.

BSB's main competitor was Rupert Murdoch's Sky Television, which uses transponders on Luxembourg's Astra satellite. Half of Sky viewers received all four channels via home dish, sold for £200 or for rent, and others got one or more channels over cable systems. Sky Movies used scrambled signals and was available for $16 a month. To speed the growth of Sky, Murdoch began to offer satellite dishes bundled with a weekly subscription fee of £4.49 ($8) (Glenn, 1989b, p. 18).

In the early phases of the competition, Sky Channel pulled ahead of BSB, despite the latter's higher signal power. BSB had incurred the high cost of its two satellites ($1.5 billion), whereas Murdoch was only leasing his on a sixteen-transponder satellite. BSB also experienced problems with program cost and with the reception of its D2-MAC signal, a problem Sky, which used the PAL standard, did not have.

In November 1990, BSB and Sky Television, having lost, respectively, $900 million and $600 million decided to merge rather than compete. The joint company operated with the trade name BSkyB. Murdoch, whose service was much more successful with one million subscribers (vs. only 120,000 for BSB) received a substantial cash payment which helped his $8–9 billion indebtedness. The merged system used at first both satellite systems and all channels, but progressed towards a single system (Astra), standard (PAL) and five channels.

Meanwhile, across the Irish Sea, in the Republic of Ireland, the government granted a DBS franchise to Atlantic Satellites, owned by Hughes Communication and James Stafford, an Irish shipping entrepreneur. Atlantic Satellites aimed also at the UK, France, the Netherlands, and parts of Scandinavia (Logica, 1987, p. 219).

Pan European and International Satellites

The international telecommunication satellite organization, Intelsat, is an umbrella organization with over 100 member countries, headquartered in Washington, D.C. It holds exclusive rights for civilian international telecommunications satellite service, although in the 1980s its monopoly began to be challenged by would-be entrants such as Orion and PanAm Sat.

In 1989, five low-power Intelsat satellites were transmitting video signals throughout Europe. The services on Intelsat satellites included Children's Channel, CNN, MTV Europe, Premiere, TV3, BBC-TV Europe, BR3, Pro7, Tele. 5, and SVT 1 and 2 (Swann, 1989, p. 56).

A second international body is the European Telecommunications Satellite

Organization (Eutelsat), founded in 1977 by twenty-six European PTTs. Its original purpose was to provide trans-European communications. However, its low-power satellites 1F4 and 1F5 are used primarily for cable and television distribution.[4] By 1987, 75 percent of Eutelsat's revenues were derived from cable (Logica, 1987, p. 157). A more advanced generation of satellites, Eutelsat II, was launched in the medium-power range. These offerings, in addition to Astra, Intelsat, and various national satellite systems, were expected to create a large supply of more than 200 transponders after 1993, half of them on the six Eutelsat IIs. Eutelsat was hampered by a need to give priority to its PTTs sponsors, by lack of managerial autonomy, and by an inability to group transponders together at convenient orbital positions.

United States

The DBS situation in the United States will be briefly reviewed here for the sake of completeness and comparison. The United States has several advantages over most other industrialized countries with respect to DBS power requirements. Its 525-line NTSC transmission format needs a bandwidth of only 4.2 MHz, in contrast to the 5.5 MHz of a European 625-liner. This corresponds to a further gain of 2.5 db/W, although at the expense of a lesser definition of pictures. Furthermore, Americans have fewer political problems than Europeans in accepting a lower-quality DBS signal at the edges of the footprint. The quality of the American television picture varies widely, partly because of a policy of localism in broadcasting, which leads to hundreds of different stations with limited signal strength. There was also greater willingness if not eagerness in the United States to add as many transponders as possible—which favored medium over high power—because the forces opposing a multichannel television environment were much weaker than those in Europe.

For these reasons, the United States moved toward medium-power satellites. This trend was complemented by a convergence from both directions of the power scale. "Pure" DBS projects scaled down their power demands and found medium power technically adequate and economically superior. Equally important, cable television program networks, previously users of low-power satellite signals (10–20 watts), grew interested in using medium-power transmission signals (around 50 watts) that could be marketed to households as "satellite-direct" where cable television was unavailable.

Although the FCC granted ten conditional construction licenses for high-power DBS to private interests, none have operated. Only one medium-power DBS system actually operated in the United States: USCI, a consortium of Prudential Insurance, General Instruments, and the Galesi investor group, initiated service in late 1983. One and a half years later, the company ceased operations, having gained only 10,000 subscribers. Even with a considerable tax-loss carry-forward, it was unable to attract a buyer.

Another major DBS project was promoted by Comsat, the U.S. designated satellite carrier in Intelsat. Initially it envisioned four satellites covering the United States with some overlap. Each satellite was to have three transponders of 230-watt strength, and the project's cost was expected to be over $1 billion, comparing poorly with rival delivery systems. Whereas the high-power Comsat system required a $75 capital investment per household reached and program channel supplied, other technologies were considerably cheaper: cable television was $17, microwave Multipoint Distribution Service was $15, and Satellite Master Antenna TV was $12 (Henry, 1985). In the face of this market pressure, the project was first scaled down and then completely abandoned in 1984.

Many observers of USCI's dismal failure and Comsat's troubles concluded that DBS was dead in the United States. But with equal justification, one can say that DBS is alive and well, and gaining the interest of a new and promising set of major media firms.

This seeming contradiction resulted from the development of DBS in ways not anticipated by the original governmental and corporate planners. Such "supply-side" television, similar in approach to that taken by Western European governments, missed the market because it generally underestimated the difficulties of the technology itself as well as those of subscription marketing and program acquisition. Yet although major corporations foundered in "real" DBS, a demand for "quasi"-DBS emerged virtually spontaneously from the consumer end all across the United States. Spearheaded by do-it-yourselfers and promoted by small entrepreneurial businesses, hundreds of thousands of people set up satellite antennas in their backyards and farms, and the home "dish" antennas soon numbered more than 2 million.

The key impetus for the expansion on the ground is the equally rapid expansion in the sky. Fueled by the expansion of cable television and the drop in satellite transponder costs, a large number of program suppliers emerged to fill the multichannel cable medium with a variety of program wares ranging from the Eternal World Television Network to the Pleasure Channel. All these programs could be received via satellite without any payment to the program providers. In fact, until 1985 an antenna owner *willing* to pay a fee to a program supplier had no mechanism to do so.

When there was only a small number of private backyard satellite receivers, the cable television operators and their program providers shrugged off the matter as transitory and as a reflection of a demand that was caused by the often tortuous process of awarding municipal cable franchises. They responded negatively only when programs were resold to third parties without permission or royalty payment. (In several Caribbean countries, American program suppliers are largely powerless to inhibit unauthorized commercial distribution.) With the growing numbers of TV receive-only (TVRO) owners, however, it became evident that quasi-DBS reception was not transitory but permanent in the following areas: low-density areas that were not likely to be reached by cable; cabled urban and suburban settings where viewers sought to avoid payment of the often substantial cable subscription fees or where they sought added diversity; and apartment house settings, where landlords were setting up unregulated Satellite Master Antenna Television (SMATV) distribution. The potential and real revenue losses galvanized the cable industry into legislative, judicial, and organizational action. The losses also led the industry to begin recognizing the potential of the market and to view it as a natural extension of its activities and an opportunity rather than a rival.

There were several approaches to the prevention of backyard satellite reception. Some municipalities banned TVROs, partly for aesthetic reasons. Antenna vendors were challenged in court for knowingly selling equipment to be used for the reception of unauthorized signals. A much more effective approach, however, involved reaching the source of program supply. For cable operators to be protected from "free" DBS, the key condition of excludability needed to be fulfilled. At a substantial cost, the market leader HBO thus introduced the scrambling of satellite signals.

Scrambling originated as a defensive move to terminate piracy. It immediately gained commercial potential, however, since it enabled program providers, including HBO, to sell their programs *retail* to satellite viewers, instead of *wholesale* through cable operators. In the landmark Cable Communications Policy Act of 1984, Senator Barry Goldwater, the conservative champion of high-tech individualism—and owner of his own satellite dish antenna—successfully sponsored a provision that guaranteed the right to receive for private viewing any satellite channel without payment obligation, unless the supplier encrypted the signal and had operational marketing mechanisms to supply these programs. The legislation created an incentive for the more popular satellite channels to set up a DBS retailing system, at least in noncabled areas. A cable program supplier's desire to set up such a direct marketing system must be distinguished from its ability to maintain it in a competitive environment. In effect, HBO was asking TVRO owners to pay $400 for unscrambling equipment (which would be incompatible with many of the TVROs, and would thus require further costly modifications) and a monthly fee of $13 thereafter. A backyard pirate has no reason to consent to such domestication. Although HBO is the most popular pay channel, there are substitutes for it. To succeed in signing up satellite viewers, HBO would have to be joined by other channel suppliers in adopting scrambling. Given the often high cost of doing this, it is not surprising that program suppliers did not initially join HBO in offering a "scrambled package."

The other possibility for creating an economic foundation for hybrid DBS was for program suppliers to follow the traditional pattern of commercial broadcasting and become advertiser supported. More specifically, the satellite signal could have advertising messages inserted into programs for "satellite-direct" viewing. Receiving the same programs for retransmission to households via cable, the cable operator could either retain the commercials and benefit from their revenue or excise them. Several minutes of lag would accumulate periodically, but on a majority of programs realtime is not important.

To succeed in scrambling, the major program suppliers would have to behave oligopolistically, since they would have to agree on and enforce joint action. In the past they had not been able to do so, given competition. Therefore, the involvement of the cable operators, as distinguished from the program providers, became significant. In effect, major cable operators could organize a "scrambling cartel" by insisting on carrying only those channels that had been scrambled by their program providers. It makes perfect business sense for the cable operator to insist on a program provider's scrambling, since free satellite reception of unscrambled signals diverts some of its customers. It also facilitates the entry into redistribution DBS as local agents of program suppliers, protecting them from competition with their own program suppliers.

Given these realities on the ground, the space segment adjusted. Since 1986, HBO has offered "satellite-direct" service. Other cable channels followed suit. In 1989, there were thirty-one scrambled services available to home dish owners (*Cable and Station Coverage Atlas,* 1989). Viewers may subscribe directly from HBO, or, in areas where cable franchises operate, from cable operators acting as service agents.

Thus, direct satellite reception is alive in the United States as a supplement to cable distribution, especially in areas where cable is unavailable or expensive. Recognizing this market niche, in 1990 several major consortia announced DBS plans. One was to launch the four-satellite, 108-channel Sky Cable service that brought together NBC (one of the three major commercial networks), Hughes Communications (the satellite firm owned by General Motors), Cablevision (a major cable distribution and program packaging firm), and News Corp. (Rupert Murdoch's U.S. holding, which would benefit from his European DBS). Another system included AT&T, using its communication satellites and providing billing and subscription information via the telephone network's signaling channel (*Satellite Week,* 1990, p. 5).

Conclusion

DBS has been both a failure and a success. Defined as a high-powered satellite, it turned out to be, at least during the 1980s, an obsolete concept that kept going, even after being recognized as such, from sheer momentum, absence of analysis, and political and economic muscle. There are very few subscribers to such a type of DBS. Though the numbers of viewers reached by DBS that are published appear large [e.g., 10 million in the Netherlands, 6 million in Belgium (Glenn, 1989a)], in reality they are virtually all regular cable television viewers who receive the program via their cable head-end, which could almost as well receive them from a vastly cheaper low-power telecommunications satellite. On the other hand, DBS is a sensible way to go if it is based on more economical medium-power, multitransponder satellites such as Luxembourg Astra, the Eutelsat II generation, or the Sky Cable project planned for the United States. The target audience of direct reception, instead of encompassing the entire population as planned in the past, is becoming those for whom cable transmission is uneconomical or as yet not available. The latter is especially the case in countries only partially cabled: France, the United Kingdom, Italy, Spain, Portugal, and Greece. (In several of these countries, however, cabling is steadily progressing, thus reducing the market for direct satellite reception.) Medium-power satellites hence appear to be a sensible compromise that permits an economic reach of both cable head-ends and households.

29

Conclusion: The Evolutionary Stages of Broadcasting

The preceding country-specific and general chapters of this book have shown the extraordinary evolution in broadcasting systems. Different societies contribute their own distinct features based on their history, politics, geography, demographics, and economics. But these differences should not obscure certain central themes. We can discern five stages of evolution in the broadcast systems of democratic countries. Table 29.1 summarizes them for Europe.

Stage 1: Early Private Broadcasting

Most European countries moved in the 1920s through the stage of early private broadcasting. Entry barriers into radio were low. Amateurs played an important role, often through clublike broadcast associations. Radio was a highly individualistic affair, not unlike computer "hacking" in the 1980s. Amateurs popularized radio and made many technical contributions. But they were soon pushed aside by radio set manufacturers seeking to develop markets and by the state jealously guarding its highly profitable and strategic monopoly over telecommunications. It had taken centuries of effort to establish a postal monopoly and then to integrate telegraphy and telephony into it (Noam, 1991). Radio communications were considered an integral part of this monopoly. In consequence, amateurs found themselves suppressed both in the conduit function (by low power requirements, limited frequency allocation, etc.) and in content (e.g., no transmission of music, political topics, or business information). But the spirit of amateur radio lived on, beyond its early "ham" practitioners. It re-emerged in the 1970s and 1980s in the many movements for community radio that sprang up across Europe.

Radio manufacturers viewed broadcasting merely as a way to increase the sale of radio sets; in several countries manufacturers themselves provided programs to create a critical mass of listeners. Manufacturing and broadcasting operations reinforced each other. Hence, vertical integration made economic sense during this stage. A governmental role in the licensing of listeners' sets was sought by industry to protect it from radio set imports (e.g., in Britain, Germany, Belgium, Netherlands, Austria, and Spain). The link of broadcasting

Table 29.1 The Stages of Broadcasting*

	Early Private	State Broadcasting	Independent Public	Privileged Private	Open Broadcasting
Austria	—	1924–1966	1966–	—	—
Belgium	1923–1931	1931–1960	1960–1987/9	1987/9 [a]	—
Denmark	1920–1925	1925–1959	1959–1988	1988– [b]	—
Finland	1921–1934	1934–1958	—	1958–	—
France	1921–1938 [c]	1938–1986 [c, d]	—	1986–	—
Germany	1923–1927	1927–1949 [e, f]	1949–1987	1987– [g]	—
Greece	1924–1936	1936–1990	—	1990–	—
Iceland	—	1930–1986	—	1986–	—
Israel	—	1936–1965	1965–1990	1990–	—
Ireland	—	1926–1960	1960–1988	1988–	—
Italy	1924–1929	1929–1975	— [h]	—	1975– [i]
Luxembourg	1929–1940	1940–1945 [j]	—	1945–	—
Netherlands	1919–1924	—	1924–1990 [k]	1990–	—
Norway	1923–1933	1933–1980	1980–1990	1990– [l]	—
Portugal	1925–1930	1930–1991 [m]	—	1991–	—
Spain	1923–1934	1934–1989 [n]	—	1989–	—
Sweden	1923–1933	—	1933–1991	1991–	—
Switzerland	1922–1931	—	1931–1986	1986– [o]	—
Turkey	—	1924–1990 [p]	—	—	—
United Kingdom	1920–1926	—	1927–1954 [q]	1954–1990	1990– [r]
United States	1920–1926	—	— [s]	1926–1980	1980– [t]

*Western Europe. Eastern Europe: state broadcasting until 1989; thereafter, varied transitions.

Notes

[a] Wallonia 1987; Flanders 1989.
[b] Local public experiments; limited opening to commerical providers after 1989.
[c] Mixed private-public 1931–1945.
[d] Limited independence 1975–1986; Reform Law passed 1982.
[e] Partial private ownership until 1932.
[f] In East Germany until 1990.
[g] First Land, Lower Saxony, in 1984.
[h] Independence established in 1975.
[i] Legalized in 1976, restrictions on national networking until 1991. Private near monopoly in networking.
[j] German-controlled.
[k] Limited entry of associations.
[l] Local entry after 1984.
[m] Also private radio until 1975, then mostly nationalized.
[n] Substantial private and official organizations' radio throughout.
[o] Experimental.
[p] Independence during 1967–1970; some after 1983.
[q] With residual state prerogatives.
[r] Limited realization.
[s] Educational broadcasting created in 1920s.
[t] Limited opening after 1972.

with manufacturers did not last long, however, because exclusion of other radio set producers was difficult, even after enlisting the governments in licensing sets. But the other form of vertical integration endured, that of distribution of programs and their production.[1]

The public's fascination with radio turned out to be enormous. As radio's influence on mass audiences was recognized, it seemed dangerous to concentrate this power in private hands. The period was one of major social and political divisions: general strikes, depressions, popular fronts, fascism on the right, Bolshevism on the left, prewar confrontations, the war itself, postwar reconstruction, and the cold war's ideological and military stalemate. Governments did not wish to abdicate control over this medium to a few privileged owners.

Four policy options existed. The first was to do nothing, on the expectation that a profit-maximizing private broadcaster would stay fairly centrist in terms of programming and politics in order to maximize audiences, or that the totality of stations would provide adequate balance. But this required a long-term faith in economic rationality and the assumption that a private broadcaster would not subsidize his political views. It was, after all, an era of press empires run not by corporate bureaucracies but by strong-willed men with definite agendas.

A second and related policy option was to reduce any single broadcaster's power by structural rules that would localize and decentralize private media. Abundant radio would then undercut the power of limited radio. This was the approach taken in the United States, where radio was localized and ownership decentralized. What the U.S. government did not do, however, was to eliminate the concentration of program provision, partly because legal instruments were less adequate. In consequence, powerful program networks emerged.

The third option was to deliver control to a few privileged owners, so long as that privilege was state controlled. In much of Europe, on the other hand, a fourth policy approach to potential private media power was to concentrate it instead in public hands, through a closely controlled state monopoly.

Stage 2: State Broadcasting

Most European countries established a state system in the 1920s and early 1930s. Exceptions were small countries, such as Luxembourg and Monaco, which have remained in the 1st stage and function primarily as "broadcast havens." Some other countries permitted a mixed public–private system, such as the Iberian dictatorships, as well as France and Belgium. But almost everywhere else a government operating monopoly in broadcasting was added to the existing licensing monopoly, either as a state administration or through an exclusive state-controlled private-law company. In Sweden and Britain, the government's role was more limited, but residual powers were still substantial.

This led to state radio, often a consciously wielded tool of government. It is easy to see this for the various dictatorships of the era, but even in the Scandinavian democracies governments used radio for their purposes, and the restrictions of the British government over diversity of political voices on BBC broadcasting is not a proud chapter in its history. Winston Churchill could not raise his warnings against the policy of appeasement even once over the BBC, because he did not represent the government or the official opposition.

Radio was also being centralized. Though in technical terms it was a local medium, it was prevented from becoming so by politics and economics.

The emergence of television strengthened state broadcasting still further. TV shows are more expensive to produce than radio programs, and their broadcasting requires a much broader spectrum. Because the number of television viewers was small at first, it could support only a limited number of channels. To put them into the hands of private interests (in the 1950s) after two decades of ideological conflicts seemed unwise. The approach of state control was strengthened.

This also suited the interests of print publishers. Newspapers and magazines were (and are) highly influential and often were tied to political parties. When radio emerged, publishers rarely sought direct entry. The novel medium, with its unfamiliar technology, and with its music, entertainment, and drama orientation seemed as far removed from their newspaper activities as film was. Although there were exceptions (especially in Sweden and Finland), overall, the limited involvement by publishers is extraordinary in early broadcasting. Beholden to the print model of media, they viewed themselves in the news*paper* business and missed the broader opportunities of radio. But they were concerned nevertheless, because their economic well-being depended on advertising, and their political power was helped by an absence of comparable channels of mass communication. Radio was threatening on both scores, and with television, the danger of competition was greater still.[2] Hence, newspaper publishers usually supported a nonadvertising system of public broadcasting and also saw to it that radio's role in news coverage was restricted. For example, in the United Kingdom and Switzerland, radio news had to be provided by a press agency.

In the decades that followed, radio was used effectively by strong political leaders, and it made them stronger still—Hitler's exhortations to expansion, de Gaulle's calls for resistance, Churchill's mobilization of Britain's spirit, FDR's fireside chats to regenerate America's optimism. Radio's auditory appeal was powerful (witness the mass hysteria following Orson Welles' "War of the Worlds" broadcast). It was a perfect tool for influencing the public. In the political age of the masses, the radio provided the link and the control. It was an excellent and cheap means of one-way exhortation, and it even paid for itself. Governments could not afford to let it be in the wrong hands, and they did not.

Stage 3: Independent Public Broadcasting

Broadcasting has not yet passed from the stage of state control even in parts of democratic Europe (e.g., Greece, Turkey, Spain, and Portugal). Politically agitated and economically less developed countries are only now hesitatingly leaving this phase. France was in it only a few years ago. Eastern Europe is contemplating the transition.[3] But most other countries turned away from state broadcasting earlier and moved to the next stage, independent public broadcasting free of direct government control, and based on national public monopoly institutions.

In the late 1950s, European societies began to become less polarized. Transfers of power and coalitions among moderate left and moderate right parties became fairly normal. But changes in government were destabilizing to the broadcast institutions themselves if they were not provided with a more civil service-like status. The institutions themselves, developing professional standards as they grew enormously with television, sought as much independence as possible. Similarly, the political parties in power could reduce the risk of being totally shut out in a period of declining electoral fortune by sharing broadcast powers with the present opposition. There was less at stake, and control over broadcasting could be eased. The new medium, television, added to this change. Television, though a powerful presence, was less prone to demagogic abuse than radio. Marshall McLuhan observed that Hitler was made by radio and would have been unmade by television. This observation is factually incorrect insofar as Hitler never appeared on radio before assuming power, and thus cannot be said to have been "made" by the medium. But the broader insight is probably correct. As democracies stabilized, party or government television became less acceptable, and shared control was introduced. Thus, the governmental control of broadcasting was relaxed through much of Europe in the 1960s in favor of a more independent but public status.

A nonpartisan institution could command broad political support. A partisan one, on the other hand, opened itself to political retaliation in the form of an opening of entry barriers. Those broadcast institutions that disregarded this danger lost their status of exclusivity when the opposition gained power. This happened, for example, in France and Greece. In Italy, independence came to broadcasting only in 1975, too late to stem the tide of private television, which was legalized within a year. Such countries as France, Greece, and Italy largely skipped the stage of independent broadcasting.

By creating independence, the government in effect provided the opposition with a share of control of content, personnel, and finances. But this set dynamics in motion that ultimately undermined most of the public broadcasters.

There were three basic institutional courses of independence. One was separatism—broadcasting was divided among different political movements. This was done in the Netherlands formally through time allotments within joint channels and in Italy informally by allocation of control among the three channels. Such a system, however, proved to be too inflexible to accommodate new and different voices and interests. The second approach was internal pluralism of personnel. Most positions were appointed according to party affiliation and according to some formula, and appointees protected their party's interests from within. This model was followed, for example, in Germany and Austria and led to a high degree of politicization within the broadcast institutions. The third approach was genuine independence of the institutions, and this meant, in effect, a substitution of the program (and sometimes political) preferences of producers and reviewers over those of the viewers or their political representatives.

All these approaches led to dissatisfaction. Many viewers did not feel their program preferences were met; others were turned off by party wrangling or by a perceived bias in reporting. This dissatisfaction was the background to the emergence of pressures that moved the broadcast system into its fourth and next phase, the stage of limited private television based on a mixed system of public and privileged commercial television. But it was only one factor. As important as the specifics of politics and technology are, they are primarily manifestations of more general and fundamental forces. Human economic activity centered originally on agriculture and later on industrial production. It has moved increasingly in the direction of production and processing of information. (It has been said that 90 percent of all scientists who ever worked are alive today.[4]) In the first half century of printing, between 1450 and 1500, approximately 20 million books were produced (Curran, 1982, p. 217). That is not a small number, but it is dwarfed by today's figure by a factor of about 50,000! In the United States alone, about 2.3 billion books were distributed in one recent year (1987) (Dessauer, 1988). And this number does not even include the countless reports and other book-like products generated. The amount of paper used in the United States has increased in the last ten years by 66 percent (Fisher, 1990), to about half a pound per person per day (or, in terms of pages, fifty pages per person per day). The number of those active in informational activities rose rapidly.

Educational levels rose. Whereas in the past, a university education was the exception, it became much more common.[5] Production of goods shifted to greater knowledge intensity, either in the manufacturing process itself, in the product, or in its applications. Thus, as societies advanced, they increased informational inputs, outputs, intermediate goods, and knowledge workers. Information became a key resource and product. Electronic mass media—television, radio, recordings, video productions, and so on—were part of this dramatic increase.

On the *production* side, more people are proficient in media production than ever before. Equipment cost dropped continuously while its performance rose. In the process, video production moved from the arcane art of specialists to a more broad-based form of communication. Today it is in the process of joining the mainstream of human expression. Signs abound. Colleges send out video surveys of their facilities, and applicants return their own video biographies. Speakers who cannot attend an engagement in person send a tape instead. Friends or relatives send each other a Season's Greetings videos showing their family's activities over the year. Self-improvement instructional video materials are available on many subjects. Thus, society's total potential for video production has increased continuously and enormously on the amateur and professional levels. A TV system of two or three channels and a total of perhaps ten hours of prime airtime per day cannot handle the increased production ability of an entire society, any more than two or three magazines could. Since commercial production is affected by what can be distributed, the bottleneck in distribution backs up into production, reducing it below what it would be in a more open system. Manifestations of this phenomenon are the huge numbers of people trying to "break into" television production, news, plays, and commentary. Although that is also true for other attractive endeavors, the difference here is that the scarcity is state sponsored. In an age in which video expression becomes prevalent, the broadcast system makes individuals' right to video access conditional on an official institution's right to select and allocate scarce resources. It is the benign equivalent of the Soviet Union's past practice of allocating printing paper only to approved authors.

Meanwhile, on the *consumption* side of television, similar discrepancies emerged. Viewers became more selective in their program choice. Subjected to increasing information flows, they had to resort to screening those flows on which they most wanted to spend their limited time and attention. When a TV set in the living room was still a novelty, viewers would accept almost anything (even the test pattern), but over time they became more discriminating. Furthermore, as incomes rose, the value of time increased, and with it the reluctance to waste it on a program that was only mildly desired. Similarly, increasing education played a role by encouraging a more active attitude toward program choice.

These factors contributed to a greater differentiation of viewing patterns than in the past and to a greater centrifugalism in the mass audience. In some instances viewers did not necessarily want programs different from those already provided by the public broadcasters. But they wanted them at the time of their choosing. In other instances, the programs offered were not aimed at the center of the taste distribution and left audience segments unserved. In consequence, when VCRs made time shift viewing and video rentals possible, their sales rose rapidly (Table 29.2). The growth was not random. A country with large commercial broadcast TV choice, such as Italy, had a VCR penetration of only 19 percent, much lower than that in other countries where broadcasting was more limited. (Penetration in Spain was 39 percent; in France, 45 percent; in Germany, 52 percent; and in the United Kingdom, 66 percent.) Audiences got used to the notion of control over their viewing, and to pay money for that control. Their selections of video cassettes indicated furthermore a different mix of programs from those provided regularly by the public broadcasters.

All this provided clear signals that the electronic distribution of programs would fill pent-up demand, and it was therefore not surprising that the supply sector was energized. Among the most insistent potential entrants were publishers. For some it was a preemptive move in order not to let others control a major share of any new media market. But for others it represented a forward step in their own understanding of their role—no longer a print publisher, but a producer, packager, and distributor of *information*.

Thus, both the demand and supply sides were ready for a more varied menu. The problem was the bottleneck in the pipe connecting them. This was partly

Table 29.2   Penetration of VCRs and Cable Television (% of TV Households)

Country	Video Cassette Recorders		Cable Television		
	1981[a]	1989[b]	1981[a]	1989[c]	1989[b]
Austria	4.0	37.0	6.0	12.8	18.0
Belgium	3.0	45.0	75.0	88.0	92.0
Denmark	5.0	40.0	0.0	17.9	30.0
Finland	1.5	47.0	4.0	25.4	30.0
France	2.0	45.1	2.5	1.2	1.0
Germany	4.0	52.3	4.0	23.0	34.0
Greece	1.0	40.0	0.0		0.0
Iceland		60.0			0.0
Israel		53.0			[d]
Ireland	3.0	30.0	18.0	31.4	44.0
Italy	1.0	19.5	0.0	0.0	0.0
Luxembourg		54.0		69.1	
Netherlands	4.0	46.0	60.0	80.4	90.0
Norway	8.0	50.0	21.0	31.2	30.0
Portugal	1.0	28.0	0.0		0.0
Spain	1.0	38.9	0.0		6.0
Sweden	5.0	46.0	0.0	22.4	22.0
Switzerland		48.0	29–34	67.2	68.0
Turkey		37.0			0.0
United Kingdon	6.5	66.4	8.0	1.4	1.0
United States	1. [e]	64.6[f]	19.9[e]	65.1	52.8[f]

Sources and Notes.

[a] *Television Today and Television Tomorrow*, 1983, Toby Syfret, ed., JWT Europe.

[b] TBI, *World Guide '90*, New York.

[c] Euromedia Investor, 1989, Paul Kagan.

[d] Pirate cable reaches 5% of the population.

[e] 1980 data. From Television Bureau of Advertising, Inc., *Trends in Television*, (annual).

[f] Television Bureau of Advertising, Inc., *Trends in Television*, (annual).

alleviated by the emergence of video cassette recorders. But for direct electronic communications the bottleneck was still strong, jealously guarded by the
established broadcast institutions and their client interests, and by those who
had been persuaded that a limited system of video information distribution was
socially more valuable. For a long time, a principled discussion had been postponed because the physical limitation of spectrum scarcity seemed to set a
natural and low ceiling on channels. This was never correct, because the scarcity was to a certain extent self-imposed and spectrum was being allocated to
various official uses without regard for its opportunity cost. The emergence of
dozens of low-power stations, as well as the locating of frequencies for all
kinds of new national broadcast channels once the political will was there,

demonstrated that the ''scientific'' spectrum argument had been carried much too far.

Change began with radio, where the stakes and the entry barriers were lower than those for television. Indeed, the restrictions had become porous, and pirates were embarrassing the official system by defying persistent efforts to close them down and by their popularity with audiences. In many instances, radio liberalization became merely the ratification of reality. It created a legal and organized model for the new broadcast environment, and it changed attitudes by demonstrating the vitality of entry and the absence of one-sided political (i.e., right-wing business) control.

In any event, spectrum allocation became less relevant because of the emergence of a key new distribution medium, cable television. It is difficult to overestimate the impact—past, present, and future—of this form of distribution. Many European countries established wide-ranging cable networks in the 1980s. The numbers in Table 29.2 speak for themselves. In many countries, cable penetration was high and rising. Whereas the less developed countries of the south had little to show, in the north the smaller countries were being densely cabled.[6]

In most smaller countries, cable television did not emerge pursuant to a governmental blueprint of media or technology policy (Denmark is a partial exception), but as relatively modest and frequently local efforts at improving reception and carrying additional signals, especially those of larger neighboring countries, whose programs supplemented the sparse local fare.

In that sense, the large public broadcasters, by their attraction to neighboring countries, undermined the foundation to their own exclusivity. How did that happen? Once these distribution pipes reached into many households, they were eagerly filled with additional programs of other public stations, typically from adjoining countries, because those were the only ones readily available. And it seemed only fair to let the rest of the population watch programs on cable that their fellow citizens nearer to the border could already receive over the air. But soon, commercial offerers found a way to reach cable head-ends, starting with the Sky Channel.

Once these commercial offerers were ready to serve, the basic question of admissibility of commercial programs could no longer be postponed. The old justifications for limited television had become irrelevant; physical scarcity of channel capacity was not the problem. Even though early cable systems had only five to fifteen channels, it was well understood that the number could be much larger. In the United States, newer cable distribution networks carry fifty to 100 channels and soon 150. See also Table 3.2(c). Even more channels can be supported if multiple coaxial lines are used in parallel or through fiber transmission. If anything, the problem for the cable network is how to fill their channels with attractive programs, which has shifted the burden of proof radically.

As the availability and cost of channels dropped, the traditional system became dependent on law and politics rather than on physics and economics to protect itself. Although it seems acceptable to have a state monopoly on providing the only two or three channels, it is a different matter when it comes to fifteen or more. At the same time, generalized opposition to commercialism in media was not easy in societies where newspapers, magazines, books, video-cassettes, and films were mostly commercially produced and distributed and where public broadcasters themselves often carried advertising.

The independent public system had been fostered by the steady growth in license fee revenues. But when the number of TV households reached its natural ceiling, the broadcast institutions became more constrained financially, and hence politically, and less able to expand into new media activities. At the same time, they had to support a very expensive production and administrative apparatus with civil-service like work protections. The decisive policy turned out to be whether to permit advertising-supported foreign cable channels, but in most instances that decision received little attention in comparison to those given to the question of terrestrial private television. Yet the cable decision was the critical one, because it carried its own inherent logic: once foreign commercial cable channels could be imported, it made no sense to limit domestic ones; indeed, it seemed vindictive to permit foreign media advertisers to capture domestic markets while gagging own's one.

This then led to the next logical step of liberalization, domestic cable channels. But once that bridge was crossed, it was difficult to argue against commercial terrestrial broadcast channels. After all, if it is acceptable on cable, why not over the air, assuming availability of spectrum? Furthermore, it seemed unfair to let people in the cities have television program options that were unavailable to the rural population or to areas not yet cabled. Thus, terrestrial commercial broadcasting emerged soon thereafter.

Technology played a function in this change, but it would be inaccurate to ascribe to it a central role and to hide basic societal decisions behind the alleged relentlessness of technology. Technology was enabling but not determinative. Terrestrial broadcasting required licensing, not new technology. Italy is full of stations using venerable broadcast technology. Other countries use cable television, which at its core is not an especially innovative technology and which was available in the 1950s and 1960s, though with fewer channels (but certainly much more than the two or three over-the-air broadcasts). Satellites were more of a technological advancement, but their role as a direct-broadcast medium was still minor by the end of the 1980s. Satellites were important as a *wholesale* medium for cable retail distribution, but this also could have been accomplished by more traditional means, such as telephone lines, microwave transmission, and even postal parcels, at a slightly greater effort. Videocassette recorders are also a technological advance, but their role as a viewing option was not directly helpful for opening broadcasting. They serve in many ways as a substitute for electronic transmission and can thus even reduce the pressure of demand for additional channels. The impact of VCRs was more indirect, by making consumers used to control over their viewing and by strengthening a low-cost production sector.

Stage 4: The Television of Privilege

Most European countries liberalized broadcasting and permitted commercial broadcasting in the late 1980s. The United Kingdom, however, opened entry for the ITV cartel in 1954, and Finland established the MTV-YLE duopoly in 1958. (Luxembourg's broadcasting has always been a private monopoly.) A main jolt to the traditional system occurred in Italy, where in 1976 the broadcast monopoly collapsed almost overnight and the public RAI was supplemented by hundreds of local stations. But that was considered an aberration at the time. Despite strenuous resistance, within the last few years almost all European countries have opened up (see Table 29.3), in what future generations may consider a tidal wave: Germany, in 1984; France and Iceland, in 1986; Belgium, in 1987; Denmark and Ireland, in 1988; Spain, in 1989; Israel, Netherlands, Greece, and Norway, in 1990; and Portugal and Sweden, in 1991.

The parallelism in timing suggests similar societal forces at work, as well as cross-border interactions. As one country opened up, its neighbors' viewing options were enhanced. Restrictive policy became less defensible if sensible neighbors had opened their own media without the sky falling in. Furthermore, European integration made national restrictiveness harder to maintain. In Brussels, the European Commission, usually less tolerant of national monopolies than member countries' governments, established principles and expectations of free flows of media productions at least within the Community. Thus, country A could not restrict the carriage on cable of a channel from member country B if A permitted its own commercial programs to be shown. Although the jurisdiction of the EC Commission was in dispute, but Brussels became a force pushing to reduce national restrictiveness. Its influence also affected non-EC countries of Europe.

The liberalization that occurred in the late 1980s should not be confused with an open system. It is merely a partial opening, and it leads into the fourth phase of television: the television of privilege. It is privileged in the sense that entry is still highly restrictive, and allocated by governments in large measure for reasons of politics and favoritism. In France, for example, the Socialists awarded control over private channels to their allies Rousselet, Seydoux, and Ribaud. The conservatives added their own favorites, Hersant and Bouygues. Even when direct political connections were not rewarded, allocations went to influential media firms. In Germany, both main private channels and a pay channel are owned by major publishers. In Belgium, both private channels are similarly dominated, as is the single private channel in the Netherlands. In Spain, all three channels went to consortia with heavy publisher interests. In Greece, the first two TV licenses were allocated to publishers, with others in the wings. If governments' opening of television had been aimed at enhancing diversity of television, the sensible policy would have been to *avoid* giving licenses to publishers in order to increase media diversity, and to add voices rather than to amplify existing ones. But existing voices were amplified. *The television of privilege is the television of media concentration.*

Table 29.3 Changes in Broadcast Channels 1980–1990

	Television Channels 1980			Added Television	
	National Public 1980	National Private 1980	Regional 1980	Additional Public National TV	Additional Private National TV
Albania	RTS(1) [a]				
Austria	ORF(2) [a]				
Belgium	RTBF(2) [b] BRT(2)				VTM* RTL-TVi
Bulgaria	BTV(2) [a]				
Czechoslovakia	CTV(1)		2	Ch.3	
Denmark	DR(1)			TV2 (nat/8reg)	
Finland	YLE(1 1/2)	MTV(1/2)		YLE(1/2)	MTV(1/2)
France	TF1 A2 FR3 [c]				TF1 (privatized) Canal Plus La5* M6*
Germany	ARD [c] ZDF DDR(2) [d]		ARD3 [a]		SAT-1* [e] RTL-Plus* [e]
Greece	ERT/YENED(2)			ERT	
Hungary	MTV(2) [f]				
Iceland	RUV(1)				Stod-2 TV1
Ireland	RTE(2)				TV3

326

& Radio Channels, 1980–1990			
Additional Public Regional TV	Additional Private Regional TV	Additional Radio	Additional Cable Channels
			3-Sat (public w/ARD SBC)
		40	TV5 (public, w/others)
			Filmet* (w/others)
			Canal Plus Belgique
	Masesba 10		
	19 operating 52 planned	277	
		65	PTV
	Tele- Monte Carlo	1600 w/11 networks	La Sept (public, w/others)
			Sports 2/3 (public)
			TV5 (public, w/others)
			Canal Enfants
			Canal Infos
			Canal J
			Canal Humor
			Canal Sante
			Cine Cinema (pay)
			Cine Cinefel (pay)
			Paris Premiere
			Planete
	>10	190	5 nationally carried public regional 3rd program
			3-SAT (public, w/others)
			1-Plus (public, w/others)
			La Sept (public, w/others)
			Premiere*
			Pro-7
			Tele-5
			Music Box
			Sportkanal
			several regional cable stations
	Mega*	520	
	Antena TV		
	TV-100		
	New Channel*		
	TV Plus		
	Seven X TV		
Studio Budapest	TV-S NAP-TV	4	
		4	
		1 nat. 25 local	

Table 29.3 Changes in Broadcast Channels 1980–1990 (*Continued*)

	Television Channels 1980				Added Television
	National Public 1980	National Private 1980	Regional 1980	Additional Public National TV	Additional Private National TV
Israel	IBA (1)				Ch. 2
Italy	RAI(2)	partial networks	RAI (regional) 537 (private) [g]		Canale 5 Italia-1 Rete-4 (Several partial networks, incl. Globo MonteCarlo)
Luxembourg		RTL			[h]
Netherlands	NOS(2)			NOS	RTL-4
Norway	NRK(1)				2nd channel under discussion
Poland	PRT(2) [i]				1 expected
Portugal	RTP(2)				2 new channels under discussion
Romania	RTR(2) [k]				
Spain	TVE(2)				Antena3* Canal Plus* Tele-5*
Sweden	SR(2)				private 3rd channel planned
Switzerland	SBC(3) [l]				
Turkey	TRT(1)			TRT	
United Kingdom	BBC(2)	ITV [c]			Channel 4 C5 (planned)

& Radio Channels, 1980–1990			
Additional Public Regional TV	Additional Private Regional TV	Additional Radio	Additional Cable Channels
			4 planned ISTV planned
	approx. 450	>3000	
		6000 pirates up to 350 local and 25 reg.	Filmnet* (w/others)
	>100 community TV	>400 community radio	TV-1 TV-Norge
1	ITI; several expected	2	expected (Warsaw and Cracow)
		600 pirates 4 licensed 50 unlicensed [j]	
ETB-Euskal Cadena-Catalana Telemadrid TV3; Canal 33 Valencia; Camal Sur	TV de Galicia TV de Catalunya	1856 additional stations (private 18% official 82%)	
		25 local >100 community stations w/2300 community groups	TV3 (London based) Filmnet* (w/others) SF-Succe* TV-1000 TV-4
	5	>37	3SAT (public, w/ORF, ARD) Paysat* (private, w/others) Telecine Romandie* EBC* TV5 (public, w/others)
3			Music Box Satellite 2, 3 planned
S4C		3 national planned 300 community planned	BSkyB (5-9) Super Channel Music Box Arts Channel Bravo Children's Channel Eurosport ScreenSport

329

Table 29.3 Changes in Broadcast Channels 1980–1990 (*Continued*)

	Television Channels 1980			Added Television	
	National Public 1980	National Private 1980	Regional 1980	Additional Public National TV	Additional Private National TV
United Kingdom (*continued*)					
U.S.S.R.	Gostelradio (l)		4 republic 122 local	Gostelradio (l)	
United States	PBS	ABC NBC CBS	267 public 746 private (including network affiliates)		1
Yugoslavia	JRT(2)		8 (16 programs)		

Notes

*Publisher participation

[a] With regional stations.

[b] Serve language communities.

[c] Regional structure.

[d] German Democratic Republic stations, renamed 1989 DFF. Integrated 1990 into FRG system.

[e] Available in most regions.

[f] Including 3 regional studios.

[g] Including network affiliates.

[h] RTL foreign ventures listed under other countries.

[i] Including 8 regional.

[j] Mostly on FM, the government plans to allocate 600 licenses for new FM stations.

[k] Since 1990 RTRL.

[l] One for each major language.

& Radio Channels, 1980–1990

Additional Public Regional TV	Additional Private Regional TV	Additional Radio	Additional Cable Channels
			Premiere CNN Lifestyle TV3
122 local	Nika TV		
83	358	1960	Started-Up after 1980 and existing in 1990: Arts&Entert.; Amer. Christ TV; Altern. View; Amer. Movie Classics; Black Ent.; Bravo; Cable Vid Store; Cinemax; CNBC; CNN; Comedy Ch.; Country Music; C-Span II, Discovery; Disney; E! Ent. TV; Eternal Word; Family Guide; FamilyNet; Financial News; FNN/Sports; TV Comedy; Headline News; Hit Video; Home Shop Net I; Inspirational Net; JC Penny; KTLA; KTVT; Learning Ch.; Lifetime; Mind Ext. U.; MTV; MSG; Nat. College TV; Nick a/Nite; The Nashville Net; Nat Jewish TV; Nostalgia Ch.; Playboy; Prayer Ch.; QVC Net; Request TV; Request 2; Silent Net; Sino Vis.; Sports News; Sports Ch.; TNT; Travel Ch.; USA Net; Vh1; Videi Jkbx; Viewers Choice 1, 2; VISN; Weather Ch.; WPIX; WSBK. Operating before 1980: C-Span I; ESPN; Family Ch.; HBO; Galavision(Spanish); Movie Ch.; Nickelodeon; Showtime; Trinity Bdcast Net; TSB; Univision; WGN; WWOR
2	Tele-vjesnik(1)		

In many instances, the license allocations were without clear criteria and explanation. Yet they constitute huge financial windfalls. Even where the licenses did not go to present friends and future allies, they still are a favor granted and one that can be withdrawn. In a very real sense, the foundation of a media enterprise is a piece of paper issued by the government and denied to others. *A television of privilege is a television of limited independence.* The absence of independence does not mean that these television channels will extol the government in power. But it implies caution in being identified as oppositional. The television of privilege tries to make no political waves. The American experience in the first decades of television provides ample evidence for self-imposed caution.

On the program content side, the television of privilege disappoints those seeking high cultural quality. This is not because the medium is commercial. After all, print publishers and film producers are also private, and they turn out many works of high cultural standards (as well as of low ones). Rather, the commercial TV system often has low program standards because it is *limited,* and therefore serves mainly the broad center of the taste distribution. In terms of the model of Chapter 4, the diversity spread is low. Structure affects performance. If only a handful of books were permitted to be published, in all likelihood, only potboilers would make it. The point of an open media system is only partly to provide more entertainment. The other important part is to provide diversity and choice. And this can be accomplished structurally only to a minor extent in a limited private system. *Economic logic leads the television of privilege to be limited in terms of cultural standards and of choice.*

It is true that some of Britain's ITV program are of high quality, and it is therefore tempting to conclude that the profits of the limited system are required for high-quality productions. But that assumes that artistic creativity is based on a patron system: The crumbs from the table of privilege pay for its hymns, as under feudalism. But creativity is just as much, if not more, derived from the interplay of lively minds, and an absence of powerful organizations' ability to constrain a restless spirit. These are all more likely to flourish in an environment of many avenues of production and distribution, although such a system is not a sufficient condition. The logic of the argument that monopoly profits are required to support artistic endeavors could equally justify, say, a single monopoly oil company in the United States on the theory that its monopoly profits could lead to greater donations to the arts. Or it would justify a single national newspaper, because by cutting duplicative commentators one could best support the remaining ones and select only the greatest talent. It is likely that under a more open system certain prestige projects will not be funded. (Even that is arguable; after all, each new channel would have to invest in creating positive audience identification.) But overall, the greater number of possibilities for video talent is likely to lead to greater program originality. *The television of privilege restricts avenues of creativity.*

Next to restrictiveness, the other tendency of limited private television is toward oligopolistic behavior. In the United Kingdom, the ITV companies established a cartel system among themselves, and a cooperative arrangement with their rival BBC. They did not compete in the acquisition of programs. In other countries, a collaborative arrangement of the private and the public stations emerged in several instances. In Belgium, RTL-TVi, the sole station licensed for French-language private broadcasts, entered into a formal agreement with the public RTBF to pool advertising through sales by joint agency, and to "coordinate" media buys, program schedules, and type of programs. In Austria, it appears that private television will be permitted only as a collaboration of publishers and the public ORF. In Finland, the public YLE and the private MTV had for years a system of tight cooperation.

Little can be said in defense of coordinated private broadcasting. If a collaborative new channel were desirable outside of a few unavoidable areas, it would be best to provide it as another public channel, not as a noncompeting but profit-making enterprise.

Similarly, the incentives to vertical integration of production and distribution are strong and flourish with the market power in the distribution stage. The example of the United Kingdom, where a television of privilege was established in 1954, is instructive. High-cost inside productions proliferated while independent producers languished. It took government action to open one network (Channel 4) for independent producers—with spectacular success; and it took government action to open, at least partly, the rest of ITV and the BBC.

The British example is useful in another way. There was a broad-based opposition to further opening. Not only was the BBC, with its public broadcast arguments and its supporters, opposed to lowering of barriers to entry, but the private ITV companies were as well. In Finland, the private MTV similarly resisted new commercial entrants. And in the United States, broadcasters generally obstructed in the 1970s an expansion of cable television's ability to provide additional programs. It is easy for all incumbents to agree on the undesirability of further entry and to oppose it. It is therefore likely that in other European countries a future further opening of television will be contested by a formidable coalition of the public broadcasters, private broadcasters, and influential parts of the publishing industry that have obtained television licenses. *The television of privilege is the television of further exclusion.*

But is such exclusion stable? After all, the monopoly system has already broken down. Would the duopoly system prove more resilient? The answer is probably no. For all the efforts that they will undoubtedly expend, media incumbents will be subject to the same forces that led to the demise of the entrenched monopoly—entrepreneurial innovation, audience demand, producer dissatisfaction, multichannel delivery on cable and DBS, imported channels, and so on. But it will take time for those forces to lead to the next phase of television, the open television system. In Britain, it has taken more than a third of a century to get close to the beginning of that next stage, at least in political terms, and even then change has been due more to government initiative than to grass-roots dissatisfaction. However, it is unlikely that other countries will take that long, especially those with multichannel cable distribution.

Perhaps most significant, there is no principled argument on behalf of the television of privilege. A public broadcast monopoly has certain arguments in its favor. Some, like spectrum scarcity, are weak; others entail value judgments such as the unwillingness to leave media power in private control. But there is little to justify giving valuable television licenses to only a few entities and to exclude the rest of society from broadcasting unless one advocates a nightly shared societal experience. It is argued that

1. "Too much" television will not survive. (In that case, no entrants will be forthcoming, or they will fail.)
2. High profits are needed for quality programs. (That argument has been dealt with earlier.)
3. One could, after all, buy up a license from an existing holder. (But the purchase price would include the capitalized monopoly rents, thus creating a barrier to entry that is very expensive to pass; and the new participant would have to pass muster with the government.)
4. Open entry will lead to a chaotic structure. (It need not be more orderly than in print publishing.)
5. It will lead to a private monopoly, similar to Berlusconi's in Italy. (Obviously, general antimonopoly rules should not be suspended for television.)
6. It will lead to control by foreign interests. (This too can be dealt with through structural rules.)

Perhaps the best one can say about privileged entry is that it permits society and other parts of the media system to adjust gradually to a more open system. In Italy, local broadcasting was opened abruptly, without any preparation in the program provision end. As a result, most programs were imported and/or inferior. A gradual liberalization therefore may have advantages in some situations. But one should not overvalue advance preparation. The various DBS projects of European countries had many years of planning time and still were in disarray, even after launch, about basic aspects of usage, target audience, and standards.

Another positive aspect to privileged entry is that it is generally more palatable to opponents of openness in television, who tend to believe that the less there is of it, the better. Actually the opposite is the case: The most questionable system is a highly profitable restricted private medium under the protection of the government and run by its private-sector friends.

Stage 5: Open Television

Whenever a revolution takes place in countries with state broadcasting, the rebels' first targets include the television station. But in an open system of broadcasting, which station would one occupy to silence the previous regime? *In open television, no single media entity or point is dominant.*

It is a system in which, on the *conduit* side, numerous means of transmitting television exist: over the air by regular broadcasting, over coaxial cables, by telephone fiber networks, by domestic satellites, and by international satellites.

These conduits can be accessed freely by *content* providers, who put program channels together, domestically and from abroad. The content providers, in turn, draw on the providers of *creativity,* the producers of the actual programs, both at home and internationally. These functions are filled by both private and public entities of different sizes and specialization, on the local, regional, national, and international levels. Some organizations may be integrated vertically, across the three functions; some may be integrated horizontally, across several conduits; and some may be integrated geographically, across various countries. Some are huge and international (including public organizations); others are local and nonprofit. But none control access, transmission, content provision, or program creation.

No country in the world is close to this system, and its description here is idealized. But some countries are gradually moving in that direction in a process of liberalization of electronic media.

We have observed that the state phase of broadcasting was associated with radio and that the independent public stage was linked to broadcast TV. Privileged television is initially linked to several new forms of media, most particularly cable television, and to a lesser extent satellites and videocassette recorders. These media, however, are not containable. They lead, together with the addition of telephone-carried switched television, to the stage of open television.

In the United States, where there never was a state broadcasting phase, the radio system was moderately open, though with powerful national networks and privileged award of transmission power (Barnouw, 1982). With the advent of television after World War II, however, broadcasting moved into the stage of privileged entry. Many licenses were allocated to already existing media interests. When cable television emerged as a competitive transmission, it was restricted for several years. For a long time, the triumvirate of ABC, CBS, and NBC dominated, supplemented by an underfunded and highly fragmented public broadcasting system.[7] In time, however, the system began to be opened by various small steps. No dramatic event such as a legislative act marks the evolutionary shift into the beginning of the open phase. But if a date must be picked, it would be 1980, when the FCC, in a four-to-three decision, eliminated most restrictions on distant broadcast signals that a cable system could carry. (Earlier actions had already removed some of those barriers.)

In Italy, the abrupt opening of local broadcasting led to open conditions in the local submarket of television. But national television is restricted in Italy, advertising support is the only viable way to provide channels (i.e., the economic foundation of the production sector is still lagging), foreign channel provision is nonexistent, and the industry structure is highly concentrated. Italy is therefore only at the beginning of an open system. The United Kingdom is also only at that early stage, but the Broadcasting Act of 1990 indicates a recognition of change from the privileged system to a more open and varied distribution system.

The independent system was frequently pluralistic (particularly in comparison with the state system), in the sense that spokespersons of various political parties could address viewers. Political diversity was thus enhanced. But one should not equate balance with access and free speech. The party-pluralist system accommodates primarily official views. There is little room for the maverick individual or group. Yet the point of free speech is not to make it available to authorized voices. Their views are already disseminated in numerous other ways. A system is only open when it can be accessed without the approval of any official entity. This does not mean indiscriminate access for the tedious, the extreme, and the self-indulgent, any more than a newspaper must carry their articles. The difference is that such individuals and groups can start their own newsletters or magazines and try to gain influence. But in state or independent television they had no way to do so. It was closed. Although occasionally such a voice may have been put on for contrast, it was at the discretion of the monopolist or privileged broadcaster (i.e., a favor and not a right). *In contrast, open television is a system that enables access* although it does not assure it. Economic barriers remain.

One would expect the restrictions of avenues of expression to have been intolerable to the moderate political left. However, much of the left opposed the liberalization of media, viewing it largely as strengthening business interests. As a tactical perspective, and looking only at the stage of privileged television, this is correct, but in more historical terms it is short-sighted to argue against openness and accessibility. Casting itself as the party of restriction may harm the left in the long run as much as the Catholic Church's restrictiveness against book publishing has remained part of its image even after centuries. There were important exceptions to the narrow perspective. In France, the Socialists took the initiative in opening broadcasting after decades of conservative state television. In Italy they supported local private television once it got started. But in Scandinavia it took conservatives to establish community broadcasting, an initiative that should have been a natural one for social democrats to make rather than to oppose. Northern Europe was significantly more dogmatic about mass media than southern Europe.

The liberal center supported liberalization, but it usually had only limited political clout. Hence, it was primarily the right, typically Christian democratic parties, that enacted change. For traditionalists, support for liberalized media was also a shift from traditionalist positions, such as resistance to values of consumption and sexuality. On the other hand, traditionalists believed their political values to be in better hands in limited private media than in independent public ones. They too were taking a short-term perspective. In time, their promotion of modernism will undermine the foundation of several of their support groups.

Both conservatives and social democrats interpreted media largely along an axis of class analysis—pro– or anti–big business—rather than along the dimension of modernism and traditionalism. They focused, sometimes obsessively, on ownership and control rather than on the more fundamental issues of the environment created by the structure of media.[8]

One of the key features of open television is that its economic foundation is different from that of present television. It is also likely to be costlier than in the past, and hence to benefit most those with an ability to pay. However, in no way could past European public television be described as "free." It was based on a regressive tax that, for color sets, ranged in 1990 from $100 a year in Italy to $250 a year in Denmark.

The impact of new forms of distribution is less important in its contribution to the creation of additional channels in a quantitative sense than in its change of their underlying economics. For a long time, broadcasting's economics were highly unusual. In economic terms, it was a pure public good—consumption could not be restricted (nonexcludability), and no single consumer's use imposed a cost on others (nonrival consumption). As a result, broadcasting could be provided only inadequately by regular market transactions. Two models of financing emerged: advertising support (in the private and frequently in the public system), and a use tax (license fee) in the public one. Both methods left audiences with a considerable "consumer surplus" of benefit above price. How big the difference is can be gleaned by considering what would happen if movie theaters were not permitted to sell tickets but were supported only by advertising carried on the screen. The result would almost certainly be lower revenues, and therefore fewer movie houses and film productions. In 1990, a movie ticket sold in New York City for about $7. Even that includes a consumer surplus, since a good number of viewers would presumably pay more if a system of price discrimination could be devised. In contrast, the advertising revenues raised in a movie theater from advertisements per person, even with multiple interruptions of the film, would be between only $0.30 and $0.60. Unless audiences multiplied ten to twenty times, the theaters would be less well off.

Multiplied, the consumer surplus in television is huge. For the United States, it was estimated in 1973 as the equivalent in today's dollars of $56 billion (Noll, et al., 1973). Thus, anything that could shift this benefit from users to providers would have a major impact on production and distribution.

Cable television, VCRs, and encrypted broadcasting transformed television from a public into a private good (using the economic term that is based on nonexcludability and nonrival consumption, and which is independent of ownership). (A private good could be provided by a public agency, such as rail transport, and a public good could be provided by a private firm such as broadcasting.) By maintaining control over the transmission path and thus establishing excludability, it became possible to sell "television tickets." This creates direct exhibitor–viewer relations and leads to greater incentives to entry, to a better chance for entrants to survive economically, and to the possibility of concentrating on niche audiences rather than only on mass audiences. *The television of openness is based on market transactions comparable to those found in publishing. It is costlier to users.*

The future will also likely see a much greater separation of the content, conduit, and creation functions in television. *Conduit services* (broadcast transmission, cable transport, satellite services, telephone-fiber links) are likely to be offered by specialized organizations, typically with a hardware orientation. On these transmission paths, *content providers* (program packagers) will offer programs to audiences, either as bundles of channels, separate channels, or specific programs. These firms will be, in effect, video publishers. They will shape and select program offerings and sell them to end users. Their skills are those of editors and marketers. The third major segment is that of the *providers of creativity,* the producers of programs. Consumers are not interested in transmission or packaging per se, but in the programs they deliver. Program production requires skills of artistic creation as well as putting creative talent and financing together.

Pure archetypes may be rare, but the separation of the three functions—conduit, content, and creativity—may become more pronounced over time, because they require very different skills. Their vertical integration makes most sense economically in an environment of market power, in particular in distribution. But where there is no such power at any stage, private and public packagers could select among various programs offered to them by private and public producers and could pick various transmission paths, domestic and international, to reach viewers, configuring an optimal distribution in terms of temporal sequencing and spatial transmission segments that create interconnected ''networks of networks'' in time and space.

In an environment of great diversity in program availability, transmission media would similarly be free to carry program providers of their choice. (Videocassette stores are an example.) On the other hand, where the distribution is more limited and market power in transmission exists, such choice must be supplemented with a strong element of access rights, known as *common carriage* (i.e., the ability of program provider to access transmission in a nondiscriminatory fashion based on the prevailing market price). The absence of such common carriage provisions would otherwise reduce the likelihood, in particular, of controversial programs to be carried. The economic logic of the transmission carrier may be to restrict such programs, because they may have negative spill-over effects on the remainder of the programs, and may subject the conduit to political and regulatory pressures. But such a decision may be socially and economically inefficient, because it would restrict some programs even if audiences wish to view them. In such a situation the requirement of nondiscriminatory carriage at market rates makes sense. For example, transmission of television programs by telephone organizations over fiber is a technical likelihood in the future. If they have market power, it is inadvisable from a public policy perspective to permit pick-and-choose power over the programs provided by others for their carriage.[9] On the other hand, such a requirement imposed on a single-frequency broadcasting system would be unreasonable. But if a transmission organization controls most of technical broadcasting, as is often the case in Europe, where PTTs may have a technical broadcast monopoly, it too should have to serve indiscriminately as a common carrier.

Whereas the old system favored the conduit end of television in the form of the monopoly broadcaster, the television of openness strikes a balance between content, conduit, and creation. Consequently the environment of an open television will not be neat and logical, but a collage of shifting offerings and alliances. But the print sector is not neat, so why should video be? Simplicity is easiest in a restrictive environment. *Open television is an untidy system.*

But suppose the opposite happens, and open television becomes too tidy? In Italy, private broadcasting became very concentrated, even without privileged entry, and this raises the question of whether television generally will tend to be concentrated in an open environment. There are basically two scenarios:

1. Entry barriers and scale efficiencies in TV are such that a "natural" monopoly exists. (This is highly unlikely but theoretically possible.)
2. Various forms of anticompetitive behavior lead to dominance.

In either case, structural policies could deal with that problem (e.g., by limiting the market of any single dominance). *Openness does not mean the absence of any and all regulation.*

This leads to the next question: What is the nature of the regulatory system? Within many countries, the form of state control has been changing. Under state television, governments operated all broadcasting, either directly or through a fully owned and controlled corporation. In the phase of independent television, supervision was based on appointees. Only a very limited regulatory mechanism was necessary (e.g., for the supervision of fundamental political matters and the setting of the license fee).

However, liberalization, with its private and community stations and cable distribution, required a different approach. Licenses had to be awarded; operating conditions set; and their fulfillment enforced in light of new developments. A regulatory structure became necessary. One response was to lodge regulation in an independent or semi-independent agency. This was the model in the United Kingdom of the IBA, the Cable Authority, the telecommunications agency Oftel, and the new Independent Television Commission (ITC). In France, the state Ministry of Information eventually gave way in the 1980s to the Haute Autorité, the CNCL, and then the Counseil Supérieur de l'Audiovisuel, with each step providing additional independent powers. In Germany, the various states created semi-independent *Medienanstalten*. This trend resembles the creation, in the United States, of the Federal Communications Commission in 1934 and of the state public utility commissions decades earlier. In many European countries, such independent bodies, often with executive, judicial, and quasi-legislative power, were not usual, and their creation is a change in the administrative process with significance beyond television.

The existence of regulation also raised the question of its locus in the emerging European supranational system of governance. European harmonization of regulation is often subsumed under the shorthand of "1992," the date when it is supposed to occur. In the process, will Brussels become Europe's regulatory capital for electronic media? Will the European Commission be in charge of broadcasting? It is unlikely that member states' role will disappear. In Germany, for example, the role of the Länder dominates that of the federal government and is fiercely guarded. By analogy, Europe's television policy will have a strong federated component. But this still leaves room for Europe-wide policies on technical compatibility, advertising, and property rights. The European Community is also likely to prevent discrimination in program imports from a member state to others and may try to prevent member states from acting as a "broadcast haven."

The European Community harmonized certain television regulations during the 1980s, following its Green Paper "Television without Frontiers." This approach may accelerate but will not likely change qualitatively to a centralized system. On an *attitudinal* level, however, the notion of a unified Europe will be strengthened through the efforts toward 1992, and cannot fail to instill national media policies that are less territorial than those in the past.

Media regulation is not likely to be a zero-sum game. National governments may lose control without Brussels or others necessarily assuming it. They may also lose it to lower levels of government. The openness of television means less centralism. Local broadcast stations and cable networks emerge. In part, they provide locally produced programs by community groups. However, the fundamental economics of production suggest that for commercial providers most purely local programs are not attractive. The role of local distribution outlets therefore is based less on local production and more on local *selection*, tailoring different program and channel packages based on the sociodemographic characteristics of the area. This is not unusual; bookstores also have different assortments, depending on location, even if they share certain basics. *The television of openness enhances local control over selection, even if production and distribution are national and international.*

No doubt there will be efforts to increase E.C. centralized regulatory power in order to solve the national inconsistencies. But even where uniform policies for television exist, they are likely to clash with a myriad of other societal concerns, such as those for telecommunications, cultural development, protection of children, or technology development. There are not enough "degrees of freedom" to deal with all problems without internal contradictions.

This is most obvious for the program side, but it is also increasingly the case for technical aspects, given the numerous interests and participants. It was relatively easy to set standards for FM radio and black-and-white television, but it was impossible for color television, because of governmental disagreements. Even where these disagreements could be bridged at the highest European political levels for MAC, the next phase of standards, they could not command the multiple interests—set manufacturers, chip makers, broadcasters, satellite operators, and so on—to fall into line. At the beginning of the 1990s, MAC was in disarray, and the standard for high-definition television was subject to ferocious international political infighting. Even if these differences could be resolved, it is far from certain that the marketplace would abide by it.

What is the consequence? The major fault may be the premise that uniform standards should be set at all. The notion of standards is dear to engineers and civil servants, but it is essentially a static notion, because it transforms change and transition into a bureaucratized process. Standards are useful for coordinated development and production, but they are also confining to innovation (Besen and Johnson, 1986; Farrell and Saloner, 1986; David, 1987). In the past, uniform television standards were unavoidable. But they will not be in the future. A television set will be less of a "dumb" reception terminal and more of a "smart" signal processor. It will be, in effect, a computer that transforms incoming informational inputs into visual and audile outputs. There is no reason such computers could not handle multiple standards. In computers, it is routine that various software types and hardware boards are offered to make features and systems possible. Similarly, a new type of broadcasting could be introduced by its provider persuading users of its advantages, instead of the present system of requiring a multinational, multi-industry accord. As the life cycle of television generations shortens, which is likely with a merger of television and computers, the old system will become too unwieldy. Consumers' television sets thus must be capable of accepting various standards; that is, they must become open. *Open television as a transmission medium leads to open technological standards.*

The television of openness also transforms the nature of the mass audience. Viewers in time discovered that they would rather not constantly be part of a great national community, the mass audience, and that they instead belonged to subaudiences, to distinct taste publics. Of course, there are distinctly national events, but not nightly. Producers learned that it was often more satisfactory to address specific audience segments than to be all things to all people. And advertisers recognized the advantages of targeting specific audiences rather than general ones (assuming that the cost of advertising time is not directly proportional to its effectiveness).

This spells out a transformation of the mass audience, at least of the territorial, nation-state-oriented variety. The future audience will be less aggregated along spatial and temporal dimensions and more individualized in the sense that each individual will be able to shape his own program environment out of multiple mass-oriented offerings. In that sense, viewing will be more active. A system of video-on-demand, in which the viewer dials up a video library for the desired program, which is then transmitted electronically, illustrates the direction.[10]

Mass audiences will instead often be aggregated across national frontiers and along the dimensions of interest and taste. Cultural units thus become transnational. For centralized states this is a challenge. Historically, states have distrusted groups with cross-border allegiances—rebellious youth culture; proletarian solidarity; ethnic, religious, and linguistic minorities with allegiances beyond the border. *Open television weakens national cohesion and strengthens both particularism and internationalism.*

Like the United States, Europe goes through cycles of confidence like a manic-depressive. At the beginning of the 1980s, *Eurosclerosis* was the buzzword, replaced at the decade's end with *Europhoria*. Europeans tend to feel small and fragmented, as if their principal countries do not have sizable populations and speak languages prevalent around the world. (Eleven European countries have languages shared by more than 100 million native speakers in Europe and overseas.) The process of integration, the evolution from a Europe of hostile nation-states into a larger whole, inspires individuals and institutions alike and generates innovation where traditionalism reigned. On the other hand, some bad ideas get taken surprisingly seriously if they are packaged as inter-European collaboration. In the name of Europe, outsiders can be restricted, and compromises among European countries may come at their expense. In the field of electronic media equipment, Asian countries are especially excluded. In one instance, the French government harassed Japanese VCR manufacturers (whose primary fault was offering a better product at a cheaper price) by creating a customs checkpoint that seemed to specialize in slow processing, in the out of the way city of Poitiers (openly chosen for its symbolism as the site of the defeat of the Moslems in 732). Fortunately, some of this cultural and economic nationalism has been overcome in the building of a united Europe. It was often feared that the opening of television would undermine European culture and lead to domination by American firms. This criticism tended to idealize the quality of European public television and to be anachronistic in its view of U.S. television, which had progressed beyond its three-network oligopoly to a multichannel environment. The European reality, after a decade of its own media transformation, looked much different from what had been feared. By the beginning of the 1990s, there was very little direct U.S. media presence in Europe, much less than one would expect in an open environment, given the U.S. strength and experience in this field. Where American firms took an imaginative initiative (e.g., the Luxembourg Coronet satellite project, which introduced the concepts of medium-power DBS satellites as quasi-common carriers separated from the content side), the plan was discredited and blocked by rival European interests and governments as a "Coca Cola" satellite. After the American founders were forced out, the project proceeded as a purely European venture and became highly successful. In the United Kingdom, many cable franchises were awarded to U.S. and Canadian firms, but little cable was actually put in place, and the foreign firms were called in to remedy the domestic unwillingness to invest. But if cable becomes successful this presence might be curtailed in a different political environment.

In contrast, several European media firms have moved aggressively in the international sphere. CLT, Berlusconi, Bertelsmann, Murdoch, Kirch, Maxwell, Havas, and Kennevik have all been more active and nimble in crossing the borders of their home base than American media firms. These European individuals and firms have created internationally diversified media companies. The main exception to the relatively low U.S. presence is provided by actual programs. Here Hollywood has benefited from the larger European demand for programs, the slower growth in European program production, and its established strong distribution channels; and its sales have increased substantially.

Moreover, the related fear of a decline of the public broadcast institutions had not materialized. In the environment of open television, public television will continue to play a major role, partly because certain types of programs are not provided otherwise and partly because of the public institutions' strength and experience.

They are still very large enterprises. Of Europe's six largest television networks in terms of 1988 television revenues, five were public broadcasters: ARD (Germany, $3.5 billion); BBC (United Kingdom, $2.1 billion); RAI (Italy, $1.7

billion); Fininvest (Italy, private, $1.5 billion); RTVG (Spain, $1 billion); and ZDF (Germany, $0.85 billion). The public broadcasters also have among them four of the ten largest advertising incomes.

However, the structure of public broadcasting began to change from its national orientation. It started to include also regional, local, and community channels, on the one hand, and international public channels, on the other hand. Similarly, a stronger separation of production and programming emerged. In the future, the revenues of the license fee may also be allocated to subsidize the production directly of valuable programs by independent producers for transmission on any channel, public or private.

Earlier, we associated the stage of state broadcasting with radio and that of independent broadcasting with television. What technology is similarly characteristic of open television? It would be natural to consider cable television and satellites as the prime candidates, and that would be correct in some sense. In another sense, however, the infrastructure of transmission is secondary to a viewer, just as the nature of reservoirs and pumping stations is for the user of tap water. From the viewer's perspective, the difference to his environment is the availability of greater *choice,* not the existence of a coaxial wire in the house. And this choice is exemplified by the emergence of a fairly humble but significant technology—the hand-held remote control device. It would be wrong to view it merely as a convenience. The use of the device implies the establishment of some viewer control, the creation of a *reverse channel* of communication, if only for a few yards. Whereas traditional radio and television were strictly a one-way channel, remote control now symbolizes the emergence of two-way communication.

There is something significant in the creation of viewer "remote" control. Radio and broadcast television appealed to the ear and eye, both basically passive ways of receiving internal and external inputs. A remote control device, on the other hand, extends the human hand and establishes an active output. Most viewers actually feel some personal satisfaction as they switch away or cut off the sound from a bad program, a tedious speaker, or a jarring advertising message.

There is no reason to expect that the habit of literally taking viewing into one's hand will be containable. In time, the reverse channel will grow in length. Technologies are becoming available that make its extension possible. Cable television already has elements of it (so-called addressability) and experimental two-way capacity. Switched cable architectures will provide more of such capability. Similarly, the broadbanding of telephone networks will create point-to-point video transmission with two-way communications, which may be primarily infrastructure for video distribution. The point is not that much video will be sent back upstream; more significant is the creation of continuous selectivity and control. Viewers can call up the program of their choice at the time of their choice from a variety of sources. Viewing thus can become a frequently individualized affair within mass distribution, like the reading of books, although there will still be room for mass audience simultaneity.

As these changes unfold, there will unavoidably be nostalgia for the good old days. People tend to remember the program highlights of their youth and to attribute their absence to the new environment. In the United States, there is also a myth about the "golden age" of early television. Yet when these early programs are watched now, one cannot help but be disappointed often if today's standards are objectively applied.

It is likely that some fine programs will not be made in the future, just as no one illuminates manuscripts as beautifully as the scribes of monasteries (the Middle Age's public media institutions, made obsolete by the commercial Gutenberg), or builds cars like Hispano-Suiza, or performs music like the Beatles. On the other hand, many new types of extraordinary creations will no doubt emerge.

The revolutionary changes in Eastern Europe at the end of the 1980s demonstrate the impossibility of impeding the free flow of information over the long term. Similarly, the cumulative impact of the opening of media in West Europe will lead to a very different media environment. Except for unusual events, the electronic hearth around which entire societies congregated nightly will be no more. But this communal experience of constant information sharing has been only an ephemeral episode in the history of mankind. It clashes with a more individualistic media past and a more information-rich future. It is a system based on scarcity of content production and scarcity of conduits. As these conditions change, the structure of television evolves. Though economic barriers and political restrictions will be formidable, and though the path will be full of new problems, in time we shall experience a television of openness, open to the access of new voices—commercial and nonprofit—open across frontiers, and open to viewer choices. Television will become part of the environment, just as print has become centuries ago. It will contain some that is good, much that is bad, and most that is casual. That is, video will become an everyday event, and devoid of its present special status as the national integrator that leads to anxieties over its control. And it will flourish without cultural high priests and public officials guarding its entrance, just as print communication does today.

Notes

Chapter 2

1. Imports may even vitalize an otherwise declining movie environment. French Minister of Culture Jack Lang, otherwise a long-time critic of U.S. media, viewed Hollywood as a potential benefactor of French movie houses that were otherwise closing, by reducing the lure of "free" television competing "unfairly" with movie exhibitions. According to Lang, "What counts is the vitality of cinema on the big screen, not where it comes from" (Riding, 1990).

2. A more sophisticated analysis of flows based on market share and the concept of "cultural discounts" is Hoskins and Mirus (1988.)

3. Prices would be equal to marginal cost in a fully competitive system if media products would not be differentiated. But the absence of such homogeneity is the essence of cultural production, and it is therefore not likely that programs would be bid for at marginal cost in a competitive demand situation. The differentiation of outlets by suppliers in a release sequence, discussed in Chapter 3, is aimed to establish differentiated pricing above marginal cost.

4. There are, for example, three Asian-language channels (Nippon Golden Network, The Asia Network, and Ultravision), three Spanish-language services (Telemundo, Univision, and Galavision), and the International Television Network, which broadcasts a variety of foreign programs (Applebaum, 1989).

5. The large literature, much of it dealing with media imperialism, includes, e.g. Schiller (1969), Fejes (1981), Varis (1985), Noam and Millonzi (1991), Collins (1988), and Hoskins and Mirus (1988).

Chapter 4

1. These preferences are assumed to be given and discrete rather than continuous.

2. Similarly, the use of a single-peaked distribution other than the normal would not alter the basic analysis but would complicate the computations. A twin-peaked distribution, however, would make a difference.

3. Within a given distribution of program preference, a broadcaster could occasionally scatter the pitch of its program in order to reach outlying program preferences, on the assumption that an audience, once tuned in, exhibits a delay in moving back to its primary program preference. This also does not change the basic analysis.

4. The impact of additional signal power on the reception range drops quickly for

345

VHF and UHF transmissions, which do not follow the curvature of the earth. Adding antenna height quickly reaches structural and practical limits.

5. We choose a linear weight:

$$-c = 1/Z(Z + P)$$

Z is a constant, defined so that $c = 1$ when $P = 0$ (i.e., a neutral weight at the peak of the distribution). The smaller Z is, the greater is the weight given to income. Audience consumption power is

$$C = \tfrac{1}{2} Hp_2 \cdot 2B \cdot 1/Z(Z + P_2) = B(2\pi)^{-1/2} e^{-1/2\, P_2^2} 1/Z(Z + \Gamma_2)$$

To maximize, we set

$$dc/dP_2 = B(2\pi)^{-1/2} [Ze^{-1/2 P2} (-P_2) + e^{-1/2 P_2^2} + P_2 e^{-1/2 P_2^2} (-P_2)] = 0$$

We have

$$e^{-1/2 P_2^2}(-ZP_2 + 1 - P_2^2) = 0$$

Since the left-most part of this expression is always positive, we can solve for a maximum at

$$P_2 = -Z/2 + [(Z^2/4) + 1]^{1/2}$$

We find that if we do so, the greater the income weight, the more the maximizing pitch will be shifted to the right. In other words, when audience income is factored into the broadcaster's profit-maximizing quality pitch, the result is that program pitch is actually raised in terms of quality.

6. With more than two parties, however, different platforms could emerge; yet coalitions would tend to push the equilibrium toward the center, although unstable non-centrist solutions are also possible. This corresponds to the analysis of public choice theory voting behavior (Mueller, 1979).

7. A variant exists if a coalition government needs to satisfy its several constituencies. For example, if the winning coalition comprises two parties—one to the left and one to the right of V_c in Figure 4.2—the program pitch may be set at or near V_c to serve both coalition parties. This could leave the programming pitch considerably off center.

8. For purposes of the analysis, we assume a quality weight, W, which is linearly proportional to the program quality pitch, $W = 1/M (M + P)$, and $P = 0$, so that the weight is neutral for the centrist pitch P. The optimal pitch P is then the one that maximizes the audience multiplied by program quality weight. This optimization can be extended with the inclusion of the goal of a wide band of programs. But even within a wide band, the basic strategy question remains what the average pitch will be.

Similar to the case of income-weighting, differentiation yields as maximizing P the right of center, at

$$P_7 = -M/2 + (M^2/4 + 1)^{1/2}$$

9. That smaller triangle is given by $n \cdot m/2$, where n is the distance between $P_x + B$ and $P_y - B$ (i.e., $n = P_x - P_y + 2B$). Height m is given by the relation

$$m = (2\pi)^{-1/2} e^{-1/2 P_x^2} (P_x - P_y + 2B) 1/2B$$

and the triangle is

$$T = n \cdot m/2 = 1/4B \ (P_x - P_y + 2B)^2 \ (2\pi)^{-\frac{1}{2}} \ e^{-\frac{1}{2}PX^2}$$

Chapter 5

1. The magnitude of the revenue from pay TV alone is substantial. Even in pay-cable's early years (1981), pay-TV companies paid some $375 million for movie rights; in comparison, the two largest U.S. movie theater chains, General Cinema and United Artists Theater Circuit, both controlling hundreds of theaters, paid Hollywood $155 and $144 million respectively (Guback, 1982, p. 171).

Chapter 6

1. In the last ten apocalyptic months of the regime, however, Hitler spoke only once to the German people.

2. The Reichspost and the RRG, however, used the Eiffel Tower in Paris during the Occupation to broadcast temporary transmissions.

3. ZDF, in contrast to the ARD stations, had no authorization for radio broadcasting. After exerting significant pressure, it received it in 1990.

4. There was no advertising on the third channel until the broadcast authority in Hesse, the state most opposed to commercial television at the time, began to carry it in order to undercut the potential advertising market for future private systems. This led to the curious spectacle that the political left advocated more advertising on public television, whereas the right opposed it.

5. In 1981, the Germany Monopoly Commission criticized the Bundespost's cable equipment procurement and development practices that were channeled through a working group of nine manufacturers: "The manufacturers that are included in the working group obtained through their participation a significant development advantage over manufacturers that are not involved" (Monopolkommission, 1981, p. 34). Following an order from the Federal Cartel Office, foreign producers and other German producers were allowed access to the catalogue of standards. The Monopoly Commission also noted that "concerning [master antenna] systems that are to be newly erected, the result is that the DBP has left for itself many of the profitable projects, while it gives permits when conditions are unfavorable" (Monopolkommission, 1981, p. 64).

Chapter 7

1. The 1984 law recognized four types of private local broadcasters: advertiser-supported-only stations, such as NRJ (about 40 percent of the stations); "associative" broadcasters (29 percent), which are run by groups as clubs and derive no part of their revenues from advertising; association stations, which have advertising support (13 percent); and mixed association stations, which have advertising and government subsidies (19 percent) (Opitz, 1990, p. D47).

2. In 1986, the British independent broadcaster Granada acquired a share of between 3 and 5 percent in Canal Plus, which was later sold.

3. The legislation gave the government the authority to sanction direct transmission

facilities on rooftops regardless of local decisions. The law was aimed particularly at the Eiffel Tower, owned by the City of Paris and controlled by the then oppostion leader Jacques Chirac, also the Mayor of Paris.

4. Another satellite program venture is TV-5, a low-power satellite channel that was started in 1984 as a joint operation of the French-speaking public broadcasters in France, Belgium, and Switzerland, later joined by Canada. Each partner supplies programs, primarily highlights of its past programs, on alternate days.

5. Although teletext usually uses the vertical blanking interval while regular television program transmission takes place, it is also possible to broadcast it continuously rather than intermittently. Teletext was broadcast by special transmission all day in Paris and Lyon, and nationally over the FR3 network during breaks in regular television programming (*L'Expansion,* 1985).

Chapter 8

1. In fairness, the BBC is more cost conscious than many other broadcasters. In Germany, as the BBC's Alasdair Milne, then Director General noted, television drama productions use ten to seventeen days of expensive studio time for a one- and one-half-hour play. At the BBC, on the other hand, it is unusual for a drama production to take even four days. BBC crews also tend to be smaller than at other public broadcast institutions.

2. In 1986, for example, before cable channels were added: 54 percent versus 46 percent, of which BBC2 had 9 percent and ITV's Channel 4, 9.4 percent (Tunstall, 1986, p. 115).

3. Control Board Minutes, Nov. 6, 1928; Eckersley to Reith, p. 337. The papers relating to this scheme have been lost (Briggs, 1965, p. 358n).

4. Lord Hunt, a civil servant and former secretary to the Cabinet, was a member of the boards of IBM and Unilever; Sir Maurice Hodgson was chairman of British Home Stores, a company active in the use of video equipment; and Professor James Ring, the third member, was a physics professor at Imperial College and a member of the IBA board.

5. The minister for information technology, Kenneth Baker, a man with a computer business background, had overoptimistically argued in 1982 that interactive services were the "raison d'etre for the expansion of cable television" (*Sunday Times,* Dec. 5, 1982—as quoted in Dornan, 1984, p. 26).

6. The White Paper struck a conciliatory but vague note on the issue of foreign programming:

> The Government's intention is to require those seeking a franchise to specify the proportion of material of British or European Community origin which they intend to include in their services . . . The Government accepts that in the early years cable operators may need to use a significant amount of overseas material if cable is to get going [U.K. Department of Industry and Home Office, 1983, 51–52].

To drive this point home, the home secretary announced in a press conference on the White Paper that eventually a 14 percent ceiling on imported programming would be imposed, identical to the one for ITV.

7. In general, the consortia were grab-bags of media companies, financial institutions, electronic firms, and newspaper publishing companies. Aberdeen Cable Services,

for example, was formed by the Aberdeen Trust, British Telecom, ATC, MMG, Rockall Scotia Resources, Fortronic, Royal Bank of Scotland, and Clydesdale Bank.

8. The DTI therefore imposed a number of conditions on cable licenses. One of its objectives was to make sure that cable systems would have the potential to provide voice telephony in the future. This condition includes an obligation to seek an interconnecting agreement with the operator of another public telecommunications system, such as British Telecom or Mercury, when a customer requests a service that requires such a connection. When an interconnection agreement cannot be reached, the director of the telecommunications regulatory agency Oftel can arrange for an agreement. Cable operators and communications systems connected to it must also permit value-added services such as banking or information provision by other parties. The obligation does not arise except when it would impede the sound commercial development of the cable system by interfering with the cable operator's own plans.

9. Companies pursuing the switched development included GEC, Thorn-EMI, Rediffusion, and Cabletime, a joint venture of the American firm Times Fiber and United Engineering Industries.

10. Defining "switched star" and "tree and branch" in legally precise terms is a problem in itself because a variety of hybrids exist. The DTI required certain performance characteristics as a basis for judging whether a fifteen or a twenty-three year license should be granted. Data service capability and interactivity must be provided. There must be a commitment to permit data service of 64 kbps with access from the cable system to the public switched telephone network.

11. The Peacock Committee report, mentioned earlier, also examined the forms of common carrier obligation to be applied to broadcasting and cable television in the United Kingdom. The report recommended that British Telecom (BT) replace copper circuits with optical fiber and be permitted to carry and offer television signals. These recommendations implied end-to-end competition between BT and any other cable operators, which seemingly went contrary to the government's intention of using cable systems to stimulate controlled local competition in telephony.

The U.K. Cable Authority, although opposed to the committee's recommendations, urged the government to reexamine the telecommunication duopoly of BT and Mercury, with an eye toward the participation by cable operators.

Cable television was also discussed in the government's White Paper in 1988 dealing with broadcasting. It sought to separate cable operations from program provision. However, after protests by the industry, a decision on video carriage by telecommunication providers was delayed until the 1990 duopoly review of BT and Mercury (Home Office, 1988, p. 30).

One of the largest U.K. operators, Windsor TV, carries telephone traffic to a central hub where it is routed through Mercury's long-distance network.

12. The Murdoch media empire, unprecedented in its spread, is a complex construction. The major Murdoch family holding company is Cruden Investments, which in turn, owns another holding, News Corporation, Ltd. (NCL), domiciled in Sydney (Biebl and Manthey, 1985, p. 122). NCL in turn owns two holdings, News Ltd. in Australia and News Corporation Investments in Europe. News Ltd. owns Australian papers and major private television stations in the principal cities of Sydney and Melbourne, and a majority of one of the two Australian domestic air carriers. News Corporation Investments owns yet another holding, News International in London. News International in turn owns newspapers in Britain, including *News of the World, Today,* the *Sun, The Times,* and the *Sunday Times.* The Australian holding and the European holding jointly

own still another holding company, this one for American property News America Publishing, the fifth holding company in the chain of ownership.

13. Subsequent satellite services—a constantly changing cast—were, from the United States, Bravo, a classic movie channel; Cable News Network (Turner); Discovery Channel, and MTV Europe. British channels were The Children's Channel (British Telecom, Thames Television, Central Television, and D. C. Thompson), Eurosport, Lifestyle Television (W. H. Smith, D. C. Thompson, Yorkshire TV, and TV South), and Screen Sport (W.H. Smith and the American ESPN).

14. Radio 1 provides pop music and news and has roughly 30 percent of the total audience; Radio 2 has light music, jazz, and sports and has 20 percent of total audiences; Radio 3 transmits serious music, drama, poetry, and talk shows and has 2 percent of the total; and Radio 4 offers news and current affairs with additional material for educational broadcasting and general entertainment, accounting for 12 percent of the total. The remaining 36 percent of the audience listens to BBC local radio, commercial radio, and so on (Stephen Hearst, communication). No license fee is charged for radio listening. BBC's worldwide reputation is based partly on its radio World Service, perhaps the most credible source of international radio news. World Service is financed by the Foreign Office.

15. The government's restrictive technical specifications, however, reflected its reluctant attitude which was based partly on fears of ethnically oriented radio. In 1989, twenty community radio stations were licensed.

Chapter 9

1. Although Italy has a higher density of broadcast stations than other countries, the absence of multichannel cable television makes the comparison somewhat misleading.

Chapter 11

1. A barrier for cable has been its legal inability to provide high-order services that include interactivity. Data transmission is the exclusive province of the RTT.

Chapter 15

1. The reality, however, was at times more complex. In the early 1950s, political parties could effectively veto programs, since representation of all parties was required in controversial programming. By refusing to participate, a party could prevent a program altogether. This veto system lasted until the mid-1950s. The popular movements also often challenged Sveriges Radio and tried to shape programming.

Chapter 26

1. This section is based on research by Andrew Blau, and benefitted from the Hans Bredow Institute's *Handbuch*.

2. Some of the departments include Central Television and Central Domestic Radio, each of which in turn includes administrative and editorial departments, literature and

drama, youth programming, and so on; the central editorial office of the Correspondents Network; the main editorial office of Letters and Sociological (i.e., audience) research; and various print publications.

3. In 1990, the French media firm Havas announced signing an exclusive agreement to sell advertising time in the U.S.S.R. (Toy, 1990, p.114).

Chapter 27

1. Sound and data are inserted into the line-blanking interval of the FM video system, and bursts of data at about 20 megabits per second are inserted into the line-blanking interval. This results in a transmission rate of about 3 megabits per second, enough for video and up to eight high-quality sound channels. The format is also suited to encryption, an important factor in the provision of pay programs.

Chapter 28

1. This rhetoric of cultural identity contrasts with the reality of French state activity in broadcast exports to Africa; the official Radio France Outre-mer distributes daily satellite-delivered compilations of French newscasts and talk shows for rebroadcasting to Africa (Morley and Mann, 1986). France also has a 40 percent involvement in the major African commercial radio station, the Gabon-based Africa No. 1, which was started in 1981 and has been highly successful in terms of audience and as an advertising outlet for French companies. The powerful station reaches much of Africa, and its popularity hurts indigenous broadcasters.

2. The difficulty in developing traveling wave tubes (TWTs) of more than 100 watts caused the project's main technical problems and was the primary reason for its delay. Initially, Thomson and AEG developed different systems, but the French ultimately agreed to the AEG tubes for both satellites.

3. Kopernikus was used by the other German commercial networks Tele 5 and Pro 7, the pay service Premiere, and several regional public broadcasters (Kirk, 1990).

4. Eutelsat-1F4 in 1989 carried 3Sat, EBC, FilmNet, Galavision Europe, Landscape Channel, PACE, RTL-Plus, SAT-1, Sky Channel, Super Channel, Teleclub, TV-5, and Worldnet. Eutelsat-1F5, in 1989, carried NRK, RAI-1, RAI-2, TVE-1, 3Sat, and Canal Course.

Chapter 29

1. In the United States, the system of program networks and independent stations partly separated the two, except that some stations were owned by program networks. Independent stations produced their own programs.

2. In the United States, commercial television indeed contributed to the demise of general circulation magazines such as *Look, The Saturday Evening Post,* and for some time, *Life.* In Europe, in contrast, the same type of magazine survived.

3. Eastern Europe is not discussed in detail, because its past led to evolutionary dynamics different from those of democratic Europe.

4. In the United States, lawyers increased 141 percent between 1960 and 1980; accountants, 103 percent; authors and writers, 57 percent; engineers, 61 percent; postsec-

ondary teachers, 224 percent; and other teachers, 106 percent (U.S. Census Bureau, communication, August 1990).

5. In the United States, in 1983, 12.5 million (5.3 percent of the population) were students attending universities and colleges, 3.5 times as much as in 1960, and 1.4 times as many as in 1970. (U.S. Department of Commerce, 1990, p. 128). In Germany, there were almost 1.5 million college students (2.4 percent of the population) in 1983, 2.2 times the number in 1970. French higher education attendance in 1983 was 1.1 million (2.0 percent of the population), 1.4 times as much as in 1970. In Italy, the number rose to 1.1 million (1.8 percent of the population), an increase of 60 percent. And in the United Kingdom, in 1983, 581,000 British students attended college, or 1 percent of the population, 20 percent higher than in 1970 (European Community, 1986).

6. Some of the larger countries were lagging. Italy had some cable, but only prior to the opening up of broadcasting. In the United Kingdom and France, despite governmental efforts at establishing cable as technology development projects, cable progressed only slowly; but one can expect that British cable television will see larger investments and penetration rates in the 1990s. In Germany, the Bundespost telephone administration strongly pushed cabling, but with German unification the investment priorities shifted into basic telephone service in East Germany.

7. The way things have been changing, PBS may end up as the last public system, except for the BBC, without advertising, though with sponsorship messages that are very close to commercials.

8. Occasionally, empirical research was mandated to accompany the opening of a new distribution mode, but even such valuable contributions to an understanding of the immediate effects were no substitute for a long-term interpretive analysis, of which there was little.

9. To anticipate this, the New York State Public Service Commission established in 1989, as the first state in the United States, a set of common carrier requirements, drafted by the author, on the mass media carrier obligations of telephone carriers.

10. The expression of culture itself is changing. It will be more of a video culture, not just in entertainment and mass audiences, but increasingly in small-group and even individual communication. With abundance the style of communications will change. Communicating via television becomes a more casual event. At the same time attention span for any individual message is limited. Hence, the style of ''sound-bite,'' capsules of facts and analyses, will become more prevalent and continue to simplify the nature of political discourse. In entertainment, plots will become increasingly simple, episodic, and nonlinear. And the content is likely to be conceived with an international audience in mind.

References

Chapter 1

Cryan, Thomas J., James S. Crane, Michael S. Marcil. 1988. The Future of Sports Broadcasting: An International Question. *Seton Hall Legislative Journal,* 10(2):213–273.

Gans, Herbert J. 1972. The Politics of Culture in America: A Sociological Analysis. In *Sociology of Mass Communications,* ed. Denis McQuail. New York: Penguin, pp. 372–385.

McQuail, Denis, and Karen Siune, eds. 1986. *New Media Politics: Comparative Perspectives in Western Europe.* Beverly Hills, CA: Sage.

Media Perspektiven. 1989. June.

Noam, Eli M. 1991. *Telecommunications in Europe.* New York: Oxford.

Robbins, E. D. 1967. The Postmaster General and the Pirates. *EBU Review,* March, p. 52.

Chapter 2

Applebaum, Simon. 1989. Prepare for an Onslaught of "Melting Pot TV" Channels. *Cablevision,* May 8, p. 24.

Collins, Richard. 1988. National Culture: A Contradiction in Terms? International Television Studies Conference.

Commission of the European Communities. 1984. *Television without Frontiers:* Green Paper on the Establishment of the Common Market for Broadcasting, Especially by Satellite and Cable. COM (88) 300 final, June 14.

Fejes, Fred. 1981. Media Imperialism: An Assessment. *Media, Culture, and Society.* pp. 79–124.

Home Office and Department of Industry. 1983. *The Development of Cable Systems and Services* (White Paper). London: Her Majesty's Stationery Office.

Hoskins, C., and R. Mirus. 1987. A Study of the Economic Social Cultural Reasons for the Significant International Popularity of Television Fiction Produced in the United States. Edmonton: University of Alberta.

Knops, Tilo Rudolf. 1989. Heiliger Krieg: Sechzig Jahre Europäische Filmkampffront. *Medium,* January–March, pp. 44–48.

Milne, Alasdair. 1983. A View from the Brits: Westward No. *Channels* 3(2):63–64.

Morgan, Janet. 1985. The Flood of Information—the Age of Cultural Conflicts. In *Medientrends.* Hamburg: Intermedia Centrum, pp. 33–44.

Noam, Eli M., and Joel Millonzi, eds. 1991. Media Americanization, National Culture, and Faces of Integration. In *The International Market in Film and Television Programs.* Norwood, NJ: Ablex Publishing.

Pryluck, C. 1986. Industrialization of Entertainment in United States. In *Current Research on Film: Audiences, Economics, and Law.*, ed. Bruce A. Austin. Norwood, NJ: Ablex Publishing.

Schiller, Herbert. 1969. *Mass Communications and the American Empire.* New York: Kelly.

Variety Weekly. 1990a. Natives Fill In Français for U.S. Players. May 2, p. 110.

———. 1990b. Rub-a-Dub of Dante's Lingo on the Track. May 2, p. 178.

Varis, Tapio. 1985. International Flow of Television Programmes. *Reports & Papers on Mass Communications.* Paris: UNESCO. No. 100.

Chapter 3

Baumol, William J., John C. Panzar, and Robert D. Willig. 1982. *Contestable Markets and the Theory of Industry Structure.* New York: Harcourt Brace Jovanovich.

Brock, William A. 1983. Contestable Markets and the Theory of Industry Structure: A Review Article. *Journal of Political Economy* 91(6):1055–1066.

Dunnett, Peter J. S. 1990. *The World Television Industry: An Economic Analysis.* London: Routledge.

Henry, Jane E. 1985. Economics of Pay-TV Media. In *Video Media Competition*, ed. Eli Noam. New York: Columbia University Press, pp. 19–54.

Kellner, Hella, and Hendrik Schmidt. 1979. Programmangebot und Mediennutzung. *Publizistik* 24(4):353–369.

Jackson, Allen. 1985. Has Cable TV Diversified Away the Vast Wasteland? Center for Telecommunications and Information Studies, Working Paper Series No. 270. New York: Columbia University.

Noll, Roger G., Merton J. Peck, and John J. McGowan. 1973. *Economic Aspects of Television Regulation.* Washington, D.C.: Brookings Institution.

Okun, Arthur. 1975. Rights and Dollars. In *Equality and Efficiency, the Big Tradeoff.* Washington, D.C.: Brookings Institute, pp. 1–31.

Pool, Ithiel de Sola, Hiroshi Inose, Nozomu Takasaki, and Roger Hurwitz. 1984. *Communications Flows: A Census in the United States and Japan.* North-Holland: University of Tokyo Press.

Shepherd, William. 1983. Concepts of Competition and Efficient Policy in the Telecommunications Sector. In *Telecommunications Regulation: Today and Tomorrow*, ed. Eli Noam. New York: Harcourt Brace Jovanovich.

Spence, Michael, and Bruce M. Owen. 1977. Television Programming: Monopolistic Competition and Welfare. *Quarterly Journal of Economics* 91: 103–126.

Sterling, Christopher H., and Timothy R. Haight. 1978. *The Mass Media: Aspen Institute Guide to Communication Industry Trends.* New York: Praeger.

Veljanovski, Centro, and W. D. Bishop. 1983. *Choice by Cable: The Economics of a New Area in Television.* Lansing, U.K.: Institute of Economic Affairs.

Waterman, David. 1985. Prerecorded Home Video and the Distribution of Theatrical Feature Films. In *Video Media Competition*, ed. Eli Noam. New York: Columbia University Press, pp. 221–243.

Chapter 4

Beebe, J. H. 1977. Institutional Structure and Program Choice in Television Markets. *Quarterly Journal of Economics* 91:15–37.

Gans, Herbert. 1974. *Popular Culture and High Culture*. New York: Basic Books.

Howard, Herbert H., and Michael S. Kievman. 1983. *Radio and Television Programming*. Ohio: Grid.

Levin, Harvey. 1971. *The Invisible Resource*. Baltimore: Johns Hopkins University Press.

Mander, Jerry. 1978. *Four Arguments for the Elimination of Television*. New York: William Morrow and Co.

Mueller, Dennis C. 1979. *Public Choice*. New York: Cambridge University Press.

Noam, Eli M., 1985. Local Regulator's Rewards for Conformity in Regulation. *Public Choice* 45(3): 291–302.

Owen, Bruce M. 1975. *Economics and Freedom of Expression: Media Structure and the First Amendment*. Cambridge, MA: Ballinger Publishing Co.

Poltrack, David F. 1983. *Television Marketing, Network/Local/Cable*. New York: McGraw-Hill.

Rothenberg, J. 1963. Consumer Sovereignty and the Economics of Television Programming. *Studies in Public Communication* 4:45–54.

Spence, Michael A., and Bruce M. Owen. 1977. Television Programming: Monopolistic Competition and Welfare. *Quarterly Journal of Economics* 91:103–126.

Steiner, Peter O. 1952. Program Patterns and Preferences, and the Workability of Competition in Radio Broadcasting. *Quarterly Journal of Economics* 66:194–223.

Wildman, Steven S., and Bruce M. Owen. Program Competition, Diversity, and Multi-Channel Bundling in the New Video Industry. In *Video Media Competition*, ed. Eli Noam. New York: Columbia University Press. pp. 221–243.

Wiles, P. 1963. Pilkington and the Theory of Value. *Economic Journal* 73:183–200.

Chapter 5

Baumol, William J., and Ward G. Bowen. 1966. *Performing Arts: The Economic Dilemma*. New York: Twentieth Century Fund.

The Bowker Annual Library and Book Trade Alamnac, 34th ed. 1989–1990. New York: Bowker.

Briggs, Asa. 1961. *History of Broadcasting in the United Kingdom*. London: Oxford.

Doebler, Paul D. 1981. The Book Industry, 1981: From "Business as Usual" to ???— The Convergence of Small Publishers, Expanding Retailers and Technologies. In *Book of Industry Trends 1981*, ed. John P. Dessauer. Book Industry Study Group.

Ehresman, Julia, ed. 1984. *Bowker Annual of Library & Book*, 29th ed. *Trade Information*. New York: Bowker.

Eisenberg, A. L. 1936. *Children and Radio Programs*. New York: Columbia University Press.

Eisenstein, Elizabeth. 1968. Some Conjectures About the Impact of Printing on Western Society and Thought: A Preliminary Report. *Journal of Modern History* 40(March):1–56.

Encyclopedia Britannica. 1986. History of Education. Chicago: University of Chicago Press, vol. 18.

Guback, Thomas H. 1982. Die Neuen Medien und die Zukunft der Filmtheater in den USA. *Media Perspektiven*. pp. 166–175. March.

Media Perspektiven. 1981. June, p. 494.

———. 1983. September, p. 653.

Moore, Thomas G. 1968. *The Economics of the American Theater*. Durham, NC: Duke University Press.

Motion Picture Association of America. 1990. *1990 U. S. Economic Review*.

Noble, J. Kendrick, Jr. 1982. Book Publishing. In *Who Owns the Media?*, Benjamin M. Compaine, et. al. White Plains, NY: Knowledge Industry Publications, Inc. pp. 95–141.

Noelle-Neumann, Elisabeth. 1973. Return to the Concept of Powerful Mass Media. *Studies in Broadcasting* 9:67–112.

Paine Webber Mitchell Hutchins, Inc. 1982. Cited in *Book Publishing*, J. Kendrick Noble, Jr. In *Who Owns the Media?*, Benjamin M. Compaine, et al. White Plains, NY: Knowledge Industry, pp. 95–141.

Plog, Jobst. 1987. Film und Fernsehen Zwischen Konkurrenz, Komplementarität und Kooperation. In *Rundfunk und Fernsehen*, 35(3):361–372.

Poggi, Jack. 1968. *Theater in America*. Ithaca, NY: Cornell University Press.

Pool, Ithiel de Sola, Hiroshi Inose, Nozomu Takasaki, and Roger Hurwitz. 1984. *Communications Flows: A Census in the United States and Japan*. North-Holland University of Tokyo Press.

Renz, Marianne, and Werner Taubert. 1983. Die Deutsche Filmwirtschaft in Spiegel der Amtlichen Film-Statistik. *Media Perspektiven*, September, p. 615.

Sterling, Christopher H., and Timothy R. Haight. 1978. *The Mass Media: Aspen Institute Guide to Communications Industry Trends*. New York: Praeger.

Waterman, David. 1985. Prerecorded Home Video and the Distribution of Theatrical Feature Films. In *Video Media Competition*. New York: Columbia University Press, pp. 221–243.

Chapter 6

Ahrens, Wilfried. 1989. No More Free Lunch. *Television Business International*, September, p. 12.

———. 1990. Racing for Partners in the Other Germany. *Television Broadcasting International*, February, pp. 4–5.

———. 1990. The Vision of Leo Kirch, Internationalist. *Television Business International*, May, pp. 80–86.

Bachof, O., R. Breuer, H. Ehmke, J. A. Frowein, W. Grewe, and P. Haberle. 1983. *Archiv des Öffentlichten Rechts*. Tübingen: J. C. B. Mohr. July.

Barsig, Franz. 1981. *Die Öffentlich-Rechtliche Illusion*. Cologne: Deutscher Institut Verlag.

Bausch, Hans. 1980. Rundfunk in Deutschland (Baud 3). Munich: Deutscher Taschenbuch Verlag GmbH.

Behrmann, Hannes. 1990. Mit Brüchen: Wie Weiter im DDR-Rundfunk?. *Kirche und Rundfunk*. Nr.40, May 23.

Bullinger, Martin. 1980. *Kommkunikationsfreiheit im Strukturwandel der Telekommunikation*. Baden-Baden: Nomos-Verlagsgesellschaft.

———. 1986. *Rundfunkfinanzierung im Ausland: Rechtliche Aspekte*. Baden-Baden: Nomos-Verlagsgesellschaft.

———. 1987. *Koordination im Öffentlich-rechtlischen Rundfunk*. Mainz: Zweites Deutsches Fernsehen.

BVerfGE. 1961. Judgement of February 22. 12 BVerfGE 205 (1962).

————. 1971. Judgement of July 27. 31 BVerfGE 314 (1972).

Das Bild. 1990. Mehr Werburg in ARD and ZDF? *Eastern Europe: Please Stand By*, Washington:GPO, p. 1.

Diller, Ansgar. 1980. *Rundfunkpolitik im Dritten Reich*. Munich: Deutscher Taschenbuch Verlag.

DTV. 1980. *Rundfunkpolitik: Nach 1945*, vols. 3, 4. Munich.

Engler, Jörg. 1990. Das Rundfunksystem der Bundespublic Deutschlands. In *Internationales Handbuch für Rundfunk und Fernsehen*, Hans-Bredow-Institut. Hamburg and Baden-Baden: Nomos, pp. A56–A91.

Expertenkommission Neue Medien Baden-Württemberg. 1981. *Abschlussbericht III. Kommunikationsatlas: Medien in Baden-Württemberg*. Stuttgart: Kohlhammer.

Fuchs, Gerhard. 1986. Die Geschichtliche Entwicklung des Rundfunks (Hörfunks) in der Deutschen Demokratischen Republik. In *Internationales Handbuch für Rundfunk und Fernsehen*, Hans-Bredow-Institut. Baden-Baden: Nomos, pp. B113–B116.

GDR: New Media Policy Issues. 1990. *Intermedia* 18:(3)7–8. 222 [?]

Gerber, Volker. 1990. Das Rundfunksystem der Deutschen Demokratischen Republik, In *Internationales Handbuch für Rundfunk und Fernsehen*, Hans-Bredow-Institut. Baden-Baden: Nomos, pp. A92–A107.

Glenn, Adam. 1990. German Pay TV Merger Improves Remaining Service's Survival Odds. *Broadcasting Abroad*, April, p. 4.

Glotz, Peter. 1983. Unpublished position paper.

Grosser, Alfred. 1979. From Democratic Showcase to Party Domination. In *Television and Political Life*, ed. Anthony Smith. London: Macmillan, pp. 114–141.

Hans-Bredow-Institut für Rundfunk und Fernsehen. 1990. In *Internationales Handbuch für Rundfunk und Fernsehen*. Baden-Baden and Hamburg: Nomos.

Hoffmann-Riem, Wolfgang and Christian Starck. 1987. *Das Niedersächsische Rundfunkgesetz vor dem Bundesverfassungsgericht*. Baden-Baden: Nomos.

Hoffman-Riem, Wolfgang. 1975. Medienwirkung und Medienverantwortung. Baden-Baden.

————. 1984a. Policy Research in West Germany. In Vincent Mosco, ed., *Policy Research in Telecommunications*. Norwood, NJ: Ablex.

————, ed. 1984. Tendenzen der Kommerzialisierung in Rundfundsystem. In *Internationales Handbuch für Runkfunk und Fernsehen*, Hans-Bredow-Institut. Hamburg, Baden-Baden: Nomos. pp. 32-50.

————, ed. 1987. *Medienplatz Hamburg: Projekt*. Baden-Baden: Nomos. vols. 1–6.

————, ed. 1988. Rundfunk im Wettbewerbsrecht; der öffentlich-rechtliche Rundfunk im Spannungsfeld zwischen Wirtschaftrecht und Rundfunkrecht. In *Medienwissenschaftliches Symposium: Dokumentation*. Hamburg: Hans-Bredow-Institut.

————. 1990. New media in West Germany: the politics of legitimation. In *The Political Economy of Communications: International and European Dimensions*, ed. Kenneth Dyson and Peter Humphreys. London: Routledge.

———— and Dieter Ross, eds. 1979. Strukturfragen des Rundfunks in Geschichte und Gegenwart. In *Medienwissenschaftliches Symposium: Dokumentation*. Hamburg: Hans-Bredow-Institut.

———— and Will Teichert. 1980. Aktuelle Fragen der Rundfunkpolitik: Entwicklung in der Bundesrepublik—Erfahrungen im Ausland. In *Medienwissenschaftliches Symposium: Dokumentation*. Hamburg: Hans-Bredow-Institut.

Kaiser, Wolfgang, Hans Marko, and Eberhard Witte. 1979. *Two Way Television*. Berlin: Springer-Verlag.

Kleinsteuber, Hans J. 1980. *Rundfunkpolitik: Medienpolitische Aspekte von Hörfunk und Fernsehen.* Hamburg: Landeszentrale für Politische Bildung.

————, Denis McQuail, and Karen Siune, eds. 1986. *Electronic Media and Politics in Western Europe.* Frankfurt and New York: Campus Verlag.

Kleinwächter, Wolfgang. Rundfunkwerbung in der DDR.

KtK (Commission for Development of Telecommunications Systems). 1976. *Telecommunications Report.* Bonn: Federal Ministry of Posts and Telecommunications.

Lange, Bernd-Peter. 1980. *Kommerzielle Ziele und binnenpluralistische Organisation bei Rundfunkveranstaltern: Eine Untersuchung aus wirtschaftswissenschaftlischer und kommunikationstheoretischer Sicht.* Frankfurt: Metzner.

———— and Ulrich Patzold. 1984. *Medienatlas Nordrhein-Westfalen: Grundlagen der Kommunikation.* Bochum: Schurmann & Klages.

Lerg, Winfried B. 1980. *Rundfunkpolitik in der Weimarer Republik.* Munich: Deutscher Taschenbuch Verlag.

Logica Consultancy, Ltd. 1987. *Television Broadcasting in Europe: Toward the 1990s.* London, p. 61.

Media Perspektiven. 1990. April, pp. 211–218.

Mestmäcker, Ernst-Joachim. 1978. *Medienkonzentration und Meinungsvielfalt.* Baden-Baden: Nomos.

————. 1985a. The Impact of Deregulation Trade in Services Agreements on Telecommunications Monopolies in Europe. In *Special Session of the World Telecommunication Forum: Law, Regulation, Standards of Global Communications.* Washington D.C.: International Telecommunication Union.

————. 1985b. The Influence of Political and Legal Conditions on the Development of the Media—an International Overview. In *Medientrends.* Hamburg: Intermedia Congress. pp. 124-135.

————. 1987. *The Law and Economics of Transborder Telecommunication.* Baden-Baden: Nomos.

Monopolkommission. 1981. *Die Rolle der Deutschen Bundespost im Fernmeldewesen.* Baden-Baden: Nomos.

Noam, Eli. 1991. *Telecommunications in Europe.* New York: Oxford University Press.

Noelle-Neumann, Elisabeth. 1986. *Die Antwort der Zeitung auf das Fernsehen: Geschichte einer Herausforderung.* Konstanz: Universitatsverlag.

Paulu, Burton. 1974. *Radio and Television Broadcasting in Eastern Europe.* Minneapolis: University of Minnesota Press.

Pestalozza. 1981. Der Schutz vor der Rundfunkfreiheit in der Bundesrepublik Deutschland. *Neue Juristische Wochenschrift.* 2158 pp.

Plog, Jobst. 1987. Film und Fersehen zwischen Konkurrenz, Komplementarität und Kooperation. In *Rundfunk und Fernsehen.* 35(3):361–72.

Protzman, Ferdinand. 1989. An Imposing Rival for Would-Be Time-Warner. *New York Times,* April 3, sec. 4, p. 8.

Ratzke, Dietrich. 1982. *Handbuch der Neuen Medien.* Stuttgart: Deutsche Verlagsanstalt.

Roß, Dieter. 1986. Der Rundfunk in Deutschland: Entwicklungen-Strukturen-Probleme. In *Internationales Handbuch für Rundfunk und Fernsehen,* Hans-Bredow-Institut. Hamburg and Baden-Baden: Nomos, pp. B56–B66.

Scherer, Joachim. 1985. Fernmeldepolitik als Medienpolitik. *Media Perspektiven,* March, p. 166.

Siemens, Georg. 1957. *Geschichte des Hauses Siemens*. Grieburg and Munich: Karl Alber.

Task Force on Telecommunications and Broadcasting in Eastern Europe. 1990. *Please Stand By*, U.S. Department of State. Advisory Committee on International Communication. Spring.

Tonnemacher, Jan. 1987. Telecommunications and the Mass Media in West Germany. VDI/VDE Technologiezentrum Informationstechnik GmbH.

Tracey, Michael, 1982. *Das Unerreichbare Wunschbild: ein Versuch über Hugh Greene und die Neugründung des Rundfunks in Westdeutschland nach 1945*. Cologne: Kohlhammer.

Witte,Eberhard, ed. 1980. *Human Aspects of Telecommunication*. Berlin: Springer-Verlag.

———. 1982. *Ziele deutscher Medienpolitik*. Munich: Oldenbourg.

Witte, Eberhard, 1984. *Neue Fernsehnetze im Medienmarkt: Die Amortisationsfähigkeit von Breitbandverteilsystems*. Heidelberg: Decker. vol. 130S.

Witteman, Christopher. 1983. West German Television Law: An Argument for Media as Instrument of Self Government. *The Hastings International and Comparative Law Review* 7(1):145, 210.

Woldt, Runar. 1989. The Growth of Cable TV. *Media Bulletin*, March, p. 7.

Chapter 7

Beck, Kirsten. 1985. A New French Lesson. *Cable Television Business,* March 15, p. 60.

Bertho, Catherine, et al., eds. 1984. *Histoire des Télécommunications en France*. Toulouse: Editions Eres.

Braillaird, Peter. 1988. Cable TV in France. *Intermedia* 16(3):22.

Bredin, Jean-Denis. 1985. *Actualite des Techniques de Communication dans le Monde*. Rapport Bredin—Oui à la télévision privée, mais dans l'ordre et dans la coherence. Paris: La Documentation Française. June, pp. 1–5.

Cayrol, R. 1977. Á la Recherche des Journalistes de Radio-Télévision. *Etudes de Radio-Télévision*, No. 24. November. As quoted in Kuhn, p. 438.

Dutton, William, Jay G. Blumler, and Kenneth L. Kraemer, eds. 1987. *Wired Cities: Shaping the Future of Communications*. Boston: Hall.

EBU. 1989. EBU Review Vol. XL, No. 5, May, p. 27.

EBU. 1990. EBU Review Vol. XLI, No. 2, March, pp. 31–38.

Epstein, Marc. 1988. Disaster Area Picks Itself Up. *Television Business International*, July–August, p. 42–43.

———. 1989. Canal Plus Builds a European Network. *Television Business International*, July–August, p. 8.

Kuhn, Raymond. 1980. *The Politics of Broadcasting in France, 1974–1978*. Ph.D. dissertation. University of Warwick, Department of Politics.

———. 1985a. France and the 'New Media.' *West European Politics*, 8(2):50–66.

———. 1985b. France: The End of the Government Monopoly. In *The Politics of Broadcasting*, ed. Raymond Kuhn. New York: St. Martin's, pp. 47–82.

L'Expansion. 1985. La Campagne de France du Micro-ordinateur, January 11–24, pp. 74–79.

Missika, Jean-Louis, and Dominique Wolton. 1983. *La Folle du Logis*. Paris: Gallimard.

Munich, Laurent. 1989. A Brand New Ruling Body for the French Audiovisual Industry. *Media Bulletin*, March.

Nora, Simon, and Alain Minc. 1978. *L'informatisation de la Société, Rapport à M. le Président de la République*. Paris: La Documentation Française.

Opitz, Gert. 1990. Das Rundfunksystem Frankreichs. *Internationales Handbuch für Rundfunk und Fernsehen*, Hans-Bredow-Institut, Baden-Baden and Hamburg: Nomos, pp. 42–72.

Rogers, Everett, and François Balle, eds. 1985. *The Media Revolution in America and Western Europe*. Norwood, NJ: Ablex.

Rozenblum, Serge-Allain. 1984a. Neue Fernsehangebote in Frankreich. *Media Perspektiven*. Teil 1. Canal Plus-ein neuer Fernsehkanal, February, pp. 123–131.

———. 1984b. Neue Fernsehangebote in Frankreich. Part 2. Die Verzögerungen in der Satellitenentwicklung. *Media Perspektiven*, October, pp. 743–748.

Siritzky, Serge. 1990. Canal Plus Plus Plus Plus. *Television Business International*, March, p. 56.

———, and Jay Stuart. 1990. France. *Television Business International*, April, pp. 23–31.

Television Business International (TBI). 1990. *World Guide '90*. New York: Act III, pp. 36–44.

Télécoms Magazine. 1990. Câble: Second Départ . . . No. 35. June.

Variety. 1988. Euro Air Hums with Commercial Radio. October 12.

Vedel, Thierry. 1987. Public Service Broadcasting in France: From Monopoly to Agony. In *Public Service Broadcasting in a Multichannel Environment*, ed. Robert K. Avery. New York: Longman.

———, and William H. Dutton. 1988. New Media Politics: Shaping Cable TV Policy in France. Center for Telecommunications and Information Studies, Working Paper Series No. 266. Columbia University.

Werth, A. 1967. *De Gaulle*. New York: Penguin p. 361.

Williams, Roger M. 1985. France: A Revolution in the Making. *Channels*, September–October, pp. 60–61.

Chapter 8

Ball, Adrian. 1984a. London Market to Focus on "Television Media." *Television/Radio Age*, September, pp. A1–A24.

———. 1984b. Sky Channel in Third. *Cable Age*, September 3, p. 42.

Biebl, Elmar and Dirk Manthey. 1985. Der Dschingis-Khan der Medien. *Neue Medien*, January, pp. 122–133.

Briggs, Asa. 1961. *The History of Broadcasting in the United Kingdom: The Birth of Broadcasting in the United Kingdom*, vol. I. London: Oxford University Press.

———. 1965. *The History of Broadcasting in the United Kingdom: The Golden Age of Wireless*, vol. II. London: Oxford University Press.

———. 1979a. *The History of Broadcasting in the United Kingdom Governing the BBC*, vol. III. London: Oxford University Press.

———. 1979b. *The History of Broadcasting in the United Kingdom: Sound & Vision*, vol. IV. London: Oxford University Press.

Brittan, Samuel. 1986. Birds-Eye View of Peacock. *Financial Times*, Weekend FT, July 5, p. 1.

Broadcasting. 1988. MSOs, Telcos Eyeing Europe, Asia. December 19, pp. 56–57.

Brooks, Richard. 1988. Cable TV Fails to Plug In. *Observer,* sec. 5, October 9, p. 21.

Brown, Maggie. 1988. Murdoch's Fox Is Just Ahead of the Hounds. *The Independent,* June 15.

Burns, Tom. 1977. *The BBC: Public Institution and Private World.* London: Macmillan.

Cable-Telco Report. 1991. UK Set to Ignite Unparalleled Level of Competition in Telecommunications, Much to US Players' Relief. January. p. 9.

Carter, Bill. 1989. The BBC Faces Up to Technology—and the Till. *New York Times,* December 17, p. 41.

Central Office of Information, British Information Services. 1981. Broadcasting in Britain. In *Broadcasting Around the World,* ed. William E. McCavitt. Blue Ridge Summitt, PA: Tab Books, pp. 232–263.

CSP International, for the Department of Trade and Industry. 1987. Deregulation of the Radio Spectrum in the UK. London: Her Majesty's Stationery Office.

Collier, Andrew. 1988. Competition Threatens British Commercial TV. *Multichannel News,* March 21, p. 23.

Communications Daily. 1990. New Turner Service to Widen Cable's International Reach. May 24, p. 5.

Curran, James, Michael Gurevitch, and Janet Woollacott, eds. 1977. *Mass Communication and Society.* London: The Open University Press.

Curran, James, and Jean Seaton. 1981. *Power without Responsibility.* London: Fontana.

Dornan, Chris. 1984. Fear and Longing in the United Kingdom: Cultural Custody and the Expansion of Cable Television. Working Paper in Communications. Montreal: McGill University Program in Communications.

Ducat, Vivian. 1986. Words from the Wise. *The Atlantic Monthly,* September, pp. 70–76.

Dyson, Kenneth, and Peter Humphreys. 1985. The New Media in Britain and in France: 2 Versions of Heroic Muddle? *Rundfunk und Fernsehen.* 33(3–4):362–379.

The Economist. 1985a. Byebye, Britain. August 10, p. 11.

———. 1985b. Invasion of the Little People. March 19, p. 61.

Edgar, Patricia, and Syed A. Rahin, eds. 1983. *Communication Policy in Developed Countries.* London: Kegan Paul International.

Emery, Walter B. 1969. *National and International Systems of Broadcasting.* East Lansing: Michigan State University Press.

Evans, Jane, Jill Hartley, Jonathan Simmett, Michael Gibbons, and Stan Metcalfe. 1983. The Development of Cable Networks in the UK: Issues in the Formulation of a Technology Policy. The Technical Change Centre, July.

Evans, Richard. 1988. Auctions for Radio Stations. *The Times,* January 20, p. 1.

Financial Times. 1990. TV Companies Under Starter's Orders. March 31.

Garnham, Nicholas. 1978. *Structures of Television.* London: British Film Institute.

Glenn, Adam. 1990a. British, U.S. Firms Steel for Cable-Telco Review. *Broadcasting,* September 24, p. 82.

———. 1990b. British Satellite Rivals Ready for Battles. *Broadcasting Abroad,* April, p. 7.

———. 1990c. Cable: UK Boom Is US's Gain. *Broadcasting Abroad,* April, pp. 4–5.

Hansard, Parliamentary Debates. 1922. vol. 156, col. 1226, July 12.

———. 1923. vol. 157, col. 1951, August 4.

Hearst, Stephen. 1982. Rundfunkforschung in Grossbritannien. *Media Perspektiven,* March, pp. 191–198.

Heyn, Juergen, and Hans-Jurgen Weiss. 1980. Das Fernsehprogramm von ITV und BBC. *Media Perspektiven,* March, pp. 135–150.

Hoggart, Richard, and J. Morgan, eds. 1982. *The Future of Broadcasting.* London: Macmillan.

Hollins, T. 1984. *Beyond Broadcasting: Into the Cable Age.* London: BFI.

Home Office, U.K. 1982. Report of the Inquiry into Cable Expansion and Broadcasting Policy. London: Her Majesty's Stationery Office.

———. 1988a. Broadcasting in the '90s: Competition, Choice, and Quality. London: Her Majesty's Stationery Office.

———. 1988b. Memorandum submitted by the Cable Authority. London: Her Majesty's Stationery Office, February 10.

Homet, Roland S., Jr. 1979. *Politics, Culture and Communications.* New York: Institute for Humanistic Studies.

IBA. 1983. Code of Advertising Standards and Practice.

Information Technology Advisory Panel (ITAP). 1982. *Report on Cable Systems.* London: Her Majesty's Stationery Office.

Kerver, Tom. 1986. Maxwell's Grand Plans. *Satellite Communications,* July, pp. 22–28.

Lee, Harvey. 1988a. Commercial TV's Sale of the Century. *Television Business International,* April.

———. 1988b. History Yields to Progress. *Television Business International,* May.

McGhee, Colin. 1984. BT Tel Co. Strategy for a New Era. *Cable & Satellite Europe,* February, pp. 41–44.

McKenzie, G. A. 1983. Teletext—The First Ten Years. *IBA Technical Review,* May, pp. 4–10.

Madge, Timothy. 1979. *Beyond the BBC: Broadcasters, Broadcasting, and the Public in the 1980's.* London: Macmillan.

Manchester, William. 1988. *The Last Lion. Winston Spencer Churchill . . . : Alone— 1932–1940;* vol 2. Boston: Little, Brown.

Multichannel News. 1985. Britain Gauges Interest in More Cable Franchises, January 21, p. 21.

Nadelson, Regina. 1984. The Best Television Company in the World. *Channels,* September/October, pp. 26–28.

Negrine, Ralph. 1990. British Television in an Age of Change. In the *Political Economy of Communications: International and European Dimensions,* eds. Kenneth Dyson and Peter Humphreys. London: Routledge.

Nossiter, T. J. 1986. British Television: A Mixed Economy. Unpublished report. Center for Television Research, University of Leeds, January.

O'Brian, John. 1980. A Study of the General Public's Perception of the BBC and Its Role. *Annual Review of BBC Broadcast Research Findings,* pp. 7–29.

Paulu, Burton. 1981. *Television and Radio in the United Kingdom.* Minneapolis: University of Minnesota Press.

Peitz, Gangolf. 1984. Student Radio. *Medium,* July/August, pp. 49–52.

Raines, Howell. 1988. In Tory Country, Someone to Watch Over TV. *New York Times,* June 10, sec. 1, p. 4.

Reith, J. C. W. 1924. *Broadcast Over Britain.* London: Hodder & Staughton.

———. 1975. *The Reith Diaries,* ed. Charles Stuart. London: Collins.

Report of the Broadcasting Committee. 1935. cnd. 5091, 1936.

Schubin, Mark. 1990. Television's Progress—A Global Process. In *World Guide '90,* TBI. New York: Act III Publishing, pp. 17–18.

Sendall, Bernard. 1982. *Independent Television in Britain,* vol. 1. London: Macmillan.
————. 1983. Communications Policy in the United Kingdom: A Culture Based on Makeshift Social Pluralism. In *Communication Policy in Developed Countries,* eds. Patricia Edgar and Syed A. Rahim. London: Kegan Paul International, in association with the East–West Center, Honolulu, pp. 57–93.
Smith, Anthony. 1973. *The Shadow in the Cave.* London: Unwin.
————. 1979. Britain: The Mystery of a Modus Vivendi. In *Television and Political Life,* ed. Anthony Smith. London: Macmillan, pp. 1–40.
Smith, Sally Bedell. 1983. Morning TV Is the Talk of Britain. *New York Times,* December 1, sec. 4, p. 4.
Snoddy, Raymond. 1990. US Investors Show Interest. *Financial Times Survey: International Satellite Broadcasting,* May 29, p. 6.
Taylor, Dorreen. 1987. Scottish Broadcasting, a Sense of Identity. *Intermedia* 15(4/5):72–75.
Television Business International (TBI). 1990. *World Guide '90.* New York: Act III Publishing, pp. 89–102.
Tracey, Michael. 1978. *The Production of Political Television.* London: Routledge and Kegan Paul.
————. 1991. *The Throne We Honor: Essays on Public Service Broadcasting.* London: Sage.
Tunstall, Jeremy. 1986. Great Britain. In *Electronic Media and Politics in Europe,* eds. Hans J. Kleinsteuber, et al. Frankfurt: Campus Verlag, pp. 110–134.
U.K. Department of Trade and Industry and Home Office (DTI). 1983. *White Paper.* London: Her Majesty's Stationery Office.
————. 1991. Competition and Choice: Telecommunications Policy for the 1990s. Cm 1461, London: HMSO.
Veljanovski, Cento. 1984. Regulatory Options for Cable TV in the UK. *Telecommunications Policy,* December, pp. 290–306.
Wedell, E. G. 1968. *Broadcasting and Public Policy.* London: Michael Joseph.
Wilson, H. H. 1961. *Pressure Group: The Campaign for Commercial Television in England.* New Brunswick, N.J.: Rutgers University Press.

Chapter 9

Broadcasting Abroad. 1990. Italy's Reteitalia Plugs Europe-based Co-production. June, p. 6.
Cavazza, Fabio Luca. 1979. Italy: From Party Occupation to Party Partition. In *Television and Political Life: Started in Six European Countries,* ed. Anthony Smith. London: Macmillan, pp. 76–113.
Cohen, Roger. 1990. The Ethics of Cross Ownership. *Gannett Center Journal,* Spring.
Faenza, Roberto. 1977. *The Radio Phenomenon in Italy.* Strasbourg: Council for Cultural Corporation, Council of Europe.
Grandi, Roberto. 1978. Western European Broadcasting Transition. *Journal of Communication,* 28, Summer. p. 75–78
————, and Giuseppe Richeri. *Le televisioni in Europa.* Milan: Feltrinelli.
Grizaffi, Giuseppe. 1983. Privatfernsehen in Italien. In *Rundfunk und Fernsehen,* pp. 42–50, 397.
Grossi, Giorgio. 1984. *La RAI sotto analisi.* Torino. ERI.

Johnston, Bruce. 1990a. RAI's Leash Grows Shorter. *Television Business International*, April, p. 10.

————. 1990b. RAI's Day of Reckoning. *Television Business International*, July/August.

————, Glauco Benigni, and Luca Fabbri. 1989. How RAI Won Its Fight for Survival. *Television Business International*, October, pp. 58–66.

Mazzoleni, Gianpietro. 1990. Das Rundfunk System Italiens. *Internationales Handbuch für Rundfunk und Fernsehen 1990/1*, Hans-Bredow-Institut. Hamburg and Baden-Baden: Nomos, pp. 111–123.

Media Perspektiven. 1984. November, pp. 855–864.

Ministry of Post and Telecommunications (MPT). 1985. Draft of 1985 Broadcasting Bill.

Monteleone, Franco. 1979. *Storia della RAI dagli alleati alla DC, 1944–1954*. Bari: Laterza.

Papa, Antonio. 1978. *Storia politica della radio in Italia*. 2 vols. Roma: Guida.

Radke & Dilaurenzo. 1985. Silvio Berlusconi bricht Sein Schweigen. *Neue Median*, July, pp. 126–29.

Rauen, Birgid. 1980. Italienischer Privatfunk: Vom Wellensalat Zum Wohlgeordneten Geschäft. *Media Perspectiven*, June, pp. 385–394.

Riding, Alan. 1989. Why Vatican's Voice Sometimes Bites Its Tongue. *New York Times*, September 21, sec. 1, p. 4.

Sasson, Donald. 1985. Political and Market Forces in Italian Broadcasting. *West European Politics* 8(2):67–83.

Silj, Alessandro. 1981. Italy's First Few Years of Private Television Broadcasting. *Intermedia* 9(5):12–25.

Stuart, Jay. 1988. The Emperor Comes Home. *Television Business International*, May, pp. 50–97.

Television Business International (TBI). 1990. *World Guide '90*. New York: Act III Publishing. pp. 62–65.

Variety. 1986. October 15, p. 146.

Chapter 10

Bos, Harrie, and Kees van der Haak. 1982. Der Rundfunk in den Nierderlanden. In *Internationales Handbuch für Rundfunk und Fernsehen*, Hans-Bredow-Institut. Hamburg and Baden-Baden: Nomos, pp. E48–E57.

————, and Bon van Reenen. 1990. Der Rundfunk in den Niederlanden. In *Internationales Handbuch für Rundfunk und Fernsehen*, Hans-Bredow-Institut. Hamburg and Baden-Baden: Nomos, pp. D142–D159.

Brants, Kees. 1985. Broadcasting and Politics in the Netherlands: From Pillar to Post. *Western European Politics*, 8(2):104–121.

————, and Nick Jankowski. 1985. *Cable Television in the Low Countries*. In *Cable Television and the Future of Broadcast*, ed. Ralph N. Negrine. London and Sydney: Croom Helm, pp. 74–103.

Diller, Ansgar. 1980. *Rundfunkpolitik im Dritten Reich*. Munich.

Haverman, Ferry. 1984. Dichter ist Kein Netz der Welt. *Neue Medien*, June, pp. 242–245.

Hins, Wouter, and Bernt Hugenholtz. 1988. *The Law and Economics of Transborder*

Telecommunications: Part III: Radio and Television. Hamburg and Baden-Baden: Nomos, Max Planck Institut.

Jehoram, Herman Cohen. 1982. The Unique Dutch Broadcasting on the Eve of the Revolution in Teletechnics and the Freedom of Information. In *Netherlands Report of the Eleventh Congress of Comparative Law,* Caracas. Deventur: Kluwer.

Logica Consultancy, Ltd. 1987. *Television Broadcasting in Europe: Toward the 1990's.* London.

Nuyl, Piette. 1984. Sowing the Seeds for the Pay-TV. *Intermedia,* January, pp. 9–11.

Television Business International (TBI). 1990. *World Guide '90.* New York: Act III Publishing, p. 71.

Van den Heuvel, and Hans H. J. 1981. Broadcasting in the Netherlands. In *Broadcasting in the World,* ed. William E. McCavitt. Blue Ridge Summit, PA.: Tab Books, pp. 287–298.

Variety. 1988. Quaint Dutch Broadcast System Bound to Change—But When? October 12, p. 162.

Versteeg, Dick, and Jay Stuart. 1989. Special Report: Holland. *Television Business International.* July/August, pp. 30–34.

Wigbold, Herman. 1979. Holland: The Shaky Pillars of Hilversum. In *Television and Political Life,* ed. Anthony Smith. London: Macmillan, pp. 191–231.

Chapter 11

Apeldoorn, Robert van. 1985. Les Télévisions Locales et Communautaires. Courrier Hebdomadaire, Centre de Recherche et d'Information Socio-Politiques. April 12.

BFT Studiendienst. 1980. *The Influence of Cable Television on BRT Flemish TV Viewing Figures.* Brussels: BFT.

Clausse, Roger. 1941. *La Radio Huitième Act.* Brussels.

Emery, Walter B. 1969. *National and International Systems of Broadcasting.* East Lansing: Michigan State University Press.

Epstein, Marc. 1989. Canal Plus Builds a European Network. *Television Business International,* July/August, p. 8.

Fauconnier, G. 1983. Serving Two Cultures: Local media in Belgium. *World Communications, A Handbook,* eds. G. Gerbner, and M. Sierfert. New York: Longmans.

Geerts, Claude. 1982. Der Lokale Hoerfunk in Belgien. *Media Perspektiven,* March, pp. 178–183.

Govaert, Serge, and Evelyne Lentzen. 1986. Les Médias en Flandre (2). Courrier Hebdomadaire, Centre de Recherche et d'Information Socio-Politiques. January 31.

Hirsch, Mario. 1985. Gespann der Giganten. *Neue Medien* 8:118–122.

———. 1986; 1990. Das Rundfunksystem Belgiens. In *Internationales Handbuch für Rundfunk und Fernsehen 1986/87; 1990/91,* Hans-Bredow-Institut. Hamburg and Baden-Baden: Nomos, pp. E2–E5, 13–17.

Lange, Andre. 1987. Belgium: The Silent Deregulation. Unpublished paper. University of Liège.

Matthias, Glyndwr. 1989. CLT: Facing the Big Chill of Change. *Television Business International,* June, p. 24.

Media Monitor. 1990a. Canal Plus Launches First Foreign Venture. September 27.

———. 1990b. Flemish to Challenge EC. May 31.

———. 1990c. Very Treasured Market. April 6.

Poesmans, Daniel. 1984. Television Viewing in Flanders. Unpublished paper.

VerLommen, Raymond. 1980. Le Statut de la Radiodiffusion en Belgique Historique et Evolution. *Etudes de Radio-Télévision* 27:29–44.

Chapter 12

Dyson, Kenneth. 1990. Luxembourg: changing anatomy of an international broadcasting power. In *The Political Economy of Communications: International and European Dimensions,* eds. Kenneth Dyson and Peter Humphreys. London: Routledge.

Hirsch, Mario. 1985. CLT/RLT: Schwierige Zeiten für Wegbereiter des Kommerzfunks. *Rundfunk und Fernsehen* 33(3–4):513–524.

Odenwald, Andreas. 1985. Die Goldfinger aus Luetzelburg. *Neue Medien,* May, pp. 14–27.

Opitz, Gert. 1986; 1990. Das Rundfunksystem Luxemburgs. In *Internationales Handbuch für Rundfunk und Fernsehen 1986/87; 1990/91,* Hans-Bredow-Institut. Hamburg and Baden-Baden: Nomos, pp. E76–E81, D132–D144.

Schmidt, Hendrik. 1985. Parforce-Ritt der fröhlichen Wellenreiter. *Neue Medien,* July, pp. 70–72.

Chapter 13

Alter, Urs. 1985. Ein verunsichertes System kampft ums Überleben. *Rundfunk und Fernsehen* 33(3–4):494–500.

EBU Review. 1989. 40(4):14.

Expert Commission for a Comprehensive Media Concept (ECCMC). 1982. *Medien-Gesamt-Konzeption.* Berne: Swiss Federal Department of Justice and Police.

Frischknecht, Jürg. 1981. Die SRG und die Lage der Nation. In *Eine Deformierte Gesellschaft,* eds. Michael Haller, Max Jauggi, and Roger Müller. Basel: Lenas Verlag Basel, p. 462.

Haldimann, Ueli. 1984. Kommerzialisierung mit Bremsversuchen. *Medium,* July/August, pp. 18–23.

Halter-Schmid, Ruth. 1980. *Schweizerisches Radio, 1939–1945: Die Organisation des Radiokommunikators durch Bundesrat und Armee. Ein Beitrag zur Mediengeschichte.* Berne: Communicatio Publica 8.

Hoepli, Goettlieb F. 1984. Die Helvetischen Kabelprofis. *Neue Medien,* June 9, pp. 248–249.

Jaques, Robert. 1987. Swiss TV: One Parent Feeds Three Siblings, Each With Own Lingo. *Variety,* April 15, p. 83.

Noam, Eli. 1980. The Efficiency of Direct Democracy. *Journal of Political Economy* 88(4):803–810.

Odenwald, Andreas. 1985. Zwei Mann in einem Boot? *Neue Medien,* July, pp. 105–115.

Pünter, Otto. 1971. *Schweizerische Radio—und Fernsehgesellschaft 1931–1970.* Berne.

Saxer, Ulrich. 1986; 1990. Das Rundfunksystem der Schweiz. *Internationales Handbuch für Rundfunk und Fernsehen, 1986/7; 1990/91,* Hans Bredow Institut. Hamburg and Baden-Baden: Nomos, pp. E147–E154, D204–D210.

Schürmann, Leo. 1985. *Medienrecht.* Bern.

SRG Medienstudie. 1986. *DRS Global Radiostudie*. Geneva: SRG, p. A85.
Television Business International (TBI). 1990. *World Guide '90*. New York: Act III Publishing, pp. 87–88.

Chapter 14

Ahrens, Wilfried. 1989. Can ORF Cling On? *Television Business International*, October, p. 26.
Bauer, Johannes M., and Michael Latzer. 1987. Symposium on Economic & Financial Issues of Telecommunications. Part 4: The Role of Telecommunications in the Infrastructure and Its Impact on Economic Growth. *World Telecommunication Forum*. Geneva: ITU, pp. 37–41.
Fabris, Hans Heinz, Kurt Luger, and Benno Signitzer. 1982; 1990. Das Rundfunksystem Österreichs. In *Internationales Handbuch für Rundfunk und Fernsehen 1982/ 83; 1990/91*, Hans-Bredow-Institut. Hamburg and Baden-Baden: Nomos, pp. E61–E65, D168–D179.
Luger, Kurt. 1983. Die Zukunft der Massenmedien in Österreich. *Rundfunk und Fersehen*, pp. 143–158.
Nidetzky, Peter. 1981. Videotext in Öesterreich. *Media Perspektiven*, July, pp. 584–588.
Signitzer, Benno, and Kurt Luger. 1984. *Socio-economic Aspects of National Communication Systems: Radio Broadcasting in Austria*. Paris: Unesco.
Television Business International (TBI). 1990. *World Guide '90*. New York: Act III Publishing. p. 26.
Wolf, Franz Ferdinand. 1985. Mit Feinkost gegen McDonald's. *Neue Medien* 15(4):111–116.
———. 1984. Alp-Druck fuer die Zwangslizenz. *Neue Medien*, January, pp. 245–248.

Chapter 15

Ahlen, Henrik. 1984. Scandinavia's Year of Change. *Cable and Satellite Europe*, February, pp. 10–12.
Aronsson, L. O. 1983. *Towards Wide Band Communications*. Stockholm: Swedish Telecommunications Administration.
Browne, Donald R. 1984. Alternatives for Local and Regional Radio: Three Nordic Solutions. *Journal of Communication* 31(2):36–55.
Engelhart, Beila. 1988. Local Television Services in Scandinavia and Finland. Stockholm: Swedish Broadcasting Corporation.
Gustafsson, Karl Erik. 1982. Die Diskussion um die Einführung von Werbung im schwedischen Fernsehen. *Media Perspektiven*, December, pp. 750–755.
Hedebro, Goran. 1983. Communications Policy in Sweden: An Experiment in State Intervention. In *Communications Policy in Developed Countries*, eds. Patricia Edgar and Syed A. Rahin. London: Kegan Paul International, pp. 137–156.
Hultén, Olof. 1984. Sweden Preparing Legislation for Cable. *Intermedia* 12(6):8–9.
———. 1986; 1990. Die Elektronischen Medien in Schweden. In *Internationales Handbuch für Rundfunk und Fernsehen, 1986/87; 1990/91*, Hans-Bredow-Institut. Hamburg and Baden-Baden: Nomos, pp. E139, D194–D201.

————. 1988. Citizen's Community Radio: Public Access in Sweden. Unpublished paper, pp. 10–17.

Nicholson, Paul. 1990. The Pay-TV Wars. *Television Business International (TBI)*. June, p. 24.

Ortmark, Ake. 1979. Sweden: Freedom's Boundaries. In *Television and Political Life*, ed. Anthony Smith. London: Macmillan, pp. 142–190.

Ploman, Edward W. 1976. *Broadcasting in Sweden*. London: Routledge and Kegan Paul.

Soderstrom, Herbert. 1981. Broadcasting in Sweden. In *Broadcasting Around the World*, ed. William E. McCavitt. Blue Summit Ridge, P.: Tab Books, pp. 299–312.

Svärd, Stig. 1982. Sweden Regulates its Media Mix. *Intermedia* 10(2):29–31.

————. 1990. Sweden. *Intermedia* 18:4–5.

Sveriges Radio. 1985. Audience and Programme Research. Stockholm. October, p. 4.

Swedish Telecom. 1983. *Annual Report*. Farsta: Swedish Telecom Printing Office.

Television Business International (TBI). 1990. *World Guide '90*. New York: Act III Publishing, pp. 84–86.

Wachtmeister, Anne-Margrete. 1990. State Channels Meet the Satellite Challenge. *Television Business International (TBI)*. New York: Act III Publishing, June, p. 28.

Chapter 16

Browne, Donald R. 1984. Alternatives of Local and Regional Radio: Three Nordic Solutions. *Journal of Communication*, Spring, pp. 36–55.

Bruce, Robert R., Jeffrey P. Cunard, and Mark D. Director. 1985. *From Telecommunications to Electronic Services: Global Spectrum of Definitions, Boundary Lines, and Structures*. Washington, D.C.: Butterworths, p. 32.

Castren, Jouko. 1987. Cable Television Act. *Teletiedotuksia*, Finnish P&T, p. 28.

Erholm, Erja, and Matti Oksanen. 1982. Television News in Finland: Competitive Viewing, Affect, Cognition and Effect. Presented to Mass Communication Division at the 32nd Annual Conference of the International Communication Association. May.

Finnish Local Radio Association. 1987. Private Local Radio Operations in Finland.

Hannuksela, Jaakko. 1987. Cable TV in the West and the Case of Finland. Working Paper Series. Center for Telecommunications and Information Studies, Graduate School of Business, Columbia University.

Howkins, John. 1982. Communications in Finland. *Intermedia* 10(4/5):53–55.

Humphreys, Patrick. 1990. The Shift is on in Finland. *Television Business International (TBI)*, June, pp. 36–40.

Kalkkinen, Marja-Leena. 1984. The Spread of Electronic Entertainment Equipment in Finnish Households. Working Paper Series. Helsinki: YLE Planning and Research Department. No. 28.

Mäkinen, Helena. 1984. Electronic Media Policy in Finland. Unpublished report. Annenberg School of Communications, University of Southern California, p. 23.

————. 1990. The Finnish Broadcasting System. *Internationales Handbuch für Kundfunk und Fernsehen*, Hans-Bredow-Institut. Hamburg and Baden-Baden: Nomos, pp. D35–D41.

MTV. 1985. *Annual Report*. Helsinki: MTV, No. 11.

Nordenstreng, K., ed. 1969. *Mass Communications and the Public*. Tapiola: Weilin & Goos.

Oksanen, Matti. 1985. Finnish Media Utilization. Unpublished report. Helsinki: YLE Research Department.

———. 1986. *Finnish Media Utilization*. Helsinki: YLE.

Paavela, Jaateko, and Jorma Miettinen. 1990. Finnish TV System to Be Reorganized by 1993. Helsinki: MTV.

Paldan, Leena. 1985. When the Radio Was Liberated—In the Finnish Style: Reflections on the Local Radio Stations. III Nordic Conference of Mass Communication Research. Fuglso, Denmark: August 18–21.

Parliamentary Committee Report. 1984. Seven Proposals for the Organization of the Finnish Broadcasting Company. Helsinki.

Sarkkinen, Raija. 1985. Structure of Television Programming in Finland. Helsinki: YLE.

Soramäki, Martti. 1984. Proposals for Reorganization of Broadcasting in Finland. Unpublished report for YLE Research Department, Helsinki. May.

———. 1990. Finland. *Intermedia* 18:4–5.

———, and Marina Osterlund. 1983. New Communications Technology and Its Regulation in Finland. Paper presented at the International Seminar on the Development of the New Media. Copenhagen, Denmark, December 10, pp. 1–11.

Varis, Tapio. 1970. Offensiveness in YLE Programmes. Studies of the Department of Planning and Research, YLE, Helsinki.

Wilo, Osmo A. 1980. *Principles of Communication*. Espoo: Weilin & Goos.

YLE Research Department. 1985. YLE, MTV and Nokia: Joint Project for a Third Finnish TV-Channel. Unpublished report. Helsinki.

———. 1986. Helsinki Television (HTV). Unpublished report. Helsinki. July 1.

Chapter 17

Browne, Donald R. 1984. Alternatives for Local and Regional Radio: Three Nordic Solutions. *Journal of Communication*, Spring, pp. 36–55.

Emery, Walter. 1969. *National and International Systems of Broadcasting*. East Lansing: Michigan State University.

Engelhart, Beila. 1988. Local Television Services in Scandinavia and Finland. Stockholm: Swedish Broadcasting Corporation.

Logica Consultancy, Ltd. 1987. *Television Broadcasting in Europe: Toward the 1990s*. London: Logica Consultancy, Ltd., pp. 414–415.

Nicholson, Paul. 1990. Norway Draws up Its TV Blueprint. *Television Business International (TBI)*, June, pp. 30–32.

Nyheim, Jan Henrik. 1984. Norwegian Broadcasting and Telecommunications. *The Norseman* 5:39–41.

Roloff, Eckart Klaus. 1986. Rundfunkpolitik in Norwegen: Aufbruch ohne Lösung. Bestandsaufnahme Regierungswechsels. *Media Perspektiven*, July, pp. 460–466.

———. and Gunnar Köhne. 1986. Das Rundfunksystem in Norwegen. pp. D100–D102.

———. 1990. Das Rundfunksystem in Norwegen. *Internationales Handbuch für Rundfunk und Fernsehen*, Hans-Bredow-Institut. Hamburg and Baden-Baden: Nomos, pp. D160–D167.

Television Business International (TBI). 1990. *World Guide '90*. New York. Act III Publishing, p. 76.

Chapter 18

Danmarks Radio. 1987. *Act No. 421 of 15 June 1973 on Radio and Television Broadcasting*. Soborg: Danmarks Radio.

GEAR-meeting. 1988. Denmark: Yearly Report. Amsterdam.

Henriksen, Frank, and Kaare Schmidt. 1980. Danish Screen Communication, Before and After. *Intermedia* 8(4/5):69–73.

Medium. 1985. Auf einer Wellenlänge. July, pp. 37–38.

Petersen, Vibeke G., Ole Prehn, and Erik Nordahl Svendsen. 1988. Community Radio and TV in Denmark Breaking a Monopoly or Introducing New Media. IAMCR XVIth conference. Barcelona. July 24–28, p. 6.

Prehn, Ole. 1986a. Lokalen Fernsehen in Danemark-Drei Versuchsjahre. *Media Perspectiven* 6:381–391.

———. 1986b; 1990. Das Runfunksystem Dänemarks. In *Internationales Handbuch für Rundfunk und Fernsehen 1986/87; 1990/91*, Hans-Bredow-Institut. Hamburg and Baden-Baden: Nomos, pp. E7–E11, D25–D33.

Qvortrup, Lars. 1984. Cable Television, Public Infrastructure or Private Business, Cable Politics in Denmark. *Le Bulletin de L'Idate: Le prix des Nouveaux Medias*, vol. 17, October, pp. 173–179.

Radio Act. 1949. Telecommunications by Radio Act. No. 188. As amended by 1 62 229 (22/6) and 1 65 213 (4/6). April 12.

Television Business International (TBI). 1990. *World Guide '90*. New York: Act III Publishing, pp. 30–32.

Chapter 19

Gunnarsdottir, Elfa-Bjork. 1988. The Transformation of Icelandic Broadcasting. *EBU Review*, September, pp. 21–24.

Nicholson, Paul. 1990. Head on Clash in Iceland. *Television Business International*, June, p. 40.

Post and Telecommunications Administration. 1987. *Telecommunications in Iceland*. Reykjavik.

RUV. Icelandic State Broadcasting Service. 1985. *Annual Report 1984*. Reykjavik.

Television Business International (TBI). 1990. *World Guide '90*. New York: Act III Publishing, pp. 57–58.

Chapter 20

Bell, Desmond. 1985. Proclaiming the Republic: Broadcasting Policy and the Corporate State in Ireland. *West European Politics* 8(2):27–48.

Connections. 1985. Green Prospects. May 24, p. 4.

Doolan, Lelia, Jack Dowling, and Bob Quinn. 1969. *Sit Down and Be Counted*. Dublin: Wellington Publishers.

EBU Review. 1990. Newsreel: Ireland. 41(2):46–47.

Kelly, Charles E. 1976. Look Back in Pleasure. In *Written on the Wind*, ed. Louis McRedmond. Dublin: Radio Telefis Eireann Publishing, pp. 17–18.

Kenny, Colum. 1990. Burke's Last Act. *Playback*, September.

Logica Consultancy Ltd. 1987. *Television Broadcasting in Europe: Towards the 1990s.* London: Logica Consultancy, Ltd.

Multichannel News. 1986. Hughes Gets OK to Build Irish Satellite System. December 22, p. 17.

Murphy, Detlef. 1990. Das Rundfunksystem der Republik Irland. In *Internationales Handbuch für Rundfunk und Fernsehen,* Hans-Bredow-Institut. Hamburg, Baden-Baden: Nomos, pp. D102–D111.

O'Carroll, Lisa. 1990. Irish Rights Battle Ending. *Television Business International,* May, p. 49.

Pine, Richard and Rory Thomas. 1986. Communication and Community: The Case of Irish Radio. *Issues in Broadcasting* 7:1–27.

Radio Telefis Eireann (RTE). 1983. *Annual Report 1983.* Dublin.

Raidio na Gaelachta. 1987. Statistics. Casala. p. 9.

Rohan, Mike. 1988. Heading Towards a Shakeout. *Television Business International,* July/August, p. 50.

———. 1989. Satellite Ads Go Local. *Television Business International,* October, p. 28.

———. 1990. Irish Pubcasters Fights Revenue Limits. *Television Business International,* July/August.

Television Business International (TBI). 1990. *World Guide '90.* New York: Act III Publishing, p. 59.

Chapter 21

Black, Gordon. 1980. Broadcasting in Gibraltar. *Combroad,* September, pp. 12–13.

de Moragas, Miguel, Rosario de Mateo, and Emilio Prado. 1986. Spain. In *Electronic Media and Politics in Europe,* eds. Hans J. Kleinsteuber, Dennis McQuail, and Karen Siune. Frankfurt and New York: Campus Verlag, pp. 251–272.

Emery, Walter. 1969. *National and International Systems of Broadcasting.* East Lansing: Michigan State University Press.

Ezcurra, Luis. 1984. *Historia de la Radiodifusión Española los Primeros Años.* Madrid: Editora Nacional.

Faus-Belau, Angel. 1986; 1990. Die Entwicklung des Spanischen Rundfunksystems. In *Internationales Handbuch für Rundfunk und Fernsehen, 1986/87; 1990/91,* Hans-Bredow-Institut. Hamburg and Baden-Baden: Nomos, pp. E168–175, D225–237.

Franuquet, R. 1986. *Historia de la Radio.* Barcelona: Edicions 62.

Gorostiaga, E. 1976. *La Radio Televisión en España.* Pamplona: EUNS.

Howkins, John. 1983. Basques Use TV to Speak Their Own Language. *Intermedia,* 11(3):20–25.

Lopez-Escobar, Esteban, and Angel Faus-Belau. 1985. Broadcasting in Spain: A History of Heavy Handed State Control. *West European Politics* 8(2):122–136.

Magdaleno, Salvador. 1989. Spain Decides. *Television Business International,* September, p. 20.

Chapter 22

Ehrhardt, Marion. 1990. Das Rundfunksystem Portugals. In *Internationales Handbuch für Rundfunk und Fernsehen, 1990/1*, Hans-Bredow-Institut. Hamburg and Baden-Baden: Nomos, pp. D188–D192.

Optenhoegel, Uwe. 1986. Das Rundfunksystem Portugals. In *Internationales Handbuch für Rundfunk und Fernsehen, 1986/7*, Hans-Bredow-Institut. Hamburg and Baden-Baden: Nomos, pp. E129–E130.

Screen Finance. 1990. Government Backs Down on Church TV Plan. March 21.

Specht, Marina. 1986. Variety Coming to Portuguese TV. *Electronic Media*, January 6.

Television Business International (TBI). 1990. *World Guide '90*. New York: Act III Publishing, pp. 79–80.

Torres, Nuno Cintra. 1989. Portugal Is Next. *Television Business International*, June, pp. 13–14.

————. 1990. The Church's Loss. *Television Business International*, April, p. 10.

Chapter 23

Ansay, Tugrul. 1986; 1990. Das Türkische Rundfunksystem. In *Internationales Handbuch für Rundfunk und Fernsehen, 1986/87; 1990/91*, Hans-Bredow-Institut. Hamburg and Baden-Baden: Nomos, pp. E181–E185, D245–D249.

Besiroglu, Akin. 1986. Recent Developments in the Turkish Broadcasting System. *EBU Review*, January, vol. 57.

Eryarar, Serhan. 1990. Media Moguls Target Turkey. *Television Business International*. September, pp. 14–15.

Karpat, Kemal H. 1964. Traditionalist Elite Philosophy and the Modern Mass Media. In *Political Modernization in Japan and Turkey*, eds. Robert E. Ward and Dankwart A. Rustow. Princeton, NJ: Princeton University Press, pp. 255–282.

Ogan, Christine. 1986. *Media Imperialism, Video Cassette Piracy, and the Case of Turkey*. Unpublished paper. Indiana University.

Salin, Haluk. 1981. Broadcasting Authority in Turkey: Its Rise and Fall—1961–1971. *Journalism Quarterly*. 58(Autumn):395–400.

Chapter 24

Avnerre, Arie. 1981. Broadcasting in Israel. In *Broadcasting Around the World*, ed. William E. McCavitt. Blue Ridge Summit, PA: Tab Books, pp. 107–119.

Bainerman, Joel. 1989. Israel's Battle to Bring Order to TV Chaos. *Television Business International*, September, pp. 14–16.

————. 1990. Cable TV Debuts in Israel. *Television Business International*, May, p. 39.

Fallon, James. 1989. Israel: Cable Ops Face Dearth of Programming. *Multichannel News*, May 15, p. 38.

Gil, Zvi. 1986. *A House of Precious Stones*. Tel Aviv: Sifriat Poalim (in Hebrew).

Gotliffe, Harvey L. 1981. *Israeli General Television: A Historical Exploration of Content and Influence*. Ph.D. dissertation.

Greenberg, Keith. 1989. Cable in Israel Emerges with a Decided American Slant. *Cablevision*, August 28, pp. 59–61.

Israel Broadcasting Authority (IBA). 1986. *Annual Report 1986*. Tel Aviv: IBA.

Katz, Elihu, and George Wedell. 1977. *Broadcasting in the Third World*. London: Macmillan.

Shinar, Dov. 1972. Structure and Content of Television in Israel. *Television and Social Behavior, vol. 1 of Media Content and Control*. Washington, D.C.: U.S. Government Printing Office.

State of Israel. 1983. *Report of the Committee on the Operation of CATV Systems in Israel*. June.

Stoney, George C. 1984. Community Video in Israel: A View from Kibbutzim. *Community Television Review*, pp. 16–17.

Television Business International (TBI). 1990. *World Guide '90*. New York: Act III Publishing, p. 175.

Viorst, Milton. 1981–82. The Tug of War in Israeli Television. *Channels*, December/January, pp. 40–42.

Chapter 25

Dimitras, Payanote. 1986. "TV, Once More A Campaign Issue." *Media Bulletin* 3(4):9.

Dimitras, Payanote, and Tessa Doulkeri. 1986. "Electronic Media Policy in Greece." in Hans J. Kleinsteuber, Denis McQuail, and Karen Siune, eds. *Electronic Media and Politics in Europe*. Frankfurt and New York: Campus Verlag, pp. 139–142.

Emery, Walter. 1969. *National and International Systems of Broadcasting*. East Lansing: Michigan State Press.

Heretakis, Manolis. 1986. "TV Penetration in Greece and its Audience." *Adie*, No. 308, June 6.

Katsoudas, Dimitrios. 1985. "Greece: A Politically Controlled State Monopoly Broadcast System." *West European Politics*. 8(2):137–151.

Lazos, Christos. 1986. "Programming and Authority in Greek Television: The Uncertain Future of State Channels." *Adie*, No. 308, June 6.

Logica. 1987. *Television Broadcasting in Europe: Towards the 1990's*. United Kingdom: Logica Ltd., pp. 374–378.

Papathanassapoulos, Stylianos. 1989a. "Greece: Nothing is More Permanent than Provisional." *Intermedia* 17(2):29–35.

———. 1989b. "Greek Politics Strangle Process." *Television Business International*, July/August.

———. 1990. "The Greeks Throw Caution to the Wind." *Television Business International*, March, p. 20.

Stuart, Jay. 1990. "Encouraging Boldness," *Television Business International*, April, p. 18.

Chapter 26

Biró, Vera, ed. 1976. *Kulturális intérzmények és szervezetek Magyarországon*. Budapest: Kossuth.

Brabec, Otto. 1988. Das Rundfunksystem der Tschechoslowakischen Sozialistischen Republik. *Internationales Handbuch*. Baden-Baden: Nomos. pp. E215–E218.

Brown, Les. 1990. The Ways of Eastern Europe. *Television Business International,* May; p. 68.

Campbell, John C. 1972. Yugoslavia. In *The Communist States in Disarray 1965–1971,* eds. Adam Bromke and Teresa Rakowska-Harmstone. Minneapolis: University of Minnesota Press.

Campbell, Robert W. 1988. *The Soviet Telecommunications System*. Indianapolis: Hudson Institute. October 31.

Dennis, Everette E., and Jon vanden Heuvel. 1990. *Emerging Voices: East European Media in Transition*. New York, NY: Gannett Center for Media Studies.

Dziadul, Chris. 1990. The Americans Open Poland Up for Cable. *Television Business International,* February; p. 9.

Gajlewicz, Michal. 1988. Das Polnische Hörfunk und Fernsehsystem. *Internationales Handbuch für Fersehen,* 1990/1. Baden-Baden: Nomos, pp. E159–E165.

———. 1990. Das Rundfunksystem Polens im Umbruch. *Internationales Handbuch für Rundfunk und Fernsehen, 1990/91*. Baden-Baden/Hamburg: Nomos, pp. D183–D187.

Guback, Thomas H., and Steven P. Hill. 1972. The Beginnings of Soviet Broadcasting and the Role of V. I. Lenin. *Journalism Monographs,* December, p. 26.

Head, Sydney W. 1985. *World Broadcasting Systems: A Comparative Analysis*. Belmont, CA: Wadsworth.

Jakab, Zoltan. 1990. Das Ungarische Rundfunksystem: Am Anfang einer Umwälzung. *Internationales Handbuch für Rundfunk und Fernsehen, 1990/1991*. Baden-Baden: Nomos, pp. D249–D255.

Jakubowicz, Karol. 1990. Broadcasting in Post-Communist Poland: Blazing New or Old Trails? Paper presented to the International Institute of Communications. Dublin, Ireland. Unpublished.

Michel, Lutz P. 1990. Das Rundfunksystem der UdSSR. *Internationales Handbuch für Rundfunk und Fernsehen* Baden-Baden: Nomos, pp. D214–D223.

Mihailovic, Radmila, and Zlatko Sinobad. 1988. "Das Rundfunksystem Jugoslawiens." *Internationales Handbuch für Rundfunk und Fernsehen*. Baden-Baden: Nomos, pp. E105–E107.

Pálfalvi, Nándor, ed. 1987. *Hungarian Television Facts and Figures 1987*. Budapest: Magyar Telvizio.

Paulu, Burton. 1974. *Radio and Television Broadcasting in Eastern Europe*. Minneapolis: The University of Minnesota Press.

Popa, Victor. 1986. "Das Hörfunk und Fernsehsystem Rumäniens." *Internationales Handbuch für Rundfunk und Fersehnesen*. Baden-Baden: Nomos, pp. E130–E134.

Popova, Rosita, and Meglena Ivanova. 1990. Hörfunk und Fernsehen in Bulgarien. *Internationales Handbuch für Rundfunk und Fernsehen 1990/1991*. Baden-Baden: Nomos, pp. D19–D25.

Posner, Steve. 1990. Television Broadcasting in Eastern Europe: Country Profiles. *Eastern European & Soviet Telecom Report,* September 1, pp. 5–7.

Remington, Thomas. 1988. Soviet Union. In *Internationales Handbook of Broadcasting Systems,* ed. Philip T. Rosen. Westport, CT: Greenwood Press, pp. 257–268.

Reuter, Jens. 1990. "Das Rundfunksysterm Jugoslaviens." *Internationales Handbuch für Rundfunk und Fernsehen, 1990/1991*. Baden-Baden: Nomos, pp. D124–D131.

Roth, Paul. 1980. *Die Kommandierte Öffentliche Meinung: Sowjetische Medienpolitik.* Stuttgart: Seewald Verlag.

Scott, Len. 1988. Hungary: State Channel Faces Competition. *Television Business International.* MIP Issue. p. 11.

———. 1989. Hungary's Early Nap. *Television Business International,* October, p. 36.

Shanor, Donald. 1985. *Behind the Lines: The Private War Against Soviet Censorship.* New York: St. Martin's Press.

Stuart, Jay. 1989–1990. The Currency of the East. *Television Business International,* December/January, p. 22.

Stump, Matt. 1990. The Shrinking World of Totalitarian TV. *Broadcasting,* September 10, p. 96.

Szecskö, Tamás. 1979. *Communication Policies in Hungary.* New York: UNESCO.

———. 1985. Teletext in Hungary. *Intermedia* 13 (4/5):81

Szendry, Thomas. 1988. Hungary. In *International Handbook of Broadcasting Systems,* ed. Philip T. Rosen Westport, CT: Greenwood Press, pp. 119–132.

U.S. Department of State, Task Force on Telecommunications and Broadcasting in Eastern Europe, Advisory Committee on International Communications and Information Policy. 1990. *Eastern Europe: Please Stand By.* Washington: U.S. Department of State.

Television Digest. 1990. 30(44):3.

Toy, Stewart. 1990. Havas: France's Media Star is Rising in the East. *Business Week,* July 16, p. 114.

Zeidenberg, Leonard. 1990a. Poland to Build Cable With US Partner. *Broadcasting Abroad,* February, p. 5.

———. 1990b. Commercial Broadcasting Struggles for Toehold in Eastern Europe. *Broadcasting Abroad,* March, pp. 6–10.

———. 1990c. Polish Delegation Seeks U.S. Aid. *Broadcasting Abroad,* April, p. 10.

———. 1990d. East Europe: "USIA Publishers Media Guide." *Broadcasting Abroad* 2(5):48.

Chapter 27

Cate, Fred. 1990. The European Broadcasting Directive. American Bar Association, *Communications Committee Monograph Series.* 1990/1. April.

Caze, Marcel. 1985. European Harmonization of the Legal Framework for Broadcasting. *Le Bulletin de L'Idate,* November, pp. 351–363.

Commission of the European Communities. 1984. *Television Without Frontiers: Green Paper on the Establishment of the Common Market for Broadcasting, Especially by Satellite and Cable.*

Crane, Rhonda J. 1979. *The Politics of International Standards: France and the Color TV War.* Norwood, NJ: Ablex.

Degnan, Kim E., and Daniel B. Freyer. 1990. HDTV Roundup. *Satellite Communications* 14(8):12.

Dornan, Chris. 1984. Fear and Longing in the UK: Cultural Custody and the Expansion of Cable TV. Working Paper in Communication. Montreal: McGill University.

Eugster, Ernest. 1983. *Television Programming Across National Boundaries: The EBU and OIRT Experience.* Dedham, MA: Artech.

European Task Force. 1988. *Report: Europe 2000: What Kind of Television?* Manchester: The European Institute for the Media.

Funkschau. 1990. D2–MAC: Requiem auf Einen Standard, June 1, pp. 24–26.

Glenn, Adam. 1989. Private Broadcaster Lobby Outlines Aims in Europe. *Broadcasting Abroad,* December, p. 4.

Greenhouse, Steven. 1989. Europe Reaches TV Compromise; U.S. Officials Fear Protectionism. *New York Times,* October 4, sec. 1, p. 20.

Information Technology Advisory Panel. 1982. *Cable Systems.* London: Her Majesty's Stationery Office.

Intermedia. 1989. HDTV: One Step . . . Two Steps? 17(5):5-6.

Margolies, Adrienne. 1989. European Harmony. *Television Business International,* April, p. 20.

Office of Technology Assessment (OTA), U.S. Congress. 1990. *The Big Picture: HDTV and High Resolution Systems.* Background Paper OTA-BP-CIT-64. Washington D.C.: Government Printing Office. June, pp. 32–33.

Papathanassopoulos, Stylianos. 1990. Broadcasting and the European Community: the Commission's audiovisual policy. *The Political Economy of Communications: International and European Dimensions,* eds. Kenneth Dyson and Peter Humphreys. London: Routledge.

Scharf, Albert. 1990. Professor Albert Scharf: Dean of the EBU. *Broadcasting Abroad,* January, p. 11.

Snoddy, Raymond. 1986. The BBC Adjusts Its Set. *Financial Times,* January 21, p. 25.

Stuart, Jay. 1989. European Quotas: Playing Hollywood's Game. *Television Business International,* July–August, pp. 6–7.

Chapter 28

Bullinger, Martin. 1985. *Satellitenrundfunk.* Hamburg: Hans-Bredow-Institut.

Cable and Station Coverage Atlas. 1989. New York: Warren Publishing.

Connections. 1985. Frontiers Against Commercials. May 10.

Evans, Rowena, Jean-Luc Renaud, and Wilfried Ahrens. 1989. The Last Frontiers of European Television. *Television Business International,* October, p. 69.

Funkschau. 1990. D2–MAC: Requiem auf Einen Standard, June 1, pp. 24–26.

Glenn, Adam. 1989a. Satellite TV on the Rise in Europe. *Broadcasting Abroad,* October, p. 9.

———. 1989b. Sky Promotes Dish Sales. *Broadcasting Abroad,* November, p. 18.

———. 1990a. Battle of Britain Being Fought in the Air. *Broadcasting Abroad,* June, p. 8.

———. 1990b. British Satellite Rivals Ready for Battle. *Broadcasting Abroad,* April, p. 7.

Graham, George. 1990. A Burning Obligation. *Financial Times,* May 29, p. 4.

Henry, Jane E. 1985. Economics of Pay-TV Media. In *Video Media Competition.* New York: Columbia University Press, pp. 19–54.

Kirk, Don Lewis. 1990. New Option for Networks. *Financial Times,* May 29, p. 4.

Logica Consultancy, Ltd. 1987. *Television Broadcasting in Europe: Towards the 1990s.* London.

McCartney, Neil. 1985. Probleme Beim Sprung Über den Ärmelkanal. *Neue Medien,* May, pp. 138–140.

Morley, Meg and Sally Mann. 1986. Retaining Family Ties. *Connections,* January 27, pp. 3–4.

Müller-Romer, Frank. 1989. Satelliten und Kabelrundfunk. In *Internationales Handbuch für Rundfunk und Fernsehen 1988/9,* Hans-Bredow-Institut. Hamburg, Baden-Baden: Nomos, pp. A1–A23.

Neue Medien. 1984. Das Hindernisrennen des Unternehmens Coronet. February, pp. 42–48.

Nicholson, Paul. 1990. State Channels Meet the Satellite Challenge. *Television Business International,* June, pp. 28–30.

Pirard, Theo. 1989. Will Short-Term Attitude Hurt Tele-X? *Satellite Communications,* March, pp. 55–58.

Pool, Ithiel de Sola. 1991. In *Technologies Without Boundaries,* ed. Eli Noam. Cambridge: Harvard University Press.

Satellite Week. 1990. Sky Cable Receives Closer Look at NAB, April 9, 12(15):5.

Scherer, Joachim. 1985. *Telekommunikationsrecht und Telekommunikationspolitik.* Baden-Baden: Nomos Verlagsgesellschaft.

Snoddy, Raymond. 1990. Going for Quality. *Financial Times,* May, pp. 1–2.

Swann, Nicola. 1989. Satellites Around the Globe—A Brief Overview of the Major TV Carriers. *Television Business International,* May, p. 56.

Vedel, Thierry. 1987. New Media Politics & Policies in France from 1981 to 1986: What Is Left? Center for Telecommunications and Information Studies, Working Paper Series No. 123. Columbia University.

Chapter 29

Barnouw, Eric. 1982. *Tube of Plenty: The Evolution of American Television.* New York: Oxford University Press.

Besen, S., and L. Johnson. 1986. *Compatibility Standards: Innovation and Competition in the Broadcast Industry.* Santa Monica, CA: The Rand Corporation.

Curran, James. 1982. Communications, Power, and Social Order. In *Culture, Society, and the Media,* eds. Michael Gurevitch et al., London: Methuen.

David, Paul A. 1987. Some New Standards for the Economics of Standardization in the Information Age. In *Economics Policy and Technological Performance,* eds. Paula Dasgupta and Paul Stoneman. Cambridge, MA: Cambridge University Press.

Dessauer, John. 1988. *Book Industry Trends 1988.* New York: Book Industry Study Group.

European Community. 1986. *Education and Training, 1985.* Luxembourg's Statistical Office of the European Community, pp. 70–72.

Farrell, Joseph, and Garth Saloner. 1986. Installed Base and Compatibility: Innovation, Product Preannouncements and Predation. *MIT Working Papers.* No. 411. February.

Fisher, Lawrence J. 1990. Paperless Office Evolves With Paper, But Less of It. *New York Times.* August 5, p. 1.

McLaughlin, John F., and Anne Louise Antonoff. 1986. Mapping the Information Business. *Program on Information Resources Policy.* Cambridge, MA: Harvard University Press.

Noam, Eli M. 1991. *Telecommunications in Europe.* New York: Oxford University Press.

Noll, Roger G., Merton J. Peck, and John J. McGowan. *Economic Aspects of Television Regulation.* Washington, DC: Brookings Institution.

Porat, Marc U. 1978. Communication Policy in an Information Society. In *Communications for Tomorrow,* ed. Glen Robinson. New York: Praeger.

U.S. Department of Commerce, Bureau of the Census. 1990. *Statistical Abstract of the United States 1990: National Data Book,* 110th ed. January, p. 128.

Index